Public Administration and Policy

Public Administration and Policy
Governing in Challenging Times

EDITED BY

Martin W. Westmacott
University of Western Ontario

Hugh P. Mellon
King's College, University of Western Ontario

Prentice Hall Allyn and Bacon Canada
Scarborough, Ontario

Canadian Cataloguing in Publication Data

Main entry under title:

Public administration and policy: governing in challenging times

Includes bibliographical references.

ISBN 0-13-780636-1

1. Public administration—Canada. 2. Political planning—Canada I. Westmacott, M.W. (Martin William), 1943–   . II. Mellon, Hugh.

JL75.P82 1999   351.71   C98-931262-5

Prentice-Hall, Inc., Upper Saddle River, New Jersey
Prentice-Hall International (UK) Limited, London
Prentice-Hall of Australia, Pty. Limited, Sydney
Prentice-Hall Hispanoamericana, S.A., Mexico City
Prentice-Hall of India Private Limited, New Delhi
Prentice-Hall of Japan, Inc., Tokyo
Simon & Schuster Southeast Asia Private Limited, Singapore
Editora Prentice-Hall do Brasil, Ltda., Rio de Janeiro

ISBN 0-13-780636-1

Vice President, Editorial Director: Laura Pearson
Acquisitions Editor: Dawn Lee
Associate Editor: Sharon Loeb
Copy Editor: Ann McInnis
Production Editor: Melanie M. Meharchand

Production Coordinator: Peggy Brown
Permissions/Photo Research: Susan Wallace-Cox
Cover Design: Sarah Battersby
Cover Image: PhotoDisc
Page Layout: Janette Thompson (Jansom)

1 2 3 4 5 WEB 03 02 01 00 99

Printed and bound in Canada.

Visit the Prentice Hall Canada Web site! Send us your comments, browse our catalogues, and more. **www.phcanada.com** Or reach us through e-mail at **phabinfo_pubcanada@prenhall.com**

Contents

Contents

PREFACE

We have prepared a collection of readings on key issues of debate in the field of public administration. Our various contributors are each expert in their field, but they have consciously attempted to craft their comments with an undergraduate audience in mind. The essays are organized into eight sections: (1) introduction to public administration and the relation between politics and administration; (2) politics, accountability, and government administration; (3) the design and reform of institutional arrangements (the examples of aboriginal land claim negotiations, provincial-municipal relations); (4) the collection of policy information by governments through commissions and think tanks; (5) various public policy debates (regulation, privatization, and budgetary strategy); (6) education policy as a selected case study in public policy; (7) the strengths and weaknesses of advanced information technology in government; and (8) concluding insights on administration from past and present senior federal bureaucrats. With each section, there is an introduction and a list of suggested discussion questions.

The contributors have been drawn from across Canada. They include both academics and bureaucratic professionals. All have endeavoured to explain fundamental issues and concepts, relate them to real-world situations, and offer challenges for further academic reflection. Their contributions have been much appreciated.

As editors we were in the position of depending upon numerous individuals for advice, information and friendship. It was our good fortune to be the recipients of the assistance of many capable and thoughtful individuals.

Our contributors displayed a high degree of expertise mixed with a ready spirit of cooperation. All have laboured to convey their subjects with sensitivity to the interests and likely backgrounds of undergraduate readers.

Recognition is also due to The University of Western Ontario and its affiliate, King's College. These institutions have supported our efforts in diverse ways. Research monies, library support, documentary collections, and other resources have been made available so as to facilitate our work.

Friends and family members have been sources of comfort and compassion amid the hectic pace of deadlines and work pressures. Their thoughtfulness will long be treasured. Colleagues such as Ross Gibbons and Andrew Sancton deserve note for their helpfulness.

Thanks is also due to those who reviewed the text at various stages of its development, particularly Laurent Dobuzinskis and Steven MacBride of Simon Fraser University and Richard Sigurdson of University College of the Cariboo.

Prentice Hall and its staff have been readily available for consultation and reaction. Their competence and encouragement have helped to bring this project to timely fruition.

Several key individuals merit personal recognition and special thanks. Both of us are grateful for their helpfulness and are appreciative of their unfailing good humour. Jane Borecky of King's College and Lynn Hill of The University of Western Ontario have provided assistance and professional skills which have been of tremendous help. Jane has helped bring order to unruly prose, computer glitches, and mounting piles of paper. She and Lynn have assisted us throughout this project and have contributed significantly.

M. Westmacott

Hugh Mellon
London, Ontario

LIST OF WEBLINKS

PART I   INTRODUCTION

Liberal Party
liberal.ca

New Democratic Party
ndp.ca

Progressive Conservative Party
pcparty.ca

Reform Party
reform.ca

Bloc Quebecois
blocquebecois.org

Ontario Hydro
hydro.on.ca

Auditor General
oag-bvg.gc.ca

PART II   POLITICS, ACCOUNTABILITY, AND GOVERNMENT ADMINISTRATION

Cabinet Ministers and Portfolios
canada.gc.ca/howgoc/cab/cabind_e.html

Parliament of Canada
parl.gc.ca/english/index.html

Canadian Parliamentary Affairs Channel
screen.com/CPAC

Members of Parliament (House of Commons)
parl.gc.ca/english/members/alpha/alpha_a.htm

Parliamentary Calendar
parl.gc.ca/english/calpre/htm

Members of the Senate
parl.gc.ca/english/senate/bio-e/bio-e.htm

Senate Committees
magi.com/~sencom

PART III   RESTRUCTURING INSTITUTIONS

Nunavut Planning Commission
npc.nunavut.ca

Canadian Department of Indian and Northern Affairs
inac.gc.ca/index.html

Royal Commission on Aboriginal Peoples
indigenous.bc.ca/rcap/rcap.html

Inuit Tapisat of Canada
infoweb.magi.com/~itc/itc.html

Alberta Municipal Affairs
gov.ab.ca/dept/ma.html

Canadian Information by Subject
nlc-bnc.ca/caninfo/ecaninfo.htm

PART IV   GOVERNMENT, INFORMATION, AND POLICY IDEAS

Globe and Mail – Search Keywords: Somalia Inquiry
theglobeandmail.com/docs/top/search/query.html

Privy Council Office
pco-bcp.gc.ca

C. D. Howe Institute
cdhowe.org

Fraser Institute
fraserinstitute.ca

List of Weblinks

PART V   POLICY DEBATES

Alberta Gaming and Liquor Commission
   gov.ab.ca/gov/agency/galc.html

Alberta Alcohol and Drug Abuse Commission
   gov.ab.ca/aadac

Canadian Radio-television and
   Telecommunications Commission
   crtc.gc.ca

Canadian Broadcast Corporation
   cbc.ca

CTV (CFTO) Homepage
   baton.com/ctv.htm

Department of Finance
   www.fin.gc.ca/fin-eng.html

PART VI   POLICY AND ADMINISTRATION—DEBATES IN EDUCATION: A CASE STUDY

Political Ideologies
   keele.ac.uk/depts/po/thought.htm

Mindscapes: Political Ideologies
   Towards the 21st Century
   mghr.com/college/0075526115.html

Veterans Affairs Canada
   vac-acc.gc.ca

Canadian Education on the Web
   oise.utoronto.ca/~mpress/eduweb.html

PART VII   INFORMATION, TECHNOLOGY, AND GOVERNMENT ADMINISTRATION

Canadian General Standards Board
   w3.pwgsc.gc.ca/cgsb

Electronic Frontier Canada
   insight.mcmaster.ca/org/efc/efc.html

Human Resources Development Canada
   hrdc-drhc.gc.ca

Statistics Canada
   statcan.ca/start.html

PART VIII   SENIOR PRACTITIONERS' INSIGHTS

Canadian Centre for Management Development
   ccmd-ccg.gc.ca

Prime Minister of Canada
   pm.gc.ca

Public Service Commission
   psc-cfp.gc.ca

Canadian Federation of Students
   cfs-fcee.ca

I

INTRODUCTION

Politics and administration are often viewed as separate topics to be examined in isolation. A common refrain has been that there is no Liberal or Conservative or Reform way to shovel a street, process an income tax form, or oversee collection of vital statistics. Politics was understood to be about persuasion, election campaigns, and parliamentary debate. Administration, on the other hand, was thought to be about application of rules, budget guidelines, and management techniques.

The conceptual division seemed clear and lasting, but problems remained. Instances of administrative breakdown became political controversies as citizens asked for accountability and reform. Political forces, meanwhile, shaped the management environment and affected the recruitment of senior administrators. Matters of politics and administration now seemed interconnected. This interconnection occurs along a number of fronts, many of which are explored in subsequent chapters. Assessments of policy making, for example, require appreciation of both political forces (partisanship, public opinion, party platforms, etc.) as well as administrative topics (spending patterns, policy implementation, etc.). The same pattern of interconnection holds true for other aspects of public administration as well.

Reflecting upon the connections between politics and administration is a good starting point. The connections are many and diverse. Working through their implications will help prepare students for the diverse chapters to follow. Neither politics nor administrative conditions exist separately from each other. They are linked via such things as the institutions of government, the budget setting process, the practice of policy/program evaluation, and the sources of policy advice to which a government subscribes. Connections also occur through the value choices of decision makers, the mood of the electorate, and prevailing currents in elite administrative circles. These and many other factors illustrate the merging of political and administrative forces.

DISCUSSION QUESTIONS

1. Why do administrative issues sometimes become political controversies? Can you cite an issue where people called for more effective government supervision of a program or policy? Please elaborate.

2. With what kinds of government administration have you personally come into contact? Were you happy with your experience?

3. Compare the views of Woodrow Wilson and Max Weber. What are the strengths and weaknesses of their approaches to matters of politics and administration?

4. Do you think there is a Liberal, PC, Reform, or Bloc way to (a) build schools or bridges; (b) formulate a government budget; or (c) design new education or health care policy?

5. How would you see the relative responsibilities of cabinet ministers and senior bureaucrats? What might happen when senior bureaucratic officials advise ministers on important issues? Might they lose their objectivity? From where do governing values come?

6. Why is public administration a part of political science courses at Canadian colleges and universities? How might "public administration" differ from, or relate to, "business administration"?

POLITICS AND ADMINISTRATION: Separate, Connected, or Integrated? Looking at Possibilities

Hugh Mellon

In the 1952 United States presidential election, the celebrated military hero Dwight D. "Ike" Eisenhower triumphed. This much-heralded leader seemed intent upon extending his record of success to a different realm, that of president and political chief executive. Voter confidence in the war hero's ability to transfer his leadership abilities from wartime administration to peacetime government was evident in his victorious 1952 campaign. Others harboured doubts, however, and one of these was Eisenhower's predecessor, Harry Truman. During the pre-inauguration preparations Truman is reported to have expressed his concerns about Eisenhower to his staff: "He'll sit right here and he'll say do this, do that! And nothing will happen. Poor Ike—it won't be a bit like the Army. He'll find it very frustrating."[1] These comments reflect more than a lack of faith in Eisenhower's adaptability; they also express an awareness that executive leadership and administrative direction in government is more than simply giving orders and trusting in military discipline and obedience. Political forces such as bureaucratic rivalries, voter sensibilities, and partisanship come into play and require considered responses.

Testing the accuracy of Truman's assessment of Eisenhower is a question best left for another time. What is critical here is the exploration of the relationship between administrative and political factors. In the past, it was posited that they (administration and politics) were, in fact, separable. Modern voices regard them as fundamentally intertwined. Not only is there no easy separation of administration from politics, in reality they become intertwined in various ways. This leads to regulatory and analytical complexities. References to pertinent literature, and examination of real world cases where these issues were raised, will help suggest some of these underlying complications. Elaborating upon the links between administration and politics will facilitate appreciation of the challenges facing modern public administration. Administrative practices and principles need to be situated within a context rife with political pressures.

The following essay will proceed in several stages. The ensuing section is designed to highlight the importance of administration to the success of public sector organizations. This helps establish the fundamental connection of administration to politics—that good administration may well be good politics as well. Next will be a survey of the views of two of the major commentators in the longstanding politics/administration debate, Woodrow Wilson and Max Weber. Both authored key works which have been long studied by students of public administration. Their insights into the relationship between administration and politics will subsequently be compared with those of more contemporary observers. In the concluding segment a couple of real-world situations will be referred to in hopes of spurring discussion and further reflection about the administration/politics nexus.

BAD OR INATTENTIVE ADMINISTRATION IS BAD POLITICS

Life, not to mention large-scale government, is seldom simple and Eisenhower would be neither the first nor the last political executive to be frustrated over unfulfilled expectations of administrative performance in government. The demands of government administration are arduous, but the stakes are high. Careless or callous administration can produce severe hardship. Examples of such difficulties abound.

In mid-August 1997, the political climate of Ontario was shaken by reports of severe problems amid the ranks of the province's major public energy utility, Ontario Hydro. Nuclear reactors were to be shut down, large numbers of staff dislocated, and estimates of losses in the billions of dollars surfaced in public debate. The president of Hydro announced that he would be stepping down. Meanwhile, Premier Mike Harris observed, "It's not been well run," while Hydro Chair Bill Farlinger offered this insight: "I'll give you my own theory: that the nuclear unit was operated over all those early years as some sort of special nuclear cult....Senior management didn't dig into what was going on in this special unit to the extent we might now say they should have."[2]

As Ontario Hydro's failings were becoming public, there was also widespread discussion of another apparent failure of leadership and administration. The report of the Commission of Inquiry appointed by the federal government to investigate the atrocities and misdeeds associated with the Canadian peacekeeping mission in Somalia was released. Here, too, evidence pointed to organizational failings and inadequate leadership. Tales of torture, racism, and extreme reluctance on the part of some officials to provide needed documents to investigators were widely reported. Poor management may well have allowed a very difficult situation to become a horrifying tragedy. The Commission's conclusions carried overtones of the laments over the poor management at Ontario Hydro: "Systems broke down and organizational discipline crumbled. Such systemic or institutional faults cannot be divorced from leadership responsibility, and the leadership errors in the Somalia mission were manifold and fundamental."[3]

An autumn 1997 issue of the popular American magazine *Newsweek* featured a cover story on the alleged failings of the U.S. Internal Revenue Service. The very title of the article, "Infernal Revenue Disservice," conveyed the sense of deep-rooted organizational problems. Abuse of public trust and maladministration were portrayed as ongoing problems. At issue was the very culture of the organization and its relationship with ordinary taxpaying citizens: "There's a widening gulf between the IRS's collection agents, who actually have to meet and work with troubled taxpayers, and an ever more remote and arrogant management."[4]

This brief list of institutional and managerial weaknesses is not meant to be exhaustive. Observers of the contemporary Canadian (or American) scene could easily supplement this collection with other tales of administrative error or omission. At this point cynics may be prepared to throw up their hands and dismiss all public sector efforts at large-scale organization. However, the aim here is not to dismiss the possibilities offered by modern organizations and conscientious government administrators. Offering this selected list of organizational mishaps is instead meant to suggest the need for study of bureaucracies and the political issues they raise, not to condemn these institutions outright. Canadians receive many necessary services through the actions of governments at all levels.

Failure to examine and analyze the basics of our governing institutions and the linkages between administrative and political considerations could have serious consequences. Both the legitimacy and the effectiveness of government are at stake for, as Leslie Seidle suggests, "The present lack of confidence in how Canada is governed encompasses not only elected institutions but also the administrative (public service) sector."[5] Concerted attention to issues of public administration and government performance can be a source of useful insights into the already noted examples of organizational pathology. What is more, these insights can be applied to the efforts to implement better public policies and improve public confidence levels. Michael Atkinson has asserted that "in Canada, with some notable exceptions, the connection between institutions and public policy has not been drawn very tightly."[6] There is much to be studied and the issues are many.

One of the critical issues is the challenge of sorting out the underlying relationship between politics and administration. Are they two separable spheres each working according to a particular logic or are they, by practical necessity, intertwined and complementary? Over time students of public administration have come to recognize the wisdom of the latter understanding. Recent works have further refined this perception and elaborated upon different manifestations of interconnection. Becoming acquainted with some of the principal participants in this debate will foster understanding of the issues at stake and contribute reference points for the subsequent examination of selected real-world situations.

WOODROW WILSON (1856–1924)

One of the most noted works in the history of public administration as a field of independent study is an article by Woodrow Wilson entitled simply "The Study of Administration" which appeared in June of 1887 in the *Political Science Quarterly*.[7] Wilson's call for development in the United States of studies in administration and for utilization of businesslike models, became very influential. In fact, the distinguished scholar Dwight Waldo has noted that this "essay is *the* most significant work in the history of self-aware Public Administration, a source of seemingly endless stimulation and controversy."[8] Examining Wilson's commentary yields key insights into early assumptions about the boundaries between the spheres of administration and politics.

In the late 19th/early 20th century, there was an active movement, particularly in the United States, for the reform of government. Business and community leaders called for sound administration and curbs on the excesses and cronyism of the political process. Within this environment Wilson's endorsement of the inclusion of administrative studies within advanced educational offerings, struck a receptive chord. He called attention to the expanding role of government and yearned for more attention to the issues related to its performance and the implementation of public programs. Corruption and administrative amateurism often prevailed at the expense of sound management practice. "This is why there should be a science of administration which shall seek to straighten the paths of government, to make its business less unbusinesslike, to strengthen and purify its organization, and to crown its duties with dutifulness."[9] Phrases such as the "science of administration" and the search for a "businesslike" approach to public affairs indicate an underlying search for definable principles of management and administration which could be applied untainted by political expediency. Public administration should involve scholars seeking to forge clear rules about the proper conduct of government organizations. Partisanship and political influences were suspect and application of business models of market efficiency was to be prized.

Wilson regarded administration and politics as distinct entities. In this he was one with the forces pushing for government and civil service reform. "Most important to be observed is the truth already so much and so fortunately insisted upon by our civil-service reformers; namely, that administration lies outside the proper sphere of *politics*. Administrative questions are not political questions. Although politics sets the tasks for administration, it should not be suffered to manipulate its offices."[10] This was not a call for turning over all authority to officials. Rather, it was part of a search for a more objective way of conducting public affairs.

Observe that Wilson assigns an important responsibility to the world of politics, that of setting out and agreeing upon the tasks to be administered. Politics is a needed, yet distinct, matter. But he is calling for administration to be recognized as a field of specialization and is endeavouring to "liberate" it from the perceived excesses of the political system. To put it simply, the world of politics could produce decisions such as when to build roads or schools, or when to offer social services, or which countries to regard as international enemies. Once these judgments are made, administrative principles could be applied scientifically by a competent civil service, appointed based on ability, not political or family connections.

This conception of the purpose and significance of public administration became widely shared. Nicholas Henry has argued that "Woodrow Wilson largely set the tone for the early study of public administration."[11] Political involvement in matters deemed administrative was suspect, for it involved favouritism, compromise, and deal making. Administration, on the other hand, was seen as referring to an objective search for capability and the application of scientific rules according to businesslike models of efficiency. Once they were defined as separate functions with differing operating beliefs, the complete separation of political and administrative activities became an article of faith. Administration could be handed over to professional specialists who would act according to sound principles. At its best, Wilson's notion of the politics/administration split reflected a desire for efficiency and professional management unimpeded by crass partisan intrigue. Yet his belief in the easy separability of administration and politics was overly optimistic or, in the minds of some, naive.

MAX WEBER (1864–1920)

One of the legends in the history of the social sciences is the great German sociologist, Max Weber. Weber's impact on much of North America's public administration community was delayed due to translation obstacles, but it was worth the wait. His interests were wideranging and his ultimate influence has been profound. One of the many issues which interested Weber was the trend toward growing reliance upon officials, or bureaucrats, working within a social order rooted in legal claims to authority. These officials worked within legally defined areas of responsibility according to rules and rationality. Authority to give commands was organized and assigned on a hierarchical basis. Preparations were made so that required duties would be performed on an ongoing basis. "In principle, the modern organization of the civil service separates the bureau from the private domicile of the official, and, in general, bureaucracy segregates official activity as something distinct from the sphere of private life."[12] The bureaucratic model would function according to this and other fundamental characteristics including reliance upon written rules, formal record keeping, merit-based appointment, hierarchical organization, clear allocations of jurisdiction, and the understanding that official employment is a career choice where advancement will be based upon merit. Claims to authority resting upon either traditional or charismatic credentials would lose out against the "technical superiority"[13] of bureaucratic structures.

Weber's depiction of modern bureaucracy and its essential characteristics has been widely read and considered. Evidence of Weber's intellectual contribution can be found in the following assessment offered by Richard Stillman: "For public administration after World War II, sociologists fundamentally offered a new lens from which to view, analyze, and define the world of public administration. Max Weber's concept of bureaucracy was translated from the German and spread throughout American universities...."[14] Blau and Meyer assert that Weber's theory of bureaucracy "remains the model that most people have in mind when they think of bureaucracy as well as the one most often used in practice."[15]

In the aftermath of World War II, western governments took on expanded peacetime workloads. Governmental responsibility over such matters as macroeconomic stabilization, encouragement of advanced technology and space research, and the promotion of cultural industries increased and with this came an increase in the number of government workers. Bureaucracy and the growth in the number of officials and in the range of their influence became added to the concerns of public administration scholars and participants.

Weber's work alerts readers to the rise of the professional bureaucrat armed with authority, expertise, and access to strategic information. The strength of the officials and the "superiority" of bureaucracy posed a difficult challenge for popular control. Officialdom could pose serious potential problems. One such danger which Weber recognized would be the tendency of bureaucrats to control the flow and availability of information.[16] This relates to the larger problem of the difficulty faced by elected politicians in attempting to hold officials accountable for actions taken. Weber suggested that the politicians would be in the position of "dilettantes" facing "experts."[17] This places bureaucrats in a position of considerable influence and power. Effective checks upon their activities will be difficult given the reliance of most democracies upon legislative members (members of parliament, members of Congress, etc.) drawn from diverse, and often generalist, backgrounds. Weber hoped that political parties and strong legislatures would produce leaders "of real quality, fitted to lead a world power."[18] Some have suggested that Weber was more concerned with strong leadership than with democratic beliefs.[19] Whatever the case, his attention to the rise of modern bureaucratic organizations and to the influence of the bureaucrats who compose these organizations was insightful and timely.

Weber's account of bureaucracy raises serious questions about power, accountability, and control. Politicians find themselves dependent upon a corps of officials possessing formidable resources. Rivalry, or even conflict, between bureaucrats and democratically elected politicians would appear to be almost unavoidable. In assessing Weber's account of the relationship between bureaucracy and democracy, Waldo concludes that "The picture that is sketched is of two forces sometimes reinforcing, but also sometimes—and seemingly inevitably—in an antagonistic manner."[20]

CONTEMPORARY OUTLOOKS ON THE RELATIONSHIP OF POLITICS AND ADMINISTRATION

The accounts of Wilson and Weber present an interesting analytical dichotomy. For Wilson, politics and administration have intrinsic differences, and the limitation of political influences can facilitate better administration. In the Weberian outlook, bureaucracy is a deeply rooted social trend and representative institutions can attempt to provide a needed check upon the authority of official experts. Like most dichotomies, this one contains a modest element of oversimplification. Today, most observers would opt for the notion that political and administrative considerations are tightly linked and that a continuum would best capture the relevant possibilities.

Wilson's model of separate spheres did not hold up under scrutiny. Paving a road may seem purely administrative, but deciding how much to spend on paving and which neighbourhoods will get road improvements quickly takes on political overtones. Common challenges for any government—locating a new recreational or waste-treatment facility, reviewing the adequacy of school facilities in differing localities, responding to community requests for funds, etc.—all involve issues which straddle the line between supposedly "pure" administration and politics. The boundary between politics and administration gets blurred when one considers the underlying allocation of resources and the competition among communities of interest for desired resources and outcomes. Battles over budgets automatically involve political struggles.

Despite its conceptual limitations, the politics/administration dichotomy did serve certain interests. This contributed to its staying power. In the 1920s and 1930s, for example, the Rockefeller interests developed philanthropies interested in dealing with public policy issues. Many in American society were skeptical, though, about the public-spiritedness of the Rockefellers. They were, of course, incredibly rich and well connected. Furthermore, the business tactics of John D. Rockefeller were viewed by many as abusive and disreputable.[21] Critics feared the involvement of the Rockefellers in political issues, questioning whether they might have self-interested designs at work. Even the simple act of promoting research was suspected as a cover for building an improved public image. Use of the politics/administration division allowed the Rockefeller interests an out. Research into government matters could be defended as "administrative" and not "political." As Alasdair Roberts has asserted, the notion of separate administrative and political spheres was thereby perpetuated: "the philanthropies breathed new life into the idea at a critical stage, when many of the principal institutions within the field of public administration were first established."[22]

It is possible that the idea of separate and distinct spheres had deeper roots in the United States than in the United Kingdom or Canada. Hodgetts suggests that the notion of a strict politics/administration dichotomy "emerged naturally in the United States because of that country's formal constitutional separation of powers."[23] The parliamentary model's fusion of the executive and legislative institutions of government, through the institutions of responsible government, and cabinet and ministerial responsibility, oriented conceptions of government and administration differently. (With reference to ministerial and cabinet responsibility please note the essay by Sutherland and Mitchell in this volume.) In November of 1945 the *Canadian Journal of Economics and Political Science* carried an exchange among different commentators about the future of public administration. Note the expansive definition of the field offered by Alexander Brady from the University of Toronto: "The genuine and profitable study of public administration in a democratic state cannot be narrower than the broad frame of government, if we are to appreciate duly the ultimate end sought—the competent management of the state."[24]

One of the most important modern works to deal explicitly with the relationship of administration and politics came out in the early 1980s. *Bureaucrats and Politicians in Western Democracies*,[25] authored by Aberbach, Putnam and Rockman, offers a detailed examination of the working relationship between politicians and senior bureaucrats. Their research was cross-national and exhaustive, involving "systematic interviews with more than 1400 senior civil servants and members of parliament in the United States, Britain, France, Germany, Italy, the Netherlands and Sweden."[26] From these labours the authors fashioned differing "images"[27] of how the relationship between the senior politicians and bureaucrats might operate. Image one is the familiar, if now largely questioned, view of separate spheres of responsibility wherein administrators accept political directions and then go about putting them into practice. Their second image draws the two functions (administration and politics) a bit closer together. Senior administrators now are seen as having input into policy making, but their role is still largely limited to the provision of data and knowledge about policy implementation. The two remaining "images" bring political and administrative figures and concerns yet closer together. In the third image, both politicians and administrators are assumed to be engaged in politics and policy making. However, there are differences of scale at work. Politicians deal with the grand sweep of interests, partisanship, and communication with the electorate. For senior administrators the task is to "mediate narrow, focused interests of organized clienteles."[28] The role and workload of high level administrators and politicians blends even further together with image four. This image postulates a breakdown of the politician-administrator division at the senior levels of government. Both are understood to operate with attentiveness to political considerations and to move between political and administrative career paths. Evidence for this image relates to trends noted in various countries such as the appointment of partisans to senior administrative posts and the availability of options to move between senior administrative and political positions.

Aberbach and his fellow researchers urge readers to look beyond traditional conceptions of strict difference (politicians versus administrators) and either/or boundaries. In place of these suspect formulations, they urge attention to the "relative predominance"[29] of each group and to the strengths and weaknesses of their particular approaches to decision making. Selection of the word "relative" underlies the fluidity of the boundaries distinguishing the groups. The evidence leads Aberbach and the others to argue that "bureaucrats are oriented toward efficient problem solving, whereas politicians seek to ensure that policies meet popular demands."[30] Arguments like these have pushed the conceptual debates into new and enlightening avenues liberated from familiar, yet now ill-fitting, categories. Commentators such as Colin Campbell and Guy Peters have praised the conceptual clarification emanating from *Bureaucrats and Politicians in Western Democracies*.[31] Reflection upon this and other contributions to the growing literature on political and administrative behaviour[32] allows us to analyze more effectively the events and behaviours found existing within the world of Canadian public administration.

APPLYING THE INSIGHTS TO THE WORLD
OF CANADIAN PUBLIC ADMINISTRATION

Aside from the challenge of reading and assessing theoretical debates about the importance of administration and its relation to politics, there is the added test of applying these insights to daily situations. Becoming acquainted with the study of public administration is easier when the intellectual theory is applied directly to real-life situations. This can be illustrated through the use of several situations or issues drawn from actual experiences in Canadian politics and public administration. Reflection upon these situations or issues will lead to the recognition of several key points. First is the already noted observation about the deep linkages between administration and politics and between senior administrators and politicians. Point number two involves the regulatory challenges involved in dealing with the contemporary interrelationships among politicians and administrators. Many of our regulatory arrangements have been predicated upon the old doctrines of separate spheres. Understanding the breadth of the challenge posed by the blurring of the lines between administration and politics, illuminates another aspect of the study of public administration. First, let us turn to the basic observation about the linkages between administration and politics and its elaboration via the third and fourth images constructed by Aberbach, Putnam and Rockman. Focusing attention on real-world instances of these images fosters insights into the evolving responsibilities and influence of public administrators.

Observe, for example, the following extract from the Auditor General of Canada's[33] April 1997 *Report*. The question "What does the public service do?" is posed, and three functions are described. One is service provision and application of policy. Another is to respond to issues below the threshold of public attention. The third carries clear overtones of the already explained image number three.

> One principal role of the public service is to provide policy advice to ministers. This role is carried out primarily by the more senior members of the public service, with staff support. It involves such matters as definition of issues, consultations with interested parties, identification of options, analysis, consensus building, consultation with other sources of policy expertise, and development of recommendations.[34]

The references to defining issues for the national agenda, to building consensus in response to societal division, and to engaging in consultations with a range of interested parties, speak of more than passive implementation of orders. Modern senior administrators are obviously understood to have a broad range of duties involving the public and the shaping of interest group involvement in political debate. Put simply, this depiction suggests that the senior ranks of the public service may often help prepare the political landscape for the elected ministers.

Image four presents an even closer linkage with significant blurring of the administrator/politician categories. Turning to this possibility let us ponder the example of senior bureaucrats actually seeking elected office and then being appointed to cabinet by the prime minister. Past examples of this career trajectory include such disparate personalities as Jack Pickersgill (senior public official who served as a cabinet minister under Liberal governments and then moved on to head a federal regulatory commission in the transportation field), Lester Pearson (senior Canadian figure in the world of diplomacy and international affairs who served as a Liberal cabinet minister, leader of the Opposition and ultimately prime minister), Mitchell Sharp (senior public official who also served as a cabinet minister under

Liberal governments and who now assists the Chrétien government with advice on ethical and other matters), and, surprisingly enough, Lucien Bouchard (who went from being an ambassador to an abbreviated term as a Mulroney cabinet minister before moving on to lead a political party). Pickersgill's case stands out because when he ultimately opted to run for elected office he "was Clerk of the Privy Council and secretary to Mr. St. Laurent's cabinet, theoretically a non-partisan position."[35]

The practice of moving from the upper echelons of the public service into electoral politics continues. A modern example is the case of Marcel Massé whose long and distinguished career as a public servant spanned Liberal and Progressive Conservative governments. Under the Mulroney government, he attained the position of Secretary to the Cabinet for Intergovernmental Affairs. Given the tensions left by failed constitutional accords and federal-provincial rivalries, this was clearly a senior posting. In spite of (or perhaps because of) this impressive bureaucratic career, Massé was the focus of recruitment initiatives from both Liberals and Progressive Conservatives. In the end, the Liberals won out and in 1993 Massé became "one of the party's star candidates, hand-picked by Chrétien to run in Hull-Aylmer riding over the objections of the riding association."[36]

The permeability of the supposed walls between elected politicians and senior officials is made evident by examples like Pickersgill, Sharp, Bouchard and Massé. Massé, like others before him, brought detailed knowledge of the workings of government administration to the cabinet table. His cabinet career has included stints as Minister of Intergovernmental Affairs Responsible for Public Service Renewal and President of the Treasury Board, a critical cabinet committee responsible for overseeing spending, government labour relations, and public sector management. These postings have allowed him room to pursue his designs for modern governance: "Massé pushed his plan for a systematic and comprehensive rethinking of government from the moment he first signed on with Chrétien."[37] His influence clearly contributed to the forces propelling the Liberal government to trim public service ranks. Upon taking power in 1993, the Liberals embarked upon major employment cuts. The contrast with the Mulroney government's record is clearly drawn out by Lee and Hobbs: "The employment reductions achieved by the Liberals in the 16 months prior to the 1995 downsizing program were impressive and substantial compared to the much smaller reductions under the Mulroney government over nine years. Clearly the Liberal government has been much more efficient at terminating public servants."[38] Restraint remained a priority and in 1995–96, for example, public service separations (people leaving the system) reached nearly 20 000.[39]

Massé's appeal to diverse political parties, and his ability to wield power in both administrative and political posts, speaks to his possession of considerable talent. What is more intriguing, though, is that they also speak to the fourth image noted earlier. Conceptions such as professional administrator or politician become blurred when transitions are made so easily. This ease may have some social advantages (range of opportunities for capable individuals, broader talent pool for political leadership, provision of administrative experience to cabinet), but it also raises some serious regulatory complexities. These complexities extend not simply to the demarcation of administrators from politicians, they extend to the dilemma of grafting these and other new realities about politics and administration to society's traditional, yet often conflicting, ideas about the administrative culture in the Canadian public sector.

Before moving on to discuss the regulatory difficulties posed by this evolution, it might be useful to first note an additional example of the kinds of blurring which takes place across the presumed politics/administration divide. Governments may be tempted to select senior civil servants in accordance with their attentiveness to the governing party's cause. Deputy ministers are the senior bureaucrats who oversee the operation and administration of governmental departments. They are charged with the items noted earlier by the Auditor General's Office, advising ministers on courses of action, the credibility of interest groups encountered by the minister, the mediation of disputes, etc. What lifts this from the third image paradigm to the fourth is the added element of commitment to the spirit of a particular government's agenda. It is, of course, commonplace for incoming governments to complain that the public service they inherit is biased toward their now departing predecessors. The standard argument is that over time the civil servants have come to think like the previous government and see their career opportunities in accordance with the previous government's priorities. Yet the argument that the upper ranks of the public service are proponents of the partisan agenda of the cabinet, is now taking on a more proactive characterization. Listen, for example, to the characterization of deputy ministers in the British Columbia public service since the early 1990s offered by Norman Ruff: "From this point on, B.C. seems to have pushed at the boundary line between a program-oriented senior bureaucracy and one whose commitments and sense of accountability extends beyond programs, the legislature, or public to their authors—the governing party."[40]

Governments have for years endeavoured to control administrative conduct in hopes of promoting public confidence and raising the level of public service performance. As already noted, there is a longstanding, widely held assumption that administration can be separated from politics and that public servants have a duty to accept political direction and then perform their work in an objective manner untainted by partisanship and party loyalties. The parliamentary model of government provides political direction via the cabinet and its position at the nexus of representative politics and administration. As Sutherland and Mitchell recount elsewhere in this volume, ministers are deemed to be responsible and answerable for the actions of their departments. As the political heads of departments and ministries, cabinet ministers were assumed to be accountable to Parliament and to the public for administrative performance. This was assumed to allow members of the general public to have a focal point for their complaints about unfair or inappropriate treatment. This ideal was (and generally still is) seen as part of a value system shaped by ultimate political control over administration, provision of equal service to all, encouragement of public service professionalism, and reliance upon ministers to act responsibly. While this value system may have appeal for many, analysis of its underpinnings raises questions. In a society with a Charter guaranteeing free expression and association, where do we draw the lines for political involvement by public servants? What are the legal implications of the Charter? Why are there debates over the meaning and feasibility of ministerial responsibility in the modern age? How do we gauge what is appropriate conduct on the part of those working for government? How should a public organization react if the political expressions of its employees irritate the government and/or the general public? These and other issues continue to generate lively controversy. Various institutions (courts, human rights commissions, academics, etc.) have made useful contributions to elements of this controversy. However, important disputes persist. Kenneth Kernaghan and John Langford published a superb work in 1990 on the importance of the ethical issues associated with responsible bureaucratic conduct. In regard to the basic issue of public service neutrality, they reported, "Moreover, not only public servants but judges, legislators, journalists, and academics as well are uncertain or in disagreement as to the current meaning of the public servant's duty to be politically neutral."[41]

Even if there were to be agreement on what neutrality would involve, there are indications that political and social forces intrude via other avenues. The heralded search for professional neutrality and strict reliance upon objective merit may not be a completely accurate depiction of actual Canadian experience. For example, have Canadians or, more to the point, has the Canadian government always wanted a "neutral" public service? There is a long history of controls and monitoring being applied in Canada to test the loyalty of public servants and to screen those believed to be politically misguided. Fears about those perceived to have political beliefs deemed undesirable led to elaborate screening mechanisms, what Hannant calls "the infernal machine." "The evidence shows that the RCMP did not begin to screen civil servants to search for Soviet spies. What gave birth to the machine was the fear of domestic communism."[42] Have we as Canadians, or has our government, always been wholly committed to hiring the best people available? Our national record on this front is also open to some discussion. In various ways, for example, barriers were placed in the way of women seeking public service employment: "In 1921 formal restrictions were placed against the employment of married women."[43] For 34 years this hurdle persisted. Married women who wished to work either had to exhibit their financial need or engage in subterfuge. Even then, their employment possibilities still rested on the hope that an inadequate number of males would be available.

To get a sense of an actual dispute in the contemporary regulatory environment let us examine a case written up in the 1995 *Annual Report* of the New Brunswick Ombudsman.[44] Bear in mind that constitutionally Canada is a federation and, as a result, the provincial governments have their own spheres of authority. With this they have considerable freedom in the operation and organization of their governing institutions. The Office of the Ombudsman is a Scandinavian innovation which has spread around the world. It refers to an individual charged with examining bureaucratic conduct or administrative practices, and attempting to rectify wrongs in a straightforward and effective fashion. At issue for the New Brunswick Ombudsman was the following scenario. An individual was involved in a provincial employment program called the N.B. Job Corps. This program offered opportunities for workers between 50 and 65 who would have difficulties re-entering the work force. In exchange for volunteering with community efforts, individuals "are guaranteed a work placement of 26 weeks each year" for which they can "receive taxable monthly benefits to a maximum of $12 000 per year."[45] The individual in question consulted his or her (the individual was anonymous in the *Report*) supervisor about the possibility of running as an independent candidate in a provincial election. The supervisor responded that remaining in the N.B. Job Corps was incompatible with being an electoral candidate. The basis of the incompatibility was the provincial *Civil Service Act* which contained restrictions on political involvement. Such types of restrictions are a common way of promoting the idea of a neutral public service.

Dissatisfied with this outcome, the individual approached the Ombudsman's Office. Due to the supervisor's answer and the obvious time limitations resulting from the electoral process, the individual lost the opportunity to run. Yet the person did receive good news from the investigation by the Office of the Ombudsman. They sided with the individual because the employment program differed from employment in a more "regular" bureaucratic position. The root of the problem was the evident failure to contemplate this eventuality when either the *Civil Service Act* or the N.B. Job Corps were developed. The Ombudsman's "Office recommended that political restrictions regarding persons in special employment programs be clarified and that information be distributed to all managers and individuals involved with such programs."[46] An apology was extended to the individual and the results of the Ombudsman's findings were transmitted to relevant personnel. Further inquiry to the Office of the Ombudsman revealed[47] that the N.B. Job Corps is now slated for termination. In light of this, the *Civil Service Act* has not been amended.

This New Brunswick case is illustrative of a broad trend throughout the world of Canadian public administration: the difficulty of applying traditional nostrums to an era of new service delivery approaches and widespread contracting-out of responsibilities. In the past, government programs were generally offered by large teams of public servants. Benefits to those in need usually came in the form of cheques or vouchers. Both of these approaches are under attack. There are those within the New Public Management School who advocate that governments should contract out service provision to others. Governments are encouraged to generate market competition among these providers.[48] If others will manage recreational facilities or collect urban refuse, does the relevant government still need to employ public servants to perform these tasks? Opting to contract out such responsibilities raises questions about continued adherence to past beliefs about the character of the public service. New questions are spawned by the ongoing experimentation in the field of social services. New employment creation strategies which feature payment for work and community service further undermine past assumptions about how to define civil servants.

Analysis of these debates lends support for the already noted hypotheses. The first is that the apparently simple question of defining who or what a civil servant is has layers of underlying difficulty. The second is that traditional calls for political neutrality or for neutral objectivity within the public service are inadequate in an era of Charter protections and rights consciousness, mixed with contracting out of services and other new organizational arrangements. This generates a third observation, that efforts to regulate the boundaries of politics and administration inevitably encounter important practical and legal difficulties.

In closing this discussion, let us explore a case where these matters were argued all the way up to Canada's Supreme Court. It relates to a former CBC on-air figure who held a leadership position in a union, many of whose members were dubious about the benefits of the then-emerging Canada–U.S. free trade. Meanwhile, the negotiation of such a trade arrangement was a primary political objective of the prevailing federal government, that of Brian Mulroney. Fearful for their public image and journalistic stature, CBC executives acted to restrain union activism and the resulting clash illustrates the blending of political and administrative elements and the challenge of setting appropriate social standards for the future. In this instance the ruling executives at the CBC did want a neutral group of broadcast professionals, but their strategy had not accounted for political freedoms and rights of expression.

Dale Goldhawk worked as host of a CBC radio program. The program's theme was discussion of current controversial issues through in-station guests and telephone calls from across the country. Mr. Goldhawk became president of the Alliance of Canadian Cinema, Television and Radio Artists (ACTRA) and, as such, he naturally took on the role of speaking out on issues of concern to the members of the Alliance. One of these issues was Canada–U.S. free trade, an issue which gripped Canadians during the election campaign of 1988. Goldhawk authored an anti-free trade piece in a union periodical. The CBC became alarmed about perceived partiality on Goldhawk's part against the free trade initiative. Their intervention led to negotiation of an agreement that Goldhawk would give up his position as host, pending the election day. This did not end matters and CBC continued to pressure Mr. Goldhawk. He offered to give up speaking out on behalf of his union, ACTRA. CBC executives found this unacceptable and an ultimatum developed whereby Goldhawk could either give up the union presidency or relinquish his position as program host. Goldhawk's actual on-the-job performance was not apparently the issue. The CBC's head of current affairs (radio) stated that "Dale's journalism has been impeccable throughout, yet concerns arose over the perception of bias."[49] Mr. Goldhawk opted to remain as radio host, a not unsurprising choice given his career aspirations and professional interests. It was not a choice made willingly. Goldhawk publicly lamented, "Where do we draw lines here? Does no journalist who works at the CBC have any right to take an active role in their union?" ACTRA filed a formal complaint asserting that the CBC had unduly interfered with legitimate union activity. ACTRA's General Secretary declared that the CBC "is attempting to muzzle journalists who exercise their right to participate fully in the activities of their union."[50] The complaint went to the relevant regulatory agency for labour disputes within federal jurisdiction, the Canada Labour Relations Board, which ruled in favour of Goldhawk and ACTRA and their ability to speak freely and engage in public debate. Furthermore, "the CBC could offer no evidence to the labor board that Goldhawk's work performance was influenced by his union position."[51] Nonetheless, CBC executives were dissatisfied with the outcome and subsequently appealed first to the Federal Court of Appeal and then to the Supreme Court, but the appeals were all in vain.

The regulatory judgment and the court appeals raised esoteric questions involving labour law and judicial review of regulatory board decisions which are beyond the scope of this paper. Despite this, the fundamental question throughout the long dispute is easily understandable. Did the CBC have a right to restrain Mr. Goldhawk's performance of his duties? Arising from this is the larger conundrum of how to reconcile regulatory models which assume neutrality and separation of public service administration from political factors, with modern guarantees of free speech and association as well as union involvement in public debate. There is no simple answer, but these issues need to be raised.

CONCLUSION

Is public sector administration important to the study of politics (or political science)? This introductory essay offers several reasons why that question should be answered in the affirmative. First is the obvious yet often overlooked reality that poor or abusive administration of public programs often results in a large price tag, raises interest group and media concerns, and produces unhappy constituents. The second rationale relates to Truman's perception of Eisenhower's expectations and relates to the political factors that may impinge upon smooth implementation of executive orders. Such factors can include voter sentiment, rivalry among differing agencies or political leaders, citizen utilization of Charter rights and freedoms, and interest group lobbying. Weber's early insights offer another argument about the relevance of administration which is the power possessed by the modern bureaucracy and the difficulty of holding bureaucratic institutions politically accountable for their actions. Related to this argument are the new insights offered by modern scholars about the evolving relationship between senior politicians and bureaucrats. There are empirical examples supporting their arguments and uncertainty remains about the implications of these developments. Finally, there remains what might be called the pragmatic dilemma of how society may wish to regulate administrative performance and behaviour in light of modern trends and pressures.

Political studies or political science has a long history of being concerned with these sorts of topics. Reference has been made to some of the distinguished contributors to the public administration literature. Their insights are fruitful sources of ideas and reference to them can help shape our research questions. There is much that remains to be sorted out and much that will challenge our powers of analysis. The issues raised by this and the succeeding chapters are indications of some of the interesting debates offered for students of public administration.

NOTES

1. David McCullough, *Truman* (New York: Simon and Schuster, 1992), 914.

2. Both quotes are found in William Walker, "A Nuclear Cult 'Ran Reactors'" [Toronto] *The Toronto Star* 14 August 1997: A1. For further information on the issue one may note Stan Josey and Jane Armstrong, "Hydro Shock: 7 Reactors to Shut, President Quits" [Toronto] *The Toronto Star* 13 August 1997: A1, A17.

3. Canada, Report of the Commission of Inquiry into the Deployment of Canadian Forces to Somalia, *Dishonoured Legacy: The Lessons of the Somalia Affair* (Ottawa: Canadian Government Publishing, 1997): Executive Summary–1.

4. Michael Hirsh, "Infernal Revenue Disservice," *Newsweek* 13 October 1997: 34–5.

5. Leslie Seidle, "Introduction," *Rethinking Government: Reform or Reinvention*, ed. Leslie Seidle (Montreal: IRPP, 1993), 7.

6. Michael Atkinson, "Introduction," *Governing Canada: Institutions and Public Policy*, ed. Michael M. Atkinson (Toronto: Harcourt Brace Jovanovich, 1993), 5.

7. Woodrow Wilson, "The Study of Administration," *Political Science Quarterly*, 2:1 (1887): 197–222. Wilson, of course, later went on to serve as president of the United States.

8. Dwight Waldo, *The Enterprise of Public Administration* (Novato, California: Chandler and Sharp, 1980), 11. The italicized word is italicized in the original.

9. Wilson, "The Study of Administration," 201.

10. Ibid., 210. Italicized word is italicized in the original.

11. Nicholas L. Henry, *Public Administration and Public Affairs*, 3rd ed. (Eaglewood Cliffs: Prentice-Hall, 1986), 20.

12. Max Weber, "Bureaucracy," *From Max Weber: Essays in Sociology*, ed. and trans. H. H. Gerth and C. Wright Mills (New York: Oxford University Press, 1958), 197.

13. Ibid., 214.

14. Richard J. Stillman II, *Preface to Public Administration: A Search for Themes and Direction* (New York: St. Martin's Press, 1991), 127.

15. Peter M. Blau and Marshall W. Meyer, *Bureaucracy in Modern Society*, 3rd ed. (New York: Random House, 1987), 19.

16. Weber, 233.

17. Weber, 232.

18. Martin Albrow, *Bureaucracy* (London: Macmillan, 1970), 48.

19. See, for example, Albrow, 49.

20. Waldo, *The Enterprise of Public Administration,* 87.

21. For an account of the issues related to the Rockefeller philanthropies and public reaction, see Alasdair Roberts, "Demonstrating Neutrality: The Rockefeller Philanthropies and the Evolution of Public Administration, 1927–1936," *Public Administration Review*, 54:3 (May/June 1994): 221–8.

22. Ibid., 227.

23. J. E. Hodgetts, "The Intellectual Odyssey of Public Administration in English Canada," *Canadian Public Administration*, 40.2 (Summer 1997): 179.

24. Alexander Brady, "The University and the Study of Public Administration," *Canadian Journal of Economics and Political Science*, 11.4 (November 1945): 520.

25. Joel D. Aberbach, Robert D. Putnam and Bert A. Rockman, with the collaboration of Thomas J. Anton, Samuel J. Eldersveld and Ronald Inglehart, *Bureaucrats and Politicians in Western Democracies* (Cambridge: Harvard University Press, 1981).

26. Ibid., vii.

27. The distinctions among the images are made clear in chapter 1 of the book, pp. 1–23.

28. Aberbach et al., 9.

29. Ibid., 252.

30. Ibid., 253.

31. See, for example, Colin Campbell, SJ, and B. Guy Peters, "The Politics/Administration Dichotomy: Death or Merely Change," *Governance*, 1.1 (January 1988): 82. This issue of the Journal contains several interesting essays inspired by, or resulting from, the debates entered into by the Aberbach et al. volume.

32. In addition to works cited here see, for example, Donald J. Savoie, *Thatcher, Reagan, Mulroney: In Search of a New Bureaucracy* (Pittsburgh: University of Pittsburgh Press, 1994); and David Osborne and Ted Gaebler, *Reinventing Government* (Reading: Addison-Wesley Publishing, 1992).

33. The Auditor General of Canada is a servant of Parliament appointed to monitor the Public Accounts and the expenditure of public funds. The Auditor General oversees a staff and their reports provide analysis of spending and management practices and indicate possible improvements.

34. Canada, "Maintaining a Competent and Efficient Public Service," *Report of the Auditor General of Canada to the House of Commons* (Ottawa: Minister of Public Works and Government Services of Canada, 1997): 1–9.

35. Hugh Winsor, "The Power Game: Pickersgill's Clout Set the Standard" [Toronto] *The Globe and Mail* 19 November 1997: A4.

36. Edward Greenspon and Anthony Wilson-Smith, *Double Vision: The Inside Story of the Liberals in Power* (Toronto: Doubleday Canada, 1996), 107.

37. Ibid., 114.

38. Ian Lee and Clem Hobbs, "Pink Slips and Running Shoes: The Liberal Government's Downsizing of the Public Service," *How Ottawa Spends 1996–97: Life Under the Knife*, ed. Gene Swimmer (Ottawa: Carleton University Press, 1996), 373.

39. *Report of the Auditor General,* 1–14.

40. Norman Ruff, "Provincial Governance and the Public Service: Bureaucratic Transitions and Change," *Politics, Policy, and Government in British Columbia*, ed. Ken Carty (Vancouver: UBC Press, 1996), 170.

41. Kenneth Kernaghan and John W. Langford, *The Responsible Public Servant* (Halifax: IRPP, 1990), 79.

42. Larry Hannant, *The Infernal Machine: Investigating the Loyalty of Canada's Citizens* (Toronto: University of Toronto, 1995), 242.

43. J. E. Hodgetts, William McCloskey, Reginald Whitaker, and V. Seymour Wilson, *The Biography of an Institution: The Civil Service Commission of Canada 1908–1967* (Montreal: McGill-Queen's, 1972), 486.

44. Office of the Ombudsman, *Annual Report 1995* (Fredericton: Office of the Ombudsman, 1997), 84–5.

45. William J. Milne, *The McKenna Miracle: Myth or Reality?* (Toronto: University of Toronto Press, 1996), 77.

46. Ombudsman, *Annual Report 1995,* 85.

47. Correspondence dated October 6, 1997, to the author from Ellen E. King, Ombudsman for New Brunswick.

48. For a useful discussion of this from a Canadian perspective see Leslie A. Pal, *Beyond Policy Analysis: Public Issue Management in Turbulent Times* (Scarborough: Nelson, 1997), 54–62 and 156–83.

49. "Goldhawk Retires During Election" [Toronto] *The Globe and Mail* 11 November 1988: C10.

50. Lorne Slotnick, "CBC Union Promises to Fight Forced Resignation of President" [Toronto] *The Globe and Mail* 25 November 1988: A10.

51. "CBC Violated Labor Code, Court Rules" [Toronto] *The Toronto Star* 15 May 1992: A24.

POLITICS, ACCOUNTABILITY, AND GOVERNMENT ADMINISTRATION

The public administration of democratic societies takes place within an environment shaped by the values and institutions of constitutional governance. As the fundamental rules, values, and understandings which guide political life and judicial rulings, the constitution is the foundation for social and political order. Elements of a constitution come from differing sources; examples include, but are not limited to, centrally important documents, traditions and conventions, court rulings on the interpretation of fundamental matters such as the interpretation of Charter rights or the division of federal and provincial powers, etc. Constitutional proprieties must be adhered to in the conduct and oversight of administrative behaviour and decision making. A fundamentally important consideration of Canada's Constitution and democratic institutions is that the bureaucracy and the practice of public administration should be accountable to the democratically constituted government.

Within the Canadian political system the primary nexus of accountability works through cabinet and the respective ministers within the cabinet. Formally, executive authority (executive authority relates to the power to execute decisions, to direct the bureaucracy, and to exercise ultimate political and administrative leadership authority) continues to reside with the monarch of the United Kingdom and his or her Canadian designate, the governor general. Effective executive authority resides with the prime minister (or premier) and her or his cabinet. Ministers owe their allegiance to cabinet and it functions with a degree of solidarity under the leadership of the prime minister. They actually direct the priorities of the government, oversee administration of public affairs, and supervise the public purse. Each minister is expected to be accountable for events within her or his assigned portfolio (field of functional responsibility, for example, Finance, Health and Welfare, and Justice) and is expected to answer questions about affairs within this portfolio arising from members of parliament, the media, representatives of other levels of government or interest groups.

This section provides complementary examinations of the arrangements for accountability provided by the Canadian constitutional order. Accountability is a complex concept, but basically it refers to the responsibility of governments to be responsible to the House of Commons and to be aware of their need to account for the trust and resources with which they have been entrusted by the citizenry. James Mitchell and Sharon Sutherland outline the basics of ministerial responsibility and place its operation within Canada's long constitutional heritage. This situates the lineage of the concept and illustrates how deeply it is interwoven into the constitutional order. David Docherty brings Parliament into the discussion and points out the activities of MPs. Parliament refers to the monarch/governor general, the Senate, and the House of Commons. In most cases the House of Commons is the scene of the most intense action and Docherty illuminates the workload of parliamentarians and the expectations people have of their performance. This ties neatly into the themes introduced by Mitchell and Sutherland, for the operations of Parliament (Question Period and the debate of public bills, for example) are structured around the authority and accountability of cabinet and individual ministers. Together, these two readings emphasize the constitutional importance of democratic control of government operations and the built-in mechanisms for accountability.

DISCUSSION QUESTIONS

1. Why should governments care what other people think? Why should they consider the views of MPs? senators? representatives of other levels of government? the judiciary? the media?

2. What is ministerial responsibility? Why should ministers receive this heavy responsibility? What might be the strengths and weaknesses of such a system?

3. Would you like to be a cabinet minister? Why or why not? Is there a portfolio that would appeal to you? Why or why not?

4. How do you envision the collective deliberations of cabinet? How do you think it would feel to sit around the cabinet table, catch the prime minister's eye, and start to speak out on an issue of national concern? What kind of expectations do you have of cabinet meetings and decision making?

5. Do you ever watch the proceedings of the federal House of Commons or your provincial legislative assembly? of your local government? What are your impressions? Why?

6. What role is played by our parliamentary institutions and the work of the MPs of the various parties? Do these institutions and the MPs contribute to the accountability of government? How?

7. What implications do you draw from Docherty's commentary? Why?

8. Can you imagine possible improvements that would make parliamentary proceedings more salient in the eyes of average Canadians? Would you like to be an MP? Would it affect your response if you knew you would never receive a cabinet appointment? What opportunities would be offered by being an MP?

MINISTERIAL RESPONSIBILITY: The Submission of Politics and Administration to the Electorate

James R. Mitchell
and S. L. Sutherland

Ministerial responsibility is the defining principle of our system of parliamentary and cabinet government, a system that is generally known as *Westminster* government.[1] Ministerial responsibility ensures the democratic accountability of ministers to the elected legislature. It also has the core democratic virtue of making the bureaucracy subservient to the elected government and, through the government, subordinate to the electorate.

Our purpose in this chapter is to explain the doctrine of ministerial responsibility in something like an ideal form.[2] Our presentation of the ideal includes, in addition to doctrine, a description of how government organizations are structured, and a description of how answerability relationships work in the three phases of public policy creation—from ideas through implementation to learning about the consequences. Near the end of the chapter we acknowledge some of the more serious complications in Canada's political system.

Our basic argument in support of Westminster government, which we expand upon below, can be put in a nutshell as follows. The advantage of making politicians responsible to citizens is that the politicians' duty to *explain* compels them to take charge of problems as those problems are brought to their attention in the House of Commons and in the media. Out of that selective attention to problems as they arise come two advantages. First, the power and authority to make changes to policy are reserved for elected politicians—not non-elected (appointed) officials. Second, the question of how much a minister can "really" know about the activities of his or her huge department simply does not matter; the minister need only exercise competent leadership in a small number of areas of current interest.[3] These are two of the features that have made the Westminster model such a successful form of democratic government in so many different parts of the world. Westminster government is the only form of government that makes elected politicians uniquely responsible for what happens as a result of the administrative actions of the state.

Bureaucracy

We call the modern state "the administrative state" because the modern era is in many ways the era of administration or bureaucracy. A bureaucracy can be defined as a hierarchical organization in which people:

(a) work for purposes, and toward goals, that are approved at the top of the organization;

(b) provide their labour for fixed salaries, the level of which is determined for a class of employees rather than on an individual basis;

(c) work, almost without exception, under fairly close supervision; and

(d) can be disciplined or displaced on grounds of incompetence.

Although they are constrained in many ways by law, regulation, and the constant scrutiny of Parliament, public servants also enjoy a fair degree of autonomy in their work: they cannot be told to disobey the law, nor can they apply or suspend sanctions to members of the public for irrelevant reasons; and they generally have some role in deciding their own conditions of work. In addition, public servants have a certain autonomy or range of discretion in how they interpret their jobs and in how they reason in individual cases. Speaking very generally, discretion is less and supervision is more intense at the low end of the hierarchy. Nevertheless, in the highest positions, and in jobs where an individual's work will be seen by the minister, all work is subjected to intense study by many persons.[4]

Bureaucracies existed long before democracy emerged. In fact, democracy has had to find ways to fit the principle of popular control over the actions of the state around the bureaucratic fact. Historically, the only experiments with democracy that were not supported by bureaucracy were the city-state democracies of ancient Greece, in which citizens (adult free males) were chosen by lot to perform administrative tasks for short periods.[5] Yet even in Greece, the inevitable standing armies were led by professionals.[6]

There are really only two options for keeping bureaucracies from becoming dictatorships of permanent officials. Klaus König distinguishes between two "styles" of government control: "civic culture" bureaucracies, such as those of the Anglo-American democracies, and the "classical" bureaucracies of Europe. The civic culture governments evolved almost seamlessly over time from the British tradition. They control their bureaucracies by making them work closely with the political executive and making them subservient to the values of the political regime.[7] The countries that have followed this tradition (notably the United Kingdom and the countries of the "old" Commonwealth) have been able to maintain continuous political leadership of administrative activity because there have been no historical upheavals of such force that it became necessary for bureaucracies to function without such leadership.

In continental Europe, by contrast, and all the way through the 20th century, republics have alternated with monarchies and dictatorships with democracies, with periods of intense civil strife between. We tend to think of France as having been a republic since the revolution in 1789. Yet two empires punctuated the next century, those of Napoleon Bonaparte from 1799 to 1815 and of his nephew Louis Napoleon from 1852 to 1870. Indeed, in some cases in European history, and as recently as in Italy after World War II, bureaucracies have provided law and order, run schools and hospitals and collected taxes—have provided government essentially on their own account—when the political executive was discredited by war or caught in a turmoil of dissolving coalitions.[8]

In continental Europe, therefore, the *continuity* of the elected executive could not constitute a "regulative idea" (König's words) to prevent the servants of the state from abusing their power for their own ends. In much of Europe the regulative idea was the idea of the *state itself* as the provider, directly under the rule of law, of civic order and care. This notion led to the elaboration of complex and detailed codes of public law, of which administrative law is a part. In France, the *Code Civil* or *Code Napoléon* of 1804 was to influence the development of law in many countries. To this day in continental Europe, administrative law provides a central if not the main principle for control of officials' actions. In turn, public officials are specialists in public and administrative law and "civil servant" is a professional designation.[9]

This distinction between civic culture and legal polities that we have just described may be somewhat too sharply drawn for the end of the 20th century, because the Anglo-American countries are increasingly developing their own bodies of public law and administrative law. Canadians saw the constitutional entrenchment of the *Canadian Charter of Rights and Freedoms* in 1982. This is a foundational public law (sometimes called "political" law) and a central element of the written part of Canada's Constitution. Administrative law, which provides for verification of the purely technical legality of bureaucratic action, as well as elements of fairness, is also an increasingly imposing part of the public law of even the countries that have followed British traditions of government. König himself notes that it is now more appropriate to distinguish between (a) "managerial" (Anglo-American) countries, where politicians have maintained power to quickly and completely change many features of government, and (b) the "legalistic" continental nations, where governmental change has been much slower and more superficial.

Bureaucracy, in short, is an essential underpinning of the state. If not watched carefully, the state apparatus may well end up serving only itself. There are basically two strategies for preventing this: leadership of administration by the political executive (the British system), or correction of administrative action by judges (the continental system). Individual bureaucratic values or the personal goodness of officials is not enough to guarantee the integrity of public administration in either strategy. In our system, it is the political route for control of bureaucracy that has been followed. We explore below the relationships that make political domination of bureaucracy possible.

Responsibility

As noted above, in our system responsibility is the foundation of the regime. We should begin by saying something about responsibility in general. The *Concise Oxford Dictionary* says that an actor is responsible when he or she is liable to be called to account by someone for some thing, or for its absence.[10] When applied to governments, responsibility means that governments cannot be autocratic—they must continually account to a body such as an elected assembly or legislature for what they do.

The secondary meaning of "responsible" offered by our dictionary is that the actor in question will be treated *as though* he or she were the "primary cause" for any given result (italics added). In the governmental context, where political actors are supported by public servants who act on their behalf, this means that those who hold the power of the government (ministers) must be ready to answer personally for whatever happens within the scope of their public office. Whether they knew of an action before the fact or participated in its planning is, except in cases of criminal action or their own personal involvement in poor decisions,[11] completely irrelevant. They cannot pass off political responsibility for the effects of public policy onto their officials, no matter who did what or when.

Both of these two threads are essential for an understanding of ministerial responsibility.

THE RESPONSIBLE MINISTER
IN RESPONSIBLE GOVERNMENT

The master plan for government that Canada inherited from Great Britain is called, interchangeably, "Westminster government" or "responsible government" or, more informally, "cabinet government." The adjective "Westminster" refers to the style of government that developed over time in the old palaces of Westminster that still house the House of Commons and the House of Lords, the representative institutions of government in Britain. In Westminster government, there is a formal "head of state"—in Britain's case the Queen, and in Canada's case the Queen acting through the Governor General—in whose person the authority of the state resides. This is an authority that is exercised on behalf of the Queen by ministers who are accountable to a democratically elected legislature. In practical terms, the most important function of the head of state is to formally designate who will lead the government after an election. More generally, it is to ensure that, even in times of political crisis, there always *is* a government led by elected politicians.

"Parliament," it never hurts to remind the reader, has three parts: the House of Commons, the upper house (the Senate in Canada), and the Crown or the Crown's representative. The approval of all three authorities is necessary before a bill can become law. Except in this sense of approving legislation, "Parliament" does not provide the government of the day. That is the task of the ministry, which is drawn from the majority party in the House of Commons and keeps its seats there, so that it is both part of the House and also the directing committee of the House. In other words, Westminster or responsible government is, above all other things, *party* government, provided by the representatives of the voting (enfranchised) population. We explain the meaning of this statement below.

The Executive

The active part of the "executive," the one that actually exercises the power and authority of the state on a daily basis, has always had two distinguishable parts. The directive or commanding force in Westminster government is termed the *political executive*, or the ministry. This consists of those members of parliament from the majority party who are sworn to office as ministers and who serve as the legal and administrative heads of departments.[12]

As the discussion on bureaucracy will have alerted the reader, Westminster government also includes a *permanent executive*, namely the civil service or bureaucracy, which in Canada is called the "public" service at the federal level. This is composed of all the people working in the dozens of departments and agencies of the government. The public service is deemed "permanent" not because public servants are in their jobs for their whole lives, but because their positions are not directly and immediately affected by an electoral change from one party majority to another. Public servants may leave as they wish or can be fired if they are found incompetent, but they cannot be replaced simply because the governing party has changed. The public service *executes* the operational and advisory tasks that are given to it by the political executive according to the lawful authority of Parliament.

A responsible government is one that has a continuing constitutional obligation to the legislature, and ultimately to the electorate, to either give a satisfactory account of itself or be defeated. The government's duty to answer for its actions in the House of Commons puts both ministers and officials on notice that they must be prudent and act responsibly. That is, every public official, elected or appointed, must act according to principles and for reasons that can meet the tests of publicity and debate, and be found reasonable in the context of the times.

Political Parties

Political parties can be described as the "motor" of responsible government: they provide new ideas while respecting political tradition and political realities. Equally important, they recruit and train people with the stamina and brain power to meet the demands of public office. Ideally, that training is an apprenticeship in progressively more responsible public offices. In the most general sense, party government provides for the continuous existence of cohesive groups of people who act as political rivals, each group held together by a set of beliefs plus, of course, a shared desire to exercise power. These partisans offer their leadership to the public. Parties and elections therefore give the electorate a self-renewing cluster of future-regarding partisans of more or less known ability who are prepared to take over the leadership of the House of Commons, if given the chance.

By winning a majority in the House of Commons, a political party earns the right to govern—that is, to provide political direction to the country and administrative leadership to the departments of government. But responsible government also means that the majority party may at any time lose a vote of confidence in the House of Commons and thus lose its right to govern. In the case of a clear defeat, the prime minister is then obliged to go directly to the Crown to ask for a dissolution of the House, which will bring about an election.[13]

The possibility of defeat—of complete loss of power—illustrates the principle of responsibility at work: in the case of a confidence vote, signals from the public are magnified by debate in the House of Commons. The requirement that the government meet the House to face questions and criticism means that it cannot avoid hearing unwelcome truths, such as that it is behaving in an unpopular manner ("arrogant" or "distanced") or that it is on a track that the public does not want, such as refusing to investigate the safety of medicines or food products, or failing to react "responsibly" to changes in the economy or the market, or raising taxes for purposes the public did not foresee or approve.

In brief, then, one can say that the political executive (that is, the prime minister and cabinet) is the steering committee for the majority party whose mandate derives from popular support that is given only temporarily (that is, every five years or less) to the members of the House of Commons. As noted, that support can be taken away at any time during those five years. The plans and actions of the executive, and its performance in governing the country, are exposed to the test of publicity by the continuing watchfulness of all the members of the House of Commons—both the members of the opposition parties and the private or backbench members of the governing party. They are also subject to the scrutiny of the media, who daily bring the actions of the government to the attention of the electorate.

Ideally (yes, again), our system of responsible government ensures that the political executive will be closely tuned to the wants and needs of the public. It also provides that if the government proves seriously unresponsive, incompetent or deceitful, it can be dismissed by a simple majority vote of the House.[14] All of this, of course, is the ideal. In practical terms the quality of our democracy depends very much on the competence and sense of responsibility of the members of the House of Commons (see David Docherty's chapter in this volume). And it of course depends very heavily on the individual MP's capacity, as the ears and voice of his or her constituents, to try to understand what is behind individual complaints, so that public policy problems can be identified. We briefly recall some of the short-comings in actual practice below. But, perfect or imperfect, it is important to remember that under our system the House of Commons cannot and should not try to govern. That is the job of ministers. Nor can the House be held responsible for policy choices or still less for outcomes. Members of parliament are there to criticize the performance of the government, to question its platform and agenda, and to contest its standing with the public.

THE RULES OF RESPONSIBLE GOVERNMENT (CABINET GOVERNMENT)

To say that "Parliament" (that is, the Commons, the Senate, and the Crown taken together) is sovereign means, for our purposes, that the principles set out above will be respected. It means, among other things, that any given government—and, by extension, the Parliament of which it is the active force—is not limited by measures passed by previous Parliaments. A Parliament cannot, without full publicity and constitutional amendment, foreclose the future by limiting the range of options open to future governments. Yet no government, no matter how large its majority, has unlimited authority. It will always be limited in its range of options by the law, by the division of powers entrenched in the Constitution, by the fundamental rights of persons protected under statute or entrenched in the *Charter of Rights and Freedoms*, and to some extent by custom, political tradition, and culture.[15] Besides, the actual agenda of the government will be restricted by rough-and-tumble politics between ministers, divisions in its own body of supporters (the total of which, including both leading personnel and backbenchers, is called "caucus"), the size of its majority if it has one, its standing with the public, the character of the opposition parties, the economic situation, and the state of Canada's relationships with other nations, to name only a few factors.

The foregoing are the most basic principles and challenges of Westminster government. From them one can understand more easily how the various elements of our system fit together and how they work.

1. The Department and the Arm's-Length Organizations

The basic organizational entity in the Westminster system is the department. This can be defined as an organization with a minister at its head, both in legal terms and those of daily administration. Powers are formally assigned in law to the minister, not to the department as an organization.[16] Except in regard to pressing or interesting issues, those powers are normally executed *on behalf of* the minister by officials who are accountable up the departmental hierarchy to the minister. Constitutionally speaking, those officials are simply "part of" the minister.

We also need to say a few words about organizations that are *not* ministerial departments; that is, about the mixed group of bodies that deliver public policy but nevertheless operate at arm's length from the minister or the cabinet. In Canada this category includes a variety of organizational types. There are "crown corporations" (the Crown being the symbol for the state in systems that have been inherited from Britain) such as Atomic Energy of Canada Ltd., which are set up to carry out commercial or quasi-commercial activities. In some cases these entities are supported by appropriations (money voted in the House of Commons) while others operate on a purely or partly commercial basis. The category also includes boards and other agencies such as the National Energy Board and the Canadian Transportation Agency that perform regulatory or other administrative functions where it is deemed to be in the public interest to separate those functions from the minister and the department. And it includes bodies such as the Canadian Human Rights Commission and the Canadian Radio-television and Telecommunications Commission that carry out various kinds of quasi-judicial functions, again in areas where decision making is deemed better left to an independent, specialist body than to a minister or to the courts.

Although nondepartmental organizations have a long history in the Westminster tradition, experience has shown that the degree of independence of arm's-length bodies, and the absence of the minister from their daily affairs, is often only a matter of timing. Such separation from politicians may last only until an event or a series of problems raises the public interest enough to put the issue onto the political agenda. At this point the government must provide explanations to Parliament and to the public to assure them that things are being properly managed, even if at arm's length. Eventually, the government may have to step into the affairs of the organization. An example is the slow trajectory, from the late 1970s to the late 1990s, of the issue of the safety of the blood supply. This has gone from being a matter under the jurisdiction of a private body (the Red Cross) to one where the federal and provincial governments collectively have taken over this function. While neither the political executive (the cabinet) nor the permanent executive (the public service) had direct responsibility in the past for running the blood supply, the fact is that the government *always* has political responsibility for the public interest, just as it has what could be called "architectural" responsibility for designing the relationships between various kinds of public bodies. Where the public interest dictates a change in those relationships, governments will eventually act. As a principle of parliamentary sovereignty, as we have noted above, the arrangements put in place by past governments cannot permanently distance future governments from pressing concerns. While we take up this point again below, it does not hurt to say clearly now that this irresistible transmutation of issues from technical delivery tasks to the highest and most urgent policy concerns, and vice versa, makes nonsense of all attempts to separate, in principle, policy making from administrative work.

It is perhaps also important to clarify that we are not claiming that the accountability arrangements under Westminster rules always function flawlessly and immediately. What we are saying is that they function *politically*. The competition between the government and the opposition tends to lead to the identification of problems, to publicity, and to discussion and study, followed by argument, publicity, more discussion...and eventually by action. Some political challenges are far more difficult than others. For example, finding the techniques and maintaining a significant element of civilian control over policing and over the military (see Peter Desbarats in this volume) are both stressful and painful, and full of political traps. This is why we are calling parties—which provide the candidates who are ready to be elected to public office—the motor of democratic government.

2. Individual and Collective Responsibility

Ministers are both *in* and *of* Parliament, almost always the House of Commons.[17] Each minister is constitutionally responsible (answerable) for what is done or proposed by the minister, by the government acting in the area of authority of the minister, or by those acting under the authority of the minister.

A government must provide effective answerability by individual ministers to the House of Commons at the same time as it politically manages the House of Commons to maintain its voting majority. These two forms of responsibility are most often signalled under the terms *individual ministerial responsibility* and *collective ministerial responsibility.*

Under individual ministerial responsibility, the minister of the day provides answerability in the House of Commons and to the public for any event or problem in his or her sphere of legal responsibility, no matter how far back in time it occurred. Thus, the Minister of National Defence was properly forced to answer in 1996 and 1997 with respect to the alleged murder of a Somali civilian by Canadian peacekeepers, an event that had occurred under a previous government.

Although ministers must accept political responsibility for the actions of officials, this should not be taken to imply that a minister is personally "guilty" of what their officials have done, or that the minister should resign if officials have made a mistake. Quite the opposite, it is the minister's duty to accept responsibility before the House, to take all necessary steps to ensure that the error or misconduct is not repeated, and then to report back to the House on the corrective action taken. To do this the minister must stay in office. If every serious mistake by an official required the resignation of a minister, there would soon be no one left to serve in ministerial office. That is not what is intended by the term "responsible government"![18]

3. Ministerial Solidarity

Our system requires that ministers stand or fall together as the government of the day. Because the government must keep the confidence of the House in order to remain in power, and because under responsible government the legislative program must be identified with the government as a whole, the prime minister will generally arrange for a show of cabinet solidarity whenever any individual minister is the focus of a vote of non-confidence by the opposition. Thus an expression of lack of confidence in one minister will lead the prime minister to put the survival of the government on the line. Such solidarity is always at least partly strategic or "political," because the prime minister will have checked beforehand that the mood of the House is in favour of supporting a particular minister. The government's House Leader and its "whips" or party managers always see if there are enough supporters to win a vote, and also make sure that the supporting MPs come out to vote. If this cannot be done, or if the vote would show division in the caucus, the prime minister will usually speak to the minister and obtain his or her resignation.

4. Cabinet

Cabinet is both a political entity and an administrative body, yet it has no formal standing in law.[19] As an administrative body, cabinet is a tool for leading administration and for coordinating administrative directions across the whole of government. Because ministers are sworn in to their duties as heads of departments, and departmental action must be mandated by the minister, the cabinet is the very heart of executive government. As a political entity, the cabinet is the prime minister's committee for finding agreement and setting directions for the government as a whole, as well as for political debate and strategic planning. It is also the steering committee for management of the government caucus and of the business that will be put before the House of Commons.

It is not necessary that all ministers be members of cabinet, and in Britain this has certainly not been the case. In Canada it is only since the first Chrétien government in 1993 that the theoretical distinction between the ministry and the cabinet has had meaning in practice. Before that, all Canadian ministers were in cabinet.[20] While British cabinets have usually averaged between 20 and 22 members, the Canadian federal cabinet operated between 1974 and 1993 with 35 to 40 members. Since the arrival of the Chrétien government in November 1993, Canada has followed the British practice of having some junior ministers who work outside cabinet under the wing of a minister holding a cabinet portfolio, working with a cabinet that is somewhat larger than the British cabinet, but smaller than before.

5. Ministers and Officials

It is a principle of Westminster government that the bureaucracy is separate from the political executive and that its personnel should not include political appointees. Instead, career officials are appointed, evaluated and promoted on criteria of merit and suitability for their work. Appointment and promotion are overseen by an independent agency—in Canada's case, the Public Service Commission, an organization that is itself staffed by career officials.

Ministers have final authority over the actions of officials in their departments. This means that even though the tenure of departmental officials is not in the hands of the minister, officials are accountable through the deputy minister, their hierarchical superior, to the minister, and are subject in the last analysis to the lawful commands of the minister.[21] Thus it can be seen that in Westminster government, accountability runs from officials to the minister to cabinet to the House of Commons, and from the House of Commons to voters.

THREE PHASES OF ACCOUNTABILITY: FROM IDEAS TO EXECUTION TO AFTERMATH

This discussion of *who* is responsible *to whom, for what,* can be made more concrete by identifying three stages of activity in the translation of ideas into public policy, beginning with the development of law and moving through the execution of policy to the final phase of accountability for the impact of policy as it is understood and described by citizens (not by scientists). Relations between the different parliamentary actors and the bureaucracy shift depending on which stage of policy making is at issue, and which public policy question is under consideration.

The three phases relate to the life of individual issues, events or problems. Much of the first phase of any issue, the policy-developing activity, takes place between the permanent executive and its political masters and in the party and the caucus, but also between government and interest groups or individuals, and indeed within Parliament itself. The legislative phase takes place wholly within Parliament, although outsiders may be called as witnesses or may lobby politicians. The answerability phase ideally takes place in the House of Commons, although events are very often precipitated by the media. Urgent or newsworthy events crowd other topics out of Question Period, and find their way into debates on motions and even divert committee work scheduled long ago for other topics. On any given day, the House and its committees could be discussing what to do about illegal immigration (what policy to put in place); arguing over amendments to legislation to regulate reproductive technologies; or blaming the government for allegedly trading with a country under UN sanctions.

See Figure 1 for a graphical portrait of the three stages.[22]

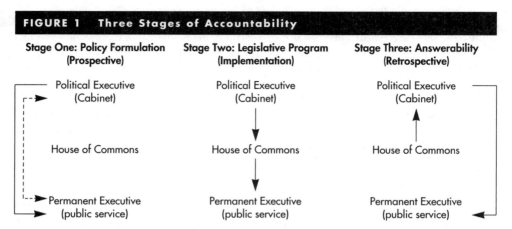

FIGURE 1   Three Stages of Accountability

Stage One: Policy Formulation (Prospective)	Stage Two: Legislative Program (Implementation)	Stage Three: Answerability (Retrospective)
Political Executive (Cabinet)	Political Executive (Cabinet)	Political Executive (Cabinet)
House of Commons	House of Commons	House of Commons
Permanent Executive (public service)	Permanent Executive (public service)	Permanent Executive (public service)

A solid line indicates an authoritative or command relationship, while a dotted line indicates influence. The influence or power flows in the direction indicated by the arrow. Information is a constant and flows in both directions.

Stage One: The Prospective Stage of Policy Analysis

This is the stage of political thinking and thorough review of the various instruments by which a policy can be transformed from idea to action. The public service plays an important but not exclusive role in providing advice to ministers. As the left column suggests, policy formulation takes place by virtue of multiple flows of information and influence, with consultation going in all directions between those who have a role in the discussion. What is not shown on the chart is the influence exercised by those with political power who act from beyond the representative institutions of government: the party leadership, business and other interest groups, outside experts and individual citizens. The fact that the content of public policy can be affected by non-elected persons does not destroy the democratic legitimacy of a decision, because once something has been decided, the minister in whose jurisdiction it falls will take responsibility both backward and forward in time (until replaced).

Stage Two: The Legislative or "Command" Stage

Because the political executive normally controls the majority in the House of Commons, this phase sees the transformation of policy proposals (in the form of bills) into statutory law. This second or legislative phase signals the undeniable responsibility of the government for the measures that are being taken, at the same time as it establishes the right of the government to tell the bureaucracy to begin implementation and execution. The term "command" is alone almost enough to describe the flow of power.

During this phase, depending on the importance attached by the government to a particular piece of legislation and the detail with which it has been worked out before tabling, the House of Commons operates more or less directly on signals from the government. The votes of the government caucus will be much as the government wishes. Only "friendly" amendments will be entertained from the opposition—those that help the government to capture the original intention of the bill. Nevertheless, although it is in "command mode" the government does not usually act like a steamroller. Even if it is unlikely to lose a vote in the House, it may choose deliberately to "lose" (allow to die) many bills that have enemies or have been shown to be flawed under the examination of a House committee. A good deal of legislation is allowed to quietly stall and then drift off the legislative agenda between sessions of Parliament, when the slate is officially wiped clean.[23]

Stage Three: The Retrospective Cycle of Political Discussion and Evaluation

This third phase is the stage of assessing the effectiveness of policies, of administration, and of political conduct in the House of Commons. It is all made possible by the principle of responsibility—the duty that each minister has to answer for him or herself and for the administrative activities of the department. This phase is both *ameliorative* (that is, it offers the possibility of remedies or improvements) and *educational* (in the sense that both politicians and the public can learn from it). Ideally, the members of the House of Commons weigh the actions of the executive from the perspective of their own role under the Constitution, namely that they jointly have the power to defeat the executive and the responsibility to do so in extreme situations. Even if this power is seldom used, its mere existence signals that no government is so secure that it cannot be voted out at any time by the representatives of the electorate. Ideally, it makes the debate in the House of Commons into a form of public education, not only in terms of accountability and punishment, but about what governments can and should try to accomplish.

The third column of Figure 1 shows that the political executive can demand answers from the appointed or permanent executive (its bureaucrats), and that the House of Commons should normally address itself to, and if necessary blame, the elected political actors. To do otherwise—that is, to blame actors other than ministers—is to undermine not just the current operations of the system, but also its lines of control and thus the principles of democratic answerability.

Some elaboration may be useful. Ministers have exclusive rights in regard to policy advice that is provided by officials, including "political" advice about how a given policy or method of achieving it compares with others for meeting the political program of the government. Constitutionally speaking, because the bureaucracy does not have a separate place in the Constitution but, as we have seen, is legally a part of the minister, one can think of this advice as taking place in the "mind" of the minister and thus being in its nature private and deserving of privacy. But there is a practical reason as well—if the advice of officials were to become a matter of public knowledge, it could reveal that a minister had ignored that advice. The opposition would take this to mean that either the minister had acted irresponsibly (by not taking into account the professional judgment of officials or the "facts" as reported), or that the advice of the officials had been judged incompetent and ignored by the minister. Either opinion would create a split between the minister and the public service. The first would discredit the minister, and the second would make the public servants useless to both the present and future governments.

It is for this reason that Westminster government has evolved the convention that ministers are not obliged to disclose the advice they have received from their officials,[24] nor (except under special circumstances) can officials be compelled to reveal what they have advised their minister. Ministers will be held responsible and forced to answer for their policies or actions, and they have the right to change direction and be held accountable for the consequences.

The importance of the retrospective phase in Westminster government cannot be overemphasized. It ensures that the political executive and the members of the bureaucracy will recognize that explanations can be required and that both, therefore, will take care to act responsibly. The retrospective phase concentrates attention on concrete means by which public distress and anger can be answered, and on how problems can be made lighter. It also casts important light upon the moral-political qualities of the executive. Obviously, the retrospective phase presents the most danger for both public servants and politicians. But because public servants know that their minister can be forced to explain or justify the outcomes of any policy or program, they prepare by briefing the minister as fully as they can on issues that may present trouble.

The accountability "conversation"—whether between ministers and the opposition or between ministers and their officials—operates on what might be called a "disaster-bring-forward" basis. By this we mean that the system forces urgent matters to the foreground of the minister's attention. The world of politics creates a political agenda of only a few items at a time, because of the limited scope for attention of both politicians and the public. This means that any one minister will have only a small number of troublesome or difficult files to master at any one time. Thus the practical scope of ministerial responsibility is not so vast as to exceed the capacity of an intelligent person working hard, although experience does help (see below). Thus arguments for forcing political accountability down to officials (that is, to blame them directly) on the grounds that ministers cannot possibly know about everything that falls within their area of responsibility are fundamentally misguided. Ministers do not have to know about everything; they need only know about what is important, whether in substantive or purely political terms.

In our system, information is squeezed upward: ministers want to ask and officials want to inform them. Admittedly, the minister usually will know little about any particular issue at any given time unless it is a priority or an emergency. What is important is that the minister quickly learn the *relevant* pieces of information, and that he or she has the authority to explore and investigate as thoroughly as any situation warrants or his or her interests and powers allow.

WHAT IS A "RESPONSIBLE" CIVIL SERVANT?

Many commentators on government divide the sense of accountability of the public servant into two categories:

  (a) internal or mental, and
  (b) external or enforced.

In the *external* and more objective category lies the responsibility or accountability which is owed upward by public servants through the bureaucratic hierarchy to the deputy minister and then to the minister. This is an accountability for all the lawful actions undertaken by officials under the terms of reference of their office, as well as an accountability for their daily performance at work—quality, speed, self-motivation, collegiality, thoroughness and more—that will be constantly evaluated by bureaucratic superiors.

Internal or subjective responsibility is thought to be the internal sense of duty or obligation of the public servant to work with the grain of the system, giving frank and complete advice free of deliberate bias, thinking of the public interest or the common good in the exercise of discretion, and doing one's duty to subordinates in the sense that one tries to ensure that they have a steady supply of relevant work and that they are treated fairly.

The subjective responsibility of the official is sometimes expected to fill in the gaps that always exist in the practical measurement of performance: unclear delegation, discretion, problems of managing autonomous professionals such as scientists, and the general imperfections of the various management methods that are used to measure the quality and amount of work accomplished inside government. (While we do accept that the overwhelming majority of public servants have a strong sense of probity and of their place, we also think it would be folly to depend upon subjective responsibility where a structure or institution can be called upon.)

THE MAPLE LEAF BRAND OF PARLIAMENTARIANISM

Is ministerial government and ministerial responsibility worth defending? We have not yet mentioned the difficulties inherent in the Canadian situation. All we can do in the space remaining is to signal the most worrisome: the issues that will have to be addressed by future generations of politicians and voters. The hardest issues, we think, are the odd marriage between the twin pillars of our Constitution, parliamentarianism and federalism, and some related issues having to do with the effective running of party government: leadership charisma or "presidentialism," minority situations, third parties, and faithless or volatile electorates.

Federalism is a formula for diffusing and dispersing political power, creating new veto points, new sites for negotiation between governments, and also very significant constitutional rigidity. Those who believe that state power is in its nature dangerous praise federalism for its power-diffusing characteristics. Westminster government, on the other hand, is a device for centralizing power in the hands of elected politicians and then arranging for them to account for themselves. The various intersections of these two different approaches to democratic government can be hard to chart and defend.

We should also note the issue of the so-called "creeping presidentialism" in parliamentary systems that is made possible by the focus of the media on the person of the prime minister. This extra-constitutional centralization of power in one personality (elected to the House of Commons only by his or her own riding's voters and elected leader of his or her party only by party activists), to the extent that it occurs, is not good news in an already-centralized system such as ours. The institution of the American presidency is incomparably weaker than the institution of the Westminster Cabinet. The central textbook on the American presidency of this century relies on the word "influence" rather than "power" to describe that institution.[25] Under responsible government, by contrast, the reverse side of the coin of "creeping presidentialism" is that the government can actually govern.

We have also said that Westminster government is above all *party* government. The requirement for an effective government, and for a credible alternative as the party of opposition, fits uneasily with situations of minority government, third parties, regional parties, and electoral volatility. Minority government has been a frequent occurrence in Canadian political history up to the 1980s. Despite an electoral system designed to give disproportionate advantage to the parties with the largest numbers of supporters, of the dozen Canadian governments from 1949 to 1980, five were minority governments.

Under minority governments, the opposition can press for the resignation of ministers regardless of facts, simply because the government realistically does not have the number of votes to extend ministerial solidarity in the face of political attack. Under majority governments, by contrast, ministerial solidarity and therefore the voting support of the government caucus in the House of Commons will be refused only to ministers who are apparently at fault in some very obvious and personal way. It is again not necessary that any allegations be proven. Rather, if the voting majority of the caucus of the government side does not want to be associated in the public mind with the blameworthy deed or the person being blamed, the minister being attacked will not be saved.

A true coalition government is something that has never existed at the federal level in Canada. In a coalition, two or more parties provide ministers and share power in cabinet. In our system this situation would confuse responsibility and therefore confuse the entire governance system. For example, it could lead to the naming of a series of governments from the same House of Commons (that is, without an intervening general election) in the Italian or French style, thereby cutting the link between the government and the electorate. Coalition government also could turn the Governor General into a more "presidential" figure (though appointed, not elected), because he or she would have to be called upon regularly to create governments.

A related threat to party government in Canada is electoral volatility. This is the phenomenon under which large numbers of constituencies return new members in a general election. At the federal level in Canada, the membership of the House of Commons is changed by voters in general elections at a rate that strongly exceeds that in Great Britain, and even more dramatically exceeds the rate of party turnover in the United States. The proportion of MPs who decide not to run again is also high at the federal level.[26] This leads to a lack of continuity of political leadership, exemplified by the fact that many individuals become ministers at their first election. The overall result is that too much time is spent by ministers and MPs in learning the basics of parliamentary government. Ministers who lack experience get into difficulty more often than do seasoned politicians, and ordinary members may be defeated before they learn how the House works to make the governors answerable to them.

CONCLUSION

Democracy—as a way of making governments responsive to people—depends on an uneasy blend of two attitudes in the population. It requires first a degree of deference and acceptance by the population of what government does; at the same time, it relies on the population to participate in political parties and to be vigilant in watching over government action. Too few Canadians join and work for political parties, and not enough of us are faithful to one party from election to election. Many Canadians, when they do take an interest in politics, seem to want the instant gratification of having governments respond directly to their immediate wishes.

Hugo Young has written an article provocatively subtitled, "After the People's Lottery, why not the People's Gallows? It is, after all, what the people seem to want." He insists that the trend among political leaders to claim *direct* responsiveness to the will of "the people," measured by polls or referenda on single topics, is offensive to constitutional democracy in large-scale or national settings:

> The people is an entity...that is out of place in the parliamentary system...[where] the popular will works through the filter of representative democracy. Parliament, not the people, is sovereign: an arrangement that constrains the power of demagogues and protects minorities against coarse majority self-interest.[27]

The Canadian combination of inexperienced politicians and increasingly inexperienced bureaucrats (because of cuts to strength added to normal turnover) poses a real danger to effective government. Our Constitution depends on an effective link between the political level and the bureaucracy. To maintain such a connection requires experience and mutual respect, which is developed over time. The alternatives are three:

(a) rule by bureaucracy—unacceptable in a democracy;
(b) a complete system of administrative law, which has its own imperfections; or
(c) a messy and non-accountable inversion of our system in which politicians claim they can do little and bureaucrats by default or design take on responsibility and political power.[28]

In our opinion, therefore, our choices as citizens are quite clear: either we work with our present system of cabinet and parliamentary government, or we bear the consequences of diluting political capacity and answerability. We believe the gradualist, pragmatic option of working to improve what we already have is the better course. This does not mean that we are stuck with the status quo. In fact, parliamentary government is a supremely flexible form of government. It keeps the two dimensions of policy and administration in dynamic balance, allowing each to transform itself as required into the other. The mutability of administration into policy through the expression of public demand means that problems will be defined, debate will take place, and governments will attempt to justify in public their responses or their inaction. In this way, governments are forced to show their character.

By making politicians accountable to the elected representatives of the public on a daily basis, and to the public itself in elections, the system forces both politicians and the public to learn from mistakes. Indeed, in the phase of retrospective responsibility, the House of Commons is what today would be called a "learning organization."

It can well be said that responsible government is a superior form of constitutional plumbing, because it can bring a sure, even if imperfect, flow of something that can be recognized as democracy into an imperfect world.

NOTES

1. We explain the use of this term and some equivalents below, under the next major heading.

2. We have benefited from the formulation in Robert Parker's *The Administrative Vocation* (Sydney, Australia: Hale and Iremonger/RIPAA, 1993), 119–21.

3. Of course ministers certainly have the authority to do more fundamental work if they have the ability and time.

4. On the other hand, people who are not working under ministerial leadership, such as police and welfare officers, can have significant degrees of discretion. In such cases, the administrative law becomes more important as a mode of control.

5. In this way the potential for one person to accumulate power was prevented.

6. For more on direct democracy, see David Held, *Models of Democracy* (Oxford: Polity Press and Basil Blackwell, 1987).

7. This does not mean that there are no differences between American government and the other Anglo-American democracies such as Canada. The United States is a unique case among world governments, having placed most of the authority that normally stays with the executive into the hands of the Congress. And quite unlike all other presidential governments, in the United States

the President has very limited authority. See Giovanni Sartori, *Comparative Constitutional Engineering* (New York: New York University Press, 1994). Nevertheless, the point that American politicians have the wish and the mandate to control bureaucracy remains undeniable.

8. See Klaus König, "Three Worlds of Public Administration Modernization," paper delivered at the Round Table of the International Institute of Administrative Sciences, Quebec City, July 14–17, 1997.

9. It may be useful to note that in continental Europe the idea of the state (the political *community*) as the regulator or umpire is considerably more acceptable and more clear than it is in countries that have emerged from the British tradition. In the latter, the political "regime" (the evolving set of rules and *processes* for conducting public business) has traditionally served as the focus of loyalty and identification for both politicians and their bureaucracies. The emphasis on process fits very well with political liberalism, which has an historical and geographical affinity for capitalism.

10. Eighth edition, (Oxford: Clarendon Press, 1990): 1026.

11. If a minister is accused of a criminal offence, as opposed to a civil offence, he or she will be investigated by ordinary police, charged if there is enough evidence, and tried in a court. No minister's status as part of government will protect him/her from trial, and government personnel cannot be pardoned before trial, as is sometimes done by the president in the United States.

12. Not all ministers head departments. There are nonministerial portfolios such as President of the Privy Council or Leader of the Government in the Senate. Not all ministers need to be in cabinet. See below.

13. It can happen that a government, defeated in a surprise vote, will ask the House of Commons to confirm its wishes in a second round of voting. Lester Pearson refused to resign after a tax bill (a money bill, and thus arguably a matter of confidence) was defeated in 1968, instead waiting a couple of days and then calling a specific vote of confidence. By contrast, Joe Clark, prime minister for less than a year between 1979 and 1980, accepted his government's defeat in a budget vote and asked the Governor General for a dissolution.

14. Alternatively, a government that is half-way or more through its five-year maximum can decide that the signals from the public mean that the government is in danger of stalling for lack of a mandate or even of falling and thus the time has come to call an election. Alternatively it may calculate that the polls say its chances are good for reelection at the moment.

15. The weight of tradition has begun to appear less significant with the fiscal crisis in state finances, which is almost worldwide, the advent of tough-minded conservative politicians, such as Ralph Klein in Alberta and Mike Harris in Ontario in the 1990s, and the push toward "globalization" or worldwide free trade.

16. This is a generalization. There are cases where departmental officials hold powers vested directly in them that are independent of the minister, such as the *Customs Act*. These cases are limited in scope and come about to satisfy concern about partisan interference in routine administrative functions that could affect the rights or property of individuals.

17. No government in recent times has exceeded the informal quota of two senators per cabinet; the leader of the Government in Senate plus, at most, one senator holding a departmental or coordinating responsibility. The reason is that senators cannot be called to answer in the House of Commons, and it would outrage the House if a significant portfolio were placed in the hands of a person beyond its reach.

18. See, on ministerial responsibility and ministerial resignation from Confederation forward, S. L. Sutherland, "Responsible Government and Ministerial Responsibility: Every Reform Is Its Own Problem," *Canadian Journal of Political Science* 24:1 (March 1991): 92–120; and S. L. Sutherland, "The Consequences of Electoral Volatility: Inexperienced Ministers, 1949–90," *Representation, Integration and Political Parties in Canada*, ed. Herman Bakvis (Toronto: Dundurn Press, 1991), 303–54.

19. The formal term for ministers acting collectively under the leadership of the prime minister is "the Governor in Council"—that is, the governor general acting on the advice of his or her ministers.

20. Prime Minister Kim Campbell went part of the way to making cabinet smaller during her months as prime minister (she won the Conservative Party leadership and took over as prime minister on Brian Mulroney's resignation in June 1993). She reduced the size of cabinet to 25 and the number of departments from 35 to 23. Some of her changes were undone when the Liberals came to power in November 1993, but her basic plan remained in place.

21. There is a view, known as the doctrine of "official independence," which holds that, as part of the permanent part of government, officials have a duty to safeguard the regime fundamentals and past practices of government against ministerial predators, and to do so by *passive* resistance, without risking their positions. We are not in agreement with this doctrine. Officials who cannot bring themselves to work on behalf of the lawful program of their minister are behaving politically without an electoral mandate. If they are unable to be "professionally loyal" to the government, they should resign and oppose it from outside.

22. This chart is adapted from Sutherland and Mitchell, "Parliament and Administration," *Public Administration and Public Management, Experiences in Canada*, eds. Jacques Bourgault, Maurice Demers and Cynthia Williams (Les publications du Québec, 1997), 29. It is reprinted with the publisher's permission.

23. Bills that have died on the order paper at the end of a Session may be reintroduced in a new Session at the stage they were at previously, if there is unanimous consent in the House.

24. Strictly speaking, the convention as now expressed in the *Access to Information Act* is that the government cannot be obliged to divulge advice to ministers on matters coming before cabinet (i.e., issues for decision).

25. Richard Neustadt, *Presidential Power* (New York: Wiley, 1960). There are many successive editions.

26. See the Bakvis volume, op. cit.

27. Hugo Young, "Who Governs Britain: Parliament or People?" *Guardian Weekly* 12 October 1997: 14.

28. Daniel Cohn, "Creating Crises and Avoiding Blame," *Administration and Society* 29:5 (November, 1997): 584–616.

PARLIAMENTARIANS AND GOVERNMENT ACCOUNTABILITY

David C. Docherty

One of the primary functions of the Canadian House of Commons is something called "accountability." While the concept of accountability may seem relatively straightforward, what is meant by accountability today differs between students of politics, observers and critics of Parliament, and in fact members themselves. Among other things, this means that there is great room for debate about the proper representative role for members of parliament, and whether or not they are properly performing this role.

Unfortunately, because the accountability function of Parliament means different things to different people there is not even agreement about what Parliament is doing wrong (or not doing). This is true even among members of parliament, some of whom think the concept of accountability should be broadened to reflect a more modern, complex understanding of representation. While not limited to a split between government and opposition parties, there is some truth to the cliché that depending upon where your seat in Parliament is located your understanding of accountability will change. At present, the more traditional notions of accountability are being challenged by members of parliament and new, more "responsive" understandings of accountability are being introduced into the work-world of the House of Commons. This is an interesting time for those who follow Parliament, as it seems that members of parliament are sitting on a fence, debating whether to cross to the other side and venture into relatively uncharted territory, or to turn back and return to the traditional understandings of their roles and duties.

This chapter begins by examining the traditional understandings of accountability in the House of Commons. It also provides some evidence as to why this conventional form of accountability has been found lacking in recent Parliaments, namely the overwhelming advantage that cabinets have historically enjoyed over opposition and government backbench members. The chapter then describes the more recent challenges to these traditions that have arrived on the Canadian political scene in the past ten years. The chapter concludes by suggesting that parliamentarians remain divided over the optimum type of accountability and how the House of Commons should be reformed to provide a more salient form of accountability. It is argued here that the most successful reforms may be the least obtrusive.

ACCOUNTABILITY IN HISTORICAL PERSPECTIVE

In Great Britain, the House of Commons was the original "check" on the power of the monarch. As Philip Norton informs us, as far back as the 14th century the Commons "had begun to use its power of the purse to ensure that public petitions were accepted by the King."[1] Thus began the journey of parliamentary power over the monarch. Today this power is regarded as what Franks calls the "simple theory of parliamentary accountability."[2] In a nutshell, Parliament is the bottom line of governmental responsibility, whether that government was run by a king (in the case of 14th century Britain) or a prime minister and his or her cabinet (in the case of modern Canadian politics).

Today, in Westminster-style governments such as Canada and Great Britain, ministers are responsible for the actions of civil servants in their departments and must answer for these actions in the House of Commons. Members of parliament are responsible for ensuring that ministers account for the actions of themselves and their civil servants. Franks suggests that the increased size and structure of government in the last half of the 20th century have made the accountability link between the public service and their ministers increasingly difficult to monitor.[3] Sharon Sutherland and Jim Mitchell in the preceding chapter have dealt effectively and in more detail with the accountability of ministers. This chapter will concentrate more specifically on the other side of the accountability equation, namely, how the public holds the government accountable through their individual members of parliament. For if ministers, in charge of departments, are the link between Parliament and the civil servants, then Parliament, or more specifically the House of Commons, is the link between the public and the government.

Citizens, at least in theory, expect their members of parliament to ensure that the government is doing what they said they would do. There are a number of mechanisms that members of parliament (outside of cabinet ministers) have at their disposal to provide this service. Traditionally in Canada all of these mechanisms have been funnelled in some manner through political parties. In fact, prior to 1993, it was difficult in Canada to talk about accountability and members of parliament in the absence of some recognition of the role of political parties in the House of Commons.[4] For despite the few years of "loose fish" members of parliament during the Macdonald era, there has never really existed a Golden Age of Parliament in Canada, where the Commons was the centre of power and the cabinet answerable to the members.[5]

It has only been since the election of Jean Chrétien as prime minister and the emergence of the Reform Party as an official party in the House of Commons that accountability has broadened beyond the sole domain of political parties. Parties still dominate members' activities and actions, and the executive still reigns supreme over the legislature, but challenges to these authorities have become more common since the 1993 election. Part of this challenge has been due to the rise of the populist Reform Party which initially ran on an anti-party ticket, citing party discipline and strong leadership as a problem, not a solution, for the accountability question. Another attack has come from the Liberal backbench, where non-cabinet ministers have decided that their political future rests not with the favour of the prime minister, but rather the votes of their constituents. The result of these challenges, to be discussed in more detail in the final section of this chapter, has been to re-question what constitutes accountability in the House of Commons.

Perhaps the most obvious vehicle for accountability in the House of Commons has been Question Period. For a number of good reasons, this is the favourite method of accountability for members of opposition parties. First, the relative openness of the process provides opposition members with the opportunity to ask cabinet ministers questions about their ministries or their own behaviour on the record. Questions are not restricted to bills or resolutions presently in front of the chamber, but can be on any issue regarding any activity in which the government is or is not engaged. The free flowing nature of Question Period, its spontaneity, and the possibility that ministers will be caught unprepared on any issue causes it to be the most covered daily event on Parliament Hill. It is the one time of day (when the House sits) that the opposition has the opportunity to publicly embarrass the government. If successful, opposition members are rewarded with potentially national news coverage. At times, the successive hammering away at ministers by opposition members has resulted in significant damage, changing political "situations" into outright "political scandals."[6]

Other avenues of accountability for members of parliament include the legislature as a vehicle for stopping the passage of bills. As Franks so bluntly points out, the duty of the House of Commons is not to create legislation, but rather to pass or defeat it.[7] Opposition parties use the Commons to keep the government accountable by opposing legislation at the second and third reading stage. Opposition parties, and often government backbenchers, can also use legislative committees to this end. The committee system achieves most of its accountability successes in studying the nitty-gritty details of legislation and in holding public hearings on various bills and issues. Pieces of legislation that are contentious or that lack broad public support are often subject to close scrutiny by members of the public. This type of accountability is not directed at the behaviour or transgressions of ministers but rather at stopping legislation that is politically unpopular. The success of this type of accountability is questionable. During times of majority governments, most legislation that reaches the committee stage will eventually become law, albeit in an often modified form. As Jonathan Malloy's examination of the very unpopular Goods and Services Tax legislation suggests, the committee system is often a better method of allowing public dissension to be recorded than it is to be reacted to.[8]

Government members have one further opportunity to check the authority and direction of cabinet, namely through caucus. Prior to introducing legislation, cabinet must ensure that they have the support of their backbenchers. Proposed legislation is occasionally modified to mollify concerns that individual government MPs might have about the "saleability" of legislation to their constituents "back home." On other occasions, the government might go so far as to back away from plans to introduce legislation or change policy based on vocalized concerns from the backbench. During the Mulroney years, for example, then Justice Minister Kim Campbell's plans to introduce gun control legislation were derailed by the vociferous reaction of the self-proclaimed "dinosaurs" in the PC caucus.

It is difficult for academics to understand the full impact of caucus as a mechanism of accountability. In order to be effective, caucus operates under a curtain of secrecy. Members are free to speak their mind and criticize their leader and cabinet ministers, knowing that what they say will not be repeated outside the walls of the caucus room. Like cabinet, however, once a decision is made, all members are expected to publicly back the position of the majority. It is only when cabinet ministers first take their appeals to the public or underestimate the reaction of their backbench, as Kim Campbell initially did with gun control, that political observers can verify the effectiveness of the government caucus as an instrument of accountability.

The House also keeps the cabinet accountable through the employment of the Auditor General. The Auditor General and his or her office provide yearly audits of various government departments and agencies. The yearly report of the Auditor General is often a source of great embarrassment to the government as tales of highways to nowhere and economic development projects gone broke come to light. The Auditor's report is jumped on by opposition politicians and reporters alike, who seize the opportunity to question the government's ability to properly manage the nation's finances. The report often requires some reaction on the part of government ministers. For example, the day the 1997 Auditor's report was released, Opposition politicians zeroed in on one item in particular. An appointed official at the federal Labour Relations Board had a habit of both claiming for expenses not incurred and going over the limit for expenses he did assume. Knowing this would be a question in the House, the Minister of Labour had to initiate the termination of this official prior to that day's Question Period.[9] In this instance it was the combination of the Auditor General and the fear of Question Period that was used to successfully keep the executive accountable.

While the role of the Auditor General has rightly been criticized in recent years, it is important to recognize that the Auditor reports not to the cabinet but rather to the House of Commons.[10] It is in this way that the Auditor is part of Parliament's accountability process, and not simply an internal fiscal check mandated by the government.

As a legislative body, then, the Parliament (or more specifically the House of Commons) provides its members with a number of tools they can use to keep the government accountable. Some of these are aimed at ensuring that cabinet is continually responsible for the day-to-day operations and actions of their departments. This is the more classic understanding of accountability. These same tools are used to ensure that ministers are conducting themselves properly and are not guilty of crossing ethical or legal borders.[11] Other methods are better suited to ensuring that the government is at least aware of any public concern over the direction of their policies.

THE PROBLEM WITH ACCOUNTABILITY

At first blush, it would seem that accountability should not be a problem. After all, the opposition and, to a lesser degree, the government backbench has all of these methods of keeping the government accountable at their disposal. Yet the problem of accountability has grown in the era of the modern Parliament. Part of the reason for this failure can be laid at the feet of members themselves, who have forsaken accountability for publicity and grandstanding. A larger share of the blame rests with the high levels of turnover in the House which robs the House of effective members. Finally, some of the responsibility must rest with the prime minister and the decisions he or she makes about selecting cabinet ministers.

It is true that Question Period remains the single most important and successful vehicle for keeping cabinet accountable for its actions. Vigilant members and keen research by opposition caucus personnel have rooted out many departmental and ministerial transgressions that find the national spotlight through Question Period. Even those departmental problems that first come to the fore via the media (such as John Fraser and the "tainted tuna" incident) are maintained as an issue when opposition members embarrass the government during Question Period.

However, Question Period has also been responsible for damaging the reputation of Parliament. The thrust and parry of debate has caused members to say things in the heat of the moment (insults to other members for example) that often make members of parliament look more like schoolyard children than national leaders. During the first term of Brian Mulroney's tenure as prime minister, four Liberal backbenchers formed what they called "the Rat Pack." They saw their job as not necessarily holding the government to account, but of embarrassing the government at every opportunity. Question Period was one of the best vehicles for achieving this goal. But in doing an effective job, these Rat Pack members also helped bring the entire Commons into disrepute.[12] Parliament suffered at the hands of a group of very successful opposition members. This has not helped the survival of the more traditional form of accountability. Canadians do not see the relevance of Commons activities to their day-to-day lives.

Stopping legislation as a method of accountability has never been a serious tool at the disposal of members of the Commons. While there was a period of relatively numerous minority governments (between 1962 and 1980 five of the seven Parliaments were minority governments) this represents an anomaly in Canadian history. Canadians have historically been led by majority governments and since 1980 this has been the case. Even after the 1997 election, where for the first time there were five parties officially recognized in the House, the victorious Liberal Party emerged with a majority, admittedly a slim one. The dominance of party discipline in Canada means that it would be almost unheard of for a majority government to have a piece of their legislation defeated.[13]

In order for federal legislation to be defeated during a majority Parliament, some government backbenchers would have to stay home or vote against their leadership. Beyond threats to their future promotion, government backbenchers have another very good reason to respond to the party whip—the threat of an unexpected election. As long as all or most legislation that the government introduces is regarded as matters of confidence, it is unlikely governments will fear large scale defections from their backbench. So even when legislation may not "technically" fall under the confidence umbrella, as long as the government acts like it does, then backbenchers will rarely stray from the end of the whip's lash.[14] Thus, as Atkinson and Thomas argue, the reality of modern Parliament in Canada has been "the inversion of responsible government," where cabinet controls the Commons instead of the other way around.[15]

Changing legislation in committee is a more common method of altering the government's plans. However, the power of committees is very much limited. First, most committees are chaired by government members who hope to parlay their ability to speed legislation through a committee into an eventual promotion to the front benches. And all Commons committees, even those chaired by opposition MPs, reflect the distribution of seats in the legislature, so that the majority still favours the government. Second, committees that examine legislation must report their bills back to the House prior to third reading. If any changes made in committee contravene government policy, the executive maintains the ability to recommend alternative amendments in the House prior to the third and final reading of the bill. Third, standing committees that examine different areas of government policy can and often do issue reports that are at least mildly critical of the government. Yet the cabinet is not required to respond to these reports in any meaningful way. As a result, there is an understandable lack of enthusiasm among backbenchers to spend time and energy on investigations and reports that have little chance of being implemented.

The most successful form of accountability in the Commons is one open only to backbench members of the governing party, namely, the caucus system. Thomas notes that, more so than other caucuses, the role of the government caucus is "one of communication and consultation."[16] Communication usually takes the form of cabinet letting the private members know their legislative and policy agenda. Consultation usually means private members attempt to rein in cabinet or conversely to tell them to go a bit further in different areas. In rare circumstances the insistence of backbenchers has been taken as a signal that cabinet should either hold off or hurry up with particular plans. As indicated above, in even rarer circumstances, the government has dropped budgetary or legislative agendas in the face of a possible backbench revolt. Here members are convinced that if the government were to proceed with a particular item, it would cost the member his or her job come next election. Yet this vehicle of accountability is a victim of its own success. The secrecy of caucus means that political observers are uncertain as to how strongly the backbench can influence the executive. An effective prime minister can often convince private members to go along with government plans, assuring them that the party can ride out any temporary dips in popularity.[17]

The Auditor General has a mixed record in accountability. While an embarrassment to the government, the Auditor's report is a delight to the opposition parties and reporters alike. The Auditor's report has often been the cause of great discomfort to governments of the day, pointing out areas where cabinet ministers should have been more responsible with tax dollars. Further, the Auditor's report is given careful scrutiny by the Public Accounts Committee, an all-party standing committee of the legislature. As a result, members are given a further opportunity to use the Auditor General's findings to keep the accountability spotlight on ministers.

Yet beyond the semblance of power of this office, there is little to suggest that it plays an integral role as an instrument of accountability, at least in terms of its relationship with members of parliament. First, the Public Accounts Committee has little actual control over the Auditor. The committee cannot direct the Auditor to investigate any particular department or agency of the Crown. Nor can they scrutinize the workings of the office of the Auditor General. Successive auditors general have interpreted their mandate as one which requires them to provide comment on the correctness or incorrectness of various government decisions. This has been criticized by some scholars as moving beyond their accounting role and into one of policy making.[18] While the public might initially see the attractiveness of such a move, it does come at the expense of members of parliament performing that duty. Additionally, the Auditor General's report has little staying power beyond a two- to three-day deluge of overspending stories. The net result of these developments may have prompted former Public Accounts Committee Chair Jean-Robert Gauthier to muse that the Auditor General's office may well be "building up populist appeal and street power at the expense of representative institutions of government and Parliament."[19]

Beyond these institutional barriers preventing members from properly performing their traditional "accountability" functions, there is a larger, even more formidable obstacle hindering them from keeping cabinet on its toes, namely, ability. The men and women sent to Ottawa who do not make it in into cabinet tend to lack the expertise necessary to ensure accountability. This is not to suggest that private members are not as talented as those who make it to cabinet, but simply that, as a group, private members have less parliamentary experience and know-how than members of cabinet. This lack of legislative experience affects both opposition and government backbenchers. In doing so, it therefore limits the accountability effectiveness both in the legislature and in caucus.

It is generally accepted that most members of parliament undergo a learning period when they first enter the Commons. This "apprenticeship period" is the time when members learn the formal and informal ropes of legislative life. Few members come to the Canadian Parliament with experience in municipal office and even fewer have served as representatives in a sub-national office (provincially or territorially). As a result, like any change in one's profession, the first few months are spent simply familiarizing oneself with one's new work environment. The parliamentary work environment, however, is quite different than most others. Members have two offices, constituency duties, parliamentary responsibilities in the legislature and committees, caucus responsibilities, and many other new and different jobs.

The duration of this apprenticeship period is fluid and disagreement exists among academics and politicians over its true length.[20] However, almost all politicians and students of Parliament agree that it takes up at least the first half of a rookie member's term of office. Members are not the most effective legislators during their first few years in office. More so than most professions, becoming a competent politician takes time.

The problem is further exacerbated when members of the cabinet have already gone through this apprenticeship phase. On balance, prime ministers are inclined to go with experienced legislators over incoming MPs when selecting their cabinets. As a result, at the beginning of each Parliament, the cabinet has an advantage, in terms of parliamentary knowledge and savvy, over many of their own backbench colleagues and the opposition members. Table 1 delineates the average number of years of experience of government leaders compared to the government and opposition backbenches at the start of each of last five Parliaments.[21]

Since 1980 the average number of years of experience of the Canadian cabinet far outweighs that of private members on both sides of the Speaker's chair. The decimation of the Progressive Conservative and New Democratic parties in 1993 made this advantage all the more extreme. The executive under Jean Chrétien's first government had an average of two full terms' experience, compared to just over one year for opposition MPs. The two new parties in 1993, the Official Opposition Bloc Québécois and the Reform Party, had an average of just eight months' experience between them when the 35th Parliament began. The experienced cabinet was off and running on policy and legislation while many new MPs were still literally finding their way around Parliament Hill.[22]

Government backbench members fare little better than their opposition counterparts. When a new government takes over, as was the case in 1984 and 1993, the government backbenches experience a surge in the number of rookie politicians. These members, at least for the first half of the Parliament, are less likely to challenge the more experienced cab-

TABLE 1 Legislative Experience by Position					
	Average Years of Experience				
Position	**32nd** **1980–84**	**33rd** **1984–88**	**34th** **1988–93**	**35th** **1993–97**	**36th** **1997–**
Government leaders	8.5	7.0	7.4	8.0	11.1
Government backbench	4.7	2.0	4.0	3.2	4.1
Opposition parties	5.5	6.5	4.8	1.2	2.8

Source: Adapted from Docherty, 1997.
Note: Government leaders include the prime minister, cabinet ministers, the chief government whip, and the chair of caucus.

inet members during caucus meetings. Thus, the cabinet enjoys a double advantage in terms of experience, the first over the opposition and the second over their caucus. The accountability function is weakened both in the legislature and outside it (in caucus) when such conditions exist. And in Canada they exist regularly.

This same advantage exists even when a majority government is returned to office, as was the case in 1988 and 1997. Many private members from the governing party are now sophomores and are well past the apprenticeship period, but they still lag behind the cabinet in terms of experience. In the most recent election of 1997, the return of the Progressive Conservatives and New Democrats to official party status also meant the introduction of a whole new class of rookies, allowing cabinet to maintain its experience edge over the opposition.

In sum, the traditional form of parliamentary accountability in Canada's Westminster-style parliament has not been an effective method of keeping the activities of the executive in check. Although the instruments at the disposal of legislators have not been formally altered, they no longer allow members to properly perform their accountability functions. More complex government, a devalued opinion of Question Period, and high levels of turnover leading to an experience gap between the executive and the backbench combine to seriously weaken one of the most important functions of the Commons.

PROPOSED SOLUTIONS TO THE PROBLEM OF PARLIAMENTARY ACCOUNTABILITY

Considering the relative lack of success that parliamentarians have met with when trying to perform their accountability duties, it is hardly surprising that calls for reform of Parliament have arisen from both the opposition and government sides of the House. The problem, however, is in finding reforms that actually provide a more efficient system of accountability in terms of legislative responsibilities. Parliamentarians may have been too quick to question or blame the merits of traditional accountability when looking for answers to the problems that face Parliament today.

There is little dispute that Parliament, and the men and women who serve in it, have lost some of their credibility with the public.[23] The explanations behind this loss of respect are too many and varied to discuss in this chapter (or indeed perhaps in this book). However, some of the loss of faith can be traced to the problems discussed above. Even if not dressed in the academic jargon of accountability and representative versus responsible government, it is not difficult to accept that the behaviour of politicians during Question Period, the secrecy of caucus, and the dominance of party discipline have contributed to the declining respect that citizens hold for Parliament and politicians in general.

Many Canadians, for example, believe that most politicians "lose touch" with their constituents soon after they are sent to Ottawa.[24] The feeling that members answer to their party leader and whip and not to their constituents has discredited the House of Commons in the eyes of many voters. It also suggests that voters either recognize that members of parliament cannot properly perform their accountability duties or that they do not see this as important. In response to some of this criticism from the public, members of parliament have turned to looking at new and different ways of providing accountability for their actions, both individually and collectively as a parliament. Some of the more interesting and controversial experiments in this "new accountability" since 1993 have included challenging party discipline, elimination of opposition critic roles, recall of members during their term in office, and reform of the committee system.

Given the number of challenges to the traditional notions of accountability, the question for observers of Parliament in the aftermath of the 1993 and 1997 elections was quite simple: Could these changes, and the new style of representation they would instil, provide a better, more effective form of accountability?

Challenging Party Discipline

Traditional parliamentary accountability is characterized by members of parliament who hold cabinet accountable for government actions and decisions. Backbench members are responsible for this watchdog function and, if they fail to do it, are held to account by voters. Yet led by the Reform Party's success in 1993, many members of parliament have been making overtures to a different type of accountability, namely, accountability of private members for representing constituency demands. This new accountability suggests that all members must first and foremost be accountable to their constituents for their day-to-day activities in the House. How do members do this? By acting in direct accord with the wishes of the majority of their constituents even if it means ignoring party discipline and their party leader.

This move to a new accountability and the popularity of the Reform Party is not a simple cause-and-effect relationship. The Reform Party rose quickly and successfully for a number of reasons, most of which can be traced to the feeling among Western Canadians that, despite the election of the Conservative government in 1984 and a significant Western presence in the cabinet, Ottawa was still ignoring the needs of the West.[25]

Critical to Reform's understanding of democratic rule, however, was that members should be accountable to their constituents for any actions or votes in the Commons. Members who work within this understanding of governance are what Eulau describes as "delegate" style politicians.[26] These individuals see themselves as delegates of their constituents. Only on matters of economic policy, where Reform had a clearly staked-out position of deficit and spending reductions, are Reform MPs expected to toe party lines. A number of Liberal candidates quickly picked up on this theme of constituency representation, promising to answer to constituents first and Jean Chrétien second.

A necessary condition for any move to more of a delegate style of representation is the relaxing of party discipline in the legislature. It has also been suggested that an easing of party discipline should not adversely affect the more traditional forms of accountability. Hold more free votes in the House of Commons, this argument goes, and members will be freer to question ministers of the Crown and to perform their accountability function. At the same time, members will be provided with the opportunity to place their constituency ahead of their party, and in doing so regain public respectability. Yet as two bills in the previous Parliament illustrate, this is easier in opposition than it is in government, and even then there are limits that cannot easily be exceeded without damaging the internal cohesion of parties.

In 1994 the Liberal government ran into its first challenge on party discipline with then Justice Minister Allan Rock's gun control legislation, Bill C-68. Popular in urban areas, C-68 was immensely disliked in much of rural Canada. For some new rookie Liberals, then, this became the first opportunity to defy their leader. The first rebellion was met with a stinging rebuke by leader Jean Chrétien, who removed some dissidents from their favoured committee positions. While some responded by falling back into line, nine government members did vote against C-68 on third reading.

These nine were not further disciplined by their leader. However, some Liberal members who voted in favour of the legislation did see their colleagues as taking an easy way out. Suggesting that it was easy for these rural MPs to vote against a bill they knew would pass, many urban MPs felt a stronger solidarity with those rural MPs who stood by the government. In future, backbench members thinking of voting against their government would have to consider more than simply the threat of losing a cherished committee spot. They would also have to contemplate the reaction of their own peers. It is one thing to pick an issue you feel strongly about and vote against the cabinet; it is another to distance yourself from your entire caucus.

This power of peer persuasion and caucus solidarity was highlighted two years later when Allan Rock introduced Bill C-33 which dealt with hate crimes against gay and lesbian Canadians. This time, however, it was the Reform Party which learned a painful lesson. In speaking out against the legislation, two Reform MPs, Bob Ringma and David Chatters, made what might charitably be described as unfortunate and derogatory remarks about gays and lesbians. Partially in response to this, Reform MP Jan Brown made public her concerns about the more extreme views of some of her colleagues. The response of Reform leader Preston Manning illustrated just how important caucus solidarity and secrecy really is. Ringma, Chatters and Brown were all suspended from the caucus. Ringma and Chatters soon returned to the caucus and Brown eventually resigned to sit as an independent. The lesson to outsiders was clear: speaking ill of your colleagues in Parliament holds a greater punishment than does making discriminatory remarks about a segment of the Canadian public.

For those hoping that a relaxing of party discipline would help lead to a new, different type of accountability, the experience of these particular pieces of legislation must have been disheartening. Until party leaders and all party members are willing to embrace wholesale reform of party discipline, members will be dissuaded from speaking out against their party, and will not vote against their party leaders on critical issues. Party discipline is at present an integral part of the Canadian parliamentary system, and goes hand in hand with the traditional approach of accountability. Occasional rebuffs from individual members will be tolerated. But changing accountability through party discipline is not a viable option at present.

Finally, the whole question of placing constituent concerns ahead of party views is questionable from a practical point of view. It is a rare issue where a politician has a concrete sense of public opinion in his or her riding. It is one thing to say that you are going to vote according to your constituents' wishes; it is another to actually know what these wishes are. Using letters to the editors of local newspapers, calls to the riding office, and feedback in town-hall meetings may give MPs a sense of the extreme or energized views of people, but it does not provide a sophisticated measure of public opinion. Claiming that you are acting as a delegate of constituency concerns does not necessarily make you more accountable to that same public.[27]

Disguising Accountability with Civility

Immediately after the 1993 election, the Reform Party decided to abolish the role of the cabinet critic and replace it with "discussion groups." In the past, opposition leaders appointed from their caucus a "critic" for each minister. These shadow cabinet members were responsible for keeping their respective ministers accountable. By contrast, the discussion groups (each consisting of four to five MPs) would be responsible for a given policy field. The benefits for accountability were only indirect. The foremost goals of this move were to improve the civility inside the House of Commons, and to improve the public's respect for Parliament by removing the negative and adversarial connotations of the "critic" role.

Reform believed that discussion groups would increase the level of debate in the House and decrease the level of overt conflict. Discussion groups were presumed to be more informative and less confrontational than the more adversarial role of "critic." It was hoped that this would not only bring a greater sense of decorum into the Commons, but would also elevate the style and substance of parliamentary debate and discussion. Among other outcomes, a more civil chamber would more likely be a parliament that the public would hold in higher regard. But there were to be some indirect benefits to accountability. In the absence of a raucous Question Period, insults and accusations would be replaced with detailed questions and answers. Opposition members would therefore learn more about the government's plans for the future, and in doing so increase the opposition's watchdog capacity.

However, all that this experiment really accomplished was to compound the Reform Party's problem of inexperience. Not only did rookies not develop expertise in any one specific policy field, but they did not develop the necessary contacts with civil servants in any one department or in any one minister's office. As a result, their questions were less organized, they did not generate national media exposure, and they often had no single plan of attack on the government. They simply could not perform their watchdog role. As a result, ministers were in fact less accountable for their actions than they might have been had Reform not tried a kinder, gentler approach to the critic's role. It was hardly surprising then that this move lasted just one year and that by July 1994 the Reform Party had a shadow cabinet. A shadow cabinet may be confrontational, but it does keep the government on its toes.

Recall as the Ultimate Weapon

In the 1997 election the Reform Party introduced another of their plans to alter the concept of accountability, specifically the right of voters to recall their members of parliament. Popular in the United States and present in British Columbia at the provincial level, recall is supposed to ensure that elected members do not disregard the concerns of their constituents between elections. If enough citizens sign a recall petition (the Reform Party plan stipulated 50 percent of eligible voters within a given constituency) then a new election (a by-election) would be held in that riding. The sitting members would be free to contest that election, assuming they got their party's nomination (or ran as an independent), but would run knowing that at least half of the voters wanted them fired. The accountability link under recall is more direct than the Reform experiment with discussion groups. Like the relaxing of party discipline, this proposal attempted to change the accountability connection from an executive-legislature relationship and to a legislator-voter coupling. Members would "lose touch" at their own peril, knowing that they could be held to account at any time and not just at election time.

Yet despite the seeming appeal of recall, it did not emerge as a major election issue in 1997, and there appears to be little pressure on the government to initiate such a scheme.[28] Supporters of recall argue that it makes members accountable for campaign promises. If they fail to keep their promises, voters do not have to wait until the next election to defeat them. Opponents argue that recall simply places more power in the hands of interest groups which may or may not have ties to a targeted riding. A member might face a recall fight, not because he or she is a bad representative, but because an opposition party or interest group sees that member as particularly vulnerable. As such, recall may be a good way to challenge a government, but it is an ineffective method of accountability.

Reforming the Committee System

That leaves the committee system as a potential area for reinvigorating the traditional understanding of parliamentary accountability. And it is here that some promise for reform rests. Surveys of members of the 34th and 35th Parliaments found that committee work was constantly referred to as a source of both promise and frustration.[29] Promise that it provided an avenue to utilize backbencher strength and knowledge, and frustration that the fruits of their committee labours were rarely considered by the government.

Important committee reports on a variety of issues from the CBC to national unity have repeatedly been shelved by governments. Not only does this severely limit the value of their work, it demoralizes members from viewing the committee system as an active agent of government accountability. Knowing that the government will not listen to their plans, committee members often revert back to their partisan selves, and minority reports are not uncommon.

Near the end of the 35th Parliament, the Liaison Committee—a parliamentary committee of standing committee chairs—released a report recommending a series of reforms to the House of Commons.[30] Many of these proposed reforms address the accountability and effectiveness problems presently faced by committees. The Liaison Committee recognized that the root of these problems can be traced back to the changes made a decade ago that were actually intended to give committees more power. Prior to 1985 special investigations by a committee could only be undertaken at the behest of a cabinet minister. When such a direction was given "committee members of all parties could proceed on the assumption that their work would be taken seriously by the government."[31] Now laden with more independence, committees often examine policy areas that may be a low priority to ministers. The Liaison Committee's report recommended closer ties between a minister and the committee(s) responsible for his or her policy area. The aim of this proposal is to maintain committee independence while encouraging the government to respond to their work.

Allowing committees greater discretion in directing their staff and others may also increase accountability. While committees have the freedom to investigate issues, they often lack the resources for a full investigation. The Liaison Committee has recommended that committees be allowed to "permit their staff to travel at committee expense on fact-finding missions relating to an inquiry."[32] In a similar vein, Jean-Robert Gauthier has argued that a more influential Public Accounts Committee which could direct the Auditor General to investigate different branches of government would go a long way to increasing the accountability of Parliament to the public.[33]

Finally, in an indirect response to the problem of resources and experience, the Liaison Committee recommended that committee chairs be given a larger budget and that chairs be allowed to serve longer terms. In terms of resources, the Report points out that committee chairs have fewer resources (in terms of staff) than parliamentary secretaries who assist ministers (often by appearing in front of committees during hearings on bills). If committees are to be effective they must have the resources to operate properly, and this includes proper staffing for the chair. In terms of experience the Liaison Committee reflects that some of the most effective committees have had chairs who have served for at least a full legislative term. While nothing can be done about electoral turnover, having less turnover in the chair's position will help offset the experience advantage which most cabinet ministers enjoy over their parliamentary peers.

Most members of parliament face obstacles in properly administering their accountability duties. All members initially face an experience problem. Until they are comfortable with the formal and informal rules of parliamentary life, they are not able to keep up with experienced and parliamentary savvy ministers. But even once members gain valuable experience and legislative know-how, keeping tabs on the government is not an easy task. Nor does it help that the public sees much of parliamentary work as theatre, and not very attractive theatre at that.

This has prompted some MPs to attempt to improve accountability and legitimacy (in the eyes of the public) at the same time. The Reform Party has been at the centre of many of these proposals. And while many of their attempts have failed, their success in 1997, moving from third party to Official Opposition, suggests that their message still finds public favour. Nonetheless, changes which allow members more independence from the party whip may improve the reputation of the Commons, but it is doubtful they will do much to increase accountability.

Challenging longstanding traditions of party discipline does not even have the support of all backbenchers, let alone party leaders. Nor is it likely that party leaders or a government would provide more power and influence to backbenchers. Leaders are not inclined to cede power if it means opening themselves up to more scrutiny. Discussion groups only exaggerate the problem of inexperience, and play into the hands of veteran cabinet ministers. Recall may keep individual members on a short leash from the public, but it does little to encourage individual members to keep the executive accountable. Instead, it merely threatens the stability of parliaments where the government has a plurality or a slim majority of seats.

Given the proper resources and power, members of parliament can act as watchdogs on ministers and departments. At the same time, the best method of improving the accountability function of MPs might best lie in the least extreme types of reforms. Altering the less scrutinized committee system may be a more viable target. The types of changes proposed by the Liaison Committee do not challenge the authority of leaders, compromise the adversarial nature of Parliament, or call for backbenchers to become active policy initiators. They do, however, open some window of opportunity to make members more effective participants in the policy process. This alone may help to restore some credibility to Parliament by allowing members to fulfil their traditional accountability roles.

NOTES

1. Philip Norton, *Does Parliament Matter?* (New York: Harvester Wheatsheaf, 1993), 14.

2. C. E. S. Franks, *The Parliament of Canada* (Toronto: University of Toronto Press, 1987), 227.

3. Ibid., 228–29.

4. Prior to 1993 it was difficult to talk about the individual member of parliament without recognizing the primary role of his or her political party. Paul Thomas in 1985 argued that legislative behaviour in Canada is synonymous with party behaviour. See Paul Thomas, "Parliamentary Reform through Political Parties," *The Canadian House of Commons Observed: Essays in Honour of Norman Ward,* ed. J. Courtney (Calgary: University of Calgary Press, 1985).

5. For a discussion of the different concepts of parliamentary government see Franks, chapter 2. See also Samuel Beer, *Modern British Politics* (Markham: Penguin Books Canada, 1982). And

Anthony Birch, *Representative and Responsible Government* (Toronto: University of Toronto Press, 1964).

6. During the Mulroney era, for example, opposition members effectively crippled the government from pursuing its own agenda by continually hammering at scandal-prone ministers during Question Period. Sinclair Stevens and Erik Nielsen are just two ministers whose ministerial fates were sealed thanks to daily negative press coverage of them responding to opposition questions. For a full discussion of "situations" and "scandals" see Maureen Mancuso, "The Politics of Shame: Leaving in Disgrace," *Leaders and Leadership in Canada*, eds. Maureen Mancuso, Richard Price and Ronald Wagenberg (Toronto: Oxford University Press, 1994).

7. Franks, 5–7.

8. Jonathan Malloy, "Reconciling Expectations and Reality in House of Commons Committees: The Case of the 1989 GST Inquiry," *Canadian Public Administration* 39:3 (Fall 1996): 314-35.

9. Scott Feschuk, "Lavish Labour-Board Chief to Be Fired" [Toronto] *Globe and Mail* 3 December 1997: A12.

10. See Sharon Sutherland, "The Politics of Audit: The Federal Office of the Auditor General in Comparative Perspective," *Canadian Public Administration* 29:1 (Spring 1986): 118–48.

11. Again, see Maureen Mancuso.

12. Undergraduates who may not recall the first Mulroney government (1984–88), or, the Rat Pack, might be interested to know that all four members of this group went on to achieve some success in their political careers. Sheila Copps was the deputy prime minister in the Chrétien government from 1993 to 1997, and was reappointed to cabinet after the 1997 vote. Don Boudria is also in the current Chrétien cabinet and Brian Tobin is premier of Newfoundland. The fourth member, John Nunziata, was removed from the Liberal caucus in 1995 when he publicly chastized his government's failure to abolish the Goods and Services Tax. He was the only independent candidate to win a seat in the 1997 General Election. While the Rat Pack managed to hurt the image of Parliament, they did not do it at the expense of their own political careers!

13. Of course some legislation and government motions are defeated but when this occurs it is usually preceded by a government declaration that the issue at hand is to be considered a "free vote" where their own members are not bound by the party whip.

14. Budget bills, resolutions of non-confidence and the Speech from the Throne are generally regarded as matters of confidence. Other bills and resolutions are less easily categorized. Governments have lost some motions and bills without resigning. However, when a government decides a particular bill should be treated as a sign of confidence, it automatically becomes one. See Andrew Heard, *Canadian Constitutional Conventions: the Marriage of Law and Politics* (Toronto: Oxford University Press, 1991).

15. Michael Atkinson and Paul Thomas, "Studying the Canadian Parliament," *Legislative Studies Quarterly* XVIII:3 (August 1993): 433.

16. Paul Thomas, "Parties and Regional Representation," *Representation, Integration and Political Parties in Canada*, ed. Herman Bakvis, Volume 14 of the Report of the Royal Commission on Electoral Reform and Party Financing (Toronto: Dundurn Press, 1991), 212.

17. Ibid., 212.

18. Sharon Sutherland, "The Politics of Audit."

19. Jean-Robert Gauthier, "Accountability, Committees and Parliament," *Canadian Parliamentary Review* (Summer 1993): 9.

20. See, for example, Franks, *Parliament of Canada.* Also Sharon Sutherland, "The Consequences of Electoral Volatility: Inexperienced Ministers, 1949–90," *Representation, Integration and Political Parties in Canada*, ed. Herman Bakvis, Volume 14 of the Royal Commission on Electoral Reform and Party Financing (Toronto: Dundurn Press, 1991).

21. The original table appears in David C. Docherty, *Mr. Smith Goes to Ottawa: Life in the House of Commons* (UBC Press, 1997), 54. The original table does not include information on the 36th Parliament.

22. Of course many new members of parliament are effective right from the start of their careers. Bob Rae, for example, won a seat for the first time in a 1978 by-election and within twelve months spearheaded the downfall of the short-lived Joe Clark government! More recent (but perhaps less dramatic) examples abound, such as Jim Silye and Ian McClelland of the Reform Party in the wake of the 1993 election. Yet even these individuals faced a learning curve when they arrived on Parliament Hill.

23. Comparisons between politicians and used car salespersons seem more numerous in conversation than they do in reality. However, a now rather dated poll (1990) suggests that federal members of parliament are ranked only one notch higher than advertising executives when it comes to ethical standards. See Peter Dobell and B. Berry, "Anger at the System: Political Discontent in Canada," *Parliamentary Government* 39:3 (1990): 3–20.

24. André Blais and Elizabeth Gidengil, *Making Representative Democracy Work: The Views of Canadians*, Volume 17 of the Royal Commission on Electoral Reform and Party Financing (Toronto: Dundurn Press, 1991), 34–36.

25. Keith Archer, Roger Gibbins, Rainer Knopff and Les Pal, *Parameters of Power: Canada's Political Institutions* (Toronto: ITP Nelson Canada, 1995), 119–21 and chapter 5.

26. Heinz Eulau, "Changing Views of Representation," *The Politics of Representation: Continuities in Theory and Research,* eds. H. Eulau and J. Wahlke (Beverly Hills: Sage Publications, 1978). Eulau's original argument appeared in H. Eulau, "The Legislator as Representative: Representative Roles" J. Wahlke et al., *The Legislative System* (New York: John Wiley and Sons, 1962).

27. A more detailed discussion of Bills C-68 and C-33 and how they highlighted the problem of party discipline in the 35th Parliament can be found in David C. Docherty, *Mr. Smith Goes to Ottawa*, chapter 6.

28. The effectiveness of recall in British Columbia is questionable. The slim majority government of the New Democratic Party in British Columbia has in fact been threatened by recall. However, at the time of writing this chapter, no member of the legislature has been forced to resign due to a successful recall petition.

29. The interviews referred to here were undertaken by the author as part of a larger project. See Docherty, *Mr. Smith Goes to Ottawa.*

30. Canada, House of Commons, *Report of the Liaison Committee on Committee Effectiveness,* Chair Bill Graham (February 1997). As taken from *Occasional Papers on Parliamentary Government* (September 1997).

31. *Report of the Liaison Committee on Committee Effectiveness.* As taken from *Occasional Papers on Parliamentary Government*, 9.

32. *Report of the Liaison Committee on Committee Effectiveness.* As taken from *Occasional Papers on Parliamentary Government*, 14.

33. Gauthier.

RESTRUCTURING INSTITUTIONS

Central to the study of public administration is the examination of governing structures. These structures shape the process of governing activities and channel interactions between governments and interested groups and individuals. The design and operation of institutional arrangements therefore raises both political and administrative issues. Political concerns include the allocation of power and authority, the provisions for citizen and/or interest group input, and organizational goals and partisan evaluations of institutional operations and perspectives, among other things.

These political concerns help shape the resulting debates about organizational operation and direction. Budgets and mandates are products of political decision making. Administrative challenges such as those relating to staffing, office location, reporting channels, and priority setting all involve the merging of political and administrative considerations. Analysis of modern public sector arrangements and structures must be conducted with sensitivity to the argument made in the introductory essay, that politics and administration must be understood as interrelated, not as distinct and separate spheres of interest.

Peter Clancy discusses the politics and administration of Aboriginal land claims. The whole issue of Aboriginal claims and aspirations is charged with political and constitutional implications. Clancy's depiction of events reflects the interrelationship of politics and administration. Institutional arrangements for discussion of Aboriginal claims have to be designed carefully so as to accommodate the constraints and opportunities offered by political and administrative factors.

Clancy's discussion also offers a useful historical perspective on relations between Aboriginal peoples and the federal government. Under the terms of the *British North America Act, 1867* (also known as the *Constitution Act, 1867*) the federal government has jurisdiction over Aboriginal affairs. Many Aboriginal peoples are working toward constitutional recognition of some form of self-government. Developments on this front have also impacted upon the negotiations and institutions evaluated by Clancy.

Katherine Graham and Susan Phillips look at another set of institutional debates which bring together issues of politics and administration. Restructuring relations between provincial and municipal governments has been a major issue in the 1990s. It is an issue replete with hot button issues: Should local governments become larger in pursuit of economies of scale? Who should direct change in regard to local governments? Should richer communities have better services or amenities than poorer communities within the same area or within the same province? Do people see local governments primarily as service providers or as sites of democratic action and community involvement? These and other fundamental questions are at stake in the ongoing reviews of provincial-municipal relations and institutions.

Under the *British North America Act* local governments and undertakings are provincial responsibilities. Provincial governments design the legal-political framework for the operation of local governments. Municipalities often find themselves reacting to provincial initiatives and defending against the downloading of added administrative and financial burdens.

Graham and Phillips provide an overview of nationwide trends in provincial-municipal relations and an in-depth study of these relations in selected provinces. Their helpful commentary illustrates the importance of provincial-municipal relations, the range of political and administrative factors involved, and a clear sense of the emerging issues in this field of institutional reform.

DISCUSSION QUESTIONS

1. Why are Aboriginal land claims an important ongoing issue? What is at stake in these proceedings?
2. Explain and evaluate the evolution in federal government thinking about Aboriginal peoples.
3. What has guided the response of the federal government to Aboriginal claims? Which elements within the federal government have been involved?
4. Why has the design of an institutional framework for discussions between the federal government and Aboriginal peoples been so complicated? Why has the whole issue of institutional design and the arrangements for discussions been an ongoing source of tension?
5. How important is your local government? What bond do you or your friends feel toward your local government? Is your local government close to its citizens?
6. Why might provincial governments want to reform local governing arrangements? What criteria should guide the provincial government's reform agenda for local governments? Why?
7. Who should be in the position to coordinate the direction or pace of local government reform? Why?
8. Would it alter your sense of community if local governing units were made larger? Why or why not? Should orientations toward locally defined communities be politically significant?
9. Evaluate the overall direction of reforms in provincial-municipal relations. What factors shape your evaluation?
10. Why does the restructuring of public sector institutions involve an appreciation of the interrelationship of politics *and* administration?

THE POLITICS AND ADMINISTRATION OF ABORIGINAL CLAIMS SETTLEMENTS

Peter Clancy

This is a case which involves the structuring of new institutions rather than the transformation of existing ones. For more than two decades the Government of Canada has acknowledged that Aboriginal groups who never signed treaties retain claims of title to their traditional lands. Ottawa has also proposed arrangements for the negotiated settlement of this title, by which Aboriginal groups receive compensation in the form of benefits in return for the surrender of title to the Crown. Fashioned in innovative ways, the terms of settlement can offer the prospect of new developmental institutions to empower Aboriginal communities. Equally, the terms can intensify their marginality if minimal solutions are imposed.

Clearly the settlement process is preeminently political, in the sense that it seeks to reconcile distinct and conflicting interests through designated state channels. In fact, the claims settlement process is a unique institutional mechanism. It can be approached as a political subsystem in its own right, never isolated from the broader state but driven nonetheless by its own norms and procedures.[1] The comprehensive claims negotiating process is of particular interest to students of politics and administration, given the complex interplay of popular and bureaucratic interests. In addition, since the roster of outstanding claims remains lengthy, an understanding of experience to date may have a bearing on future settlements as well. In this chapter the Inuit claim in the eastern Canadian Arctic (known as the Nunavut claim) is offered as an illustrative case.

Since 1971 the Inuit of the eastern Canadian Arctic have pursued the recognition of their Aboriginal claim to lands. (The term Nunavut can be translated into English as "the People's land.") Over the years this has been advanced by several Inuit organizations against a federal state which has been cautious and reluctant at best, hostile and obstructionist at worst. Until 1973 Ottawa denied the existence of Aboriginal title in law. Thereafter, the federal government stipulated a negotiated settlement process within a particular set of parameters. For the eastern Arctic Inuit the negotiations spanned a marathon 16 years before the Nunavut Final Agreement (NFA) was enacted in 1993. This political milestone marked both an end and a beginning, closing the negotiating process while opening a crucial new phase of implementation (which continues today). The NFA is a bold and original initiative which has already had a major influence on the next generation of Aboriginal claims strategies. In this chapter, however, we are less concerned with the substance of the Nunavut claim than with the structures which produced it.

To explain the process and outcomes of the Nunavut settlement, we must grasp a complex interplay of political and administrative forces. Three concepts will prove particularly helpful in the pages below. The first is the notion of the "policy cycle."[2] This suggests that policy results are not so much isolated events as they are stages in ongoing processes. While there is no necessary order here, neither does the process unfold at random. Particular decisions, while significant in themselves, form part of broader sequences of choice. For example, a crucial preliminary stage entails *issue definition*, in which policy problems are framed: What is Aboriginal title and what should be done about it? This serves to narrow the terms of debate and the range of eligible outcomes. It may precede or coincide with the related process of *agenda setting*, which determines the priorities for state action. Again, this can be hotly contested, since even if the terms of Aboriginal title are agreed, the degree of urgency and state commitment is a separate question. Once a policy issue becomes actionable, the task of *policy formulation* remains, in deciding the instruments and provisions for resolving the problem. In order to resolve Aboriginal claims a negotiating mechanism was designed and applied to a variety of settings including Nunavut. With draft proposals in hand, *policy adoption* is next, involving designated procedures for ratification of settlement agreement. The focus then shifts to *policy implementation,* in which the agreed provisions are put into effect. Obviously there is no strict linear order to this model. Stages may be combined or skipped, decision processes can be reset and repeated.

The second concept is that of bureaucratic politics. This captures the fact that administrative agents and agencies should be treated as interest holders as well as technical functionaries in the policy process. A state structure is far from unitary and homogeneous in its internal composition, and political self-interests are integral to administrative operations, as agents assert and defend their core mandates against the external challenge which new policy may present. Bureaucratic politics assumes greatest importance where decision processes are insulated from societal pressures (such as closed elite negotiating formats) and they can be particularly potent at the policy formulation stage.

The third and final concept is that of institutional logic. Every state structure, large or small, expresses certain underlying values and logic in its operating procedures. In this, the claims negotiating process can be compared to the judicial hearing, the regulatory proceeding, or the annual budget cycle. Each depends upon a distinctive decision-making routine, whose very terms embody a mobilization of bias. Archer et al. point out, however, that there may be more than one set of principles involved. If so, it is necessary to "pay attention to the defining core of principles as well as to the alternative visions, the different definitions, the contested alternatives that are posed both within and without the institution."[3] Thus it happens that claims politics can unfold within a stipulated negotiating context, while the protagonists may also be working to transform or supplant that context.

THE ERA OF COMPREHENSIVE CLAIMS: SETTING THE AGENDA

The opening of the Aboriginal claims era, in 1973, was a signal development. Only four years earlier Ottawa had declared in a White Paper its desire to abandon special programs for Indians.[4] The federal position on Aboriginal rights in non-treaty areas was uncompromising. As the White Paper declared, "Aboriginal claims to land...are so general and undefined that it is not realistic to think of them as specific claims capable of remedy...."[5] Such sweeping rejections energized the Canadian Aboriginal movement, which dismissed this contention along with the entire White Paper edifice. Instead, the advocacy of Aboriginal rights became a centrepiece of the political program advanced by Indian, Métis, and Inuit organizations ever since.

In fact, the 1969–73 period saw a dramatic political struggle over the redefinition of Canada's Indian policy agenda. A number of forces stirred this intense political ferment. A pan-Canadian mobilization through Indian organizations forced the withdrawal of the White Paper in 1971. In addition, the legal doctrine of Aboriginal rights had acquired a strong intellectual foundation by that time and several tribal groups pressed cases for recognition through the courts.[6] As a result of the 1972 election the Liberals were reduced to minority status, leaving the New Democrats with considerable parliamentary leverage to exercise on behalf of the Aboriginal movement. After a rich series of hearings the House of Commons Standing Committee on Indian Affairs and Northern Development endorsed the recognition of Aboriginal title and urged the government to do likewise. This multifaceted process was capped by the Supreme Court of Canada ruling in the Calder case in January 1973. Though the Nishga tribe failed to achieve the desired declaration that its Aboriginal title to traditional lands remained intact, the majority of the judges found a continuing basis for Aboriginal title in common law.[7] Thus Ottawa's formal victory was tempered by the prospect of future litigation and unpredictable outcomes.

The Calder judgment has become justifiably famous in the annals of legal politics as a case in which the plaintiffs lost the judicial battle but won the political war. While this is accurate, inasmuch as the federal government was obliged to abandon its 1969 position, it would be wrong to conclude that Aboriginal rights were secured as a result. Subsequent developments offer a sobering testament to the differences between defining an issue, framing an institutional process, and successfully achieving results within it.

The Trudeau government recovered the initiating advantage and, within eight months, a new policy framework was in place in Ottawa. This began only weeks after Calder, when the Yukon Indian Brotherhood presented the cabinet with a formal proposal for the recognition of Aboriginal rights.[8] The same prime minister who had earlier dismissed such title as a product of "historical might-have-beens"[9] now told the YIB that "perhaps you have more legal rights than we thought you had when we did the White Paper."[10] The new policy was unveiled, following cabinet approval, in a statement by the Minister of Indian and Northern Affairs (Jean Chrétien) on 8 August 1973.

This moment is widely cited as a turning point in the politics of Aboriginal title. Certainly it marked a sea change in issue definition by conceding the *existence* of non-treaty land rights. Significant as this was, the *terms* of recognition and settlement were even more consequential.[11] For Ottawa this was about dealing with a "traditional interest in land," rather than Aboriginal title *per se*, since the government refused to acknowledge the latter concept for years to come. It was also about "honouring lawful obligations" (language carried over from the White Paper), which meant that where the Aboriginal interest had never been extinguished by treaty or superseded by law, the government was willing to reach a "settlement." This would be negotiated directly between Ottawa and "authorized [Aboriginal] representatives," with compensation benefits being offered in return for relinquishing the Aboriginal interest. Though the term "surrender" was nowhere mentioned, the intent was clear. The new policy applied to both "Indian and Inuit people" (with no explanation provided for the inclusion of the latter or the omission of Métis). This new category of comprehensive claims was presented as an extension of the specific claims (against unfulfilled treaty terms) that were already under negotiation. In this way the logic of finalization ("these claims must be settled") was extended from treaty disputes to Aboriginal title. By adopting this conceptual frame, other options such as the recognition of continuing title, or the legislating of new rights, were ruled out. In sum, Ottawa unilaterally redefined the terms of the issue in 1973, from those of "title" to those of "claims." More specifically, the political reality of Aboriginal *title*—a continuing legal status which enjoyed positive judicial recognition—was set aside while the question of Aboriginal *claims*—unfinished business in need of negotiated conclusion—moved to the forefront.

Important as it was in framing the policy agenda, the Chrétien statement marked only the beginning of the comprehensive claims settlement process. Owing partly to the sketchiness of the statement, and partly to the sheer complexity of the undertaking, many questions remained unanswered as claimant groups began to prepare their proposals. In the years that followed, Ottawa periodically altered the terms of the policy. This gatekeeping function could be exercised at several levels (illustrated in Table 1): by formal revisions to the framework proposal of 1973, by amendments to the framework by incremental adjustment, and by *ad hoc* policy responses at specific negotiating tables. In the process the federal government was not only setting out its own negotiating strategy, but was also modifying the institutional mechanisms of claims settlement. While Ottawa guarded its predominance as an initiating agent, it is important to note that Aboriginal groups were not without influence on these matters. They could lobby cabinet ministers, litigate through the courts, and innovate at the bargaining table, as illustrated in Table 1.

BUILDING NEGOTIATING INSTITUTIONS

The concept of an institution is often advanced to capture the set of values, rules and relationships which guide a pattern of state decision making. Institutions can be distinguished from the specific decisions or policy events which they may produce, in the sense that a budget making process outlines how and why fiscal policy will be fashioned, without specifying anything about the particular budgets which are developed from year to year. Similarly, the comprehensive claims negotiating institutions reflect some basic assumptions and procedural rules for seeking settlement, without completely dictating the outcome of specific results at the negotiating table. Obviously not all pertinent policy outcomes are directly determined by this institutional complex. However, where such structures exist they serve to constrain the range of possible outcomes and promote generically similar results. Several defining features of Aboriginal claims settlement shape the institutional structure in this case. Not only did the Chrétien statement signal a realignment of political interests in the north, but the time frame required to resolve the plethora of outstanding cases is measured not in months or years but in decades. (By 1978, six claims had been accepted for negotiation and by 1981 there were another 20 awaiting attention in the backlog. By 1997 five comprehensive claim settlements had been reached in the federal northlands, including Nunavut, and two more were at the agreement-in-principle stage in British Columbia and Labrador.)

TABLE 1	Federal Policy and the Nunavut Claim	
Framework Statements	**Amending Statements**	**Eastern Arctic Inuit Claim**
		1971 ITC decides to pursue claim
1973 DIAND-Chrétien statement, "Claims of the Indian and Inuit People"	1975 ONC Reports describe range of eligible benefits	1972–75 Research and preparation
		1976 First Nunavut Proposal to cabinet, later withdrawn
	1977 PMO Policy on Northern Political Development	1977 New proposal presented
		1977 Sr. Federal Negotiator says Nunavut gov't is not negotiable
		1979–80 ITC adopt new claim framework
	1980 Appointment of outside chief federal negotiators	1980 Tungavik Federation of Nunavut designated as Inuit negotiating authority
1981 DIAND-Munro statement, *In All Fairness*		1981 Wildlife sub-agreement initialled. Ottawa repudiates.
	1982 *Constitution Act, Sections 25, 35, 37*	1982–87 Inuit Committee on National Issues participates in constitutional process
	1982 Ottawa declares six claim active negotiation ceiling	1982 Land & Resources talks begin
	1982 Munro sets conditions for NWT division	1982 Ottawa accepts principle of division after NWT plebiscite
	1983 Section 25 amendment to specify "land claims settlements"	1983 Fact-finder appointed for settlement boundary overlaps
	1983 DIAND Self-Government Policy	
		1985 TFN presents to Coolican Committee
1986 DIAND-McKnight statement, *Comprehensive Land Claims Policy*		1986 Inuit Wildlife Sub-agreement re-initialled
		1986 TFN involved in Comprehensive Claims Coalition
		1987 Iqaluit Agreement on NWT division and boundary
	1989 Implementation Agreement Guidelines	1990 TFN and Ottawa initial agreement-in-principle
	1990 Ottawa eliminates six claim active negotiation ceiling	1992 Nunavut Political Accord
		1992 Inuit accept Final Agreement in ratification vote
1993 DIAND-Siddon statement		1993 *Nunavut Act* and *Nunavut Land Claims Agreement Act*
		1993 Implementation begins
		1993 Nunavut Implementation Commission plans new Territory

   Furthermore, in this situation where so little policy guidance was available in the form of law, regulation or technical expertise, the parties to the negotiations required a formal procedural framework in which to work. A number of defining characteristics are evident in the comprehensive claims regime. One is its underdeveloped legal foundation. It is significant that Ottawa rejected a number of institutional arrangements which offered firmer shape and substance to the negotiating process. A glaring omission, in light of the many questions left unresolved by the Chrétien statement, was the lack of a legislative base.[12] The broad sweep of the new policy, measured in legal, financial, and crown jurisdictional commitments, certainly justified a statutory authorization. This would also have been appropriate in light of the finality of the agreements which Aboriginal peoples were being offered in order to acknowledge their historic collective rights.[13] The accompanying public debate would have highlighted the goals and expectations, as well as the potential flaws, of the proposed policy. Finally, a legislative mandate would have clarified the responsibilities of ministerial and administrative authorities in the discharge of these functions.[14] Lacking this foundation, many conceptual and strategic contradictions remained dormant for years to come, until they crystallized at the negotiating table.

   Another defining characteristic was the location of the federal comprehensive claims function within the Department of Indian Affairs and Northern Development (DIAND). This lead role in directing Ottawa's strategy was clouded, however, by the minister's complex and at times contradictory mandate. On one hand he held a "trust" responsibility under the *Indian Act*, which brought with it an obligation to assist claimant groups to attain the best possible settlements. While the minister's standing had slipped considerably through sponsorship of the White Paper proposals, his statutory trust role was taken seriously by Aboriginal people. At the same time, the dual portfolio bestowed a parallel mandate for economic development in the federal northern territories. Crown mineral and petroleum assets were seen as levers for far-reaching social and political change.[15] Frequently justified in terms of a "national interest," it sought a fast and final settlement of claims to allow resource exploitation to proceed.[16] Thus the tensions enclosed within the department were (and remain) deep-seated, leaving the minister seriously compromised in any choice between an obligation for fair settlements and an obligation to remove encumbrances against crown title.[17]

   The contradictory positions which the DIAND minister brought to the comprehensive claims process was well recognized both inside and outside state circles. In 1980 the Prime Minister's Special Constitutional Representative went so far as to propose a realignment of ministerial responsibilities to better balance the imperatives of settling claims and administering the north. Though his recommendation was not accepted, Bud Drury favoured the appointment of a new Minister for Native Peoples (outside of DIAND) who would act on their behalf.[18] Later, following the announcement of the National Energy Program in 1980, the lead role for northern petroleum exploration passed from DIAND to the Department of Energy, Mines and Resources. This led at least one commentator to predict a more positive system of "interdepartmental checks and balances," with DIAND presumably more sensitive to its Aboriginal trust role.[19] In the event, however, a new wave of constitutional and fiscal considerations (discussed below) prevented this from taking place.

   A third defining feature of the new regime was the choice of the actual negotiating mechanism. In designing any new administrative bureau, the most telling indicators are often those of location and mandate. The government had several options in 1973, and direct bilateral negotiation was only one of these. An alternative was the autonomous claims tribunal, along the lines of the American Indian Claims Commission established in 1946. Although a variation on this model had been approved in Ottawa in the mid-1960s, the draft legislation was first delayed, then superseded entirely, during the Trudeau years. In the American case a panel of commissioners adjudicated claims cases in a quasi-legal (adversarial) format. The panel was empowered to establish title and determine the extent of the liability. With appeal provisions lead to higher courts, this U.S. Commission demonstrated considerable success in clearing disputes.

Another alternative might have been modelled after dispute resolution methods followed in the labour-management relations field, where much experimentation has been evident in the postwar period. As Morse points out, there are many shared features with Aboriginal claims: a continuing relationship in law, a basic lack of trust, and fundamental conflicts of interest, to name only three. Consequently, "arbitration, fact finding, mediation, conciliation, final offer selection and legislated settlements could be utilized as parts of any new claims settlement."[20]

Clearly there is no lack of possibilities. In the absence of a formally articulated rationale, the government's calculations can only be judged in context. Both the tribunal and arbitration models involved a significant delegation of control, extending further than Ottawa was willing to accept. Certainly the courts had found fault with earlier federal positions on Aboriginal title, and this risk would carry over to a tribunal. Mediation would have injected a different sort of third-party involvement, along with a strong commitment to seek creative compromise.

In any event, the insertion of the claims negotiating function directly into the centre of a middle range "clientele department" suggested that Ottawa's overriding values were caution, incrementalism, and stability as opposed to innovation, systemic response, and developmental change. This impression is further confirmed by examining the policy mandate bestowed upon the Office of Native Claims (ONC), and its manner of implementation. Established in July 1974, it handled comprehensive claims talks for the first decade, until it was superseded by the Self-Government Sector (SGS) in the constitutional era of the 1980s. Since the modalities of settlement had neither been agreed nor imposed in advance, the result was a trial-and-error process which extended for at least the first five years.

TABLE TALKS

If issue definition and agenda setting take place largely at the macro level, and institutional mechanisms take shape at the intermediate level, then the negotiating process at each bargaining "table" illustrates the micro level determinants of settlement. Since each recognized claimant group pursues separate negotiations with the federal government, each table develops its own character. As Crowe puts it, "in each claim, the atmosphere and style of negotiation differs, reflecting regional, political and individual influences."[21] As in any extended sequence of negotiations, land claims outcomes are "path dependent" to a significant degree. It is important to remember that the basic coordinates of Ottawa's approach have evolved significantly over time, so that negotiations begun in the mid-1970s faced different parameters than those launched 10 or 15 years later. Equally, the negotiations process has a cumulative quality, extending not simply from one year to the next but also from one table to the next. The result is a complicated dialectic by which significant gains or losses at any table tend to reflect on all others.

A political analysis of table talks must recognize that time spent at the table amounts to a small proportion of total elapsed time. While it is commonly noted that the Nunavut claim was under negotiation for 16 years (1976–1992), a closer examination shows this to be a highly uneven process punctuated by the "overhead" involved in preparatory research, client consultation, strategic review, tactical delay, and acknowledged deadlock, as well as active negotiation. An accurate index of "real-time negotiations" would also require the exclusion of substantial intervals imposed by Ottawa to review claims policy (06/79 to 12/81, and 06/85 to 12/87), and intervals imposed by Inuit organizations to revise claims proposals (09/76 to 12/77) or to reorganize negotiating structures (02/79 to 12/79, and 12/81 to 09/82).

Given the complicated terms and ramifications of claims settlements, the lines of accountability between negotiators and clients also required constant effort at refinement. On the federal side, several types of personnel have tried their hand at the negotiating table. In 1973 Ottawa began the Yukon talks with an interdepartmental delegation, but later found it necessary to designate a "chief negotiator" to head the team. There was also a brief experiment of direct (DIAND) ministerial involvement followed by the appointment of a special claims representative from the senior ranks of the department. By the time the Nunavut talks began in 1976 the ONC furnished senior negotiators to all claims tables. This changed again in 1980 when Ottawa began to recruit full-time chief negotiators from beyond the civil service.

Even more problematic was the relation between the chief federal negotiator and the more diffuse set of government interests with a stake in the outcome. Ministerial involvement was guaranteed at two levels, as both federal framework policies (for example 1973, 1977, 1981, 1986) and specific mandates (to chief negotiators) for individual claims were authorized by cabinet.[22] On the other hand, during periods of actual negotiation Ottawa's chief negotiator received regular feedback from the coterie of federal officials making up the "federal caucus" which observed the talks and participated in the planning sessions. In this sense, the role of the chief negotiator is tightly suspended between cabinet mandate and administrative caucus. As one former senior negotiator aptly put it:

> The government constituency consists of the voters, the private sector with all of its varied interest groups, and the public sector with many departments, each having a cherished role and mandate. From this labyrinth, the government negotiators must extract agreement on new ideas to be negotiated, must obtain cabinet approval of the consensus and then thrash out with the native team agreements that can be ratified by both sides before legislation.[23]

From the outset of the comprehensive claim settlement process in 1973, the Aboriginal groups were invited to take the lead in proposing terms of settlement to which Ottawa would then respond. Yet as seen above, this invitation was never unconditional. Not only did the government insist that any settlement entail the surrender of all outstanding claims, but it also manoeuvred continually to dictate the negotiable terms of compensation. While the former point was explicitly spelled out in the 1973 Chrétien statement, the latter was more episodic, though no less final. It began as early as 1975 when DIAND Minister Judd Buchanan presented the Yukon Indians with an outline of federal expectations which was strongly suggestive of the James Bay agreement-in-principle.[24] Then in 1977 the PMO Paper declared that political division and northern government institutions would not be negotiable at the land claims table, and that moratoriums on exploration and development pending settlements ran counter to government priorities.[25] Speaking just over one year later, DIAND Minister Hugh Faulkner declared that the western Arctic Inuit (COPE) agreement-in-principle could be taken as a "model" for subsequent northern claims. By the time that DIAND

Minister John Munro released the revised federal framework statement late in 1981, policy revisionism was rampant in the contention that "negotiations are designed to deal with non-political matters arising from the notion of Aboriginal land rights."[26] The circle was fully closed when ONC publications boldly began to enumerate eligible forms of compensation modelled upon previous agreements.[27] Thus Ottawa worked relentlessly to narrow the scope of negotiable settlements.

John Merritt has characterized the 1973 comprehensive claims policy (as reiterated in 1981) as one of "chronic ambiguity," which clouded both the standards of negotiation and expected outcome by failing to address the broader objectives of settlements. This had a powerful effect on the bargaining situation, for "[i]n this posture of 'flexible response,' the Aboriginal parties to negotiations become accustomed to hearing terms such as 'nonstarters' and references to 'facts of life' when they present demands that conflict with their government counterparts' perceptions of political reality."[28]

Another powerful lever used to pressure Aboriginal groups into preferred lines of negotiation is the government's discretionary control of financial assistance for claims preparation. In its baldest form, Ottawa has both threatened and imposed unilateral withdrawals of funds in situations where Aboriginal strategies defied government expectations. In his eagerness to see the Cree people negotiate with Bourassa in 1973, Chrétien threatened to cut off their litigation funds. Buchanan told the Yukon Indians that realistic bargaining would be necessary in order to avoid a freeze on their claims funding, while Faulkner froze the Dene-Métis support for 18 months beginning in 1978 when the two groups failed to agree on the joint claim approach that Ottawa demanded in the Mackenzie Valley.

Even in cases where Aboriginal negotiators have achieved a conceptual or substantive breakthrough, results can be clawed back or nullified by determined federal effort. Perhaps the classic case arose at the Nunavut claim table in 1981. The subjects of harvesting rights and wildlife management were recognized as essential to any prospective settlement. Accordingly, they were pushed to the top of the negotiating schedule in the hope that early agreement would inject momentum to complete the talks. While Ottawa was willing to discuss creation of a joint representative body to advise on wildlife policy, the Inuit Land Claims team pressed for "joint management," particularly in the allocation of local game quotas.

Working in concert with the chief federal negotiator, they developed the terms of a wildlife sub-agreement-in-principle which was initialled as accepted on 28 October 1981. It established the jointly constituted Nunavut Wildlife Management Board, whose decision on any policy matter (under law) would take effect unless the relevant minister specifically disallowed and returned it for reconsideration. If the differences could not be resolved, then ministerial authority was final. This was a finely balanced compromise between delegated authority to the joint Board and a ministerial override to guarantee public accountability. Believing the proposal to be consistent with his mandate, and enjoying support at senior bureaucratic levels, chief federal government negotiator Bob Mitchell initialled the wildlife sub-agreement along with his Inuit and Government of Northwest Territories (GNWT) counterparts. Almost immediately, however, federal agencies with jurisdiction over migratory birds (Department of Environment) and over sea mammals and fish (Department of Fisheries and Oceans) rejected the agreement, and Ottawa then renounced it on the grounds that the chief negotiator had exceeded his mandate by initialling the government's consent.

At a stroke, an innovative step forward was transformed into a contentious dispute in which the integrity of the negotiating process was called into question. As the claimant party, the Inuit were angered by the perfidy of the Ottawa team, and discouraged by this stark demonstration of federal truculence.[29] In Inuit eyes, the federal government had yet again imposed new rules unilaterally for its own advantage, and there was talk of breaking off negotiations altogether. While this did not happen, the Inuit continued to insist that the agreement be honoured and, after persistent lobbying and a change of federal government and the appointment of an innovative new minister, it was "re-initialled" during the tenure of Conservative DIAND minister David Crombie.

This controversy was widely debated throughout the federal bureaucracy and touched all parties to comprehensive land claims. Despite the demonstrable need for new approaches after years of deadlock, it sent a warning to all chief negotiators of the dangers of innovative bargaining, while affirming a right of effective veto by departmental interests displeased with any element of the package. It also tended to reduce the federal bargaining position to the lowest common denominator of consensus within the Ottawa caucus.

Quite apart from the substantive issues of wildlife management, the claims negotiating process was revealed once again as a brittle and conservative mechanism with evident shortcomings. Federal officials chose to view the episode narrowly, however, as a technical problem of accountability which had to be corrected. One Office of Native Claims director exemplified this view in his comment that, "the chief federal negotiator represents the government. When he goes to the table and makes an offer, it is incumbent on him to ensure that he has his principals behind him….He is not there as a mediator; he is not there as a facilitator; he represents the government."[30] Yet if the claims negotiating process was viewed more as a political process, in which competing interests could only achieve positive results through dedicated consensus building on complex questions in a quasi-public forum, a different conclusion emerges. Robert Mitchell, who subsequently left the chief federal post at the Nunavut table, alluded to the challenge in observing that "the government wants to settle these claims very, very badly, but it is a debate [sic] as to whether it is prepared to make the moves that are necessary in order to settle."[31]

Despite Ottawa's extended boycott of the Nunavut wildlife sub-agreement, some of its terms found their way into negotiations at other tables. The wildlife sections of the Inuvialuit Final Agreement of 1984 included the ministerial override along with Board allocation of local harvest quotas. Similar provisions appeared in the Yukon talks and in the Dene/Métis 1990 agreement-in-principle, from whence they were carried over to the Gwich'n (1991) and Sahtu (1992) Final Agreements in the Northwest Territories. This clearly illustrates a "ratchet effect" by which significant advances at one table tend to be reflected at others, thereby establishing new threshold provisions of settlement.

RESETTING THE CLAIMS AGENDA IN THE 1980S

If the White Paper of 1969 triggered an initial struggle over issue definition, then the proclamation of the *Constitution Act, 1982* signified another. The 1982 amendments were of historic importance. Section 35 recognized and affirmed "the existing Aboriginal and treaty rights" of Aboriginal peoples, including rights derived from comprehensive land claims. In Section 25 a slightly different wording was adopted to protect "Aboriginal, treaty or other rights and freedoms pertaining to the Aboriginal peoples" from challenge under the *Charter of Rights and Freedoms*. Finally, Section 37 required that a First Ministers Meeting including Aboriginal leaders be convened within one year of proclamation to further identify and define Aboriginal rights. At the first of an eventual four such meetings (in 1983) Section 35 was amended to include both existing and future land claims settlements.

These provisions signified fundamental changes of legal and political position, which inevitably registered in the comprehensive claims arena. Where only a decade earlier Ottawa had refused to acknowledge Aboriginal title (acknowledging only an Aboriginal "interest in land"), Section 35 now entrenched several classes of Aboriginal and treaty rights, of which land claims settlement rights were just one. While it was left to the government and Aboriginal leaders to further "identify and define" Aboriginal rights, the question of self-government was destined to head this agenda.

The political initiatives of the 1982–1985 period had lasting effects. In particular, the "constitutionalization" of comprehensive claims agreements affected the northern negotiating context in several ways. With Section 35 protected from Charter challenges on grounds of legal or equality rights, there was far less threat of third-party litigation against the terms of settlements on grounds of discriminatory treatment. At the same time, this raised the threshold of political acceptability for government parties to the negotiations, in the awareness that the terms of final agreements would be carved in constitutional stone. The entrenchment of Aboriginal rights also served to undercut Ottawa's blanket extinguishment requirement for claims settlements, since claimant groups could no longer be expected to surrender all rights before the full parameters of Aboriginal rights had become clear. In fact, it was only a few short years until Ottawa was willing to distinguish between the surrender of Aboriginal title to "land and resources," and the continuance of other Aboriginal rights.[32]

In another respect, the recognition of claims settlement rights in Sections 25 and 35 served to level the field between the former and the northern constitutional processes. Previously, political development was viewed as a preserve of public government while claims settlements were public-private transactions, with Ottawa insisting on separate if parallel tracks for each. But if both now enjoyed constitutional standing, this created a potentially broad equivalency which made it possible to link the two processes with explicit cross-references and even overlapping provisions. Significantly, DIAND Minister Munro announced conditional acceptance of NWT division (a key Nunavut "political" demand) only six months after proclamation of the 1982 Constitution. Four years later, the McKnight land claims policy announced that self-government rights were now negotiable items, so long as they were excluded from constitutional protection. By 1990, DIAND Minister Pierre Cadieux went further, announcing that Framework Agreements on Aboriginal self-government could be included in comprehensive claims settlements. For the TFN/Inuit claim, this opened the way for agreement to negotiate a Nunavut Political Accord on the creation of the new Territory.

There was yet another way in which Section 35 rights shaped the comprehensive claims agenda. As befits any new constitutional provision, it was only a matter of time before its limits were tested by litigation. In 1990 the Supreme Court of Canada offered some authoritative answers in its ruling in the Sparrow case. On its facts, this addressed the status of federal fisheries regulation in the face of a Section 35–based Aboriginal fishing right. In this matter the plaintiff argued for self-regulation by constitutional right, while the Crown argued that Aboriginal fishing rights had been extinguished by progressive regulation. The Supreme Court decision broke new ground in several directions. It signalled that Section 35 would be interpreted generously, and it also delineated a rigorous standard for "clear and plain" extinguishment along with a test for the validity of state regulation in the face of Aboriginal rights.[33] At the same time, the Supreme Court anticipated political authorities would take the lead in defining Aboriginal rights, an invitation which has not yet been taken up.

Perhaps inevitably, the pace of comprehensive claim activity had slowed in the mid-1980s, as other avenues (such as constitutional amendment and self-government negotiations) seemed to offer more sweeping prospects of progress. However, David Crombie signalled that claims settlements were still a priority by appointing the Coolican Task Force in 1985 to review Comprehensive Claims Policy. It represented the most open and innovative reflection on Aboriginal policy in decades, with a broadly representative panel consulting widely before offering bold new foundations to an ailing policy sector.[34] Praised by the Aboriginal constituency, they were relentlessly attacked within the federal administration. An important counterweight was the Aboriginal common front mobilized in 1986 to promote the Coolican program in official Ottawa. The Comprehensive Claims Coalition (CCC) brought together nine claimant groups with proposals in the advanced stages. Two intense rounds of lobbying took place in the spring and autumn of 1986 and although they did not prove sufficient to win cabinet acceptance for the Coolican package, they did influence the extension of the McKnight land claims policy to include self-government provisions and offshore rights.[35]

It is evident that the policy juncture of the mid-1980s did not yield the clean re-definition of comprehensive claims that had been achieved in 1973. Perhaps this was inevitable, given the political and bureaucratic stakes accumulated over the first decade. Whereas DIAND still enjoyed an uncontested lead role at the time of the Chrétien statement, later ministers such as Munro, Crombie, McKnight, and their successors found that the cabinet process was strewn with departmental vetoes. Even if these could be overcome on particular proposals, the distinct and dissonant tracks of constitutional rights, self-government arrangements and comprehensive claims would never be easily blended after the final failed constitutional conference of 1987.

THE NUNAVUT FINAL AGREEMENT

Clearly there were many variations and combinations in the proposals advanced by the Inuit over more than two decades. Since a full treatment of Inuit negotiating strategies would require another study, this section will simply highlight some leading conceptual themes and terms, acknowledging that this telescopes a rich and fascinating political journey into an overly schematic summary.

It was in February of 1976 that the Inuit Tapirisat of Canada (ITC) presented the first Nunavut Proposal to Pierre Trudeau in Ottawa. This sixty-one page document offered a detailed settlement formula. It claimed private ownership of one-third (250 000 square miles or 647 500 km^2) of documented traditional lands. It also claimed exclusive hunting, trapping, and fishing rights, and a royalty from resource development, across the entire Inuit claim area. Another key element called for the creation of a Nunavut Territorial Government (separate from the Northwest Territories) as a public government for the Inuit claim area. Yet eight months later the proposal was withdrawn on the grounds that it failed to reflect Inuit concerns at the grass roots. While there have been many reviews and renewed proposals since that time, the Inuit political strategy remained strikingly faithful to these core provisions which are hallmarks of the 1993 Nunavut Final Agreement (NFA).

The Inuit (and other Aboriginal groups) also faced a challenge in reconciling the political and administrative demands of negotiating, though one of a different nature. First, they had to deal with federal officials within the settlement policy sketched earlier, a policy whose limited scope threatened to frustrate the prospects of a meaningful settlement. Second, they faced a continuing challenge of maintaining ties to the Inuit public in a negotiating context which posed dangers by its inherently elitist nature. This might be described as a problem of political triangulation, of gauging viable distances and linkages between Inuit public expectations, Inuit leadership mandates, and the negotiating autonomy required for strategic planning and tactical manoeuvring.

In dealing with Ottawa, the Inuit leadership displayed a combination of political persistence, ingenuity, and flexibility. When the 1977 federal position paper rejected the Nunavut government as a negotiable claims issue, the ITC refused to accept the bifurcation and boycotted all talks to this effect. When Ottawa refused an Inuit request for a freeze on all crown land use (i.e., resource development) in the claim region pending settlement, the political momentum shifted from the negotiating table to the Federal Court of Appeal, where Justice Patrick Mahoney found an Aboriginal right to exist under common law. A decisive turning point, which contributed ultimately to the signing of the NFA, was the adoption of the 1980 Inuit position paper *Parnagujak*. While the Nunavut Territory remained a fundamental feature, it was now treated as a project to be launched but not necessarily completed by the signing of the Final Agreement. Similarly, the previous proprietary control over natural resources was transformed into a revenue sharing proposal. A new approach to negotiation also emerged at this time, by which drafts would be negotiated and agreed by sub-topic, leading to a cumulative agreement only at the end. One of the first expressions of this was the crucial 1981 sub-agreement on wildlife, which pioneered the design of government-Inuit joint management boards for resources and environmental protection and impact planning.

The overall result is not a single document so much as a package. This begins with the highly detailed Nunavut Final Agreement (ratified late in 1992 and legislated the following year), running to several hundred typeset pages. It also includes the separate Nunavut Implementation Agreement. Earlier settlements had demonstrated that formal implementation plans, particularly for funding and staffing the authorized programs, were critical to guaranteeing results. Finally the Nunavut Political Accord set out the constitutional process for designing and proclaiming the new territory by the end of the decade. This, together with the *Nunavut Act*, paved the way for the Nunavut Implementation Commission to oversee the process.

CONCLUSION

This chapter began by introducing three concepts to help clarify both the general development of Aboriginal claims policy and the Nunavut Claim in particular. Taken together, they explain much about the lengthy duration of negotiations, the frequent suspensions and postponements, and the mixed results in terms of settlements achieved.

The policy cycle offers a useful tool to grasp the evolution of the federal claims framework, which to date has spanned seven governments and 14 ministers of Indian and Northern Affairs in 25 years.[36] Many of the intractable difficulties encountered at the negotiating table can be traced back to choices of policy definition and formulation years earlier. The circumstances of initial definition were clearly pivotal. Subsequent prospects of redefinition, while not impossible, were laden with difficulties. Our case reveals several key moments of policy definition or redefinition, including the 1969 White Paper, the 1973 Chrétien statement, and the 1982 constitutional amendment. It also reveals several points at which definitional opportunities were declined, particularly in response to the Coolican findings after 1985. A new prospect has surfaced at the time of writing, as Ottawa fashions its response to the Royal Commission on Aboriginal Peoples.

With the Chrétien framework, the institutional parameters of comprehensive claims policy were set. Once the negotiating process was routinized, it fell below the cabinet horizon, and negotiations were managed by administrative officials. This proved to be a particularly difficult environment for Aboriginal parties. On the other hand, it was highly conducive to the assertion of bureaucratic interests: in the definition of negotiating mandates, the vetting of table initiatives within the federal caucus, and the briefing of ministers for cabinet review of the outcomes.

Despite the designation of DIAND (and the ONC/SGS in particular) as the lead agency for comprehensive claims settlement, it was never an authoritative centre for either framework policy design or table negotiations. Less than four years into the process, the Prime Minister's Office redefined the settlements framework in issuing its political development paper. Later still, the *Constitution Act, 1982* elevated the role of the Department of Justice in light of the new constitutional status of Aboriginal rights,[37] while the 1983 amendment specified land claims agreements in the coverage of Section 25. By the late 1980s a new appreciation of settlement implementation costs and planning brought the Treasury Board Secretariat to the fore.[38]

A more radical fragmentation characterized relations in the negotiating process. The ONC/SGS shared with Justice the gatekeeping responsibility of screening petitions of claim. Then when the actual talks began, the ONC/SGS preeminence dissolved into the tangled web of bureaucratic stakeholders in the federal negotiating caucuses which battled intensely for control of framework policies, negotiating mandates, and their own chief negotiators' conduct at the table. By the mid-1980s this embraced no fewer than four DIAND programs, three central agencies, and four additional core departments as well as the two Territorial Governments.[39] The veto potential in such a highly dispersed structure is readily illustrated by the fate of the Nunavut Wildlife Sub-Agreement. In none of this could DIAND (much less the ONC/SGS) be considered a strong controlling agent capable of enforcing consistent terms and resisting encroachment by rival bureaucratic agendas. In this situation there was ample room for "many little 'Ottawas,'" as Doering aptly puts it.[40]

One potential counter to such bureaucratic fragmentation might have come from political direction at executive levels. Certainly Aboriginal issues were brought to the federal cabinet at regular intervals, and the deputy ministers' committee on comprehensive claims (1980) offered another potential coordinating mechanism. However, it was in the character rather than the frequency of cabinet involvement that difficulty lay. Rather than imposing either a statutory or declaratory policy framework from the outset, the cabinet delegated procedural responsibility to the administrative ranks and accepted incremental policy advice from an increasingly fragmented claims bureaucracy. On those few occasions when outside advice was enlisted (Drury, 1980; Coolican, 1986), its impact was marginalized by internal administrative resistance. Meanwhile, the deeper necessity of Aboriginal claims settlement was never seized by the cabinet in such a way as would concert administrative energies into realizing lasting results.

If the institutionalized logic of decentralized negotiations tilted the advantage toward Ottawa's agenda, then the logic of judicial policy making served Aboriginal claims groups in a similar fashion. While resort to the courts was episodic, it was no less authoritative for that fact. Favourable judgements in cases such as Calder, Baker Lake, and Sparrow played a crucial role in dictating both the terms and the urgency of settlement negotiations. The initial acknowledgement of Aboriginal rights was driven largely by the alarming implications (for Ottawa) in the Calder decision. Justice Mahoney's ruling in the Baker Lake case indicated that the unextinguished Aboriginal interest in northern lands could complicate the exercise of crown title indefinitely, and the Sparrow judgment augured well for the judicial recognition of Aboriginal rights in the event that the political negotiating process failed.[41] For Aboriginal claimants, the courts offered an appealing and effective avenue of redress when other political channels were closed, particularly as favourable findings tended to be generalized across the legal domain rather than confined to a single negotiating table.

For Aboriginal interests, the defects of the 1973 framework could only be remedied over time, by a relentless probing for constructive avenues of advance. This involved a refusal to accept the 1973 terms at face value. While the rudimentary structure of the negotiating paradigm initially allowed Ottawa to exploit its ambiguities, Aboriginal groups could also capitalize on this in the longer run. Ministers were lobbied, negotiating mandates were transformed over time, and federal negotiators were challenged with innovative and constructive formulations. When opportunities arose to redefine the Aboriginal claims framework, as with the 1982 Constitutional Amendment or the Coolican review of 1985, these were pushed to the limits of their potential. Equally, when a positive breakthrough occurred at one negotiating table, it was soon taken up at others, providing a new threshold of acceptability.

It is clear that outcomes such as the Nunavut Agreement are historic achievements, with powerful developmental potential. At the same time, the list of final agreements to have emerged from more than two decades of negotiation is disappointingly short, and the roster of outstanding claims is alarmingly long. Thus the case for a radical recasting of the comprehensive claims framework remains strong.

NOTES

1. In this chapter I adopt an instrumentalist approach to the state, treating it as an integrated complex of decision-making agencies which reflect societal forces while retaining a degree of administrative autonomy. As will be seen below, claims settlements involve a shifting cluster of executive and administrative agents.

2. For elaborations of the policy cycle model, see Leslie A. Pal, *Public Policy Analysis* (Scarborough: Nelson Canada, 1992), chapters 6–8; and Michael Howlett and M. Ramesh, *Studying Public Policy* (Toronto: Oxford University Press, 1995), chapter 1.

3. Keith Archer, Roger Gibbins, Rainer Knopff and Leslie Pal, *Parameters of Power* (Scarborough: Nelson Canada, 1995), 13.

4. A "White Paper" is a policy proposal released by a government for public discussion prior to its formal adoption as policy. Sally Weaver offers an incisive interpretation of the White Paper's development and of the state structure which produced it. See *Making Canadian Indian Policy: The Hidden Agenda 1968–1970* (Toronto: University of Toronto Press, 1981).

5. Canada, *Statement of the Government of Canada on Indian Policy 1969* (Ottawa: Queen's Printer, 1969): 11.

6. The emerging doctrine of Aboriginal title can be found in Peter Cumming and Neil Mickenberg, *Native Rights in Canada* (Toronto: Indian-Eskimo Association, 1971).

7. Among the many commentaries on the Calder case is Peter Kulchyski, *Unjust Relations: Aboriginal Rights in Canadian Courts* (Toronto: Oxford, 1994).

8. Yukon Indian Brotherhood, *Together Today for Our Children Tomorrow* (Whitehorse: Yukon Indian Brotherhood, 1973).

9. Cited in Donald Purich, *Our Land* (Toronto: Lorimer, 1986) 52.

10. Hugh and Carmel McCallum and John Olthuis, *Moratorium* (Toronto: Anglican Book Centre, 1977) 20.

11. The following citations are taken from "Claims of Indian and Inuit People," Department of Indian Affairs and Northern Development, 8 August 1973, reproduced in Bradford W. Morse, "The Resolution of Land Claims," *Aboriginal Peoples and the Law*, ed. B. W. Morse (Ottawa: Carleton University Press, 1985), 629–31.

12. Throughout the entire period since 1973, the only legislative authority for the Government of Canada on negotiations of Aboriginal claims derived from the annual expenditure estimates, specifically the votes covering the Office of Native Claims and the claimant funding program. DIAND, Audit Branch, "Comprehensive Claims" (October 1983), 2.

13. Unlike the negotiating framework and process, the *results* of settlement were always expressed in statute. The James Bay and Northern Quebec Agreement inaugurated the practice whereby governments formalized their assent with enabling legislation.

14. There is a telling parallel between the comprehensive claims policy and Ottawa's environmental assessment review policy established only four months later. Both cases reveal a determined aversion to legislative authority. In the case of the EARP this was on the advice of senior mandarins who feared litigation under an environmental statute and desired to keep a discretionary review process in-house. Thus a cabinet order was issued instead. G.B. Doern and T. Conway, *The Greening of Canada* (Toronto: University of Toronto Press, 1994), 194.

15. The genesis of this program is explored in Peter Clancy, "Working on the Railway: A Case Study in Capital-State Relations," *Canadian Public Administration* 30:3 (Fall 1987).

16. Edgar F. Dosman, *The National Interest* (Toronto: McClelland and Stewart, 1975).

17. C.M. Drury interpreted the policy tensions within DIAND somewhat differently, while concurring in that the mandate was untenable with regard to claims: "The federal minister represents in this process the interests of federal departments and agencies, the interests of the GNWT and the N.W.T. as a whole, as well as the 'special' interests of the native peoples." Special Constitutional Representative, *Constitutional Development in the Northwest Territories* (Ottawa: Supply and Services, 1980), 2.

18. Special Constitutional Representative, *Constitutional Development in the Northwest Territories* (1980), 138. In status, the position of Special Representative fell somewhere between a formal Commissioner of Inquiry and an administrative delegate of the government. Drury was directed to consult with northern Native groups on the Prime Minister's behalf, to develop constitutional options outside of the claims settlement process.

19. Peter Cumming, "Canada's North and Native Rights," *Aboriginal Peoples and the Law*, ed. B. W. Morse (Ottawa: Carleton University Press, 1985), 698.

20. Bradford W. Morse, "Labour Relations Dispute Resolution Mechanisms and Indian Land Claims," *Indian Land Claims in Canada*, ed. Bradford W. Morse (Association of Iroquois and Allied Indians, Grand Council Treaty No. 3, and Union of Ontario Indians, 1981), 343.

21. Keith J. Crowe, "Claims on the Land," *Arctic Circle* 1:4 (January–February 1991): 32.

22. The frequency of cabinet consultation varied according to the pace of negotiations, but one senior DIAND official estimated that comprehensive claims matters went before the cabinet 15 times between 1986–90, far exceeding any other area of social policy. R. Van Loon, "The Federal Perspective," *Northern Perspectives* 18:4 (November–December 1990): 8.

23. Crowe, 33.

24. The James Bay and Northern Quebec Agreement of 1975 was negotiated under "shotgun" circumstances, as a Quebec government corporation was proceeding with the construction of the hydroelectric dams and reservoirs in the settlement area while the talks were underway. The resulting agreement was widely denounced by Canadian Aboriginal groups.

25. Office of the Prime Minister, "Political Development in the Northwest Territories," *Northern Transitions*, vol. 2, eds. R. F. Keith and J. B. Wright (Ottawa: Canadian Arctic Resources Committee, 1978), 277–83. The issuance of the PMO Paper was widely regarded as an effort to reassert federal control over an issue which had been mishandled by DIAND.

26. Department of Indian Affairs and Northern Development, "In All Fairness," *National and Regional Interests in the North* (Ottawa: Canadian Arctic Resources Committee, 1984), 84.

27. "In addition to any provisions for local self-government, settlement benefits and rights may include lands, limited sub-surface rights, wildlife rights, and monetary compensation." Office of Native Claims, "Perspectives on Native Land-Claims Policy," *National and Regional Interests in the North* (Ottawa: Canadian Arctic Resources Committee, 1984), 90.

28. John Merritt, "A Review of Federal Land-claims Policy," *National and Regional Interests in the North* (Ottawa: Canadian Arctic Resources Committee, 1984), 79.

29. Chief Inuit negotiator Allen Maghagak "says the federal government is setting a poor precedent that erodes Inuit trust." *Nunavut Newsletter*, No. 2 (July 1982) 1. TFN lawyer Geoff Lester attributed Ottawa's reneging to DFO's obsessive resistance: "The real reason why they don't want to live with the agreement is because for a time Inuit negotiators persuaded government negotiators to see the world through Inuit eyes. Government agreed with the Inuit. Now government wants to change its mind. An agreement is an agreement. Government is acting in bad faith." *Nunavut Newsletter*, No. 1 (June 1982): 7.

30. Clovis Demers, "Land Claims Plenary Session," *National and Regional Interest in the North* (Ottawa: Canadian Arctic Resources Committee, 1984), 42.

31. Bob Mitchell, "Land Claims Plenary Session," *National and Regional Interests in the North*, 43.

32. The 1986 revision to the federal comprehensive claims policy stated that "it is important to recognize that the aboriginal rights to be released in the claims process are only those related to the use of land and resources. Other aboriginal rights, to the extent they are defined through the constitutional process or recognized by the courts, are not affected by the policy." DIAND, *Comprehensive Land Claims Policy* (Ottawa: 1986), 12.

33. The Sparrow decision is included in Kulchyski, *Unjust Relations*. For an early commentary see W.I.C. Binnie, "The Sparrow Doctrine: Beginning of the End or End of the Beginning?" *Queen's Law Journal* 13:2 (Fall 1990): 217–53.

34. DIAND, *Living Treaties, Lasting Agreements* (Ottawa: Department of Indian and Northern Affairs, 1985). As a policy tool, a Task Force undertakes policy review functions similar to a Commission of Inquiry, though it may lack the legal powers conferred upon the latter.

35. Terry Fenge and Joanne Barnaby, "From Recommendations to Policy: Battling Inertia to Obtain a Land Claims Policy," *Northern Perspectives* 16:1 (January–April 1987): 12–15.

36. The full list of ministers includes: Jean Chrétien (Lib: 1973–74); Judd Buchanan (Lib: 1974–76); Warren Allmand (Lib: 1976–77); Hugh Faulkner (Lib: 1977–79); Jake Epp (Con: 1979); John Munro (Lib: 1980–84); Doug Frith (Lib: 1984); David Crombie (Con: 1984–86); Bill McKnight (Con: 1986–88); Pierre Cadieux (Con: 1988–90); Tom Siddon (Con: 1990–93); Pauline Brower Con: 1993); Ron Irwin (Lib: 1993–97); and Jane Stewart (Lib: 1997–).

37. The constitutional reform file fell within the mandate of the Justice Department, in the same way that specific and comprehensive claims fell to Indian and Northern Affairs.

38. In the 1970s the financial costs of aboriginal claims settlements tended to be regarded as one-time expenditures. However the James Bay and Northern Quebec experience demonstrated that many settlement provisions required planned phase-ins. Furthermore, the 1982 amendment opened the prospect that a failure to commit adequate resources jeopardized a constitutional commitment. As Ottawa's expenditure control agency, the Treasury Board assumed ever greater significance in implementation matters.

39. An appraisal by the DIAND Audit Branch in 1983 enumerated the following: the DIAND programs of Indian and Inuit Affairs, Northern Affairs, Corporate Policy, and Native Claims; the central agencies of Treasury Board Secretariat, Federal-Provincial Relations Office, and Ministry of State for Social Development; the Departments of Environment, Justice, Fisheries and Oceans, and Energy Mines and Resources; and the Governments of the Yukon and the Northwest Territories. DIAND, "Review of the Comprehensive Claims Process," (Ottawa: Indian Affairs and Northern Development, 1983), 5.

40. Ron Doering, "Natural Resource Jurisdiction and Political Development in the North: the Case of Nunavut," *National and Regional Interests in the North* (Ottawa: Canadian Arctic Resources Committee, 1984), 127.

41. The Baker Lake case was brought by the Inuit Tapirisat of Canada on behalf of the Inuit of Baker Lake, when Ottawa refused to declare a moratorium on uranium exploration. Reginald Sparrow, a Musqueam band member, was charged for fishing with a drift net which exceeded the size authorized by the band's food fishing license under the *Fisheries Act.*

EMERGING SOLITUDES: The New Era in Provincial-Municipal Relations

Katherine A. Graham and Susan D. Phillips

…You are at a party to honour the mayor of a major Canadian city upon her retirement. The guests include local and provincial officials who seem to be engaged in a rather heated discussion. Gingerly, you ask some of the party-goers, "What are they talking about?"

"Provincial downloading," scowl the local people.

"Provincial-municipal disentanglement," beam provincial officials.

"How can the same world be seen in such different ways?" you wonder….

INTRODUCTION

Canada's cities are envied around the world. They work—clean water flows from taps, waste water gets flushed away, traffic is manageable by international standards, and it is generally safe to walk the streets. Two of our largest cities, Toronto and Vancouver, routinely make the international hit parade of the top ten places to live or work. Across the country we have eight major city-regions (Halifax, Montreal, Ottawa-Hull, Toronto, Winnipeg, Calgary, Edmonton, and Vancouver) that are arguably "world class" in character or aspiring to be so. Increasingly, they are aggressively competing directly with other world cities in the new global economy, and their diverse populations are themselves reflections of the many cultures, colours, and perspectives that make up today's world.

In light of all of this, we must ask a basic question: Is city governance in Canada equipped to deal with the sophisticated reality of a global economy and multicultural society? This chapter will explore the question by examining the relationship between Canada's city-regions and provincial governments. It will begin by exploring the meaning of the emerging governance paradigm in the urban context. It will then provide a constitutional/legal and historical context for our examination of the current provincial-municipal relationship. We will thus be equipped to examine recent developments in the provincial-municipal relationship between

73

selected Canadian cities and their respective provincial governments. This examination points to an important pattern in contemporary provincial-urban relations that involves four often contradictory processes: the granting of greater autonomy by provinces to munici-palities; forced restructuring of municipalities; the sorting out or "disentanglement" of provincial and municipal service responsibilities; and downloading of costs. We argue that provincial governments are increasingly aware that the economic and social health of their major cities is perhaps the major determinant of a province's fortunes. Nonetheless, they some-times pursue policies that show little understanding of the complex world of urban gover-nance and a province's most constructive role in it.

EMERGENCE OF THE GOVERNANCE PARADIGM

Increasingly, students of Canadian public policy and administration are confronted with the need to think in terms of "governance," rather than "government." There are a number of reasons for this paradigm shift. Beginning in the early 1980s we have witnessed the elec-tion of avowedly less statist governments at the federal level (beginning with the Mulroney Conservatives) and in the key provinces of Alberta (the Klein government) and Ontario (the Harris government). Public management gurus, led by Osborne and Gaebler's[1] dictum that governments should "steer not row," have argued in favour of an alternative to "com-mand and control" government. Governments are now seen as having both partners and competitors in public policy making and in the management of what had been traditionally direct government programs.[2] Indeed, governments at all levels have become increasingly entangled with both the voluntary and private sectors. Municipal governments in Canada have led this shift, as leaders in co-production of services with both sectors. As David Siegel has noted, "...local governments have been doing innovative things like contracting out and establishing partnerships without ever realizing that they were being innovative. The temer-ity of federal and provincial governments in describing these initiatives as innovative, because *they* just discovered them recently, speaks volumes about the neglect of local government in this country [emphasis in original]."[3] If all of this were not sufficient, the burden of debt and deficit financing has induced the federal and provincial governments, regardless of ideo-logical bent, to cut program expenditures and transfers. For example, the federal government's unilateral shift to the Canada Health and Social Transfer (CHST) significantly reduced cash payments to the provinces. This created a ripple effect, with reductions resulting in both provincial human services (social services and health care) and in provincial-municipal transfers, as provinces scrambled to make up their financial shortfall. At all levels, these developments have reinforced governments' reliance on other players, particularly on the vol-untary sector, to fill the void.

The governance paradigm implies "the collective capacity to set and achieve public policy goals."[4] To operationalize this idea in the urban context, two important precepts must be recognized. First, it is essential to move beyond the often restrictive territorial no-tion of "municipality" or "city" to think about the city-region.[5] Second, one needs to adopt an inclusive approach to thinking about the apparatus of urban government. It is more than municipal government—city councils and the administrative structure under their direct control. Rather, we must also look at the full range of local special purpose bodies (such as school boards, police services boards, public utilities commissions and so on) which are responsible for many services at the local level and the voluntary sector. The voluntary sector is increasingly called upon to work with, or instead of, government to foster social cohesion and economic well being within city-regions.[6]

Emergence of the governance paradigm has important implications for the provincial-municipal relationship in Canada. The governance paradigm implies a need for provincial governments to stand back and give cities, governments and their partners a chance to become well established. Simultaneously, provinces need to provide support, in the form of a legislative and fiscal regime which addresses the needs and interests of city-regions and the diverse populations which inhabit them. In order to understand the extent to which provincial governments are pursuing these parallel paths successfully, we require some historical and constitutional/legal background.

THE CONTEXT OF PROVINCIAL-MUNICIPAL RELATIONS

Almost all overviews of provincial-municipal relations in Canada use the idea that local governments are "creatures of the provinces" as a point of departure.[7] This catch phrase is intended to reflect the fact that Section 92(8) of the *Constitution Act* gives exclusive jurisdiction for municipal institutions to provinces. This means that provincial governments have exclusive authority to create and abolish municipalities, to change their boundaries, and to assign them responsibilities. Section 92(2) of the *Act* further reinforces provincial control by effectively limiting the sources of revenue available to municipal governments to those specifically assigned to them by a province's legislature.[8]

Until very recently all provinces in Canada have chosen to exercise their power over municipal governments in a very "hands on" way. This approach was embedded in the cornerstone of the legislation governing municipal affairs, each province's *Municipal Act*. Across Canada Municipal Acts have laid a very restrictive foundation for municipal action. Municipal governments have only been permitted to undertake those functions specifically delegated to them in this legislation. The result has been that provincial governments must give explicit approval for many municipal decisions, including both big decisions (such as political restructuring) and small ones (such as changing a municipal logo). Provinces also had to give their approval for municipalities to deal with emerging issues, not foreseen when Municipal Acts were initially passed. For example, explicit provincial permission was required for municipal governments to begin the regulation of smoking in public places. A similar philosophy underlay related provincial legislation governing specific municipal functions such as land use planning, environmental services, and social services.[9] Furthermore, with the exception of Quebec, where there is a tradition of separate Municipal Acts governing urban and rural municipalities, large and small municipal governments in Canada have been treated essentially the same. This tradition of small and large together belies the development of sophisticated local governments in urban Canada.

This regime of provincial supervision and control has long been the subject of criticism. For example, K. G. Crawford, one of Canada's leading scholars of local government in the earlier part of the 20th century, noted the basic tension, if not contradiction, between local authorities carrying out provincially imposed obligations and carrying out the wishes of local citizens.[10] More recently, others have tried to break the constitutional straitjacket by arguing that municipalities, in fact, have a strong foundation for self-rule, even though legally they are not a separate order of government. For instance, Cameron has argued that municipal governments have "quasi-constitutional status," as a result of their unique preoccupation with the territory and citizens within their boundaries.[11] Cohn and Smith have asserted that urban governments are effectively independent agents, carrying out a unique diplomatic role, particularly in the international arena.[12] More generally, there has been a pattern of thinking about provincial-municipal relations in terms of an agent-partnership continuum. At the agent end, municipal governments are seen as mere administrative arms of the province; at the partnership extreme, the two governments are conceived as co-equals in the governance of a particular municipality's territory and citizenry.[13] Traditionally, students of provincial-municipal relations, writing from a local government perspective, have expressed alarm about what they have viewed as the shift toward the agent end of the continuum, precipitated by the actions of provincial governments.[14]

Regardless of whether one agrees with these arguments, by the 1990s the importance of Canada's city-regions was undeniable. The eight city-regions, identified earlier, contained 45 percent of Canada's population by the 1991 Census. Their combined municipal budgets dwarfed those of the majority of Canada's provinces. The stakes associated with the need to "do the right thing" in urban policy and administration were increasingly high.[15] Perhaps it was time for a new era of provincial-municipal relations.

CONTEMPORARY DEVELOPMENTS IN PROVINCIAL-MUNICIPAL RELATIONS

By the 1990s, both provincial and urban governments were sufficiently dissatisfied with the existing legislative and fiscal arrangements and governing structures that they began to press for major change. Within their own areas of jurisdiction, local governments in most city-regions overhauled their political and administrative machinery. Their reforms often included increasing the democratic control of council by reducing the number of special-purpose bodies and enhancing customer service by continued innovation in management practices and service delivery mechanisms.

Provincial governments have undertaken even bigger changes, some of which have been welcomed by municipalities and others forced upon them. Three major types of reforms have been attempted to varying degrees by provincial governments. First, there has been a move to grant greater autonomy and discretion to municipalities by reworking the legislative foundation. As we will see, Alberta has been the leader in this experiment, later emulated by Ontario and closely watched by other provinces. In part, this reform is a recognition that governments of the city-regions are "grown-ups" with mature and democratic institutions capable of making many of their own decisions. It is also motivated by a neoconservative interest in simplifying government by streamlining the number of regulations and the size of administration. Increased autonomy has been welcomed by most large city governments, but often feared by small municipalities who rely upon the administrative assistance available from Municipal Affairs departments as part of their mandate for overseeing local affairs.

The second reform is "disentanglement"—an attempt to simplify the provincial-local relationship by eliminating overlap and separating the service delivery responsibilities of governments in a clear-cut manner. This might be seen as analogous to earlier desires to create "watertight compartments" of federal and provincial responsibilities. The contemporary rationale for disentanglement, in addition to reducing costs, usually rests upon the principle of "subsidiarity."

The term *subsidiarity* refers to "the assignment of responsibility for policy and delivery of particular functions of government to the lowest level possible."[16] This concept came into prominence with the establishment of the European Union and has been used extensively in the Canadian federal-provincial context. In the realm of Canadian provincial-local relations, the principle of subsidiarity was first advocated by the Task Force on the Greater Toronto Area (the Golden Task Force) in its 1996 report.[17] The Task Force's definition of subsidiarity focused on the assignment of responsibility for service delivery and, accordingly, masked some important and thorny questions about how to achieve an appropriate allocation of responsibilities for both policy and delivery of services in the urban context. Policy and service delivery are, in fact, entangled. This reality is quickly evident when one tries to access urban services. Furthermore, as our brief case studies will illustrate, provincial governments do not have a monopoly on policy expertise. We argue that, just as the creation of a clear-cut division of responsibilities at the federal-provincial level has proven unachievable, efforts to disentangle provincial-local relations in Canada may also represent the pursuit of a mistaken goal.[18]

The third major experiment has been the political restructuring of municipalities into larger, consolidated units. Almost without exception, major restructuring of political boundaries has not come from the bottom up. Rather, it has been instigated and, in most cases, imposed on municipalities by provincial governments. The motives behind restructuring have been to establish large political units better able to compete in the global economy; to create bigger platforms and tax bases better able to withstand the downloading of service responsibilities; and to reduce costs by eliminating duplication and reducing the number of politicians. The apparent logic of amalgamation is not strongly supported by empirical analysis, however. Although arguments about the advantages of fewer politicians may have populist appeal, evidence from the scholarly literature and from case studies weighs in almost equally on whether amalgamation reduces or increases costs.[19]

All three of these reforms have taken place against a backdrop of cost cutting and downloading by provincial governments. Downloading refers to "the practice of a government imposing an obligation on another level of government to support or provide a service by mandating that government to do so (without appropriate compensation) or by simply withdrawing from the particular field."[20] In the contemporary Canadian context, downloading is a tri-level phenomenon. Reductions in federal-provincial transfers have been an important contributing factor to the reduction of provincial-municipal grants and to the cutback or elimination of provincial programs. The pressure on provincial governments has been exacerbated by the need to get their own financial houses in order. This has further challenged the task of local governance in Canada's city-regions. Downloading represents the misapplication of subsidiarity and disentanglement, when provincial governments dress up the rhetoric of responsibility transfer in these terms, while glossing over the additional financial obligations on local governments and the voluntary sector associated with these shifts.

Collectively, these reforms mark a new era of provincial-local relations. They have also created a curious paradox: the increasing complexity of urban governance is undeniable, yet the provincial response to meeting the challenges faced by city-regions has been a quest for simple "solutions." An overview of important developments in the relations between Alberta, Nova Scotia and Ontario and their major city-regions will illustrate this point and provide the basis for more specific diagnosis and development of a prognosis for the future. In its own way, each province has led in the field of provincial-municipal relations. Alberta has made a notable contribution by rethinking the foundations of municipal legislation. Nova Scotia has undertaken simultaneous restructuring of its major city-region,

Halifax, and realignment of provincial-municipal responsibilities. Finally, Ontario has embarked on a massive provincial-municipal reform agenda which has yielded important lessons concerning the process, as well as the substance of provincial-municipal reform. Taken together, the experiences of these three provinces and their city-regions provide both examples of leading edge thinking and some cautionary tales for other jurisdictions.

Alberta: Increasing Autonomy

In some respects, the Klein government in Alberta has been at the forefront in breaking the mold of restrictive approaches to provincial-municipal relations. Its most noteworthy breakthrough in this regard is the passage of a new municipal act that embodies a much less restrictive approach to provincial supervision of municipalities' affairs. The 1994 Alberta *Municipal Government Act* (*MGA*) has several innovative elements. First, it replaces the traditional restrictive approach to provincial-municipal delegation with a broad statement of legitimate spheres of municipal action. In addition, it replaces three former provincially appointed oversight agencies dealing with important municipal issues, such as planning, assessment, and boundaries, with a single part-time Municipal Government Board. Quasi-judicial boards to supervise these aspects of municipal affairs have been part of the landscape since the early 20th century. Under this legislation, the scope and detail of this type of supervision is intended to decrease. Finally, the *MGA* commits the provincial government to intervene in traditional municipal affairs and in a broad range of related fields in which there is a municipal interest (such as environmental protection, economic development, and trade) only when there is a clear provincial interest at stake.[21]

It should be evident that this legislation makes major strides in advancing the goal of giving municipal governments more control over their affairs. In the case of both the Calgary and Edmonton city-regions, it portended that they would be less subject to unilateral provincial decisions which, in the past, had sometimes affected their ability to develop.[22] Simultaneously, however, the Alberta government was moving in a contrary direction, in reforming its approach to the governance of human services. Specifically, the government established regional boards to deal with health care and with child and family services. The Calgary and Edmonton city-regions were treated no differently than other parts of the province in the implementation of this regional approach to human services.

Like most other provinces, Alberta has traditionally assumed full responsibility for the income security aspect of social services. (The notable exceptions until recently were Manitoba, Ontario, and Nova Scotia.) It has also exerted a strong role in health care, backing the construction of a significant network of hospitals in urban and rural Alberta. Each hospital was overseen by its own board, while the province retained responsibility for health promotion and funded a range of community-based health programs for different segments of the population.

By the 1990s, this province-wide pattern had come to have a rich overlay of local action in Alberta's two main city-regions. In Calgary, for example, the City's Social Services Department was playing a major catalytic role in the development and operation of a range of human services from child care to employment readiness. The word "catalytic" is precise in the Calgary context because the City had made a deliberate choice in the early 1990s to move from direct delivery of human services to strategic planning and community development. This shift had resulted in significant elaboration of the City's relations with the voluntary sector and, in the provision of services such as child care, with the private sector.

The provincial government's shift to a regional model for major human services began with the creation of regional health boards to oversee hospital and other health program spending in the early 1990s. Members of these boards were provincial appointees who, at least in early days, had to oversee provincial spending cuts to health care, hospital closures, and rationalization. One board was established for each of the Calgary and Edmonton city-regions. In 1994 the Alberta government announced the creation of 17 provincially appointed Children and Family Services authorities, with boundaries coterminous to the health boards. The full implementation of this regional approach to human services is to be completed in 1998.

Although this Alberta initiative is still in its early days, we can see that it poses three important issues for provincial-local relations in the city-region context. The first concerns local autonomy and accountability. Theoretically, the shift of provincial authority to regional boards can be conceived as a constructive effort at devolution. One might possibly be tempted to reflect on this approach's resonance with the principle of subsidiarity. In reality, the early days of the health boards were filled with argument and acrimony, as members were variously accused of being lackeys of the provincial government's cutback agenda or of being special interest pleaders for a particular hospital or program. Regardless of the merits of these accusations, the issue of local public accountability of these provincially appointed boards emerges. Particularly in the city-regions, concerns are raised about the visibility and direct accountability of the regional boards, but also about their relationship with local, democratically mandated councils.

The second issue concerns who, in the city-region context, is best equipped to sound out, interpret, and mediate local preferences. Advocates of local government, such as Crawford and Cameron, would argue that this is an essential role of local government and, further, that local government is uniquely equipped to carry it out. Regardless of who is best placed at the policy level, one must consider the relative strengths of a staff serving a special purpose board versus those of a sophisticated and integrated civic service, such as is found in places like Calgary and Edmonton. It would seem important to capitalize fully on the expertise of the social services and planning staff of city-regions, at the very least. The extent to which this will occur under this regional model remains an open question.

Finally, the issue of sustaining and building on links with the voluntary sector under this model must be raised. As discussed above, the City of Calgary has a long history of relations with the local voluntary sector. These relations are both deep and diverse. In recent years the City has placed particular importance on working in a complementary manner with the voluntary sector, as part of its strategic approach to human services. In their early days the regional boards' connections to the voluntary sector do not have the same breadth or depth. We must wait to see the extent to which these will evolve. In the best case, they will. In the worst case, the regional boards will be seen as agents of increasing provincial government control and containment. This will increase the distance between the provincial government and the voluntary sector, on which it would increasingly like to depend.

In summary, then, the Alberta case suggests some great promise and some potentially difficult and dysfunctional times in provincial-local relations.

Nova Scotia: Disentangling and Restructuring

One of Canada's worst man-made disasters occurred in Halifax in 1917 when two ships, one of which was filled with munitions, collided in Halifax harbour. The resulting "Halifax Explosion" razed a large section of the city and resulted in hundreds of casualties. Almost 60 years later, the fusion of four municipalities to form the Halifax Regional Municipality was not quite so cataclysmic. There have, however, been some hot spots and fireworks since the launch of the new Municipality in 1996. In terms of provincial-municipal relations, they have concerned the costs of transition to the new municipality and the province's capacity to deliver its new social service responsibilities and to build necessary links with voluntary agencies in the social sector.

Creation of the Halifax Regional Municipality and the "service exchange" of responsibility for income support and transportation between the Nova Scotia government and the new Halifax represent excellent examples of the confounding effects of the search for simple solutions to complex problems in provincial-municipal relations.

The Halifax Regional Municipality officially came into existence on 1 April 1996. It amalgamates the former cities of Halifax and Dartmouth with the Town of Bedford and Halifax County. The new Halifax covers more territory than the province of Prince Edward Island. It combines densely populated urban areas with small outlying communities and extensive tracts of unoccupied land.

The Government of Nova Scotia announced this new municipality in 1994, following the recommendation of a commission into local government in the area. The province dismissed efforts by some of the affected local councils to have their own recipe for restructuring accepted as special interest pleading. Local government unification was seen as the path to regional economic prosperity and service efficiency by advocates within the provincial government and by local business interests. The region also has a number of environmental challenges, such as the cleanup of the Halifax harbour, which advocates thought could be addressed only by an amalgamated government. Finally, establishment of a large single-tier municipal government for this large area was seen as a way of containing costs or realizing savings as a result of eliminating overlap and intermunicipal competition. It was thought that financial pressures, resulting from the levelling up of service standards and salary levels for employees of the former municipalities to the highest level, had been avoided by provisions for the transition. Under these provisions, the provincial government ruled out changes in municipal employees' collective agreements for a specified period and provided for different service levels and tax rates in different parts of the region.

Coincident with the birth of the Halifax Regional Municipality, the government of Nova Scotia undertook a service exchange, whereby it assumed full responsibility for the funding and administration of income support (the former municipalities had paid a share of income support and had been responsible for service delivery). In return, the new Halifax received full funding responsibility for its transportation services. This exchange was thought to be "revenue neutral." Advocates saw it as disentangling provincial and municipal responsibilities, leaving the new regional municipality with responsibilities more in line with the municipal government's traditional role of providing services to property.

Haligonians are still struggling to see the virtues of their new municipal arrangements. The unforeseen costs of transition and the provincial government's disinclination to deal with them have been major issues between the new Halifax government and the Province of Nova Scotia. Despite the transitional rules, municipal unions have been pressing for salary equalization. The differentials are particularly apparent in protective services like fire and policing, making the public pressure more acute. Other costs are coming to the public's attention and causing concern. For example, the need to rebuild the water system in the former City of Dartmouth was well known to municipal and provincial officials before amalgamation, but it is a big financial pill for residents outside of the area to swallow, even if a differential tax structure means that Dartmouth ratepayers pay the lion's share. These and other cost issues resulted in storms of protest in the first year of the new municipality's existence. The 1997 resignation of the provincial Premier (a former mayor of the City of Dartmouth) on the grounds of self-acknowledged unpopularity, is at least partly due to the province's handling of the Halifax restructuring.

There have also been difficulties associated with the quest for disentanglement through service exchange. Specifically, the provincial government experienced difficulty in staffing to meet its new responsibilities. This was more than a matter of having warm bodies in place to process applications and cheques. Supervising provincial officials lacked the requisite knowledge of the Halifax community and, more specifically, its network of community organizations. It is interesting that in the period leading up to the exchange, staff from the Halifax Regional Municipality were meeting with the Halifax Community Network, an organization of over 70 community agencies and groups, to strategize for dealing with community issues and priorities. Depending on one's point of view, this is either ironic or a reflection of the strong gravitational force between the local state and the voluntary sector in urban Canada. The second interpretation certainly has implications for provincial-local relations, and argues for a strong local role in human services, as well as services to property.

Ontario: All at Once

Since the early 1950s, provincial-local relations in Ontario have displayed two sometimes contradictory characteristics. First, there have been moments of bold provincial action which have significantly changed the character and substance of local government. Examples include establishment of the Municipality of Metropolitan Toronto in 1953; consolidation of a myriad of small school boards into county or regional boards in the 1960s; and creation of regional governments in most of the province's city-regions from 1969 to 1974. These moments of bold unilateral provincial action have been counterbalanced by an apparent reluctance by successive provincial governments to push on other difficult provincial-local issues. For example, successive Conservative, Liberal, and New Democratic Party governments were unwilling to undertake significant local government restructuring, following the drop in electoral support experienced by the once all-mighty Conservatives after their 1969 to 1974 reforms. A similar pattern became evident in other areas of local concern—notably health care and education. There was much provincial-local consultation but little agreement or closure. In the case of education, school boards and the public were bewildered by a series of rapid-fire changes in educational philosophy at the provincial level, which took on the character of "flavour of the month." In this policy environment, school boards adopted their own coping mechanisms, resulting in significant differences in programming across the province. These differences were exacerbated by the variations in financial capacity among boards, depending on their local property tax assessment base. In the early 1990s intense negotiations occurred between the Rae government and the Association of Municipalities of Ontario (AMO) to disentangle provincial-municipal responsibilities. These negotiations fell apart over disagreement that the proposed scheme was really revenue neutral for municipalities and municipalities' bitterness over the province's unilateral imposition of the Social Contract which, among other things, reduced provincial-municipal transfers.[23]

Election of the Harris Conservatives in 1995 ushered in a new era of provincial-local relations in Ontario. As suggested above, this government was not unique in its interest in taking on difficult issues. It can, however, be thought of as unprecedented in its willingness to take on many difficult provincial-local issues simultaneously and to act with daring speed in announcing reforms, while letting the fallout associated with implementing its bold policies rain down. Ontario Supreme Court Justice Borins, reviewing the legality of the Harris government's actions in creating a single city out of the former Municipality of Metropolitan Toronto and its six area municipalities, commented that the Harris Government had exhibited "mega-chutzpah" in the scope of its reform and in ignoring popular opposition to the move. This phrase characterizes other aspects of the government's provincial-local agenda as well.

In brief, since the 1995 election, the Harris Government has introduced a new *Municipal Act* modelled after the Alberta legislation; created the new City of Toronto and an amalgamated City of Kingston, both of which came into being on 1 January 1998; significantly reduced the number and powers of school boards in Ontario; announced a process whereby it will appoint a commissioner to arbitrate reductions in the number of municipalities in each of the Ontario counties, in the event of a local failure to reach agreement on municipal restructuring; and begun the process of major restructuring of regional health care systems in the province, through establishment of the Health Care Restructuring Commission, again with arbitration powers to close hospitals and restructure health care delivery across the province.

The government also spoke to its ideological credo of less government by invoking the voluntary sector to take up the challenge of filling fields to be vacated by the government and assisting the province in implementing major new initiatives such as work-for-welfare. In the latter case, the voluntary sector bit back, informing the government that the sector lacked the level of basic financial support from public coffers needed to fulfil this part of the government's agenda. Some community groups also indicated that they were not inclined to participate in implementing workfare under the restrictive terms of the program.

As if this were not sufficient, the Harris government had also undertaken a major realignment of service responsibilities that most municipalities see not only as a change in who does what, but as significant downloading of who pays. In 1996 the province established a blue ribbon panel—chaired by David Crombie, former mayor of the City of Toronto and federal cabinet minister—to examine the full range of provincial and local responsibilities, to determine principles and to make specific recommendations on how best to overhaul the funding and delivery of a wide range of provincial and local government services. The mandate of this aptly named "Who Does What" Panel included recommendations concerning taxation and assessment, social services, education, public health, and a variety of services related to public infrastructure (the so-called "hard" services). Its overall role was to reduce waste, duplication, and the overall cost of government. Embrace of the concept of disentanglement was an important underpinning of this mandate.

The Panel worked intensively from May until December of 1996 and produced its recommendations, as directed, in a series of letters to the government, each dealing with a specific topic and delivered as soon as deliberations concerning the particular matter at hand were concluded.

Four principles guided the work of the Who Does What Panel. First, it concluded that the traditional role of municipal government should be sustained. Specifically, municipalities should have a strong role in the provision of services to property and general infrastructure (hard services), whereas "soft" services, such as education, health, and welfare, were seen as most appropriate for the provincial government. The panel's debate about this principle was intense, as some members who were representatives of large urban governments saw themselves as having a central role in human services. Regardless, adherence to this principle would lay the foundation for the Crombie Panel's conception of disentanglement. The second principle adopted by the Panel was that income redistribution should be funded by the province. The third was that, to the greatest extent possible, only one level of government should be responsible for spending decisions and that this responsibility should be coupled with the responsibility of raising the funds to pay for those decisions. Finally, the Panel worked under the guiding principle of revenue neutrality—that whatever service exchange took place, neither level of government should incur greater costs. In short, there should be neither downloading nor uploading of costs as a result of its recommendations. Adherence to this principle prompted the Panel to send a concluding letter to the province, realigning its original recommendations that both education and social services be provincially funded. These services could not both be provincially funded without a net cost to the province. Accordingly, Crombie recommended that education be left on the local property tax base.

The Ontario government moved with great speed in adopting many of Crombie's recommendations. Appropriate announcements were made during the week of 13 January 1997—commonly known as "megaweek." This was an amazing week of announcements by provincial ministers concerning everything from responsibility for ambulance services to property tax reform. Beyond the sheer volume of announcements, the government startled observers by departing from Crombie's recommendations in key areas, suggesting that it had already made its decisions on these matters before hearing the Crombie Panel's recommendations. Specifically, it increased municipalities' share of income support costs and child care. It also assigned municipalities full responsibility for long-term health care, public health, and social housing, as well as the hard services of transit and sewer and water infrastructure. The Ontario government decreed the revenue neutrality of its plan by indicating that, in exchange, it would assume greater responsibility for education funding by removing education from the residential property tax.

The Harris government's resolve that these and other megaweek announcements would be a *fait accompli* was foiled by widespread criticism of its plans. Objections from local government quickly escalated in intensity. In general, they were based on disbelief in the government's numbers and the realization that local government had been assigned responsibilities with highly variable or increasing costs, such as income support and long-term care, while the province had kept the more containable and predictable field of education finance for itself. Any sense of relief within big city governments that there was continuing recognition of their vital interest and role in human services was eclipsed by the financial picture and by the Province's announced intention to closely control human services delivery at the local level. Local governments thought they were justified in demanding "Pay for say." This demand, however, fell on deaf provincial ears.

This was certainly not disentanglement, and municipalities' own financial analysis provided mounting evidence of provincial downloading. Furthermore, the principle of subsidiarity had been left in the dust, especially when one thinks of it in the context of Crombie's recommendation concerning which level of government should undertake income redistribution, or when one grapples with the need for province-wide services. (For example, why should local residents pay for ambulance services on the province's highway network, when many of those requiring assistance may not be not local residents?) Moreover, the service exchange was not even disentanglement since it further entangles, rather than separates, provincial and local roles in social services.

Objections came from other important sources as well. Specifically, a group of notables, including David Crombie and Anne Golden (who had delivered a report on the future of the Greater Toronto Area to the government in 1996), published a letter critical of the government's scheme, particularly urging the government to remove social services from the local tax base. The Metropolitan Toronto Board of Trade also weighed in, criticizing the government for doing too much too quickly, especially in Toronto where the megacity furor was at full pitch.

In the face of these and other criticisms, the Harris government was drawn into negotiations with municipal governments, represented by the Association of Municipalities of Ontario and a coalition of big city mayors. In May 1997 it announced changes to its initial allocation of responsibilities that were generally welcomed by municipalities. In summary, it reduced the local share of social assistance and child care costs. The categories of social assistance costs which were now subject to municipal expenditure remained expanded, however, as outlined in the megaweek announcement. The Province also reassumed responsibility for funding long-term health care. To balance this off from a financial standpoint, the province would assume only half the cost of education. It would still control all education expenditure, however, as it assigned itself power to set education property tax rates across the province—a significant encroachment into local powers of taxation.[24]

Throughout this process, provincial ministers steadfastly maintained that the realignment would be revenue neutral, even though they had been unable to provide figures for individual municipalities indicating what the actual impact would be. Final funding arrangements for individual municipalities were not announced until December 1997, although the changes would take effect 1 January 1998. These final figures confirmed the fears of municipal officials that this was, in fact, an exercise in downloading. Indeed, Mel Lastman, the newly elected mayor of Toronto, publicly called the Premier a "liar," noting that the annual cost to the City would be $164 million.[25] Larger cities are intended to take a harder hit than smaller centres and were declared ineligible to draw upon a special provincial fund designed to help municipalities deal with budget shortfalls. The provincial reasoning is that the big cities can more readily make up the shortfalls by finding efficiencies in how services are delivered.

In the aftermath, the state of provincial-local relations in Ontario can only be described as precarious. Municipalities have been left scrambling to make up the losses, to undertake new services, and to find efficiencies in existing operations in a very short time frame. This comes at the very time that the shift to a new assessment system has made calculation of the revenue side of municipalities' budgets difficult. Nowhere is this more acute than in the new City of Toronto, where property tax assessment has long been a contentious issue. In addition, the new regional school boards, established under 1997 legislation, have yet to find their sea legs. Their provincial-local relations are just beginning, although the Province's inability to conclude development of a funding formula to provide these boards with a budget suggests difficult early days.

For its part, the various ministries of the Ontario government seem poorly equipped to oversee implementation of their political masters' dramatic moves. It remains to be seen if the current government can move beyond *ex cathedra* announcements to the work of successful implementation of its grand designs. One is reminded of the giraffe who, smitten with a beautiful butterfly, pondered how to establish a relationship. The giraffe asked a wise owl what to do. "It's easy," said the owl. "You just have to turn yourself into a butterfly." "How do I do that?" asked the giraffe. "Oh, I couldn't possibly say," replied the owl, somewhat miffed at this question. "You see, I'm a policy owl." This is how the Government of Ontario seems to see itself in the contemporary provincial-local context.[26]

CONCLUDING OBSERVATIONS

The above three cases reveal a number of interesting trends in provincial-municipal relations in Canada.

Perhaps most fundamental is the observation that significant change in the provincial-local relationship is afoot. The Alberta *Municipal Government Act*, which broke the traditional strictures of provincial control over municipal affairs, has been a harbinger of provincial-municipal negotiations in other provinces to achieve similar reform. Although the details differ in each case, all three provinces have embraced the creation of new consolidated units for governance at the local or regional level. In Nova Scotia and Ontario, where the emphasis has been on restructuring to achieve bigger units of local government, this development arguably portends a shift to greater local muscle in the provincial-local relationship. In some localities, this may result from increased political and administrative capacity at the local level. In the case of the major city-regions, which have been our main focus, this is less likely to be a prominent factor because predecessor governments already had this capacity. Instead, we suggest that major city-regions will gain intergovernmental momentum as a result of the high political stakes associated with provincial governments achieving success in their agendas of local government reform and restructuring. In each Canadian province, the majority of voters live in city-regions, such as those which have been our focus. Provincial government actions to consolidate urban governments or to reallocate provincial-local responsibilities will be widely felt.

Our second concluding observation concerns provincial governments' capacity to implement the significant agenda of change which they have launched. In each case there are signs of difficulty. At the policy level there is a clear provincial role, especially given the difficulties that major city-regions in Canada have experienced in restructuring themselves.

Currently, cabinets in all three provinces that we have scrutinized are replete with former local politicians and senior officials. The Premier of Alberta, and the Premier of Nova Scotia who oversaw creation of the Halifax Regional Municipality, are both former mayors of large cities. The Minister of Municipal Affairs and Housing in Ontario, who has overseen the Harris government's municipal reforms, is the former head of the Toronto Transit Commission. In addition, the Ontario cabinet contains three former school board chairs, one of whom is the Premier. The fact that these political leaders have embraced the sometimes dramatic agendas we have described attests to a certain legitimacy and supposed understanding of municipal affairs within provincial cabinets, even if one does quarrel with the specifics.[27] In no case, however, can they be accused of being parochial upon achieving provincial office. They are attempting to set a broad course.

The source of concern, then, is not parochialism or lack of vision but the ability to analyze that vision and follow through on implementation. Some elements of provincial agendas seem to have been sketched out on the back of an envelope. This is most evident in Ontario where, for example, there is little evidence of prior analysis of the implications of creating the new City of Toronto or of thinking through how the government will allocate education budgets to school boards across the province. In Nova Scotia, analysis of the transition costs for the Halifax Regional Municipality seems to have been weak. In all three cases, the provincial government has demonstrated the need to deepen its understanding of, and contacts with, the voluntary sector. Provincial governments are seeking to engage the sector as a partner in governing at the local level, but to be successful they must learn what motivates participants in the voluntary sector and provide sufficient funds for the salaried personnel and other basic infrastructure which voluntary organizations require as a foundation for their work.

The ability of any provincial government to improve its capacity to implement its provincial-local agenda is limited by its own resources. As in virtually all spheres of provincial activity, the effect of public service downsizing has been to reduce corporate memory, expertise, and capacity. There are fewer policy owls sitting in the provincial tree. Implementation owls are on the provincial endangered species list.

Finally, our research suggests that local governments in Canada's city-regions are working very hard to respond to the policy and implementation challenges associated with the current provincial-local regime. The mistaken goal of disentangling provincial-local roles so as to relegate local governments to the provision of hard services is increasingly evident to officials in Canada's city-regions, as the human streetscape becomes harsher.

Local politicians and staff are engaged with diverse local voluntary organizations in new ways. The established tradition of using the local voluntary sector to deliver services ranging from AIDS awareness to zoo upkeep is expanding. In addition, local governments find themselves in a more deeply collaborative relationship with the voluntary sector as they cope jointly with the implications of federal and provincial government downloading and other policy change. This is the governance paradigm in action. In Canada's biggest city-regions, application of the principle of subsidiarity suggests that local governments should indeed be the centre of this action, with provincial governments (and the federal government) playing the key role in income distribution and establishment and support of basic framework policies to serve the public interest.

Applying Osborne and Gaebler's aphorism to the provincial-local context, Canada's provinces should be steering, not rowing. At this stage, the provinces we have examined seem to be trying to do both simultaneously, but with only one oar. As anyone who has ever tried this in a boat will attest, the result is to go in circles.

NOTES

The research assistance of Michael Orsini is greatly appreciated.

1. David Osborne and Ted Gaebler, *Reinventing Government* (New York: Plume, 1992), 25–48.

2. Peter Aucoin, *The New Public Management: Canada in Comparative Perspective* (Montreal: Institute for Research on Public Policy, 1995), 1–19.

3. David Siegel, "Reinventing Local Government: The Promise and the Problems," *Rethinking Government: Reform or Reinvention?*, ed. Leslie J. Seidle (Montreal: Institute for Research on Public Policy, 1993), 177–8.

4. Katherine A. Graham and Susan D. Phillips with Allan M. Maslove, *Urban Governance in Canada: Resources, Representation and Restructuring* (Toronto: Harcourt Brace, 1998), 35.

5. A city-region is defined by three criteria: 1) commutershed; 2) cohesiveness of economic and social relations that transcend local boundaries; and 3) anticipated growth. See *Report of the Greater Toronto Area Task Force* (Toronto: Queen's Printer for Ontario, 1996), 24.

6. Graham and Phillips with Maslove, *Urban Governance in Canada: Resources, Representation and Restructuring,* 35–37.

7. See for example, Allan O'Brien, "Father Knows Best: A Look at the Provincial-Municipal Relationship in Ontario," *Government and Politics in Ontario*, ed. Donald C. MacDonald (Toronto: Macmillan, 1975). Also, Richard D. Tindal and Susan Nobes Tindal, *Local Government in Canada* (Toronto: McGraw-Hill Ryerson, 1995), 189–238. Also, Peter G. Boswell, "Provincial-Municipal Relations," *Provinces*, ed. Christopher Dunn (Peterborough: Broadview Press, 1996).

8. Lionel D. Feldman and Katherine A. Graham, *Bargaining for Cities* (Montreal: Institute for Research on Public Policy, 1979), 5.

9. Graham and Phillips with Maslove, *Urban Governance in Canada: Resources, Representation and Restructuring,* 175–6.

10. Kenneth G. Crawford, *Canadian Municipal Government* (Toronto: University of Toronto Press, 1954), 3.

11. David M. Cameron, "Provincial Responsibilities for Municipal Government," *Canadian Public Administration: Municipal Government in the Intergovernmental Maze*, ed. Kenneth Cameron (Toronto: Institute of Public Administration of Canada, 1980).

12. T. Cohn and P.J. Smith, "Developing Global Cities in the Pacific Northwest: the Cases of Vancouver and Seattle," *North American Cities and Global Economy: Challenges and Opportunities*, eds. Peter Kresl and Gary Oappert (Thousand Oaks: Sage, 1995).

13. R.A.W. Rhodes, *Control and Power in Central-Local Government Relations* (Westmead: Gower Publishing, 1981), 14–39.

14. See Horace Brittain, *Local Government in Canada* (Toronto: Ryerson Press, 1951); also, Feldman and Graham, *Bargaining for Cities*; also, Rhodes.

15. See Enid Slack, "Averting a Fiscal Crisis in Toronto," *Policy Options* (December 1996), 39–42; also, Katherine A. Graham and Susan D. Phillips, *Designing the New Toronto Government: Political and Administrative Structures for the New Toronto* (Toronto: Municipality of Metropolitan Toronto, 1997).

16. Graham and Phillips with Maslove, *Urban Governance in Canada: Resources, Representation and Restructuring,* 291.

17. Greater Toronto Area Task Force, 162.

18. Andrew Sancton, "Provincial-Municipal Entanglement in Ontario: A Dissent," *Municipal World* (July 1992).

19. Andrew Sancton, "Reducing Costs by Consolidating Municipalities," *Canadian Public Administration* 39:3 (1996): 267–89.

20. Graham and Phillips with Maslove, *Urban Governance in Canada: Resources, Representation and Restructuring,* 287.

21. Ibid., 176–7.

22. Feldman and Graham, *Bargaining for Cities* 72–9; Tindal and Tindal 142–3.

23. David Siegel, "Disentangling Provincial-Municipal Relations in Ontario," *Management* (Institute of Public Administration of Canada, Fall 1992).

24. Katherine A. Graham and Susan D. Phillips, "'Who Does What' in Ontario: The Process of Provincial-Municipal Disentanglement," *Canadian Public Administration*, Spring 1998. Forthcoming.

25. The original estimate of the net annual loss to Toronto following the January 1997 announcements had been $375 million.

26. Anne Golden, Remarks to the Public Policy Forum, Toronto, 9 December 1997; David Crane, "The Harris Government—2 and 1/2 Years Later," Remarks to the Public Policy Forum, Toronto, 9 December 1997.

27. John Ibbitson, *Promised Land: Inside the Mike Harris Revolution* (Scarborough: Prentice Hall Canada, 1997), 222.

GOVERNMENT, INFORMATION, AND POLICY IDEAS

Governments often encounter demands for action. Action, however, requires preparation and central to this process is the gathering and assessment of policy-oriented information and viewpoints. Difficulties often ensue for a variety of reasons. Often people overlook the time needed for thorough collection of pertinent material. People may underestimate the degree of contention over just what is fact and what is opinion. Sometimes certain sources of information may be preferred (or discarded) for reasons of partisan or ideological compatibility. On many occasions groups will differ widely about how to understand an issue and what priority to assign it. Seeking out relevant data or opinions has associated costs that need to be assumed by somebody. Often that is someone other than those issuing the calls for action. Who then is responsible for comparing the costs to the benefits received? Furthermore, the mechanisms for information gathering involve extensive planning. Devices such as the recruitment of expert panels, the commissioning of sophisticated polling that has national validity, or the contracting out of research to outside consultants require coordination and careful organization.

The challenge of collecting policy-oriented information and soliciting informed viewpoints is receiving ever more attention from scholars. Two such scholars are represented in the following section. Donald Abelson is a political scientist concerned with the use made by political leaders and governments of think tanks. His work alerts us to the surprising size of the think tank universe and their potential degree of widespread influence. Peter Desbarats is a distinguished journalist and educator who recently served on the panel appointed by the Government of Canada to review the misfortunes associated with Canadian involvement in the Somalia crisis. In the run-up to the 1997 federal election the panel was terminated before completion of its workload. The reflections of Desbarats on this experience can serve as a useful reminder of the political dimensions of open inquiry into government administration and behaviour.

Together these two readings explore a number of fundamentally important aspects of the information collection and transmission debates. The essay by Desbarats investigates the traditional practice of recourse to public inquiries. These inquiries have usually been publicly funded and administered. Think tanks, on the other hand, have been gaining increased attention in recent years. They are funded through a variety of sources and can enjoy operating autonomy. Attention to both of these mechanisms of information gathering and assessment raises a number of topics for further reflection and study.

DISCUSSION QUESTIONS

1. Where do you go for information when you are asked about a complicated contemporary policy question? Is the dividing line between information and opinion always clear? Why or why not?

2. What is the purpose of public inquiries? Can you think of any such inquiries? What kinds of issues did these inquiries face?

3. What advantages are offered by investigation via an independent inquiry that would not be as readily available through an internal investigation by a government department? Why?

4. Examine the account offered by Desbarats of the experience of the Somalia inquiry. Why might the federal government have been anxious to shut down the inquiry efforts? What price has been paid for the premature termination of the investigation? Assess the federal government's intentions and actions?

5. What are think tanks? Provide examples of think tanks and suggest examples of their work which have found their way into the public arena.

6. Can you give a rough estimate of the size of the think tank universe? What do you think might account for their proliferation?

7. Is there any way to measure the influence of think tanks on any particular decisions or sets of decisions? Why or why not?

8. What would make for a successful think tank? Suggest possible criteria and explain the rationales for your suggestions.

9. Do we need to consider the sources of information before we regard the material presented as (a) fact? (b) opinion? (c) informed commentary? Is there a difference? Is there such a thing as objective information or straightforward facts in policy debate or evaluation of government administration? Why or why not?

10. Are there issues about which you think federal or provincial governments need to be gathering more information? Offer examples with supporting reasons.

SURVEYING THE THINK TANK LANDSCAPE IN CANADA

Donald E. Abelson[1]

INTRODUCTION

Policy institutes or think tanks, as they are more commonly referred to, have assumed a more visible presence on the Canadian political landscape since the early 1970s.[2] Although far fewer in number than in the United States, a country where think tanks have become a virtual cottage industry,[3] Canadian think tanks have nonetheless begun to attract considerable attention in the media and in some academic circles. Specializing in a wide range of domestic and foreign policy issues, think tanks have attempted, through various governmental and nongovernmental channels, to become firmly entrenched in the policy-making process by providing research and expertise to government departments, policy makers, and the public. The purpose of this chapter, however, is not to assess the influence of Canadian think tanks in shaping public opinion or public policy, a subject which would go well beyond the scope of this study, nor is it to explore the many institutional, economic, and cultural barriers they have to overcome to establish a stronger presence in the policy-making community.[4] It is rather to examine their role and function in the policy-making process and to highlight how they have attempted to compete successfully in the marketplace of ideas.

In the first section of this chapter, the various types of think tanks which have emerged on the Canadian political landscape will be discussed. Since no consensus exists on what constitutes a think tank, scholars engaged in the study of these organizations have constructed various typologies to differentiate between the many kinds of think tanks which have taken root in the policy-making community. To date, most of these typologies have been designed to describe the many types of think tanks which exist in the United States. While useful, they have to be modified to better suit the Canadian think tank experience. Some of the other methodological problems encountered in employing a typology of think tanks will be discussed. In the second section, a brief history of the rise of think tanks in Canada will be provided. In doing so, three waves or generations of think tanks can be identified. Once

the evolution of think tanks has been chronicled, attention will shift to the various channels think tanks rely on to enhance their visibility in the political arena. In the final section,
some suggestions on how to measure or assess the impact of think tanks during various
stages of the policy-making process will be offered.

DEFINING THINK TANKS

Rand in Santa Monica, California, employs 525 full-time researchers and has an annual
budget in excess of $100 million.[5] Founded in 1946, it is widely regarded as the most promi-
nent research institution devoted to the study of American defence and security issues. In contrast, at the height of its existence, the now defunct Canadian Institute for International
Peace and Security (CIIPS), employed the equivalent of 40 full- and part-time researchers
and had a budget of approximately $5 million. Yet, despite the vast differences in resources
available to these institutions, both are regarded as think tanks.

Although think tanks in Canada and, for that matter, in all advanced industrial and developing countries, share a common desire to shape and mold public opinion and public
policy, they vary considerably in terms of size, resources, areas of expertise, and the quality and quantity of the publications they produce. A think tank may consist of a handful of
people involved actively in studying a particular policy area who seek to inform and educate
policy makers and the public through a variety of channels. The majority of think tanks in
Canada (see Table 1), and for that matter in the United States, fall into this category. At
the opposite extreme, a think tank may house several hundred economists, political scientists and statisticians who provide expertise on a broad range of issues.

Moreover, as several journalists have noted, think tanks in Canada also vary considerably in their ideological orientation. The Fraser Institute in Vancouver is frequently referred
to as a conservative, free market–oriented think tank. At the other end of the ideological
continuum, the Ottawa-based Canadian Centre for Policy Alternatives (CCPA) which was
established in 1980 to counter what it considered to be the mounting and pernicious influence of the Fraser Institute, is often portrayed as a left-leaning, union-supported institution.[6] Ascribing ideological labels to think tanks, although appealing to journalists and
scholars who want to quickly distinguish one think tank from another, may lead to some
unfounded assumptions. In addition to assuming institutional homogeneity, i.e., that all
members of an institution share the same beliefs and reflect those beliefs in their publications,
attaching ideological labels to think tanks (which tends to have negative connotations) may
convince some, rightly or wrongly, to discount the integrity of their studies. Consequently,
while it is it important to be aware of the ideological predisposition of think tanks, this factor alone should not be used to differentiate between types of think tanks.

Given the tremendous diversity of think tanks which exist in many advanced industrial
countries, it is not surprising that scholars have consciously avoided trying to define these
institutions. Indeed, other than acknowledging that think tanks are nonprofit, nonpartisan[7]
organizations engaged in the study of public policy, few scholars have outlined other criteria which would allow them to distinguish between think tanks and other types of non-
governmental organizations including interest groups, religious movements, and trade unions
which also seek to provide policy advice to government. In fact, as interest groups have attempted to acquire greater policy expertise to enhance their status in the policy-making
community and as think tanks have looked to interest groups to learn more about lobbying

TABLE 1   A Selected Profile of Canadian Think Tanks in Chronological Order

Institution	Location	Date Founded	Staff	Budget Category
Canadian Council on Social Development	Ottawa, ON	1920	18 FT / 5 PT	$1 000 001–$2 000 000
Canadian Institute of International Affairs	Toronto, ON	1928	9 FT / 2 PT	$1 000 001–$2 000 000
Canadian Tax Foundation	Toronto, ON	1945	18	$2 000 001–$5 000 000
Conference Board of Canada	Ottawa, ON	1954	>190	>$20 000 000
Science Council of Canada (DEFUNCT) (figures for 1992)	Ottawa, ON	1963	29	$2 000 001–$5 000 000
Economic Council of Canada (DEFUNCT) (figures for 1992)	Ottawa, ON	1963	118	>$10 000 000
National Council of Welfare	Ottawa, ON	1968	4 FT	$500 001–$1 000 000
Parliamentary Centre	Ottawa, ON	1968	10 FT / 2 PT	$1 000 001–$2 000 000
Canada West Foundation	Calgary, AB	1971	9	$500 001–$1 000 000
Institute for Research on Public Policy	Montreal, PQ	1972	15 FT	$1 000 001–$2 000 000
C. D. Howe Institute	Toronto, ON	1973	15 FT	$1 000 001–$2 000 000
The Fraser Institute	Vancouver, BC	1974	21 FT / 13 PT	$2 000 001–$5 000 000
Canadian Institute of Strategic Studies	Toronto, ON	1976	4 FT / 1 PT	$100 000–$500 000
The North-South Institute	Ottawa, ON	1976	18	$1 000 001–$2 000 000
Canadian Centre for Policy Alternatives	Ottawa, ON	1980	6	$500 001–$1 000 000
Canadian Institute for International Peace and Security (DEFUNCT) (figures for 1992)	Ottawa, ON	1984	9 FT / 3 PT	>$5 000 000
Mackenzie Institute	Toronto, ON	1986	3 FT / 3 PT	$100 001–$500 000
Public Policy Forum	Ottawa, ON	1986	10 FT	$500 001–$1 000 000
Caledon Institute of Social Policy	Ottawa, ON	1992	3 FT / 2 PT	$500 001–$1 000 000
Pearson-Shoyama Institute	Ottawa, ON	1993	2	$100 000–$500 000
Canadian Policy Research Networks, Inc.	Ottawa, ON	1994	10 FT / 7 PT	$2 000 001–$5 000 000
Canadian Centre for Foreign Policy Development	Ottawa, ON	1996	4 FT / 2 PT	$1 000 001–$5 000 000
Canadian Council for International Peace and Security (formerly Canadian Centre for Global Security and Canadian Centre for Arms Control and Disarmament)	Ottawa, ON	1995	2 PT	$100 000–$500 000

1. These data have been extracted from the following sources: *Associations Canada*, (Toronto: Canadian Almanac and Directory Publishing Company, 1996); *Associations Canada*, (Toronto: Canadian Almanac and Directory Publishing Company, 1997); Nicoline van der Woerd, *World Survey of Strategic Studies Centres*, (London: International Institute for Strategic Studies, 1992); Murray Campbell, "Wonks," *The Globe and Mail* 2 December 1995, D1-2; various institute websites; personal correspondence.

2. FT=Full-time staff; PT=Part-time staff. When no distinction is supplied, the staff was not specified in the available information.

strategies, the institutional differences between think tanks and interest groups have become increasingly blurred.

Rather than attempting to isolate think tanks from a host of other organizations which inhabit the policy-making community, Kent Weaver, James McGann and others[8] have sought to identify the key motivations and institutional traits associated with each generation or wave of think tanks. In studying the think tank population in the United States, Weaver claims that three types of think tanks coexist in the policy-making community: universities without students, government contractors, and advocacy tanks. McGann, on the other hand, contends that at least seven categories of think tanks are necessary to account for the diversity of American think tanks: academic diversified, academic specialized, contract/consulting, advocacy, policy enterprise, literary agent/publishing house, and state-based. The typology constructed by Weaver is more appropriate than McGann's in assessing the think tank population in Canada, but still requires some modification before it can be employed as a worthwhile analytical tool. To adjust his typology to better account for the evolution of Canadian think tanks, it is necessary to eliminate some categories, collapse others into a single category and add new ones.

First, there are no private think tanks in Canada on the scale of the Brookings Institution and the Hoover Institution on War, Revolution, and Peace in Palo Alto, California which, in Weaver's words, function much like "universities without students." These types of organizations, according to Weaver, "tend to be characterized by heavy reliance on academics as researchers, by funding primarily from the private sector (with varying mixtures of foundation, corporate, and individual funding), and by book-length studies as the primary research product."[9] Composed of dozens of academics armed with PhDs in economics and political science who are free to pursue their research without being subjected to the normal administrative and teaching constraints placed on university professors, these types of institutions seek to promote, but have not always preserved, their image as repositories of nonpartisan policy expertise.[10]

Since Canada is not home to such "studentless universities"[11] it may be more appropriate to refer to think tanks which regard academic/policy relevant research as one of their principal functions simply as policy research institutions. Institutions which fall into this category are staffed by economists, political scientists, and other trained academics who conduct research on a diverse range of policy issues. The majority of their resources are devoted to research, although book-length studies are not regarded as their primary outputs. Moreover, while these types of institutions seek to shape the parameters of policy debates through their research findings, engaging in political advocacy is not considered a major priority. The Ottawa-based Conference Board of Canada, well known for its expertise in providing economic forecasting to policy makers and business leaders in the private sector, would fall into this category.

Weaver's second and third category of think tanks—government specialists or contractors and advocacy tanks—can easily be applied to Canada. There are several think tanks in Canada which rely heavily on federal government funding and which in turn regard various levels of government as their principal consumers of information, a defining characteristic of government contractors.[12] In fact, during the 1960s, a handful of think tanks or "government councils" were created by the federal government to provide policy advice in specific policy areas. Moreover, since the early 1970s, there has been a proliferation of advocacy think tanks in Canada which, like their American counterparts, "combine a strong policy, partisan or ideological bent with aggressive salesmanship and an effort to influence current policy debates."[13]

It is also possible to enlarge Weaver's typology by adding a fourth and possibly fifth category—vanity or legacy-based think tanks and policy clubs. Vanity or legacy-based think tanks are created by aspiring office holders (or their supporters) and by former leaders intent on advancing their political and ideological beliefs well after leaving office. Although far more numerous in the United States, there are a few examples of think tanks in Canada which fall into this category.

The final category of think tanks—policy clubs—may, according to Evert Lindquist, best describe the majority of think tanks in Canada. In his assessment of the impact of Canadian policy institutes, Lindquist suggests that it may be more appropriate to portray think tanks in Canada as policy clubs where academics, policy analysts and, occasionally, policy makers meet to discuss public policy issues, than as policy research institutions like the Washington-based Brookings Institution which is capable of providing long-term strategic analysis.[14] Unable to compete with the institutional expertise offered by some bureaucratic departments, Lindquist contends that the nostalgic vision of think tanks as the creators of new and innovative ideas simply does not conform to the experience of Canadian policy institutes. Although Lindquist bases his observations on the work of several policy institutes created in the early 1970s, his insights about think tanks as policy clubs can also help to account for the activities of a handful of relatively small policy shops created in the first decades of the 20th century.

Classifying generations or waves of think tanks according to specific institutional criteria does pose certain problems however. To begin with, some organizations possess characteristics common to more than one generation of think tank. In other words, although few scholars encounter difficulty distinguishing between the quality of studies prepared by the Conference Board of Canada and the Canadian Centre for Policy Alternatives, both institutions engage in similar activities. They both conduct research and, to varying degrees, market their findings. The main difference is in the emphasis these institutions place on pure research and political advocacy. To argue then that the Conference Board of Canada is a policy research institution and the Canadian Centre for Policy Alternatives is an advocacy think tank would, on the surface, be misleading.

It may be more appropriate to identify the central function of think tanks in the policy-making process, than to isolate their "unique" institutional traits. Like chameleons constantly changing their complexion to suit new environments, think tanks have altered their behaviour to compete more effectively in the marketplace of ideas. To enhance their visibility, some first and second generations of think tanks have adopted strategies employed by newer waves or generations of institutes. Conversely, some newly created institutes have looked to older generations of think tanks for ideas on how to manage their operations. In short, one generation of think tanks in Canada has not been replaced by newer ones. Rather, they coexist in the policy-making community. Recognizing that think tanks can be classified according to their principal function in the policy-making process, it is possible to observe the emergence of three generations or waves of think tanks. To begin with, however, it is necessary to discuss the period immediately preceding the first wave of contemporary think tanks.

BEFORE THE WAVE: THINK TANKS AS POLICY CLUBS

There is no consensus on when the first think tank was established in Canada. Although several scholars maintain that the growth and evolution of think tanks can be traced to the creation of the Institute for Research on Public Policy (IRPP) in 1972,[15] others have suggested that the seeds of contemporary think tanks were planted well before IRPP opened its doors. For example, in the area of domestic policy, the National Council on Child and Family Welfare was formed in 1920 to discuss and debate a wide range of issues affecting the social welfare of Canadians. It later became known as the Canadian Welfare Council in 1935 and the remaining parts of the organization led to the creation of the Canadian Council on Social Development in 1971.[16]

In the area of foreign policy, it is clear that a handful of private associations were active in discussing a broad range of issues during the first decades of the 20th century. The Round Table movement, which was established in 1908 "to create an immense nexus of influence and patronage for directing public policy in imperial and other matters,"[17] maintained an important presence in Canadian policy-making circles over two decades. There were other organizations including the Canadian Association for International Conciliation and the Institute for Pacific Relations (IPR) which also performed many of the characteristic functions of contemporary think tanks. Although little information exists on the former, the IPR, which held its first conference in Honolulu in the summer of 1925, was created "to study the conditions of the Pacific peoples with a view to the improvement of their mutual relations."[18] Like many think tanks that followed, the IPR declared itself as "non-governmental, non-sectarian, non-controversial and non-propagandist."[19]

However, of all the institutes created during this period, the most significant in the area of foreign policy was the Canadian Institute of International Affairs (CIIA), founded in 1928 as the first offshoot of the British Institute of International Affairs (BIIA, later known as the Royal Institute of International Affairs).[20] Sir Robert Borden, Canada's prime minister from 1911–1920, was elected the institute's first president.[21] Created "to promote a broader and deeper understanding of international affairs and of Canada's role in a changing world by providing interested Canadians with a non-partisan, nation-wide forum for informed discussion, debate and analysis,"[22] the CIIA has evolved into an important forum for policy discussion. Although the CIIA "is precluded by its constitution from expressing an official opinion on any aspect of world affairs,"[23] the opinions of some of its members have at times generated concern within official policy circles.[24] Based on the campus of the University of Toronto, the CIIA maintains the John Holmes Library, which contains a vast collection of materials relating to foreign and defence policy. It also publishes a quarterly academic journal, *International Journal*, which is widely regarded as the leading journal on international affairs in Canada.[25] The CIIA currently maintains 15 institute branches with a membership of 1500.

Despite being created under different and often unusual circumstances, each of the organizations specializing in foreign policy appears to conform to Lindquist's conception of think tanks as policy clubs. They were created by a small group of influential individuals who shared a common interest in discussing and debating various aspects of world affairs and Canada's emerging role in the international community. Moreover, while they did and, in the case of the CIIA, do maintain ties to policy makers, their primary goal was not to bring the scientific expertise of academics to bear on a host of policy issues. Had it been, a concerted effort would have been undertaken to recruit prominent scholars throughout Canada to fulfil this function. Their mandate was simply to stimulate debate and discussion, not to help rationalize the policy-making process, a goal articulated by several American think tanks created during the Progressive Era. The term policy club is also a fitting description for the

National Council on Child and Family Welfare which, for decades, served as a "social affairs organization."[26]

Compared to the impressive list of think tanks which took root in the United States during the first half of the 20th century, including the Russell Sage Foundation (1908), the Carnegie Endowment for International Peace (1910), the Brookings Institution (1916), the Hoover Institution on War, Revolution, and Peace (1919), the Council on Foreign Relations (1921), the American Enterprise Institute for Public Policy Research (1943), and Rand (1946), the think tank landscape in Canada remained relatively barren. Indeed, it was not until the 1960s that organizations performing the characteristic functions of more research-oriented institutions began to appear.

THE FIRST WAVE: GOVERNMENT SPECIALISTS

Policy makers were not unaware of the contributions policy experts could make in advising government. After all, by the early 1960s several royal commissions and task forces had been created to investigate particular policy questions and to make recommendations on how the government could address and resolve specific problems. However, despite the important role played by several of these bodies, they only remained in existence until their mandate was completed. What was missing in the policy-making community were permanent government organizations "dedicated to public inquiry in Canada."[27]

Recognizing this considerable gap in the governmental apparatus, the government created several councils including the Economic Council of Canada (1963), the Science Council of Canada (1966), the National Council of Welfare (1968) and the Law Reform Commission (1970) to provide ongoing expertise to policy makers. For close to three decades, members of these bodies published hundreds of reports and testified before numerous parliamentary committees. Moreover, their findings were often referred to in prominent newspapers throughout the country.[28] By 1992, however, the government's perception regarding the need for such organizations changed dramatically. In that year's federal budget, the Economic Council of Canada, the Science Council of Canada, and the Law Reform Commission of Canada were among the 21 organizations disbanded by the government.[29]

The Canadian Institute for International Peace and Security (CIIPS) which was created by the Trudeau government in 1984 to provide policy makers with greater insights into the problems and prospects for maintaining stability in the international community, experienced the same fate. Despite amassing an impressive research program over a very short period of time (1984–1992), CIIPS also fell victim to the federal government's cost-cutting measures.[30] While the federal government dismantled what in effect was Canada's premier foreign and defence policy think tank, it has nonetheless continued to fund several Canadian university–based research institutes through the Security and Defence Forum (previously known as the Military and Strategic Studies Program (MSSP) whose mandate is "to encourage the training of Canadian experts on military and strategic issues, in order to respond to present and future security requirements and arouse a nationwide interest in these issues."[31] In the area of domestic policy, the federal government has also continued to fund several policy institutes, including the Canadian Policy Research Networks, Inc. (CPRN) and the Canadian Council on Social Development, through project-specific contracts. Although these are private institutes, their existence to a large extent depends on continued government funding.

THE SECOND WAVE: POLICY RESEARCH INSTITUTIONS AND POLITICAL ADVOCATES

The creation of government councils may have helped to fill a particular void in the governmental apparatus, but considerable gaps in the policy research community remained. Concerned about the absence of an independent research institution which was capable of providing long-term advice and expertise to policy makers,[32] the Canadian government commissioned Ronald Ritchie in 1968 to consider the feasibility of creating a Brookings-style think tank in Canada. After consulting with directors of think tanks in many advanced countries and with several academics, public servants, policy makers, and a majority of provincial premiers, Ritchie concluded that a large, multidisciplinary research institution in Canada was not only feasible but necessary to supplement the policy capacity of government.[33]

Although a think tank comparable to the Brookings Institution has never taken root in Canada, Ritchie's report inspired the creation of the Institute for Research on Public Policy in 1972 and a handful of other organizations committed to examining and advising government on a host of policy issues. By the early 1970s, several new policy institutes had appeared on the political landscape including the Canada West Foundation (1970),[34] the C. D. Howe Institute (1973),[35] and the Fraser Institute (1974).[36] Within a few years, several more institutes were created. The North-South Institute (1976), the Canadian Institute of Strategic Studies (1976), and the Canadian Centre for Policy Alternatives (1980) joined the field. The growth of think tanks in Canada, however, did not end there. By the mid to late 1980s, a new group of policy institutes had sprung up. Among them were the Mackenzie Institute (1986), the Public Policy Forum (1987), the Caledon Institute of Social Policy (1992), and the Canadian Policy Research Networks, Inc. (1994).[37] Firmly entrenched in this expanding galaxy of think tanks was the Conference Board of Canada,[38] the largest think tank in Canada (although some regard it more as a commercial organization) which by 1995 was generating an annual revenue approaching $23 million.[39]

THE THIRD WAVE: VANITY OR LEGACY-BASED THINK TANKS

Vanity or legacy-based think tanks are the latest generation of policy institutes that have emerged on the political landscape. The essential basis for creating these types of think tanks is to preserve and promote the legacy that leading political figures have left. However, with the possible exceptions of the C. D. Howe Institute named after its founder and the Pearson-Shoyama Institute (1993) named after former prime minister Lester Pearson and former federal deputy finance minister Thomas Shoyama, such institutes have not yet emerged in significant numbers. It is conceivable that private and public funds could be generated to support an institute in honour of other prime ministers and provincial premiers, but there is little indication that such endeavours will be undertaken in the near future.

Notwithstanding the tremendous diversity in the mandate and ideological orientation of these institutes, they share a common desire to help shape and mold public policy. As noted, they may differ in terms of the emphasis they place on policy research and political advocacy, assuming of course that a clear distinction between the two can be made. Nonetheless, they all seek to enhance their competitiveness in the marketplace of ideas. All policy institutes engage in some form of policy research and advocacy. The main difference is in the resources they allocate to performing these related functions. In the next section, the various channels that think tanks rely on to exercise influence will be outlined.

COMPETING IN THE MARKETPLACE OF IDEAS

In observing the increasingly crowded think tank community in Canada, there is a tendency to assume, usually without foundation, that think tanks exercise considerable influence in the political arena. Indeed, given the frequency with which their members are quoted by the print and broadcast media, we are often left with the impression that these organizations are largely responsible for shaping the political and economic agenda of government. Unfortunately, few scholars have attempted to explain how to measure the influence of think tanks,[40] let alone how they seek to achieve it.

Although it is difficult to accurately assess how much or little influence think tanks wield in the policy-making process, it is nonetheless possible to make informed judgments about the nature of think tank influence. A useful point of departure is to examine the various channels think tanks rely on to exercise influence. While some strategies that think tanks rely on in order to enhance their status in the policy-making community are concealed from the public, many can be easily identified. In fact, to varying degrees, think tanks employ some or all of the following strategies to influence public policy.

- Holding open public forums and conferences to discuss various domestic and foreign policy issues. Many of these forums are televised and available to viewers through satellite television. This strategy is part of the educational function some think tanks perform. For instance, since 1988, the Fraser Institute has sponsored an annual student seminar on public policy issues.

- Encouraging think tank scholars to give public lectures and addresses at universities, Rotary clubs, and other organizations.

- Inviting selected policy makers to participate in their conferences, seminars, and workshops.

- Maintaining direct contact with high-level policy makers through informal channels, e.g., breakfast meetings between senior policy makers and think tank staffers.

- Testifying before parliamentary committees. Several experts from think tanks are frequently called upon to give testimony. Their remarks and written reports become part of the official public record.

- Enhancing their media exposure by submitting op-ed (opposite the editorial page) articles to major Canadian newspapers. Members of think tanks also appear frequently on the CBC and CTV national evening newscasts and radio programs to discuss the implications of various domestic and foreign policy issues.

- Publishing opinion magazines, newsletters, policy briefs, and journals that have wide distribution. For instance, the Institute for Research on Public Policy and the Canadian Institute for International Affairs publish Policy Options and International Journal, respectively. Moreover, several think tanks, including the Canadian Centre for Policy Alternatives and the C. D. Howe Institute, publish a variety of monographs.

- Creating home pages on the Internet. This is a new medium that think tanks are relying on to reach thousands of Internet users. Several think tanks, including the C. D. Howe Institute, the Conference Board of Canada, the North-South Institute, and the Canada West Foundation, have created home pages. By "going on line," think tanks have provided the public with an opportunity to find out information about their research programs, staff, and institutional resources. Some think tanks also include recent speeches and reports.

• Targeting the public during annual fund raising campaigns, a necessary function for most think tanks.

• Preparing studies and policy briefs for members of parliament. This is a common tactic employed by think tanks which actively engage in political advocacy.

This list is by no means exhaustive. Still, it does provide some insight into how think tanks attempt to assert influence. Having said this, two central questions remain. Are think tanks influential actors in the policy-making process? If they are, how can scholars properly assess their impact in shaping public opinion and public policy?

ASSESSING THE INFLUENCE OF THINK TANKS

The first question posed above appears to be relatively straightforward and uncomplicated. However, depending on who the question is directed to, responses may range from yes, no, rarely, at times, and more than you could possibly imagine. In some respects, all of these answers are accurate. One of the major methodological problems in assessing influence is that think tanks and policy-makers have different perceptions of what constitutes influence, not to mention how it can best be measured.

For some think tanks, having their publications or members' opinions referred to in newspapers or on radio or television newscasts is a useful measure of their institute's influence. Other think tanks, however, may look to a number of other indicators to evaluate their impact. Appearing before parliamentary committees, consulting with government departments and agencies, and publishing several books and articles a year may help some think tanks better assess their institute's performance. Yet, regardless of how think tanks measure their influence in the policy-making community, they will have an incentive to exaggerate their impact. After all, to attract potential donors and to enhance their visibility in an increasingly competitive market, think tanks must give the impression that they play a decisive role in shaping public policy. Few think tanks have been more aggressive in this regard than the Vancouver-based Fraser Institute. When asked to comment on what government programs or policies his institute has contributed to shaping in the last ten years, Michael Walker, Executive Director of the Fraser Institute, remarked:

> The Fraser Institute has played a central role in most policy developments in Canada during the past decade and it is simply too onerous a task to specify. I think that you could simply look at our published record of commentary over the past 25 years and observe that, with a long and variable time lag, our ideas have been adopted by policy makers. Of course, this reflects not only our work, but the work of others who have come to join us in pressing the case for market-based solutions to economic problems.[41]

In addition to confirming the propensity of think tank directors to embellish their institute's impact, Walker's observation highlights yet another methodological problem that must be overcome in assessing the influence of think tanks. As he clearly points out, there are several other organizations and individuals who are also committed to promoting market-based solutions to a wide range of problems. If this is the case, and assuming we are not able to observe policy makers make decisions first-hand, how do we isolate the impact of the Fraser Institute from other actors attempting to influence a particular policy? The simple answer is that, with few exceptions,[42] it is difficult, if not impossible, to do. This conclusion leads us to our second question. How can scholars assess their impact in shaping public opinion and public policy?

Acknowledging that think tanks do not specialize in every area of public policy, it may be more useful to assess their relevance during various stages of the policy-making process than to evaluate their overall influence in the political arena. In other words, while all think tanks seek to exercise influence, they may or may not be engaged actively in all aspects of policy making. For instance, some think tanks such as the Fraser Institute and the Canadian Centre for Policy Alternatives may be effective during the issue articulation stage of the policy-making process. At this stage, they may concentrate on mobilizing public opinion to support or oppose a particular government initiative. To this end, they may also hold public forums and disseminate publications which will help to define the parameters of key policy debates. However, the same institutes may not be among the organizations asked to prepare detailed studies for government departments and agencies, nor may they be among those invited to testify before parliamentary committees. As a consequence, they would have less relevance during the policy formulation stage of the policy-making process. Simply put, think tanks may enjoy a high degree of public visibility (measured, for example, in terms of media citations, funding, and size of membership) during the issue articulation stage, without being relevant during the policy formulation and implementation stages of the policy-making process.

Employing such an approach may enable scholars to more accurately assess the relative influence of think tanks during various stages of the policy-making process. Moreover, by collecting data on how often think tanks are referred to by the print and broadcast media, the number of times institutes are invited to testify before parliamentary committees and the various think tanks which are called upon to advise government departments and agencies, it is possible to make informed observations about which organizations were relevant during specific policy debates. Although pursuing this line of inquiry may not result in definitive answers to the aforementioned questions, it will hopefully discourage scholars from making unsubstantiated assertions about the influence of think tanks.

CONCLUSION

The growth and diversity of think tanks in Canada, and their efforts to become involved actively in the political arena, have compelled social scientists to think more critically about their role and function in the policy-making process. These factors have also forced scholars to reflect on the implications associated with the politicization of policy expertise, a frequent criticism launched against advocacy think tanks. Yet, to date, few scholars have paid close attention to how think tanks seek to influence the political agenda. Even less attention has been focused on the extent to which think tanks have left an indelible mark on public policy. To address these and other deficiencies in the available literature, this chapter has explored, among other things, how think tanks, as self-proclaimed reservoirs of knowledge and expertise, attempt to wield influence. In the process, some preliminary suggestions on how to assess their impact have been made. Think tanks have become permanent fixtures in the policy-making process. Future researchers must now determine the most effective methods for evaluating their performance.

NOTES

1. The author would like to thank Christine Carberry, Ian Brodie and the editors of this volume for their helpful comments on an earlier draft of the chapter. He would also like to acknowledge with gratitude the research assistance of Laura Stephenson.

2. For more on the rise of think tanks in Canada see, Evert A. Lindquist, "A Quarter-Century of Canadian Think Tanks: Evolving Institutions, Conditions and Strategies," *Think Tanks Across Nations: A Comparative Approach,* eds. Diane Stone, Andrew Denham, and Mark Garnett (Manchester: Manchester University Press, forthcoming). Also see Laurent Dobuzinskis, "Trends and Fashions in the Marketplace of Ideas," *Policy Studies in Canada: The State of the Art*, eds. Laurent Dobuzinskis, Michael Howlett and David Laycock (Toronto: University of Toronto Press, 1996), 91–124.

3. James Smith has estimated that there are approximately 1200 think tanks in the United States, about 100 of which are located in Washington, D.C. However, according to a recent directory of American think tanks, the number appears far greater. See Lynn Hellebust (ed.), *Think Tank Directory: A Guide to Nonprofit Public Policy Research Organizations* (Topeka, Kansas: Government Research Service, 1996). No comparable directory of think tanks in Canada exists. Several recent studies have chronicled the growth of think tanks in the United States. See James A. Smith, *The Idea Brokers: Think Tanks and the Rise of the New Policy Elite* (New York: The Free Press, 1991); David M. Ricci, *The Transformation of American Politics: The New Washington and the Rise of Think Tanks* (New Haven: Yale University Press, 1993); and Donald E. Abelson, *American Think Tanks and Their Role in U.S. Foreign Policy* (London and New York: Macmillan and St. Martin's Press, 1996).

4. This topic is examined by Donald E. Abelson and Christine M. Carberry in "Following Suit or Falling Behind? A Comparative Analysis of Canadian and American Think Tanks," *Canadian Journal of Political Science* forthcoming.

5. Lynn Hellebust, ed., *Think Tank Directory: A Guide to Nonprofit Public Policy Research Organizations* (Topeka, Kansas: Government Research Service, 1996), 322.

6. Murray Campbell, "Wonks," [Toronto] *Globe and Mail* 2 December 1995: D1–2.

7. To receive tax-exempt status under the *Income Tax Act* in Canada and under the *Internal Revenue Code* in the United States, think tanks must remain nonpartisan. However, while think tanks in both countries publicly claim that they do not endorse the political positions of any party and therefore are nonpartisan, many have openly acknowledged and indeed promoted their own political mandate. For more on this see, Laura Brown Chisolm, "Sinking the Think-Tanks Upstream: The Use and Misuse of Tax Exemption Law to Address the Use and Misuse of Tax-Exempt Organizations," *University of Pittsburgh Law Review* 51 (3) 1990, pp. 577–640; and Abelson and Carberry, "Following Suit or Falling Behind?"

8. R. Kent Weaver, "The Changing World of Think Tanks," *PS: Political Science and Politics* 22:3 (September 1989): 563–78; and James G. McGann, *The Competition for Dollars, Scholars and Influence in the Public Policy Research Industry* (Lanham, Maryland: University Press of America, 1995). Also see William Wallace, "Between two worlds: Think-tanks and foreign policy," *Two Worlds of International Relations: Academics, Practitioners and the Trade in Ideas*, eds. Christopher Hill and Pamela Beshoff (London: Routledge, 1994), 139–63.

9. Weaver, 564.

10. Both the Brookings Institution and the Hoover Institution have been frequently criticized for their partisan leanings. In part, this stems from the contributions individuals at these institutions have

made to supporting particular presidential candidates. For more on this see Donald E. Abelson and Christine M. Carberry, "Policy Experts in Presidential Campaigns: A Model of Think Tank Recruitment," *Presidential Studies Quarterly* 27:4 (Fall 1997): 679–97.

11. Ibid., 679–97.

12. Weaver, 566.

13. Ibid., 567.

14. Evert A. Lindquist, "Think tanks or clubs? Assessing the influence and roles of Canadian policy institutes," *Canadian Public Administration* 36:4 (Winter 1993): 576.

15. The Institute for Research on Public Policy was inspired by the Ritchie Report of 1969. Ronald Ritchie was commissioned by the federal government to determine if it was feasible for the government to create "an institute where long-term research and thinking can be carried out into governmental matters of all kinds." See Ronald S. Ritchie, *An Institute for Research on Public Policy* (Ottawa: Information Canada, 1969). For an interesting assessment of the evolution of IRPP see Evert A. Lindquist, "Behind the myth of think tanks: The organization and relevance of Canadian policy institutes," diss. U. of California, Berkeley, 1989, 363–69.

16. Lindquist, "Behind the Myth of Think Tanks," 340–46.

17. Carroll Quigley, "The Round Table Groups in Canada, 1908–38," *Canadian Historical Review* XLIII: 3 (September 1962): 204. Also see, James Eayrs, "The Round Table Movement in Canada, 1909-1920," *Canadian Historical Review* XXXVIII:1 (March 1957): 1–20.

18. Mission statement quoted in Edward D. Greathed, "Antecedents and Origins of the Canadian Institute of International Affairs," *Empire and Nation: Essays in Honour of Frederick H. Soward*, eds. Harvey L. Dyck and Peter Krosby (Toronto: University of Toronto Press, 1969) 97.

19. Ibid., 97.

20. The IPR and the Round Table Movement also played an important role in bringing about the creation of the CIIA. For more on the history of the CIIA see, Carter Manny, *The Canadian Institute of International Affairs, 1928–1939*, BA Thesis, Harvard University, 1971; J. E. Osendarp, *A Decade of Transition: The Canadian Institute of International Affairs, 1928–1939*, MA Thesis, York University, 1983; John Holmes, "The CIIA: A Canadian Institution," *Bout de Papier* 7:4 (1990): 9–10; Canadian Institute of International Affairs, "Brief History of the Canadian Institute of International Affairs," (Toronto: CIIA, 1995); and E. D. Greathed, "The Antecedents and Origins."

21. T. B. Millar, "Commonwealth institutes of international affairs," *International Journal* 33 (Winter 1977–78): 5–27.

22. Canadian Institute of International Affairs, "A Brief History," 6.

23. Canadian Institute of International Affairs, *Annual Report 1994*.

24. On the relationship between the CIIA and the Department of Foreign Affairs and International Trade (DFAIT), see Alex I. Inglis, "The Institute and the Department," *International Journal* 33 (Winter 1977–78): 88–103; and F. H. Howard, "Inside the Canadian triangle: The university, the CIIA, and the Department of External Affairs, A personal record," *International Journal* 33 (Winter 1977–78): 66–87.

25. The CIIA also publishes *Behind the Headlines*, an opinion-oriented monograph, on a quarterly basis.

26. Lindquist, "Behind the Myth of Think Tanks," 340.

27. Lindquist, "Think tanks or clubs?" 564.

28. In nine Canadian newspapers (*Vancouver Sun, Toronto Sun, Toronto Star, Ottawa Citizen, London Free Press, Montreal Gazette, Edmonton Journal, Calgary Herald, Winnipeg Daily News*), between June 1, 1985 and June 18, 1997, the Science Council of Canada was referred to 690 times. During that same period, the Economic Council of Canada received 2012 citations and the National Council of Welfare generated 863 references. Data obtained from Infoglobe. See Donald E. Abelson, "Public Visibility and Policy Relevance: Measuring the Impact and Influence of Canadian Policy Institutes." Paper presented at the annual meeting of the Canadian Political Science Association, University of Ottawa, 2 June 1998.

29. When the 1992 budget was handed down, the Science Council of Canada had a staff of 29 and an annual budget of over $3 million. The Economic Council of Canada had 118 staff members and a budget in excess of $10 million. See Lindquist, "Think tanks or clubs?" 559. For a discussion on the closing of the Science Council of Canada see, John De La Mothe, "A Dollar Short and a Day Late: A Note on the Demise of the Science Council of Canada," *Queen's Quarterly* 99:4 (1992): 873–86.

30. On the closing of CIIPS, see Geoffrey Pearson and Nancy Gordon, "Shooting Oneself in the Head: The Demise of CIIPS," *Canada Among Nations, 1993–1994: Global Jeopardy*, eds. Fen Osler Hampson and Christopher J. Maule (Ottawa: Carleton University Press, 1993), 57–81. For more on the creation of CIIPS, see Gilles Grondin, "The Origins of the Canadian Institute for International Peace and Security," *Background Paper* 6, (Ottawa: Canadian Institute for International Peace and Security, 1986); M. V. Naidu, "From an Idea to an Institution: The Canadian Institute for International Peace and Security," *Peace Research* 16:3 (1984): 2–27; *House of Commons Debates* (April 17, 1984), 3117–3161; (April 18, 1984), 3189–3210; (May 11, 1984), 3643–3657; and (June 28, 1984), 5223–5229.

31. *House of Commons Debates* (April 18, 1984), 3192. Approximately 12 institutes receive between $50 000 and $100 000 per year to conduct their operations. The MSSP was created by the federal cabinet in September 1967 and has been renewed approximately every five years.

32. In the 1940s and 1950s, a few nonprofit organizations existed which provided various services to the private sector including the New York–based Conference Board which opened a small office in Montreal in 1954 and the Canadian Tax Foundation which was created in 1946, to "conduct and sponsor research on taxation." Lindquist, "A Quarter-Century of Canadian Think Tanks," 3. However, no multidisciplinary institution on the scale that was envisaged by Prime Minister Trudeau existed in Canada.

33. Ritchie, "An Institute for Research on Public Policy." In 1968, some institutes including the Parliamentary Centre were formed to address specific needs of government. Even so, such institutes had small staffs and were not capable of offering wide-ranging expertise.

34. The Canada West Foundation has three primary objectives: to conduct research into the social and economic characteristics of the Western and Northern regions of Canada, to educate individuals regarding the West's regional economic and social contributions to Canada, and to act as a catalyst for informed debate.

35. The C. D. Howe Institute was the result of a merger between the Private Planning Association of Canada and the C. D. Howe Memorial Foundation. Much of its research focuses on monetary policy, government finance and international and interprovincial trade. For more on C. D. Howe see, Alan Ernst, "From Continentalism to Neoconservatism: North American Free Trade and the Politics of the C. D. Howe Institute," *Studies in Political Economy* 39 (Autumn 1992): 109–40.

36. Few think tanks in Canada have gained more public notoriety than the Fraser Institute. The goal of the institute according to its mission statement "is to achieve a society of economic and social well being, based upon free markets, private property rights, individual responsibility and limited government." See John Lorinc, "Hold the Fries and the Social Programmes," *Saturday Night* (March 1994): 11–15, 61; and J. Marcus, "The Prophet of Profit," *B.C. Business Magazine* (August 1983).

37. For a brief overview of these and other institutes, see Murray Campbell, "Wonks," [Toronto] *Globe and Mail*, 2 December 1995: D1–2.

38. On the growth of the Conference Board see Lindquist, "Behind the Myth of Think Tanks," 347–51.

39. Lindquist, "Behind the Myth of Think Tanks," 347–51.

40. Richard Higgott and Diane Stone are among the few scholars who have thought critically about how to measure the influence of think tanks. See their article, "The Limits of Influence: Foreign Policy Think Tanks in Britain and the USA," *Review of International Studies* 20 (1994): 15–34.

41. Response made on survey questionnaire prepared by the author in October 1997.

42. One of the clearest examples of a Canadian think tank having a decisive impact in the policy-making process is the Ottawa-based Caledon Institute and its president Ken Battle (formerly of the National Council of Welfare) who played an instrumental role in developing federal social policies affecting child and seniors benefits. According to Kent Weaver of the Brookings Institution, these two major policy innovations have earned the Caledon Institute the nickname, "the godfather of Canadian social policy." Remarks made at the session on Think Tanks, Annual Meetings of the Canadian Political Science Association, 9 June 1997, Memorial University, St. John's, Newfoundland. Although a detailed case study of the Caledon Institute's influence on social policy has yet to be written, Evert Lindquist has examined how and to what extent think tanks sought to influence three key domestic policy issues: energy, policy, pension policy and tax policy. See "Behind the Myth of Think Tanks." For a useful examination of how think tanks have attempted to resolve the problem of public debt see, Allan Tupper, "Think Tanks, Public Debt, and the Politics of Expertise in Canada," *Canadian Public Administration* 36:4 (Winter 1993): 530–46.

PUBLIC INQUIRIES:
A Case Study

Peter Desbarats

The Commission of Inquiry into the Deployment of Canadian Forces to Somalia assumed historical importance on 19 January 1997 when it became the first significant federal inquiry in Canadian history to be terminated prematurely by government order. The shutting down of the Somalia inquiry by Defence Minister Doug Young provided new stimulus for a longstanding discussion of the role and utility of public inquiries in Canada. The discussion that followed this controversial move, in the media immediately and subsequently in academic and legal conferences and journals, involved most of the points at issue in the continuing speculation about the future of such inquiries.

The termination of the Somalia inquiry ended 150 years of traditional respect by governments in Canada for the independence of royal commissions and/or public inquiries—the terms are commonly interchangeable. The uncertainty that it left in its wake may provide a motive for resolving some of the perennial issues surrounding these inquiries, either by letting the institution lapse into obscurity or by taking steps to renew and strengthen it.

The Somalia inquiry was created by order-in-council on 20 March 1995 as a result of events in Somalia in 1993 when Canadian soldiers were deployed there as part of a United Nations peace enforcement mission. The aim of the mission was to restore some semblance of law and order to Somalia to assist the distribution of aid and avert the possibility of widespread famine. The decision by Canada in late 1992 to participate in the mission led by the United States was made in the light of intensive television coverage of deteriorating conditions in Somalia. About 900 Canadian troops assigned to the mission were drawn largely from the ranks of the Canadian Airborne Regiment, a crack paratroop battalion stationed in Petawawa, Ontario.

On the night of 16–17 March 1993, Airborne soldiers captured and beat to death a 16-year-old Somali, Shidane Arone, in their camp near the city of Belet Huen. A few days later, one of the soldiers involved in the incident attempted to commit suicide while being held in custody. Following that, there were allegations by an army surgeon in Somalia, Maj. Barry Armstrong, that an earlier incident on 4 March 1993, where a Somali intruder was shot dead and another wounded at the camp, appeared to have been an execution-style killing. In addition to media reports of these and other examples of questionable behaviour by Canadian soldiers in Somalia, television networks later broadcast videos of barbaric initiation ceremonies by members of the Airborne Regiment in Petawawa as well as videos taken in Somalia showing excessive drinking, racist language and other improper conduct by members of the Airborne.

The military responded to public concern about these revelations by initiating a series of courts martial primarily involving lower ranks and by appointing an internal board of inquiry. Subsequently, the government disbanded the Canadian Airborne Regiment—the first regiment in Canadian history to suffer this ignominy—and appointed the Commission of Inquiry into the Deployment of Canadian Forces to Somalia headed by Hon. Gilles Létourneau, a judge of the Federal Court of Appeal. The two other members of the inquiry were Peter Desbarats, a journalist and educator from London, Ontario, and Mr. Justice Robert Rutherford of Toronto, a Second World War tank commander with a distinguished record of overseas service.

The terms of reference provided by the government were detailed and extensive. They included such pre-deployment activities as the training and selection of the Regiment, performance and conduct of Canadian soldiers and officers in Somalia, and allegations of cover-up of incidents in Somalia that continued to surface after the regiment returned to Canada. When the inquiry was appointed, Defence Minister David Collenette promised a full investigation into these incidents, noting that they had occurred under the previous Conservative government before the Liberals won the 1993 election.

The inquiry began its hearings in the spring of 1995 and continued up to the end of March 1997, the deadline imposed for the end of public hearings by Defence Minister Young. It submitted its report as ordered before the end of the following June and it was made public on 2 July. During the course of the inquiry there were allegations about the destruction of Somalia-related documents at National Defence Headquarters in Ottawa and the production of doctored documents by NDHQ, in violation of Access to Information legislation, in response to media requests for information. Hearings into these matters resulted in the resignation of the Chief of the Defence Staff, Gen. Jean Boyle, following the earlier resignation of Defence Minister Collenette on an unrelated matter.

Collenette's replacement, Doug Young, showed signs of impatience with the inquiry as soon as he was appointed early in October 1996. By the following month he was telling news media that he "certainly wouldn't want to be in an election campaign with the inquiry still going on, having people telling me that I'm trying to cover something up."[1] When he ordered closure of the inquiry in January, he cited the length and cost of the process and the military's need for early recommendations and reform.

The commissioners had promised a full report by the end of 1997 but this final extension was refused. As a result, the inquiry was terminated before it could hold hearings into the death of Shidane Arone and subsequent allegations of coverup, the series of incidents that had largely been responsible for the creation of the inquiry.

The minister's complaints about the slowness and expense of the inquiry process reflected long-standing concern about these characteristics of public inquiries and drew a sympathetic reaction from many Canadians at a time when restraint of government spending and tax reductions were popular electoral themes. A secondary theme used by the government at this time was the unfairness of the inquiry process on senior military officers and bureaucrats in the defence department. This also echoed questions raised frequently by jurists and lawyers about the protection of individuals who appear as witnesses before inquiries or who are publicly named and blamed during inquiries.

Some of these concerns have been evident almost from the beginning of the long history of public inquiries. According to an authoritative and unusually entertaining historical paper on royal commissions by the British parliamentarian, author and playwright Sir Alan Herbert,[2] royal commissions originally were an outgrowth and extension of parliamentary committees. "Parliament, after all, is but a large committee," Sir Alan wrote, "breeding fissiparously, like duckweed, many others."[3] When parliamentary committees were unable, for various reasons, to deal with certain matters, British governments turned to committees of outside experts for advice. Sir Alan refers to the institution of the royal commission as "the Ascot of the sport of inquiry"[4] and dates it back to the 16th century. In the 19th century, royal commissions had become so prevalent that they had provoked many of the criticisms that are common today—that they are created by governments to stifle debate and stall action on controversial matters, that they take too much time, and that they cost too much money. Sir Alan quotes an 1849 pamphlet entitled *Government by Commissions Illegal and Pernicious* as stating, "How convenient it is to stop the mouth of any member of the House of Commons, if an inconvenient answer is asked, with the proposing of a commission of inquiry."[5] He also cites a typical criticism produced, in this instance, by Prime Minister Gladstone: "Inquiries are well fitted for overloading any question with 10 or 15 times the matter necessary for its consideration."[6]

But Sir Alan also was able to identify many royal commissions that made significant contributions over the years, including a 16th century commission that proposed (unsuccessfully) remarkably modern divorce laws, an 1833 commission that created the basis of contemporary local administration in England, royal commissions of 1867 and 1872 that led to sweeping judicial reforms, and a landmark Royal Commission on Trade Unions in 1867. Interspersed among these productive inquiries were many more obscure or futile examples such as the Royal Commission on Electrical Communication with Lighthouses which sat for six years from 1892 to 1898.

Referring to an interminable series of committees and commissions on divorce reform in which he participated, Sir Alan notes one in particular that sat for five years in the 1950s, examined 113 witnesses, received more than 2000 documents, and issued a report of 396 pages. Sir Alan complained that "lawyers dominated the commission" which he described as "a mammoth affair"[7] although it is dwarfed by many royal commissions of our own era.[8]

Between the examples cited by Sir Alan and contemporary royal commissions in Canada and the United Kingdom, there is one significant difference. In 1960, appointees to British royal commissions were still serving without pay. Sir Alan felt that this was "a wondrous thing that His Majesty should still be able to get the devoted services of public-spirited men and women to act on these Royal Commissions, knowing very well that, in all probability, nothing whatever will be done as a result of their reports,"[9] although he also suggested that commissioners should be paid in order to "make it easier for eminent, able, but not affluent citizens to service in this manner." He suggested that paying commissioners would have the added benefit of making governments more cautious about appointing royal commissions. If the taxpayer knew that he was paying the salaries of commissioners, their appointment "would prick up his mean little ears," according to Sir Alan.[10]

Canada's first royal commissions of inquiry were appointed by British governments under colonial regimes. The most famous of these early inquiries was the 1838 commission of Lord Durham to investigate the causes of the 1837–38 rebellion which produced the Durham Report. From about 1825, royal commissions were also appointed by Canadian colonial authorities.[11]

The first *Inquiries Act* was passed by the Assembly of the United Provinces of Canada in 1846. This formed the basis of the *Inquiries Act of 1867,* the forerunner of Part I of the current *Inquiries Act*. Subsequent amendments added Part II, provisions to cover inquiries into the business of government departments, and Part III, powers to summon witnesses and retain counsel.[12] The final part of the current Act, Part IV, was put in place in 1934 and dealt with international commissions and tribunals.

Canadian governments have made liberal use of these powers. According to a study of public inquiries published by the Law Reform Commission of Canada in 1977, about 400 commissions had been appointed under Part I of the *Inquiries Act* since Confederation. Almost 1500 departmental inquiries had been established under Part II. Canadian royal commissions have studied such important matters as federal-provincial relations, health services, broadcasting, bilingualism and biculturalism, the non-medical use of drugs, and, more recently, the status of Aboriginal peoples and the state of the national blood supply. The Law Reform Commission in 1977 produced this balanced assessment of the long-term usefulness of these commissions:

> Some inquiries have been controversial; others have been almost totally ignored. Some have had substantial impact on government policy; the recommendations of others have been seemingly ignored, although they may have had indirect effects difficult to assess. But it is significant that much of the history of Canada could be interpreted through the work of commissions of inquiry."[13]

Contemporary concern about commissions of inquiry has focused on two distinct but interrelated aspects: the complexity, cost and duration of inquiries; and the status of individuals who appear as witnesses before inquiries.

In examining these questions, most authorities have found it useful to divide commissions of inquiry into two categories. The Law Reform Commission used the terms "advisory" and "investigatory" to distinguish between the two types. Advisory commissions "address themselves to a broad issue of policy and gather information relevant to that issue."[14]

Investigatory commissions "address themselves primarily to the facts of a particular alleged problem." These functions often overlap but "almost every inquiry primarily either advises or investigates."[15] Advisory commissions often are prolonged because of the complexity of their subject matter, the need for extensive research commissioned from outside experts and the number of parties who wish to be heard. Investigatory commissions find themselves burdened by an increasing number of lawyers representing involved parties which tends to prolong the process and significantly increase its cost.

Typical of the different types of commissions of inquiry, drawn from the author's experience, would be the Royal Commission on Newspapers (1981)[16] and the Somalia inquiry. The newspaper commission was asked to investigate concentration of ownership in the newspaper industry following the closings of daily newspapers in Ottawa and Winnipeg by two of the country's leading newspaper chains. Although counsel was retained by the inquiry, most parties appearing before the inquiry, representing newspaper corporations, journalists, trade unions, and other interested parties, appeared without counsel. The chair of the inquiry was a former editor and civil servant without legal training. Public hearings were relatively straightforward. The commission completed its work and submitted its report within a year. By contrast, the Somalia inquiry was chaired by a judge, virtually all the officers and lower ranks appearing before the inquiry were represented by their own lawyers at public expense, challenges to procedure during the hearings were frequent, there was an unsuccessful attempt by lawyers for one of the senior officers to disqualify the chair on the grounds of bias, and the inquiry had lasted for more than two years when it was prematurely closed down by the government.

The legal complexities of investigatory inquiries have led some authorities to argue that inquiries aimed at the alleged wrongdoing of specific individuals are unfair and invalid because they operate without the protection of the criminal process. It was suggested recently that this unfairness could be mitigated "if inquiries focus their critical gaze on organizations and society, not individuals."[17] This was the course ultimately followed by the Krever inquiry into the national blood supply while the contemporaneous Somalia inquiry listed specific failures by eleven senior military leaders, the majority of whom had resigned or retired from the armed forces by the time the report was published. Focusing on organizations rather than individuals reduces the possibility of legal challenges to the inquiry but it may not respond to the public's demand for individual accountability.

Criticism of commissions of inquiry, by judges and lawyers as well as the media, has led some authorities to wonder about the future of this institution. Willard Estey, a former Supreme Court justice and veteran of inquiries into airlines, banking, and the steel industry, had reached the conclusion by 1990 that "the usefulness of an inquiry as a fact-gathering and conclusion-drawing organization is on the wane."[18] But he also felt sure that "whether we like it nor not, inquiries will be here for a long time" and that "we will have these show trials periodically as a cathartic in democracy and it is not bad."[19] He proposed that some of the problems could be remedied by "a more professional approach from the government itself in staffing these inquiries and keeping control of how much they are going to cost, how long they will sit and so on."[20]

However, these are all areas that relate closely to the independence of public inquiries, a characteristic that, until recently, had seemed self-evident to virtually every authority who had written on the subject. Speaking in 1972 as a judge and former royal commissioner, Gerald Le Dain stated that "a commission of inquiry established under Part I of the federal *Inquiries Act* is an independent body which, as a matter of formal relation, is on an equal footing with the other institutions of government." He continued: "Once appointed it is not subject to anyone's direction or supervision. It is not under any degree of ministerial control although it is dependent on the government for its finances and, in theory, its mandate could be revoked by order in council. In practice it is allowed to peter out."[21] The Anthony-Lucas handbook on the conduct of public inquiries cited earlier devotes only two of its 256 pages to the subject of "government intervention." It states that "there have been occasions where the government that created a public inquiry order the inquiry to cease its activity and report by a specified date" but provides no examples of such an occurrence.[22] It states that such an event could be caused in theory by changes in the situation being studied by the inquiry or "by a desire to curtail the work of the inquiry because of excessive cost or embarrassment to the government."[23] The authors of the handbook are of the opinion that, in the end, "a government intent on limiting an inquiry can do so to the extent public opinion permits."[24] However, the authors also recognize that "there is an argument that, once the order in council creates an inquiry, the Act specifically provides that officers are to inquire and report, and an order in council cannot override the provisions of the statute by denying the commissioner the opportunity to complete the investigations and report."[25]

In light of what happened to the Somalia inquiry, it might seem odd in retrospect that such a basic matter as the independence of public inquiries from government interference or curtailment did not attract more extensive earlier attention. Apparently political scientists and legal authorities felt in the past that such an eventuality was so contrary to tradition that it was hardly worth considering at length. This, as well as the historical record, illustrates the rarity of this extreme occurrence.

In practice, tensions may often arise between inquiries and the governments that appoint them, particularly if the government's own actions are under scrutiny, but these are usually communicated and managed through dealings between the inquiry and the Privy Council Office. Following the end of the Somalia inquiry, I described this relationship in these terms:

> All three of us on the Somalia inquiry were novice commissioners. We soon discovered that the tricky question of political independence is effectively dealt with, on a day-to-day basis, through ongoing contacts between inquiry commissioners and staff and officials of the Privy Council Office. This is where crucial questions of time and money are negotiated, particularly money. It is through its control of inquiry spending that government theoretically could exert some influence on the activities of an inquiry. In practice, this has not generally been done, at least not in critical areas of activity.[26]

Although the government may communicate its impatience with an inquiry through the Privy Council Office, the Anthony-Lucas handbook observes that "at all times the financing of the inquiry must be solely within the authority and discretion of the commissioners."[27]

The decision by the Chrétien government in January 1997 to curtail the Somalia inquiry was so unusual that there were virtually no precedents for the three commissioners to follow. All made statements at a press conference several days later. My own appreciation of the situation was given in these words:

> Now the government has unilaterally broken the contract that it had made with myself and my fellow commissioners. It has curtailed our inquiry in a way that will prevent us from fulfilling our terms of reference and answering some of the most crucial questions that the government itself had presented to us. This is not just a matter of shaving a few months from our schedule, let's be clear about that. This is a drastic curtailment of our work. As far as I can determine, it is unprecedented in the history of national public inquiries in Canada.[28]

Although resigning would have been a legitimate response to the government's decision, the three commissioners announced that they would continue under protest and cover as much ground as the shortened schedule would permit. As hearings continued toward the March deadline, a legal challenge to the government's decision was launched in British Columbia by John Dixon, a Vancouver academic and civil libertarian who had been a special advisor to Kim Campbell when she was defence minister at the time of the Arone murder. Dixon was embroiled at that stage in a public dispute with officials at National Defence Headquarters over when Ms. Campbell and her staff had been informed of the Arone murder. He felt that termination of the inquiry violated his right to defend his reputation by testifying before the inquiry. Judge Sandra J. Simpson of the Trial Division of the Federal Court, rejecting the government's contention that the inquiry had dragged its heels and observing that it had worked "systematically and diligently," agreed with Dixon's contention that the government had no right to terminate the inquiry while leaving its terms of reference intact.[29] Judge Simpson defined the independence of a commission of inquiry as meaning that "it is for the Commissioners, in a situation such as this where they are compelled to investigate and report, to decide when they had heard or otherwise received sufficient evidence to enable them to make findings of fact necessary to support conclusions in their report." In her view, the government "is not entitled to decide when the Commissioners have received sufficient evidence."[30]

The government quickly resolved the uncertainty about the future of the inquiry that followed this decision by issuing a new order-in-council that the inquiry, in effect, report on whatever parts of its terms of reference it had covered by the termination date set by the government. It then appealed the Simpson ruling. Subsequently, the Federal Court of Appeal, in a decision written by Judge Louis Marceau, upheld the government's right to terminate the inquiry. According to Judge Marceau, because an inquiry is the creation of the government, it cannot "prevail over the will" of the government. It must operate "within the parameters established by the Governor in Council." In order to deal with the troubling question of unfulfilled terms of reference of an aborted inquiry, Judge Marceau decided that terms of reference do nothing more than "suggest the framework of its report."[31] This agreed with the government's position in the B.C. case that terms of reference are only "optional topics" for an inquiry, a contention that Judge Simpson had rejected when she stated that an inquiry report "cannot be a nil report or simply a list of unanswered questions."[32]

The Marceau decision illustrates the chaos that was created by the government's politically motivated decision to terminate the Somalia inquiry. By upholding the government's right to close a public inquiry for whatever reasons, including cases where the inquiry threatens to embarrass the government, it severely curtailed the usefulness of inquiries for future governments.

When a government appoints an inquiry, it places great emphasis on the independence of the inquiry and its ability to investigate all relevant aspects of a situation. The credibility of the inquiry is an essential ingredient of the government's ability to hand over to it a situation that defies ordinary political solution. If inquiries lose credibility with the public, they will become useless to governments as a means of handling these intractable and politically dangerous situations.

In the renewed debate about the future of public inquiries that followed the government's termination of the Somalia inquiry, no one has suggested an alternative mechanism. Democratic governments in particular have always needed public inquiries of some sort and will continue to need them. Somehow our laws and accepted political practice have to support a workable system of independent public inquiries. Judges and others who are asked in future to serve on public inquiries will require some assurance that their work will not be interrupted when it threatens to embarrass the government, and that their competence will not be attacked by the very government that had begged them initially to undertake the inquiry.

This, in fact, was the way things stood for more than 150 years before the Somalia inquiry. Despite ongoing concerns about the cost and duration of inquiries and the rights of witnesses appearing before them, the system worked reasonably well. The Chrétien government's decision to end the Somalia inquiry before it had completed its work seriously damaged this essential institution and it is unlikely, in view of subsequent judicial decisions, that the courts will be able to repair it.

NOTES

1. Peter Desbarats, *Somalia Cover-Up: A Commissioner's Journal* (Toronto: McClelland and Stewart, 1997), 198.

2. A. P. Herbert, *Anything but Action? A study of the Uses and Abuses of Committees of Inquiry* (London: Hobart Paper 5. Institute of Economic Affairs, 1960).

3. Ibid., 9.

4. Ibid., 23.

5. Ibid., 23.

6. Ibid., 24.

7. Ibid., 31.

8. The Somalia inquiry, for example, collected more than 150 000 documents before it had completed its work.

9. Herbert, 18.

10. Ibid., 48. Canadians who are appointed to royal commissions are currently paid $500 per working day. Per diem expenses are the same as those paid to civil servants. Judges who are loaned by their courts for duty on royal commissions continue to draw their regular salaries. Lawyers who work for royal commissions or for parties appearing before them customarily earn up to $200 an hour within a daily maximum fee of up to $2000.

11. Russel J. Anthony and Alastair R. Lucas, *A Handbook on the Conduct of Public Inquiries in Canada* (Toronto: Butterworths, 1985), 1–2.

12. Ibid., 2.

13. Law Reform Commission of Canada, *Commissions of Inquiry* (Working Paper 17. Supply and Services Canada, 1977), 11.

14. Law Reform Commission of Canada, *Commissions of Inquiry,* 13.

15. Ibid.

16. The author served on staff of the Royal Commission of Newspapers, often referred to as the Kent Inquiry after its chair Tom Kent, as senior consultant and associate research director.

17. Kent Roach, "Canadian Public Inquiries and Accountability," *Accountability for Criminal Justice: Selected Essays,* ed. Philip C. Stenning (Toronto: University of Toronto Press, 1995), 290.

18. A. Paul Pross, Innis Christie and John A. Yogis, eds., *Commissions of Inquiry* (Toronto: Carswell, 1990), 216.

19. Ibid., 216.

20. Ibid., 216.

21. Gerald Le Dain, "The Role of the Public Inquiry in our Constitutional System," *Law and Social Change,* ed. Jacob S. Ziegel (Toronto: Osgoode Hall Law School Annual Lecture Series 1971–72. Osgoode Hall Law School/York University, 1973), 81.

22. Anthony and Lucas, 150.

23. Ibid., 150.

24. Ibid., 151.

25. Ibid., 151.

26. Peter Desbarats, "The Independence of Public Inquiries: Dixon v. Canada," *Alberta Law Review* 36:1 (Dec. 1997): 253.

27. Anthony and Lucas, 42.

28. Desbarats, *Somalia Cover-up: A Commissioner's Journal,* 214.

29. *Dixon v. Canada (Commission of Inquiry into the Deployment of Canadian Forces to Somalia - Létourneau Commission),* [1997] F.C.J. No. 345 (T.D.) (QL).

30. *Dixon v. Canada (Commission of Inquiry into the Deployment of Canadian Forces to Somalia - Létourneau Commission),* [1997] F.C.J. No. 345 (T.D.) (QL) at para. 76. Office of the Commissioner for Federal Judicial Affairs.

31. *Dixon v. Canada (Commission of Inquiry into the Deployment of Canadian Forces to Somalia - Létourneau Commission),* [1997] F.C.J. No. 985 (C.A.) (QL).

32. *Dixon* (T.D.) at para. 75.

P a r t

POLICY DEBATES

There are many public policy debates ongoing at any given point in time. These debates reflect differences within society and within the political system about how various sets of issues should be dealt with. Such differences arise due to the vast range of issues and outlooks existing within both society and government. Variables such as ideological identification, partisan attachment, available public resources, the extent of competing items on the governmental agenda, political culture, the distribution of seats in the relevant legislature, and the strength of political leadership all come into play in diverse and complex ways. Students of public administration need to be introduced to examples of public policy debate and to gain a sense of the important issues at stake. Each of the three readings explores a different field of policy, thereby suggesting the multiplicity of factors which can come into play during analysis of policy making and policy outputs.

Keith Brownsey examines the motivation of the Alberta government in its decision of several years ago to privatize alcohol sales. Privatization involves making activities or procedures "private" in the sense that government opts to vacate itself from the matter at hand and turn over control to marketplace decision-making approaches. In the case of alcohol, many Canadian provincial governments have long been active as regulators of alcohol distribution and sale. Students should consider the arguments put forth by Brownsey about the actions of the Alberta government and should reflect upon the balance between the kinds of responsibilities which governments should assume and those which may, or should, be "privatized." Sorting out this balance will raise questions of ideology, institutional design, and the relationship between societal protection and the costs of service delivery and product regulation.

Michael Nolan investigates issues of cultural regulation through an account of the rise and development of the CTV network. Regulation entails government agencies setting rules or guidelines backed up by some form of legal sanction. In the broadcast field the current primary federal government agency is the CRTC (the Canadian Radio-television and Telecommunications Commission). Nolan's commentary offers insights into the work of the CRTC and its predecessors and their effectiveness in terms of their regulatory mandate.

Hugh Mellon's essay looks into the political functions served by budgets. In late February 1998, federal finance minister Paul Martin unveiled the annual federal budget statement. This event is an annual occurrence and part of an ongoing planning cycle. Provincial and local governments also prepare annual budgets which receive intense coverage as their contents have tremendous political and administrative significance. Concerns are raised about topics such as spending levels, potential tax changes, debt worries, and/or the timeline for ultimate budget approval or rejection. Mellon attempts to introduce students to the world of budget politics by offering an overview of the role played by budgets and the varying perspectives brought by different elements within the political system to budgetary matters and deliberations.

DISCUSSION QUESTIONS

1. Why do you think governments ever got involved in the whole field of alcohol distribution or sale? Do you think these original rationales carry any significance in the contemporary environment? Why or why not?

2. What kinds of factors seem to be guiding the Alberta government's decision to privatize? Why might these be politically important? Should they be important?

3. Based upon the information provided, do you think you would support or oppose the decision of the Alberta government to privatize? Why or why not?

4. Can we begin to develop certain criteria about when governments should offer certain kinds of services or control certain types of functions? Are there things which governments should do or should not do? How might we recognize them?

5. Why have Canadian governments long felt a need to regulate matters of broadcasting and culture? Are these aspirations or goals still a priority concern among the public? for you and your associates?

6. What lessons can we draw from the case of the CRTC and the CTV network? Has public regulation helped produce publicly beneficial outcomes? Why or why not?

7. What are your television viewing habits like? How important is cultural sovereignty (loosely defined as the ability of a country to control its own cultural environment and enforce cultural legislation or regulations)? Why?

8. What do you think goes into the development of a budget for a large entity like a federal or provincial government?

9. Why are budgets often the source of political controversy? What differing groups seem to get involved in debates over a provincial or federal government budget? Why?

10. Explain the various functions played by government budgets. Why do you think that the finance minister is often regarded as the second most important member of cabinet after the prime minister or the premier? Can you name (a) the federal and (b) the provincial finance minister for your province?

11. What kinds of criteria could we develop to evaluate a budget?

SELLING THE STORE: Privatizing Alberta's Liquor Stores

Keith Brownsey

INTRODUCTION

In a 14 June 1997 opinion piece for the *Calgary Herald*, Alberta's minister of energy, Steve West, reflected on the provincial government's privatization of properties and services over the previous four years. As minister responsible for the Alberta Liquor Control Board (ALCB) he had overseen the privatization of the province's retail liquor outlets as well as a number of other government services. Privatization of this and other public programs was part of the effort to curb what was described as runaway government spending. But this radical change in the focus of government was more than a simple deficit elimination scheme. It was an attempt to redefine the role of the state in Alberta while at the same time consolidating support for the Progressive Conservative government of Ralph Klein. Motivated by a neoconservative ideology and political considerations, the government cuts and privatizations were justified on economic and moral grounds.

The Alberta government was convinced that the only way to eliminate a provincial deficit of over $2 billion and an estimated public debt of $12 billion was for the state to either cut back or abolish certain of its activities. In a January 1994 speech to the province the premier, Ralph Klein, announced across-the-board cuts to all government services of 21 percent. As a result the provincial Conservatives eliminated the jobs of thousands of provincial government workers, reduced medicare benefits and hospital funding, and cut support to schools, universities and municipalities to some of the lowest levels of funding in North America.[1] While some ministries and departments suffered more or less than the stated amount, part of the deficit/debt elimination program was the privatization of government services and the elimination of public sector jobs. Privatization of retail liquor outlets in Alberta must be seen as part of this ideologically motivated effort to downsize government.

Moreover, the privatization of provincial liquor stores had a political dimension. The Progressive Conservatives in Alberta are an electoral coalition of various class elements, economic interests, and regional groupings. The provincial party depends on the support of farmers, the oil and gas industry, and small business among others. Small- and medium-sized business—those companies with under one thousand employees—is an important part of the government's support in urban centres and small towns. The privatization of liquor stores, the limits on the size of privatized stores, restrictions on what the new stores could sell, and the continued exclusion from the retail liquor trade of grocery chains is attempt by the provincial government to provide and protect the interests of a particular segment of its political support—small business.

West began his assessment of provincial privatization with a history lesson. Over the previous seventy years, he said, the Alberta government had moved beyond what was its traditional role of providing basic social programs. The province had entered into such areas as building roads, developing computer systems, selling drivers' licences, building and owning houses and apartments, and retail sales. Had not the Klein government intervened, he insisted, to halt these statist tendencies, the public sector would have continued to grow.[2]

West's list of privatized government services was impressive. The Alberta Conservatives had sold off or closed registries for drivers' licences, motor vehicle registration, vital statistics (which included marriage, birth, and death certificates), land title searches, and related products; Access Television (the province's education network); information technology functions in municipal affairs, transportation, utilities, and registries; highway engineering, design, and construction; park service and maintenance; corporate and consumer affairs; and 70 000 properties representing $1.8 billion. The minister estimated that the province had lost more than $2.5 billion on its sale of properties. This was the largest single penalty the Alberta government had incurred, dwarfing the approximately $2 billion lost on a variety of loans and guarantees to businesses such as Novatel, Magcan, Gainers, and Swan Hills to name several of the more prominent financial disasters for which the provincial government was responsible.[3] "But you know," he stated, "take your loss up front, sell for a loss and save money...."[4]

IDEOLOGY, POLITICS, AND PRIVATIZATION

The focus of West's article was the privatization of provincial retail liquor sales in Alberta. The minister claimed that selling off the ALCB outlets was "a loss leader to start the campaign on privatization" and that you "have to get something under your belt and get it done quickly." This essential first step in redefining the role of the state in Alberta had, according to West, seen the elimination of a number of regulations relating to lounges and taverns, the creation of 4000 new jobs, improved consumer services, and stable or decreased pricing of alcoholic beverages. At the same time, the province had not relinquished its obligation to prevent "the sale of liquor to minors and intoxicated persons."[5]

Privatization in the 1990s has meant the sale or the contracting out of various government services to nongovernment agencies as well as the application of private sector management techniques to the public service. While not-for-profit groups may assume the delivery of goods and services previously distributed by the state, privatization is generally the commercialization of public goods and services. It can be described, therefore, as the sale of public assets to the private sector and the application of private-sector management techniques to the public sector.[6]

The decision to privatize the retail sale of alcohol in Alberta had two dimensions: ideological and political. It was an ideological decision in the sense that the provincial government assumed that more efficiency is the purview of the private sector and that the public sector is always burdened with being less efficient. This free-market orientation permeated the privatization debate. It was political in the sense that the privatization of retail liquor sales in the province was directed to one segment of Conservative support. Although they are both arbitrary and interconnected, these categories do provide an understanding of the context for the privatization of public services.[7]

The Progressive Conservative government was ideologically committed to limiting the role of the provincial government in Alberta. Ralph Klein and his cabinet held the view that state intervention into society was intrusive, inefficient and immoral. Alberta residents had become dependent on the largesse of the state and must be weaned from it. As part of this overall policy direction, West used two arguments to defend Alberta's privatization program. The first was economic. He claimed that government needed to rid itself of various enterprises so that these enterprises could be more flexible and compete in the global marketplace. This is the idea that the private sector is more efficient than the public sector and is able to deliver goods and services in a more cost-effective fashion.[8] Three types of efficiency were defined by the provincial government: technical, economic, and social. Technical efficiency is a positivist concept that is easily measurable in terms of ensuring that the maximum output of a good or service is obtained at the minimum real cost. The privatization of provincial liquor outlets is, therefore, calculable in terms of its benefits to society in such variables as cost, convenience, and selection.

The second version of efficiency is economic. This measure is both positive and normative. Analysis is expanded to include all the resources and all the economic activities of a jurisdiction such as a province. Unlike technical efficiency, this concept addresses various questions attendant on market imperfections. In the case of liquor privatization, social costs must be factored into any evaluation of the costs and benefits. This does not simply include an increase in crime related to liquor privatization, but job loss and wage loss as well.

The third aspect of economic efficiency relates to social costs. Even more normative than economic efficiency, social efficiency must take into account broad social goals such as ending poverty, better health care, and good schools. In the case of the sale and distribution of alcoholic beverages, the social costs include such issues as addiction, crime, and public health.

The second reason West gave for privatization was moral. He stated that the only role for the state is to remove people from a dependence on government. He also argued that the production and distribution of goods and services is more appropriately handled by the free market. Privatization of state services would, the minister claimed, improve the moral character of those receiving the service.[9] The moral argument for privatization was clearly stated when West argued that privatization had forced workers to "get up in the morning a little quicker." He went on to defend the lower wages of employees in the new private outlets by stating that the jobs created by privatization were "not all at $14 to $19 an hour, but only government can pay somebody that much to put Crown Royal in a paper bag."[10]

A second motivation for the privatization of Alberta's liquor stores was not discussed in the minister's article—this was the political dimension. It was simply good politics to sell off provincial liquor stores. While the government workers' union, the Alberta Union of Public Employees (AUPE), fought a losing battle against the privatization of liquor stores, the government understood that a key segment of its electoral support—small business—favoured privatization.

Alberta has been a leader in Canada in personal and business bankruptcies since the late 1980s.[11] The vast majority of these cases have occurred in small- and medium-sized business. With the arrival of various large-scale retail outlets, a string of mergers of junior and intermediate oil and gas companies, and continuing consolidation in the agricultural sector, small businesses in the province have been increasingly hard-pressed. Not only have they faced competition from larger, better financed rivals, they have suffered from high real interest rates, and a lack of investment opportunities.[12] Apart from the volatile stock market, there were few occasions for small capital to invest in Alberta in the early 1990s.

The small businessperson also has the important, and often forgotten, function of creating employment for a large segment of the population. Small entrepreneurs invest not only for the financial benefits but also to create jobs for themselves, their families, and others. The provincial government understood this and recognized that the privatization of Alberta's government-operated liquor stores would create an investment opportunity for small- and medium-sized capital. Any employment created by independent liquor stores would fit in very nicely with the provincial government's stated objective of private-sector job creation. Moreover, the protection that the newly privatized liquor outlets have received from the provincial government, by way of preventing the sale of alcoholic beverages in large retail food outlets, has guaranteed their continued support for the Alberta Progressive Conservatives.

PRIVATIZING ALBERTA'S LIQUOR STORES

On 2 September 1993, Steve West, the Alberta cabinet minister responsible for the ALCB, announced his government's intention to close as soon as possible its 204 retail alcohol stores and replace them with private outlets. While over 600 specialty wine, cold beer, and other stores were already licensed, West's announcement effectively ended the government's involvement in the retailing of alcoholic beverages—a responsibility that had existed since 1924.

The original intention of provincially owned liquor stores was to control the sale and consumption of beer, wine and, spirits. In 1916 a provincial referendum had mandated the prohibition of alcoholic beverages. Various groups, including the Women's Christian Temperance Union and a number of Protestant denominations, had demanded prohibition as a progressive measure—they believed it would alleviate the social problems caused by the over-consumption of alcoholic beverages. Realizing that prohibition was unworkable, the provincial government opened retail outlets across Alberta in 1924. While some of the rules and regulations concerning the sale and consumption of alcohol were, at best, bizarre, the system appeared to work. The provincial government was able to mitigate some of the worst excesses of an unregulated system of alcohol distribution while, at the same time, offering reasonable access to a variety of products.

With the election in June 1993 of Ralph Klein and the Progressive Conservatives, the 70-year-old system of provincially owned and operated liquor outlets came to an end. The Klein government had received an electoral mandate to eliminate the provincial deficit. As part of their plan to reduce government spending, the Conservative government decided to sell a number of government services. The minister in charge of the ALCB, Steven West, argued that the government had received a clear message from the industry and the public that they wanted privatization. He claimed that the market would lead the way to a new free-enterprise Jerusalem: prices would decrease, selection would expand, and hours of operation and store location would lead to greater convenience. Within one year of the minister's announcement all provincially owned liquor retail outlets had been either sold or closed.

But the world did not unfold exactly as predicted—prices increased, 1500 individuals lost their jobs, and selection decreased in the majority of the new private outlets. The average product price in the private stores rose by seven percent in the first year of privatization and selection decreased in most of the stores. While the former ALCB outlets claimed to have stocked all of the 2100 products listed in their catalogues, it was soon apparent that many of the new smaller stores would not be able to match this assortment. Few of the promised efficiencies—technical, economic, and social—were apparent in the new privatized liquor outlets. In September 1993, 2104 products were listed in the ALCB catalogue and another 1221 were available through distributors, for a total of 3325 alcoholic beverages (beer, wine, spirits, cider, coolers). By January 1998 the ALCB claimed that 12 381 products were available to consumers. This was a 371 percent increase in product line in five years.[13] No store, however, has the space to carry this large number of items. Even those that have a good selection of products (some stores have claimed to have more merchandise for sale than is available) have very small profit margins. For example, the gross margin on economy brands of beer is $.49 per case—roughly five percent. Moreover, profits can be as low as one to three per cent on volume sales to restaurants and social functions.[14]

Part of the problem of low profits is due to the proliferation of liquor stores. Before privatization there were 202 Alberta Liquor Control Board stores, 30 retail beer stores, 23 specialty stores, and 49 agency stores (retailers whose primary product line is not alcoholic beverages but who are permitted to carry beer, wine, and spirits in order to service remote areas). As of January 1998 there were 701 private retail liquor stores and 69 agency outlets.[15] In Calgary the number of stores increased from 24 in September 1993 to 141 by August 1996. While provincially owned stores had monopolies on local liquor sales, within two years of privatization one Calgary neighbourhood went from one store within a 16 km radius to 30 stores in the same area. It was still possible to make a profit at these outlets but, as one retailer described it, "You can eke out a living if you are willing to work hard and manage a store yourself. It's long, long hours every day and the only day we close is Christmas."[16]

For ALCB employees the consequences of the government's privatization were dramatic. Although a severance package was offered to long-time employees, and many of the former government workers would find jobs in the new private stores, 1500 full-time, part-time, and casual workers lost their jobs. A telephone survey conducted for a study of Alberta's privatization by the Canadian Centre for Policy Alternatives revealed that eleven months after West's announcement, 44 percent of the full-time equivalent employees remained unemployed. Twenty-four percent had found part-time work and 32 percent had found full-time jobs. In terms of income it was revealed that 75 percent of those who had found work were earning less than when they had worked for the government-run stores. Wages for employees in the privatized stores were, in most cases, half of what they had been under the provincial regime. The average non-management liquor store employee wage fell from $14.39 per hour for a full-time liquor store clerk in August 1993 to a provincial average of $7.13 per hour, according to a February 1996 market survey.[17]

The Alberta government's program of privatization was incomplete and incoherent. The Progressive Conservatives dismantled a mixed system of public and private stores and replaced it with a restricted market of small retailers; large grocers, who could have offered economies of scale in cost, were excluded. At the same time, the province retained control of pricing through the tax system with a flat tax of $4 per item. Along with the lack of economies of scale, this tax may have had the net effect of raising prices—a key element that contradicts one of the stated benefits of privatization. Simply put, the government's program of restricted competition did not allow the market mechanism to work. The half-measures were designed to make the existing ALCB stores attractive to potential buyers, but instead created a segment of the retail industry that depends for its existence on the province prohibiting large retail chains and grocery stores from the business of selling alcohol.

A key feature of the government's plan was the sale of its stores. In order to achieve this goal the province was forced to exclude the large grocery chains from the process. Only independent, freestanding stores would be granted new licenses under the Alberta scheme. This was done despite the fact that market surveys had told the government that consumers wanted the convenience of purchasing beer, wine, and spirits with their groceries.

As well, one important question remains unresolved. There is an artificial barrier to market entry for large grocery stores. It is apparent to most observers that this situation of restricted competition cannot last. Yet the Alberta Gaming and Liquor Commission (on 20 March 1995 the ALCB was merged with the provincial gaming commission) claims that it has no plans to allow supermarkets or grocery stores to sell alcoholic beverages; some food retailers, however, are entering the field by opening stand-alone stores beside their regular outlets. It is through this backdoor process that the large retailers will enter the retail liquor sales market. By September 1995, 10 such licences had been given to Loblaws, IGA, and Save-On Foods.[18]

Since 1993 the grocery chains—Calgary Co-op, Canada Safeway, Save-On Foods, and The Real Canadian Superstore—have been lobbying for the ability to sell alcoholic beverages in their stores. But the hundreds of small investors, many of whom have devoted a considerable amount of personal savings to their new enterprises, fear they would fall victim to the highly competitive pricing practices of these large supermarkets. Although Save-On Foods won a court challenge that allows them to open a liquor boutique in their Edmonton store, the government response has been to limit licenses to businesses that do not exceed a limit of 929 square metres, as well as to stores in which 90 percent of the products sold are alcoholic beverages.

With pressure from both the public and the Canadian Council of Grocery Distributors, it is apparent that the current regime of small retailers cannot last. The existing system of restricted competition is, at best, transitory. It is likely to be replaced by an industry dominated by the large grocery stores. The consequence of this would be the demise of many of the small retailers, especially in the urban centres where they would compete directly with the grocery stores. Moreover, many of the 4000 jobs that have appeared in the private retail liquor business would disappear.

The results of issuing licences to grocery and other stores will be twofold. First, many of the small neighbourhood stores will disappear. They simply will not be able to compete. The larger stores may be able to deliver on economies of scale promised by privatization. Second, the grocery chains tend historically to pay higher wages and provide better benefits than the small independents. Some of the losses suffered by ALCB workers may be regained as they are hired by the supermarkets. But this produces problems for the provincial government. The Progressive Conservative government of Ralph Klein has emphasized the over 2700 jobs created by privatization. Any consolidation of this industry that results in a loss of jobs would be a direct contradiction of the espoused benefits of privatization. Moreover, Conservative support in Alberta in the 1980s and 1990s has depended on the support of rural communities as well as that of the small business community in the urban areas, primarily Edmonton and Calgary. With other political parties on both the left and right ready to exploit any discontent within this Conservative bastion, the Tories cannot afford to lose one of the key elements of their electoral coalition.

Another reason West gave for privatization was the reduction of deficits and debt. The revenue from the sale of various provincial enterprises was to pay down the provincial deficit and debt, thus freeing up funds for other services. While government stores had earned a profit of $434.5 million in fiscal 1992, the minister argued that privatization would save the province $67 million annually. Liquor Control Board assets and real estate fetched a total of $59.2 million, somewhat under their estimated market value.[19] Moreover, the government did not sell all of its stores and it has been reluctant to release figures on the expected savings. Although the province claimed it would recoup another $24 million on inventory, there are no figures available on what was received from the sale of its retail stock. Under the flat tax system, the ALCB's projected income for the years 1994–96 is $415 million per annum. This figure is down from $427.7 million in revenues for 1993 and it assumes no significant increase or decrease in the volume of products sold or consumed in Alberta.[20]

As well, there was another economic reason for privatization. The consumption of beer, wine, and spirits had been steadily declining in Canada since 1981. In 1981 Albertans consumed 3.1 million nine-litre cases of spirits; by 1993 sales had fallen 42 percent to 1.8 million nine-litre cases.[21] The province had little control over the various cultural and social trends which were at play in the decline of consumption of alcoholic beverages. In order to maintain revenues, or at least offset some of the costs associated with this decline, it was technically efficient to privatize liquor outlets. Since privatization in 1993 the sale of spirits has stabilized and in some years even shown a slight increase. With a static provincial population, the increase in sales can only be explained by more aggressive marketing and greater availability on the part of the private operators. Privatization, therefore, offered the province an economic efficiency. That is to say, it gave the Klein government a means to increase or at least maintain revenues from the sale of alcoholic beverages without being seen to increase prices. Moreover, privatization eliminated the paradox of the province promoting the sale of alcohol while, at the same time, trying to curb its consumption.

Other negative consequences of Alberta's privatization have been related social costs. The Calgary Police Service reported a 62 percent increase in liquor store–related crimes during the first year of privatization. The effect of easier access to beer, wine, and spirits on rates of alcoholism has not been calculated, but the Addiction Research Foundation of Canada as well as the Alberta Alcohol and Drug Abuse Commission have predicted an increase in what they refer to as social problems connected with alcohol.

One advantage of privatization has been an increase in convenience for consumers. Longer hours and a variety of new locations have expanded accessibility. This is especially true in rural areas where smaller communities had not been served by a government store. Still, even the convenience of the new private outlets may not be enough to justify the privatization of the government stores, especially when higher prices and less selection are considered. While there are more products available to consumers, no store carries a complete selection and customers may have to look farther afield to find their favourite brands than they did under the public system.

Despite these obstacles the new private stores appear to be surviving. As of December 1995 only 28 liquor stores or 5 percent of the 633 open at the time had closed. The failure rate was substantially less than, for example, the failure rate for restaurants in their first two years of operation. And there is a backlog of applications for new licences.

CONCLUSIONS

The motives behind Alberta's privatization were ideological and political. The Conservative government of Ralph Klein assumed that the private sector was able to deliver most goods and services more efficiently than the state. But it is here that they encountered problems. The Alberta government's definition of efficiency did not take into account various social costs such as increases in crime or alcoholism. It also did not take into account any technical and economic inefficiencies—the costs in establishing a retail liquor outlet or in lower wages and unemployment for former ALCB employees. The government worked from a model where efficiency was seen simply as a formal relationship between inputs and outputs and where it was possible to be entirely neutral between alternative methods of calculating those inputs and outputs.

With other provinces—including Ontario, Quebec, and New Brunswick—contemplating privatization, there are lessons they may take from the Alberta experience. First, Alberta's decision to privatize was ideological and political with economic and moral consequences. Efficiency judgments cannot be matters of technical expertise as the provincial government believed. They necessarily invoke disputed preferences over how society should be organized. Because of its ideological blinkers, the Alberta government made a major error when it built into its projections low costs to consumers and other supposed benefits of a free-market system. That is to say, they should not have used a contestable assignment of costs in their projections. Critics of privatization can easily use the province's own pronouncements on market efficiency in their arguments against privatization of retail liquor outlets.

Second, the process of privatization was a political act. The current system of licensing only independent retailers has created a sector that both supports the Progressive Conservative government and that depends on it for survival. In order to achieve the technical efficiencies promised by the provincial government, the barriers to market entry for the large grocery chains should not have been imposed. The current situation restricts licences to small independent stores that cannot offer the benefits that are claimed by advocates of privatization.

NOTES

1. For a discussion of these events see Kevin Taft, *Shredding the Public Interest: Ralph Klein and Twenty-Five Years of One-Party Government* (Edmonton: University of Alberta Press and the Parkland Institute, 1997).

2. Steve West, "How to Succeed in Privatization," [Calgary] *Calgary Herald* 14 June 1997: 16.

3. Taft, *Shredding the Public Interest,* 41–49.

4. West, "How to Succeed in Privatization," 16.

5. Ibid.

6. Duncan Cameron, "Selling the House to Pay the Mortgage: What Is Behind Privatization?"*Studies in Political Economy* 53 (Summer 1997): 12; Donald J. Savoie, *Thatcher, Reagan, Mulroney. In Search of a New Bureaucracy* (Pittsburgh: University of Pittsburgh Press, 1994), 14.

7. I am grateful to William C. Moore, Dept. of Economics, University of Arkansas, for bringing these concepts to my attention.

8. The best example of this thinking is David Osborne and Ted Gaebler, *Reinventing Government: How the Entrepreneurial Spirit Is Transforming the Public Sector* (New York: Plume, 1993).

9. See, for example, Nathan Glazer, *The Limits of Social Policy* (Cambridge, Mass.: Harvard University Press, 1988), for an ideological/moral argument for privatization of public goods especially in the social services.

10. West, 16.

11. Industry Canada, *Consumer and Business Bankruptcies, 1991–96* (Ottawa: Office of the Superintendent of Bankruptcy, 1998).

12. Cameron, 24–28.

13. Alberta Gaming and Liquor Commission, *Liquor Privatization in Alberta* (St. Albert, 7 January 1998).

14. Barry Nelson, "The Privatization Hangover: Liquor dealers are battling for survival," [Calgary] *Calgary Herald* 11 August 1996: C7.

15. Alberta Gaming and Liquor Commission.

16. Nelson, "Privatization Hangover," C7.

17. Douglas West, "Alberta's Liquor Store Privatization: Economic and Social Impacts," *Policy Options* (April 1997): 24–26.

18. Terry Bullick, "Alberta's Liquor Lesson," *Marketing Magazine* 11 September 1995: 9.

19. Alberta Liquor Control Board, *A New Era in Liquor Administration: The Alberta Experience* (St. Albert: Communications and Industry Affairs, 1994), 57.

20. Alberta Liquor Control Board, 55.

21. Association of Canadian Distillers, *1996 Annual Statistical Report* (Ottawa: Association of Canadian Distillers, 1997), 52–53.

CASE STUDY IN REGULATION: CTV and Canadian Broadcast Policy

Michael Nolan

The introduction of CTV Television Network Limited to Canadian viewers on 1 October 1961 brought about a profound change in the structure of the Canadian broadcasting system. The decision by the Board of Broadcast Governors (BBG), the broadcast regulator established by the Conservative government of John Diefenbaker in 1958, to license a privately owned television network had shattered the status quo. Unlike the more elitist Canadian Broadcasting Corporation whose mandate was to provide cultural and educational enlightenment through the broadcasting of quality Canadian programming, the CTV network was essentially a television vehicle for advertisers. Programs that could be sold to sponsors would be televised to the largest available audience. The CBC was accountable to Canadian taxpayers through the elected House of Commons which provided an annual parliamentary appropriation to the corporation; CTV, on the other hand, was beholden largely to the marketplace for its survival.

Indeed Spencer Wood Caldwell, the founder of CTV and a former CBC employee, was prepared to challenge the corporation and the long-held notion of a "single" Canadian broadcasting system. Since the founding of the CBC in 1936, publicly owned broadcasting stations and groups of privately owned affiliates had operated as part of one system, with the public element intended to be dominant. The CBC had regulated private broadcasters until 1958 when the BBG was established. The BBG was the first separate, independent broadcast regulator in Canada; it assumed the regulatory role that the CBC had held previously. For the first time in Canadian broadcasting history, the private sector was put on an equal legal footing with the public element.[1]

The arrival of CTV, therefore, represented a sharp break with the past. No longer would there be only a CBC television network consisting of stations owned and operated by the corporation together with privately owned affiliates; rather, two separate TV systems, one public and one private, would be in competition with each other for Canadian viewers. Both CBC and CTV were committed to somewhat separate goals and different mandates: a state-owned broadcasting service (CBC) boasting a schedule of Canadian programs that were intended to provide cultural uplift, and a separate chain of privately operated TV stations (CTV) heavily reliant on mass programming to attract advertising revenue.

From the beginning, CTV in its structure functioned as a microcosm of Canada. Arthur Weinthal, CTV's Vice President of Entertainment Programming, has explained: "As a co- operative, it has always been my observation that the network [was] a mirror image of Canada. The network like the country [was] composed of haves and have nots."[2] Of the eight original stations belonging to CTV, CFTO, Toronto; CFCF, Montreal; and CHAN, Vancouver would have been in the "have" category. CJCH, Halifax would have represented a "have-not" station. The other four founding stations were CJAY, Winnipeg; CJOH, Ottawa; CFCN, Calgary; and CFRN, Edmonton. CFRN had been licensed originally as a CBC affiliate.[3]

As an instrument of public policy, CTV can be assessed by an examination of four aspects of the network's 37-year history. The following study attempted to explain: the policy rationale behind the formation of Canada's first private TV network; its early structure; the regulatory relations between CTV and broadcast regulators; and the evolution of CTV from a cooperative to a modern company.

POLICY RATIONALE

How and why did CTV, a private network reliant on advertising, come into being especially in a country that had set lofty cultural objectives for a state-owned system of broadcasting at an early stage? Clearly Spencer Caldwell, a Winnipeg native and, in many ways, the quintessential private broadcaster, was the single individual most responsible for the birth of Canada's first private TV network. Like many other entrepreneurial-minded private broadcaster-businessmen, Caldwell anticipated that network television could become a lucrative business through the sale of air time to advertisers. He was born in Winnipeg on 11 February 1909, just eight years after Marconi had conducted his successful radio experiments at Signal Hill, Newfoundland.[4] Looking back on Caldwell's career, Harry Boyle, a former CBC executive and vice-chairman of the Canadian Radio-television Commission, has explained how the early broadcasting environment in Canada that was dominated by broadcaster-businessmen shaped Caldwell's outlook: "Men like Spence grew up in the tradition that broadcasting is a money-making proposition."[5]

Caldwell had prepared a formidable application but lost out to John Bassett, publisher of the *Toronto Telegram*, and his company Baton Aldred Rogers Broadcasting Limited in a bid for the private television licence in Toronto awarded by the BBG in 1960. The BBG had decided to allow "second" service stations in eight selected markets. Still, Caldwell recognized that the newly licensed, private TV stations in major urban centres across Canada could form the nucleus of a second television network that might be owned by the new stations and private investors. Having been denied the Toronto licence, Caldwell decided to apply to the BBG for a network that would link the private stations that the board had chosen to license. The BBG, the broadcast regulator, approved Caldwell's application to operate a private television network on 21 April 1961.[6] Thus, CTV Television Network Limited was born. Murray Chercover, President of CTV from 1968 to 1990, has explained how John Bassett "did a very quick end-run around the CBC by buying the eastern conference rights to televise the Canadian football league games." Baton decided to join Caldwell's network to be able "to exercise their rights on CFL football. When Baton broke the logjam, as it were, all the rest of them [private TV stations] came in."[7]

Why did the BBG grant Caldwell a TV network licence after denying him a station licence? Clearly the BBG recognized the prospect of greater exposure for Canadian programming with the newly licensed private stations working together in a network. Andrew Stewart and William Hull have written: "The Board's interest in the proposal lay in the opportunity it appeared to present for wider distribution of Canadian programs."[8] Gordon Keeble, a former vice-president of the communications company S. W. Caldwell Ltd. who had worked earlier with Caldwell at CBC Radio, has offered a similar explanation for Caldwell's success in obtaining the network licence. The BBG, which had introduced the first Canadian content regulations for broadcasters, saw an even greater potential for Canadian programming if the stations could be linked together: "I would think that the BBG felt that there was strength in numbers and that Canadian programming per se would benefit more from the combined efforts of all the stations than it would from eight of them making their own [programs] and shipping them back and forth."[9] Still, CTV was to undergo a major struggle in its formative years. Tensions within CTV, which had been founded with an ownership structure that had involved both the owners of some affiliated stations and outside private investors looking for early financial return, eventually became so great that the network was reorganized as a cooperative in 1966 with the affiliated stations emerging as the owners of the network.

CTV'S EARLY STRUCTURE

For the first time in Canadian broadcasting history, Canada was on the verge of head-to-head competition between two separate television networks. The structural realignment in Canadian broadcasting that the founding of CTV had created would serve to underline the two visions that had dominated the debate over the historical role of broadcasting in the Canadian cultural experience. The publicly owned CBC was modelled after the British Broadcasting Corporation and aimed at cultural uplift; the privately owned CTV reflected the United States' system of broadcasting and had no choice but to respond to commercial forces in the marketplace.

In the early 1960s when CTV was building its network service, two matters of great controversy arose: the difficulty in getting the network's investors to come to agreement and the question of network time payments to affiliated stations. In order to air its programming, the CTV network, which owned no stations of its own, had to rely on the affiliates agreeing to surrender some portion of their time for which the network paid the stations. Some stations believed that they could derive greater benefit from selling the time themselves, rather than accepting the time payments from the network for showing CTV programs.

John Bassett, a member of the first CTV board of directors, was the owner of the network's flagship station CFTO, Toronto, and he emerged as a dominant figure on the board, especially throughout the 1960s. Regardless of the influence of any single individual, the network's structure could not help but create tensions between the broadcast-owners and the non-broadcast investors in CTV. Bassett has recalled that there was "a sort of natural conflict which became very apparent early between the desires and needs of the affiliates and those of the network shareholders."[10] In a broader context, Bassett's assessment was that "it was never possible on a continuing basis really to bring the stations' and the network's needs together. And the fact that the network had no owned and operated stations of its own made it very difficult."[11]

The controversy surrounding the issue of station time payments was one that was to recur throughout CTV's history. Unlike the arrangement between the CBC and its affiliated TV stations, the payments made by CTV to its affiliates were not guaranteed; the time that the network reserved on the CTV stations had to be sold first to advertisers. Only then could the prearranged payments be made to the CTV affiliates. "What they [CTV and the affiliates] did was they took the time and they worked out a percentage deal," Bassett remembered. "They [the network] retained 25 per cent of the sale, as I remember, and the stations then got 75 per cent. But from the stations' point of view, that time had to be sold first. It was not a guaranteed payment to the stations and then the 75 per cent was split among all the stations so the [individual] station . . . would certainly not get what [it would] if it could sell that time itself."[12]

Still, a confidential report sent from CTV headquarters at 42 Charles St. East in Toronto to the affiliated stations on 4 October 1962 drew attention to the favourable economic position the stations enjoyed collectively as CTV members compared to other North American networks. The network management's report to the CTV stations explained: "Payments to the CBC affiliates range from about 28% to 60% depending on the type of program provided. The CBS network pays its affiliates a basic 30% of gross time charges less a series of deductions which leaves some stations a true net return of as little as 6%." The report noted that because CTV never intended "in its original planning to provide all the services offered by other networks it agreed to a much smaller share of revenue from time sales for itself, leaving 75% of such money for pay out to you as affiliates."[13]

Indeed, even the first year of the network's operation had exposed a major weakness in the original affiliation agreement with the CTV stations that related to "sustainers" or unsponsored programs: "Experience has shown, however, that where service is concerned, we are expected to provide as many services as any other network—except, perhaps, regular sustaining shows. On occasion, we have done that, too—even to the point of allowing you to sell spots in such shows without any kind of revenue return to us. Sustainers on CTV? Certainly not something ever contemplated in the original concept of this network."[14]

Illustrative of the steady tension between the network and its affiliates that grew in the early days, was an internal memo sent to Spencer Caldwell on 17 June 1964. The document attempted to compare the revenue positions of CBC and CTV. The memo noted: "The CBC National English TV Network makes sales of some $11 million, a figure not unlike our target for 1964–65." A comparison between what the CBC paid to its network stations including those owned and operated by the Corporation, and the amount of CTV's payments to its affiliates, was also highlighted: "The National English [CBC] TV Network makes station payments (including 0&0's) of some $3 million, while li'l ole CTV is scheduled to make over $4 million next year." The memo explained: "CBC spends 3% of total costs on affiliate payments: CTV is scheduled to spend 43%." At the end was the expletive: "It's a conspiracy."[15]

By 1966, the CTV network, which now consisted of eleven private affiliates, was virtually insolvent. The station owners wanted to assume full ownership of the network and pay off the other investors who had joined Caldwell in his bid to establish a network for advertisers. The Report of the Fowler Committee on Broadcasting in 1965 was highly skeptical of the stations assuming control of CTV and specifically recommended against such action: "The necessary private television network must not be allowed to fall under the exclusive control of the private stations, and steps must be taken to ensure adequate program performance by them, both individually and collectively." The committee, which had called for the establishment of a new Canadian Broadcasting Authority, recommended that CTV be recast "as a non-profit trust operating in the public interest."[16]

Clearly, the Fowler Committee had been critical of the level of programming that CTV had provided since its inception: "The programs provided by CTV are dominated by light entertainment and programs of mass-appeal. It has produced an adequate national news service, and has a relatively inexpensive weekly Sunday-afternoon program called 'Telepoll,' reporting the opinions of Canadians; for the rest, there are few programs of any real value or substance." In Fowler's view, a major dilemma had resulted from the network's original structure as it related to day-to-day network operations: "The essential trouble is that the CTV affiliates do not want CTV to be a success. The station operators admit, quite frankly, that CTV is a private company organized to make money, and that most of the investment in it is held by people not in the broadcasting business. If there are to be any profits from private broadcasting, the stations want the profits themselves and are unwilling to let outsiders make money out of it."[17] Although the Fowler Committee had argued otherwise, the BBG approved the application by eleven affiliated stations of CTV to assume control of the network. Thus, CTV had a new beginning in 1966 as a network owned by a cooperative of its affiliates. Each station had one representative on the Board of Directors and each had a single vote.[18] This principle of equality of ownership was to be applied throughout much of the network's history, regardless of the number of television stations an individual owner held, and eventually led to considerable internal wrangling.

REGULATORY RELATIONS

The CTV network often experienced uneven relations with the Canadian Radio-television Commission (CRTC) which succeeded the BBG as the broadcast regulator in 1968.[19] Throughout the 1970s and 1980s, the Commission repeatedly drew attention to programming deficiencies when the network's licence was renewed. Two decades after CTV had been formed as a cooperative, the CRTC was exceedingly critical of the network when it applied for a licence renewal in 1986 and demanded that more Canadian dramatic programming should be aired.

The Commission was repeatedly concerned about both the structure of the network and its programming capabilities, especially in the category of Canadian drama. As early as November 1971, the Commission had requested that CTV conduct a reorganization of its programming and corporate structure. This would allow the network and its stations "a) generally to fulfill their duties and obligations, b) to extend its services, c) to increase their ability to produce significant Canadian programs in accordance with the objectives established by the Commission and d) to improve the decision-making process of the Network." When the network's licence was renewed for a three-year period on 22 January 1973, the Commission noted at an earlier public hearing it had expressed "the desire that the Network develop more drama programming with Canadian themes, concerns and locales."[20] The CRTC was to reiterate this concern throughout much of CTV's history.

Still, getting agreement on internal policy as it related to programming and other network affairs was seldom easy given the tensions within the network owned by its affiliates. Fractious directors' meetings showed repeatedly the structure of CTV to be a microcosm of Canada where the centralized, Toronto-based Baton Broadcasting Inc. often came into sharp conflict over network affairs with the more decentralized approach advanced by Western International Communications Ltd. (WIC) of Vancouver. Both companies remained powerful private broadcasters. Almost from the beginning, rancour and acrimony seemed an integral part of the CTV culture. The adamant positions adopted towards network policy by Baton's John Bassett and WIC's Ray Peters, two principal antagonists, for many years were symptomatic of the regional tensions that still exist in Canada. The Toronto–Vancouver rivalry resulted from competing visions advanced for CTV that reflected distinctive outlooks.

"I believed," said Bassett who founded CFTO, CTV's flagship station, "that Toronto was the key market in the country. In my view, there could be no argument about that. . . . Toronto is by far more dominant in the Canadian market than any single city in the United States." Bassett's recollection was that "Peters would scream and yell and I would kid him and scream and yell back."[21]

For his part, Peters was vehemently opposed to Baton's position and any notion of the Toronto company ever getting control of CTV. As chairman of the board of British Columbia Television, he once told the Canadian Radio-television and Telecommunications Commission, "The [CTV] network management, bullied by Baton, has great difficulty encouraging the development of programs from sources other than Baton."[22] Peters took a more decentralized approach towards CTV and maintained that programs should be produced in all regions of Canada, not just Toronto, that would reflect the country's true diversity. "He [Bassett] wasn't happy at the end of each year in the spring setting up the program schedule both for station sales time and the schedule for CTV sales time, if he didn't occupy all of the programs and produce them all. Now if he ever sat down with a pencil and figured out what it was costing him to produce all those programs, what he was charging for them, he would soon figure out that he was winning the battle but losing the war. At any rate, he used to make me furious at this."[23]

FROM CO-OP TO COMPANY

Perhaps the harshest criticism that CTV received as a network was when its licence was renewed in 1987. The 1986 hearing into the licence renewal before the CRTC came in the year the Caplan-Sauvageau Report of the Task Force on Broadcasting Policy was released. CTV, the leading English TV network, was singled out along with the Global TV network for relying too heavily on talk, quiz, and game shows: "In 1984 CTV filled no less than 324 hours of its schedule with three talk shows and 260 hours with two quiz shows. These five shows, therefore, account for 82 percent of the total broadcast hours of the CTV schedule devoted in 1984 to Canadian performance categories (this, of course, excludes CTV's other Canadian programs in news, sports, etc.)."[24]

When CTV's licence was renewed from 1 October 1987 to 31 August 1992, the commission came down hard on the network for its lack of long-term strategies and demanded that greater resources be put into Canadian programming, especially the expensive genre of Canadian drama through the regulatory measure of "conditions of licence." Clearly the Commission expected a higher level of programming output from CTV as a major player in the Canadian broadcasting system: "During the five years between 1981–82 and 1985–86, CTV expended approximately $230.2 million on Canadian programs. The foregoing conditions of licence would require total expenditures on Canadian programs over the five years 1987–88 to 1991–92 of at least $403.0 million. This requirement represents an increase of 75.1% by comparison with the five-year period ending in 1985–86."[25] As CTV looked to the 1990s, the challenges the network faced were obvious both in its structure and the level of programming that was to be provided to Canadians.

John Cassaday, the successor to Murray Chercover, became network president in 1990 and took CTV into a new era. Cassaday, a former executive with Campbell Soup Co. Ltd., managed to move CTV beyond its earlier "co-op" structure to a new corporate alignment analogous to a conventional company. A new shareholders' agreement came into effect on 27 January 1993. In addition, the network agreed on new long-term affiliation agreements with its stations on 1 September 1993. It should be recalled that under the cooperative nature of CTV, each owner had an equal voice in network business affairs and an equal vote, regardless of the number of stations he owned, the contribution each owner made to the resources provided for the network's operation and the size of the respective audiences each served. Moreover each shareholder held a veto power over resolutions passed at board of directors meetings dealing with money matters, including those which called upon shareholders to cover any losses that the network might incur.[26] Baton's Douglas Bassett explained the impact of such a structure on his company, a dominant player in the network: "We could own every single television station in Canada that is a CTV affiliate except one and we would still have 50–50 partners."[27]

The new shareholders' agreement had a profound impact on the network's business affairs. CTV was able to operate similarly to a conventional company. The makeup of the board of directors was to be determined by the common voting shares held in CTV; the veto power awarded to each director was removed and all resolutions at board meetings were to be decided by a majority of votes cast. According to the new agreement reached with its affiliates in 1993, the CTV stations were guaranteed payments for their time for airing network programming, an arrangement similar to CBC affiliates, regardless of how much actual revenue the network earned. The payments to the affiliated stations were to increase from $14.8 million in 1994–95 to $21.8 million in 1998–99. Not surprisingly, the broadcast regulator perceived the CTV affiliates to be in an enviable position: "The Commission considers that CTV's compensation to its affiliates for use of their airtime is, at the very least, generous. Because the compensation is fixed in each year, and is thus independent of the network's profitability, these arrangements could affect CTV's ability to meet its responsibilities should revenues fall short of projections in any given year." The commission discounted such an eventuality but expected "the licensee's shareholders and affiliates to act responsibly should such an event occur, and ensure that the network has adequate resources to fulfil its obligations."[28]

Perhaps the most significant aspect of the new shareholders' agreement was that it contained provisions for the transfer of shares and stations in CTV and allowed for one owner to eventually control the network, a long sought objective of Baton Broadcasting Inc. Following a CRTC hearing in July 1997, the Commission gave approval to Baton to acquire majority control of CTV. Baton's application had included a complicated set of transactions that involved a merger with Electrohome Ltd. of Kitchener and a swap of assets with CHUM Limited that made Baton the majority shareholder.[29] In early November, Ivan Fecan, President of Baton, was named President and Chief Executive Officer of CTV.[30]

Baton achieved a major objective when it gained regulatory approval to become the controlling shareholder of the network. The CRTC decision relating to Baton and CTV, as reported in the *Globe and Mail*, noted: "CTV needs to have a solid controlling shareholder who can bring synergies and economies of scale to its operation and get rid of the duplicated infrastructure that exists in the organization, so that there will be money available to put into the production of Canadian programming."[31] Douglas Bassett has explained: "We always believed and I personally always believed that the network could be operated more efficiently and get better programming with having a majority owner who owned affiliates.... But it [CTV] didn't own anything. It was a 40 hour service. No stations. So if Murray Chercover when he was president or John Cassaday...wanted to go out and buy the rights to the Olympic games, they had to go to the affiliates and say 'can we get time from you?' And sometimes they would say 'yes,' sometimes they would say 'no.'"[32]

Ivan Fecan has explained that the network had to be placed on a sounder footing: "We think CTV needs to be strengthened because I think the combination of duplicate and triplicate infrastructures through the system is drawing money off the screen and out of shareholders and into infrastructure which I don't think benefits anyone." Clearly Fecan has emphasized the importance of getting greater financial resources into programming: "At the end of the day, all television is about programming. The sales people will tell you it's about sales and they're right. However if you have got nothing to watch, you've got nothing to sell." As Fecan explained, "The problem with all of this duplicate infrastructure is it drains resources away from being competitive on the screen."[33] Looking to the future, Laura Eggertson wrote in the *Globe and Mail*: "Baton will present further details of its programming promises in a new business plan to be presented to the CRTC when CTV's licence comes up for renewal in 1999."[34]

The voting interest in CTV held by WIC Television Ltd., CF-12 Inc., and Moffatt Communications Limited also passed to Baton on November 12, 1997.[35] Still another development occurred early in 1998 that created some uncertainty surrounding the private TV network. The future of CTV again became a matter of discussion when Eaton's of Canada Ltd. decided to sell its 41 percent interest in Baton Broadcasting Inc. through a public offering. In effect, this development meant that CTV was without a controlling shareholder. Electrohome Ltd. of Kitchener emerged as the largest shareholder in Baton. Robert Brehl explained in *The Globe and Mail*: "There had been an agreement between the Eatons and Electrohome to control Baton."[36]

Whatever its past struggles, the CTV television network, through its structural realignment, appeared ready to face a new era in Canadian broadcasting where a growing number of specialty TV services provided viewers with expanded choice. When CTV began broadcasting in the early 1960s, its main opposition was the state-owned CBC. In the new millennium, CTV, as an instrument of public policy, faced the challenge of providing a sufficiently attractive general-interest network service that would allow it to remain competitive in a greatly changed broadcasting universe where narrowcasting seemed to be in the ascendant.

The study of CTV Television Network Limited raises several questions for discussion about the ownership and role of private networks in the Canadian broadcasting system, the responsibilities of the private broadcast industry, and the extent to which Canadian broadcasting policies can continue to attempt to nurture cultural enlightenment. At the beginning of 1998 the future of the CTV network was again debated even though Baton had managed to attain control of the network just a few months earlier. Once again the question of the network's ownership had arisen given the decision by the Eaton family to sell its 41 percent stake in Baton. Moreover CTV continued to face heavy competition from CanWest Global Communications Corp. which, for a long period, had expressed interest in the establishment of a third network in Canada besides CTV and CBC. However, in early February 1998, the CRTC rejected the notion of a third English television network in Canada preferring instead to see more funds spent on Canadian content such as drama.[37]

A second topic for debate would be the overall responsibilities that the private industry has in its attempt to meet the public policy goals established for the Canadian broadcasting system generally. Private broadcasters have to adhere to Canadian content requirements and often to conditions of licence which are related to expenditure requirements that the CRTC can impose on broadcasters. The question of broadcast regulation and the relationship of the regulator to the private industry is a matter that has created controversy in the past. Specifically, has the CRTC been too lenient in its regulation of private broadcasters? Should the private industry be expected to make a greater contribution to Canadian programming?

In the age of death stars, the future utility of Canadian broadcasting policies and the goals of the *Broadcasting Act* are worth examination. With numerous television channels to be available through direct-to-home-broadcast satellites, will federal legislation be able to continue to have Canadian broadcasting, whether it be the public or private sector, serve as vehicles for cultural uplift? Indeed both sectors of the Canadian broadcasting system would appear to face major challenges in the future.

NOTES

1. For a discussion of the role of the BBG, see Andrew Stewart and William H. N. Hull, *Canadian Television Policy and the Board of Broadcast Governors, 1958–1968* (Edmonton: The University of Alberta Press, 1994). See also Khayyam Z. Paltiel and Larry G. Kjosa, "The Structure and Dimensions of Election Broadcasting in Canada" in *Jahrbuch des Öffentlichen Rechts der Gegenwart* (Neue Folge/Band 19, Tübingen), 355–358.

2. Arthur Weinthal, personal interview, 15 Nov. 1994.

3. Canada, *Report of the Committee on Broadcasting,* (Fowler Committee) Catalogue S2- 1765 (Ottawa: Queen's Printer, 1965): 375.

4. National Archives of Canada (NAC), MG31, A17-86-548, Spencer Caldwell Papers, Volume 3 of 3, File Caldwell Spencer—1934–1936, "Spencer Wood Caldwell," 3–4. This article in the Caldwell papers is believed to have been written by Kay Kritzwiser in 1957 but never submitted for publication.

5. Rae Corelli, "Spencer Caldwell, THE MAN WHO CHALLENGES CBC'S TV SUPREMACY," [Toronto] *The Star Weekly Magazine* 13 January 1962: 7.

6. Canada, Canadian Radio-television and Telecommunications Library, Board of Broadcast Governors, *Announcement April 21, 1961, Applications for Television Networks*, 000179.

7. Murray Chercover, personal interview, 3 Mar. 1992.

8. Stewart and Hull, *Canadian Television,* 76.

9. Gordon Keeble, personal interview, 17 Aug. 1993.

10. John Bassett, personal interview, 24 Mar. 1993.

11. Ibid.

12. Ibid.

13. Gordon Keeble Papers (privately held), "Proposal - (Confidential), from CTV to the affiliates," October 4, 1962, 10.

14. Ibid.

15. CTV Television Network Ltd. Archives (Toronto), internal memo, Vin Dittmer to S.W. Caldwell, June 17, 1964.

16. *Report of the Committee on Broadcasting* (Fowler Committee), 239, 238.

17. Ibid., 236.

18. NAC, RG 100, B49, Mf. M-3087, Board of Broadcast Governors Hearing, Ottawa, CTV Television Network Ownership Transfer, February 23, 1966, 67, 58.

19. The commission became known as the Canadian Radio-television and Telecommunications Commission in 1976. See Mary Vipond, *The Mass Media in Canada*, revised edition (Toronto: James Lorimer & Company, Publishers, 1992), 173.

20. Canada, Canadian Radio-television Commission, *Public Announcement, Decision CRTC 73-44* (Ottawa, January 22, 1973),1, 3.

21. John Bassett, personal interview, 24 Mar. 1993.

22. Canada, Canadian Radio-television and Telecommunications Commission, Public Hearing, Application by Nation's Capital Television Incorporated, *Transcript of Proceedings*, volume 2 (Hull: January 27, 1988) 360.

23. Ray Peters, personal interview, 23 Jan. 1996.

24. Canada, *Report of the Task Force on Broadcasting Policy* (Caplan-Sauvageau Report) Catalogue C022-68-1-1986E (Ottawa: Supply and Services Canada, 1986): 117.

25. Canada, Canadian Radio-television and Telecommunications Commission, *Decision CRTC 87-200, CTV Television Network Limited* (Ottawa 24 March 1987): 13.

26. Canada, Canadian Radio-television and Telecommunications Commission, *Decision CRTC 94-33, CTV Television Network Ltd.*, (Ottawa: 9 February 1994): 3.

27. Douglas Bassett, personal interview, 24 Mar. 1997.

28. Canada, Canadian Radio-television and Telecommunications Commission, *Decision CRTC 94-33, CTV Television Network Ltd.*, (Ottawa: 9 February 1994): 5–6.

29. Laura Eggertson, "Ottawa okays Baton's Control of CTV," [Toronto] *The Globe and Mail* 29 August 1997: B4.

30. Brenda Dalglish, "Baton Broadcasting Appoints Fecan to Top CTV Job," [Toronto] *The Financial Post* 8 November 1997: 7.

31. Eggertson, "Ottawa okays," B4.

32. Douglas Bassett, personal interview, 24 Mar. 1997.

33. Ivan Fecan, personal interview, 1 May 1997.

34. Eggertson, "Ottawa okays," B4.

35. Canada, Canadian Radio-Television and Telecommunications Commission, Industry Analysis Division, *CTV television, chart/organigramme #7*.

36. Robert Brehl, "Eatons Unload Baton Stake," [Toronto] *The Globe and Mail* 28 January 1998: B1.

37. Robert Brehl, " CRTC Pushes More Canadian Content," [Toronto] *The Globe and Mail* 7 February 1998: A1.

BUDGETS AND GOVERNING ARRANGEMENTS: The Political Functions of Budgets

Hugh Mellon

PREAMBLE

Governments provide annual budgets accompanied by extensive reporting of financial details. New students of public administration might at first be tempted to move on to other more apparently dynamic topics. This would be a mistake of major proportions. Budgetary politics influence events and developments throughout the political system. Their significance is evident when we look at such important yet seemingly diverse matters as intergovernmental bargaining, theories of macroeconomic management, or the parliamentary conventions of responsible government. Central to this paper are these assertions—that government budgets are fundamentally important to the conduct of modern government, and that their stature can be displayed by surveying some of the critical roles they play. What follows is a discussion of governments and budgeting with elaboration of these fundamental assumptions. Extensive supporting references will be made to events and trends from post–World War II Canadian politics.

INTRODUCTION

It is often popularly accepted that governments by their very nature have problems managing money. Many, at one time or another, have felt the urge to echo the sentiments of Adam Smith (1723–90), the early apostle of the market system, who declared, "It is the highest impertinence and presumption, therefore, in kings and ministers, to pretend to watch over the economy of private people, and to restrain their expense....They [kings and ministers] are themselves always, and without exception, the greatest spendthrifts in the society."[1] Reference to mountains of accumulated government debt and associated debt servicing costs lends support to Smith's depiction. Despite the rhetorical power of such an observation and the evidence ready at hand, there is more to the picture than profligate spending.

There is evidence that public finances in many jurisdictions are being reined in. The emerging trend in federal and provincial government budgets is the search for balanced budgets. Accumulated debts will persist, but momentum is building to begin paying these amounts down. Arguments about the pace of restraint and the ranking of debt repayment as a government priority are abundant, but there is a widespread move away from the reliance upon deficit financing which governments subscribed to over past decades. In fact, there is an emerging controversy about how federal and provincial governments should allocate their surpluses once annual budgets are balanced.

Budget making and financial administration are major (some might say "the major") challenges for any government. In his guidebook, *The Language of Canadian Politics,* McMenemy defines "budget and budgetary process" as follows: "The establishment of the government's priorities for spending among existing and proposed programs by the public administration [the bureaucracy] and the cabinet and its committees, with parliamentary scrutiny and approval. The process is complicated, and varies in detail among jurisdictions."[2] Part of the complexity is that money is not only spent, it also has to be raised. Taxation and other ways of raising money as well as a collection system must also be contemplated. Furthermore, the impact of government budget making goes far beyond administrative calculation of government financial needs and available revenues. The public sector in Canada is sizeable and any decisions involving it will ripple through the broader economy and society. There are political pressures, economic impacts, and socioeconomic considerations at work simultaneously. Budgetary issues surface in a huge variety of settings—the establishment of tax levels, the introduction of the federal Goods and Services Tax (GST), public discussion replete with political slogans for tax cutting or increased government spending, quiet lobbying on the part of organized interests for preferred policies, assorted expenditures by government agencies, etc. Capturing such diversity is a mammoth task for there is decentralization and an extensive array of actors (taxpayers, different levels of government, different agencies of government at each level, government and opposition politicians, bureaucrats, etc.) in an almost limitless number of settings. Other elements of budgetary politics also come into play. Past deficits mean that accumulated government debt and borrowing costs are on the agenda. Deficits, debt levels, potential repayment schedules, and the share of overall government expenditures accounted for by debt servicing all merit consideration. So, too, do the assessments by accountants, credit rating agencies, think tanks, media pundits, and interest groups of the impact of any particular budget or set of budgets on the state of the national or provincial economy.

Looking beyond slogans and caricatures of government financial habits involves looking at a broad range of issues which span the boundaries of political science, administrative studies, and public finance. The list of pertinent inquiries would be long, including, but not limited to, study of how different governments in different settings carry out their budget preparations, theories of budget making, financial control systems, program and budgetary evaluation strategies, interest group reactions, press coverage, the impact of party platforms and preferred ideologies, economic modelling of connections between government budgets and economic conditions and indicators, and recognition and assessment of the diverse roles played by government budgets and the differing audiences involved. Any of these or other related topics clearly merit further exploration and commentary. Responding to all of them is equally clearly beyond the scope of a single essay. This paper will opt to pursue the last of the listed inquiry possibilities—the diverse roles played by federal and provincial government budgets and the assorted audiences associated with each of the roles under investigation.

Budgets are multifaceted entities which are closely watched by numerous groups with their own interests. Recognition of the resulting complexities produces a deeper understanding of the budgetary challenges facing any government. Government budgets will be looked at in terms of the roles they play within the political system. One role is their contribution to the parliamentary conventions of responsible government. A government unable to oversee passage of its budgetary strategy will have significant difficulty maintaining its stature within Parliament. The second purpose is the control function played by budgets. Governments have publicly defined their spending and taxation proposals. Upon receiving parliamentary approval for their budget a government is not free to mislead the public or to ignore the conditions of their parliamentary approvals. This allows for evaluation of administrative and management performance which can range from review of particular expenditures and areas of expenditure to broad assessments of a government's overall performance. A third function is the involvement of government budgets within the workings of Canada's federal constitutional order and its fiscal dimensions. Canada has an involved system of fiscal federalism where large sums of money flow across governmental boundaries. The fourth political purpose of budgets relates to the interconnection between budgetary direction and macroeconomic management. Governments utilize large amounts of resources and the pattern of public sector spending and revenues has a resulting impact on business and commercial activity. Finally, there is the use of the budget by governments as a vehicle for defining a policy agenda or initiative. Budget speeches receive major publicity and arguments made here are widely reported. This list is not meant to be conceptually exhaustive, but rather to serve as an educational guide to vitally important roles played by budgets within the political system.

GOVERNMENTS, BUDGETS, AND THE CONVENTIONS OF RESPONSIBLE GOVERNMENT

The operation of Canada's parliamentary system is based upon the notion of a cabinet or ministry able to govern by virtue of their retention of support among the members of parliament. According to Andrew Heard, "the most important rule of our parliamentary system holds that a government must resign or call an election when it loses the confidence of the legislature."[3] This is known as the confidence convention. Franks points out that this serves as a check on the "enormous centralized powers of the cabinet," and that "Parliament, and particularly the House of Commons, is consequently the central forum for discussion about the use and abuse of political power, and is the source of the legitimacy and authority of a government."[4] Political power is obviously a complex matter with multiple aspects for consideration. A key element of democratic government is the ability to spend money raised from others through a variety of means, most notably public taxation. Governments spend sizeable amounts of funds for a huge assortment of reasons. They require vast resources to operate, hence the raising of money is an ongoing preoccupation. Taxation involves not simply the contribution of money by people, it also entails the implementation of a regulatory apparatus to oversee collection and the threat of sanctions for nonpayment. Monies raised by the government go toward a Consolidated Revenue Fund which is allocated to differing governmental uses through the budgetary process. Only the cabinet can introduce expenditure or taxation bills. The need of the executive (the cabinet is the functioning political executive as opposed to the largely symbolic role of the monarch) for funds provides the House of Commons with an important capability. In the words of John Stewart, "Without the consent of the House no money may be withdrawn from the Consolidated Revenue Fund for any new purpose. Without its consent no taxes may be imposed to recruit the Fund."[5]

Ascertaining who has the confidence of the House is usually made relatively easy through the existence of disciplined political parties and the frequent existence of majority governments. Members of parliament from any given party vote overwhelmingly alongside their partisan colleagues and in the event of a majority government this virtually guarantees the support of a majority of the House. Under these circumstances cabinets can dominate the public agenda and constrain the independence of ordinary elected MPs. Where no party has a majority of seats in the House, matters become more complicated. Parties struggle to gain ascendancy and interparty bargaining can be intense. Governments must maintain election readiness while continuing to govern. The twin challenges of competing for public support while working on the tough choices of governing, are intense and ongoing through the minority period. There is much that might be said about the constitutional principles at stake and their implications for our governing institutions, but three points are immediately relevant. First, governments must retain the support of a majority in the House of Commons. Second, it is this support which allows a government to raise and spend funds. Third, it is during minority periods that the ability of a government to retain the support of the House is most tested.

One of the key tests for any government is having their budget approved. If a government is unable to persuade the House of the merits of their overall financial plan then it is highly unlikely that they have sufficient support to remain in office. Passing or failing to pass the annual budget is thus a test of the confidence of the House in the government of the day. This has been a pivotal issue at various points in Canadian political history. Reference to two examples illustrates the central link between a budget and the confidence convention which guides parliamentary life. The examples relate to the fall of two Progressive Conservative governments, those of John Diefenbaker and Joe Clark. They are not the only examples of government defeats based upon budgetary disagreements, but they do illustrate two sides of the coin, namely, defeat emanating from failure to present a clear budgetary plan and defeat due to disagreement with a clearly formulated, yet controversial, set of budgetary proposals. In neither case did the government want to be removed, but in both cases they were.

From 1958 until 1962 John George Diefenbaker and the Progressive Conservatives ruled the country with a huge electoral majority. They held 208 of the 265 seats while the Liberals and the Cooperative Commonwealth Federation (forerunner of the NDP) were left with 49 and 8 seats respectively. In the ensuing election of 18 June 1962, the Conservatives were reduced to 116 with the Liberals and the NDP having 100 and 19 respectively. The Opposition parties were joined by a resurgent Social Credit Party which won 30 seats, 26 of which were in Quebec. By 1962 Diefenbaker's charisma and voter appeal had dramatically evaporated for many of Canada's urban dwellers. According to J. Murray Beck, "What Diefenbaker had done was to divide Canada along rural-urban lines more than had ever been done before. Almost everything about him had contributed to this type of cleavage."[6] As a government, Diefenbaker and his parliamentary allies struggled fitfully with issues related to Quebec, macroeconomic management, monetary policy, foreign policy, and the growth of modern social challenges. The disastrous 1962 result left the Conservatives battered and divided. Dissension within party ranks arose over Diefenbaker's indecision, his isolation from the growing population of urban and young voters, and the anti-American direction of his foreign policy.[7] Denis Smith has observed that by January 1963, the "Cabinet had entered a period of terminal breakdown."[8] A central part of this breakdown was reluctance to put before the House of Commons a complete government budget to respond to contemporary concerns and issues. This led to growing complaints in the House and general public impatience. Diefenbaker's ability to govern was dependent upon the willingness of the Social Credit and their leader Robert Thompson to support him. By early February Thompson's patience had worn thin and he informed the government via informal channels that several conditions had to be met; two of the key ones related to the introduction of a budget and up-to-date government spending proposals.[9] The decay of the government continued unabated and Thompson felt compelled to move against it. Lester Pearson and the Liberals moved non-confidence in the government. Thompson then "moved an amendment to the Liberal motion framed around the Social Credit conditions... ."[10] Both the Social Credit amendment and the Liberal motion passed 142–111. This led to "singing, yelling, and paper-throwing while the prime minister made his barely audible announcement that he would go to the governor general the next day."[11] The government was defeated and a new election was held in April of that year.

In May of 1979 Joe Clark and the Progressive Conservative Party edged out the incumbent Liberal government of Pierre Trudeau to achieve a minority government. The seat totals were PC 136, Lib. 114, NDP 26, and Créditiste 6, all out of a total House of Commons of 282 seats. While the Conservatives had a clear lead over the Liberals, they remained several seats short of majority status, 142. Nonetheless they took office and Clark indicated that he and his cabinet colleagues would govern with the same resolution as if they had in fact possessed a majority. Clark and the Conservatives encountered serious debates over the future of Canadian energy and economic policies. Their determination lasted until December 1979, when Finance Minister John Crosbie introduced the government budget. The budget soon came under attack with one provision in particular serving as a lightning rod for discontent, an 18 cents per gallon ($.04/L) increase in the tax on gasoline. Bob Rae was the federal NDP's finance critic at the time and in his memoirs Rae recalls the negative reaction. With regard to the government's strategy Rae notes that "Crosbie clearly felt he needed a tax hike to deal with the deficit problem, and chose the most direct way to get it: a consumption tax that could also double as a tool for conservation."[12] Rae and his fellow New Democrats were troubled by fears related to collection of money to pay for implementation of a Tory election promise to make mortgage interest tax deductible. For his part, Crosbie has also published his memoirs and he reminds modern-day readers of the positive elements of his budget and the applause it generated from assorted groups and commentators including "the business and financial community."[13] Yet, he too acknowledges that "the general public was far more negative because of the eighteen-cent-a-gallon increase."[14]

Events in 1979 were far different from those in 1963. The Clark government had confidently presented a budgetary direction. Political manoeuvring was certainly present. Discussions had been conducted between certain Progressive Conservatives and the Créditistes, a Quebec-based offshoot of the Social Credit forces. These conversations had not progressed, but the Créditiste leader had communicated to the Conservatives that their support for the budget could be obtained "only if the Government committed all the revenues from the 18-cents-per-gallon excise-tax increase to the Government of Quebec or to energy projects in Quebec."[15] There was also talk of a call for an increased energy tax credit, but it was all to no avail. Clark rejected the offers of support counting on disarray among the Liberals in the search for a leader to replace the now-dethroned Trudeau. This was a political miscalculation of tremendous proportions. The Créditistes opted to abstain and several

Progressive Conservative MPs had not found their way back to Ottawa in time. By a vote of 139–133 the House voted no confidence in the budget. Clark rose and declared that the vote had to be understood "as a question of confidence."[16] On the next day Governor General Ed Schreyer accepted Clark's call for dissolution of Parliament and the calling of a new election. It was an election the Conservatives would lose and recriminations against Clark's tactics and leadership would plague him until his defeat by Brain Mulroney in a 1983 leadership convention.

Budgets reflect the broad spending and revenue plans of a government. Inability to win approval for such fundamentally important matters is commonly understood as indicative of a lack of confidence in the government. Failure to maintain this confidence can be fatal. Losses on individual taxation or expenditure votes is not necessarily so fatal, though. In 1968 the Liberal government of Lester Pearson was absorbed in the race to succeed Mr. Pearson. Poor House leadership one evening led to defeat of a tax bill. Pearson counterattacked, arguing that this one vote should not on its own be seen as a vote of no-confidence; "he secured the adjournment of the House for a couple of days and then returned to introduce a motion of confidence, which was carried."[17] During the adjournment the Liberals succeeded in turning the tide in their favour.

With regard to budgets and the functioning of responsible parliamentary government there are several main considerations. The parliamentary executive or cabinet is responsible to the House of Commons and must maintain the confidence of a majority of MPs to remain as the government. A vitally important indicator of this confidence is the ability to pass a budget and overall budgetary plan. Votes on segments of this plan may not be the ultimate determinant of a government's survival, but they too are important. A government unable to organize a coherent budget or one pushing an unpopular budget must count MPs very carefully, especially if they have only a minority government status.

BUDGETS AS A GOVERNING CONTRACT

Presentation and passage of a budget is an important parliamentary event, part of the cut and thrust of partisan rivalry and jockeying for public approval. This is central to our institutional order. However, relatively few budgets result in life or death parliamentary struggles for a government's survival. Far more common is use of a budget as an ongoing check or basis for evaluating government performance and legitimacy. Budgets and the associated debates and understandings serve as control mechanisms. This example of the role played by budgets is similar to a conception found in Aaron Wildavsky's work on American budgetary politics. Wildavsky suggests that among the various ways of conceptualizing budgets "a budget may be regarded as a contract. Congress and the president promise to supply funds under specified conditions, and the agencies agree to spend the money in ways that have been agreed upon."[18] Budgets can be understood as representing an implied contract among the various elements of the political system. Part of that contract is to the electorate. Also present are connections to Parliament, to the multiple agencies of government, and to holders of government debt instruments, investors who have purchased government securities.

Governments are expected to recognize their underlying responsibility to the citizenry to act within spending and taxation commitments. This serves to control the behaviour of politicians and governments. An administrative-bureaucratic culture encompassing such fundamental administrative values as openness, transparency, reliability, written records, and honesty would serve to complement these expectations of politicians and governments. Funds allocated for specified purposes need to be spent accordingly. Raising revenues must be done in accordance with statutory guidelines. Likewise there is a normative expectation of reasonable disclosure by the government. Failure to abide by what the prevailing political culture regards as appropriate can produce political problems such as a loss of credibility. The public has become accustomed to political manoeuvring and obfuscation, but even amid the voter cynicism there are sometimes events which seem to have strayed too far over the line, even for political life. For an illustration of this possibility there is the case of British Columbia around the time of the 1996 provincial election. In late April of that year the NDP provincial government had introduced a budget and then called an election. Budgetary projections seemed buoyant; a surplus appeared imminent. Glen Clark and the NDP went on to win the election and retain office. Into late June the Clark government still seemed to be signalling a budgetary surplus. Their message was not borne out by events and in early July the press reported that "the NDP government's first balanced budget has turned out to be wishful thinking, and British Columbia will likely end up more than $200-million in the red for the 1995–1996 fiscal year when all the accounts are settled, Finance Minister Andrew Petter confirmed yesterday."[19] Opposition parties cried foul, voters complained, and moves to recall selected NDP provincial legislative members commenced. A similar example may be drawn from the 1990 Ontario provincial election campaign when the Peterson Liberals indicated that provincial finances were so healthy that tax cuts would be possible. Imagine the surprise of voters and of the incoming NDP government of Bob Rae when shortly after the election a large provincial deficit was uncovered.

The interests of Parliament are protected in several ways. Among them are the provisions for open parliamentary debate and detailed scrutiny by committees of the House of Commons and the Senate, the ability to vote no confidence in a government due to their financial management, the opportunity for formal oral or written questions to be asked of the cabinet, the access to information opportunities (discussed elsewhere in this volume by Bennett and Bayley), and the evaluation work done by the Auditor General. MPs are busy people with hectic schedules. Their ability or inclination to become expert in detailed budgetary matters is a source of concern. For this and other reasons there is great reliance attached to the work of the Auditor General, an office which answers directly to Parliament. It is not under the control of the government of the day and can thus speak freely about lapses in financial and budgetary administration. The mandate of the Auditor General applies not simply to auditing in a limited technical manner, but instead extends to broader assessments which range into questions of value received for money spent and the overall effectiveness of particular programs. His or her commentary may, on occasion, lead to tighter financial controls and/or program reassessment. Take, for example, the criticisms voiced by the Auditor General's office of "Revenue Canada for its handling of two family trusts, later identified as belonging to members of Montreal's Bronfman family. The family shifted $2-billion worth of Seagram Co. Ltd. stock to the United States in 1991 without paying capital gains tax."[20] When these criticisms were made public the issue became a focus of government study. As this essay goes to print in February of 1998, the federal government is contemplating a departure tax to deal with similar situations in future.

The departments, commissions, crown corporations, and other agencies of government have budgets assigned to them by cabinet and operate with varying degrees of autonomy.

Implicit in Wildavsky's contract notion is the sense that in return for budgeted funds, the organizational units will adhere to budgetary guidelines and reporting requirements. These reporting requirements involve the ministerial responsibility principle (discussed elsewhere in this volume by Sutherland and Mitchell). Setting departmental budgetary allocations is often one of the most controversial challenges facing any government. Departments compete against each other for scarce funds and quarrelling cabinet ministers have to protect their organizational interests while comparing the relative worth of such disparate items as search and rescue equipment, assistance for the destitute, cultural promotion, education, and court administration. The resulting quarrels have been intense in recent years as government cutbacks and restructuring efforts have been used to deal with debt-related problems. In the case of the federal government there was a concentrated program review exercise which was commenced in 1994 by the Chrétien government. Reports[21] on this experience have revealed the departmental competition which was sparked as senior administrators attempted to protect bureaucratic "turf" and the attached budgetary allocations. Ministers also have more personal political motivations to protect and promote spending levels, particularly in locations relevant to their potential reelection. As Bakvis and MacDonald remind us, "most ministers cleave strongly to the belief that such expenditures will improve the odds. Both ministers and constituents realize there is an extra cachet associated with being a minister in terms of doing good things for the riding ...."[22]

There are also close connections between government budgets and those who hold government securities and those credit rating agencies who assess borrowers. The federal and provincial governments have collectively and individually amassed a large debt. Financing this requires borrowing and the better your credit rating the better the terms. As a borrower you become very concerned over how the financial and investment communities assess your budgetary conditions. One of the constraints which results from high levels of indebtedness is dependency upon the reactions of this community. Impressing them with reduced debt levels and budgetary streamlining may win improved ratings and hence reduced borrowing costs. Those in the financial and investment community closely monitor financial performance and budget statements. It should not be surprising that Paul Martin's first budget was accompanied by extensive efforts at consultation with concerned groups. Attention to reactions has continued. Shortly after the introduction of the 1998–99 federal budget, Prime Minister Chrétien made a point of travelling to New York to speak on behalf of the government's financial performance and the moves toward a balanced budget.

There are multiple groups who regard the budget as a control upon government performance and who understand the budget statement as an implied contract from the government of the day. Budget numbers are keenly watched by an assortment of political actors. These actors all have different and often competing interests. Credit rating agencies look to see reduced debt and clear financial controls. Purchasers of government bonds want security of return. Ministers have to respect the austerity agenda set by their leader and finance minister, while dealing with the political incentives to protect budgets and spending commitments. Opposition MPs are on the look-out for evidence of misspending and deviation from budgeted commitments. Amid the differing perspectives of these and other political actors there is the shared sense that the annual budget should be honoured by the government. Their actions have been guided by its commitments and capricious or hidden variation from budgeted promises will engender controversy as shown by the earlier noted B.C. and Ontario examples.

GOVERNMENT BUDGETS AND THE DYNAMICS OF FEDERALISM

Among the many elements of Finance Minister Paul Martin's budget of February 1998, was the promised introduction of several measures related to postsecondary education. Among these was the announcement of a Millennium Scholarship Fund to begin in the year 2000. The Fund is to offer scholarships to more than 100 000 students annually and will operate with a $2.5 billion endowment. In support of these and other proposals the federal government stressed their perception of a national problem and the need for resolute action. Martin declared that broadening access to education would enhance equality and social mobility; "There is no better way to reduce the gap between rich and poor, no surer way to widen the mainstream, no more meaningful way to reduce the numbers of those left behind, and no better way to provide a higher quality of life for Canadians."[23] Yet, on the day following Martin's speech, *The Globe and Mail* reported that "Several officials privately conceded yesterday that the budget's language about the millennium fund has been toned down because of Quebec's concerns, particularly in the wake of last week's negative reaction to Ottawa's Supreme Court of Canada reference [dealing with the constitutionality of separation]."[24] The Quebec government, supported by many from across the province's partisan spectrum, had opposed the federal government's initiative of asking the Supreme Court to delineate the legalities of potential provincial separation. Many in Quebec questioned whether such a matter was appropriate for the courts given its political character.

Other provinces were also troubled by the federal announcements related to education. Their reaction was fuelled by several sources. One is the distribution of powers within Canada's federal order. Jurisdictionally the provincial governments have the vast bulk of authority over this subject. Ottawa has evaded this kind of situation (provincial jurisdictional authority coupled with a federal government urge to implement something in spite of jurisdictional barriers) by relying upon their "spending power," the expenditure of federal funds via cost-sharing agreements or fiscal transfers to help accomplish what would be difficult, if not unconstitutional, for them to accomplish directly. The more important source of provincial annoyance was consternation over a federal call to action on education despite a prolonged period of federal cuts to the transfers which helped the provinces respond to the expensive policy fields like education and health care. Postsecondary education had been covered by the Established Programs Financing (EPF) arrangements which had also governed federal transfers for health, another field where the provinces have jurisdiction. The 1995 Martin budget had lumped EPF with the Canada Assistance Plan transfers (related to social welfare expenses) and created a block transfer, the Canada Health and Social Transfer (CHST). A block grant is one where Ottawa provides provinces with set blocks of money instead of agreeing to pay a certain proportion of ultimate program delivery costs. Stephen Brooks asserts that "the CHST institutionalizes the ad hoc freezes and caps on transfers that both Liberal and Tory [federal] governments imposed from the early 1980s."[25] Barker points out that "The CHST went further than merely limiting transfers—it actually reduced them."[26] Successive federal governments withdrew financial support from what were once shared subjects of interest, leaving the operational costs and daily responsibilities up to the provinces. Provincial politicians lament that it is too easy for federal governments to simply state that they will only pay a set amount rather than honour past commitments to pay a certain proportion of the actual operating costs. The February 1998 federal budget was met by grumbling from Ontario Finance Minister Ernie Eves who lamented that, while taxpayers had made the balanced budget possible, their views had been ignored. "Surely then, you can listen to what 73 per cent of Canadians have to say and what all 10 provinces unanimously have to say, and that is please restore some of the basic health care, the post-secondary funding, and they chose not to do that."[27] Bear in mind that the Millennium Scholarships will be offered by the federal government, not apparently through a shared-cost or other transfer. In response to such provincial protests, federal ministers stress their jurisdictional and institutional limitations. Bargaining with 10 provinces, each of whom has ultimate primary jurisdiction and operational control over what gets spent, is a daunting task. As a result, they argue that they exercise national leadership for provinces in recognizing national concerns and intervening selectively in the interests of what should be Canada-wide priorities. With reference to the Millennium Scholarships, the federal budget also reports that with regard to the board which will oversee the Scholarship fund, "The Council of Ministers of Education, Canada—representing provincial governments as well as the post-secondary education community—will have a role in identifying directors."[28] Time will tell how much consultation with provincial governments actually takes place.

Over the past 10 years, provincial and municipal governments have become increasingly concerned with "offloading," the transfer of spending responsibilities to more junior levels of government (federal to provincial, provincial to local). The term refers to instances where the transfer is done without cooperative consultation and it may in fact have been carried out unilaterally. If, for example, the federal government cuts back supports for language training for new immigrants, then provincial education budgets will feel the effect. Meanwhile, provincial cuts in a field like rural policing or firefighting will mean increased service costs and responsibilities for local level governments. Restraint at one level of government will have repercussions up and down the jurisdictional chain.

In the Scholarships case it will be up to future researchers to explore whether Canadians are witnessing national leadership or federal grandstanding and whether the provinces are justifiably annoyed by a credit-seeking federal government or are missing the big picture amid jurisdictional intransigence. This is admittedly a melodramatic depiction of the research challenge, but the example of the Millennium Scholarship does illustrate some of the stresses associated with the fiscal dimension of Canadian federalism. Within the Canadian federation jurisdictional authority, financial resources, and political leadership are neither coincident nor universally agreed upon. Take as an added example of intergovernmental rivalry, the field of taxation authority and the use of sales taxes. The *British North America Act* (also known as the *Constitution Act, 1867)* restricts the provincial governments to direct taxes only while the federal government can levy any kind of tax. Despite this delineation, provincial governments worked and schemed to be able to levy sales taxes, a form of taxation ordinarily considered as an indirect tax. Their labours were ultimately successful in persuading the Judicial Committee of the British Privy Council that they had found a way to adhere to the strict letter of the Constitution.[29]

Provincial success in breaching the jurisdictional barrier does not mean provincial accommodation of federal sales taxation initiatives, though. In the latter part of the 1970s Jean Chrétien was federal finance minister and he attempted to persuade his provincial counterparts to roll back sales taxes to spur on the national economy. Jacques Parizeau, his Quebec opposite number, turned the federal proposal on its ear for he "had reshaped an across-the-board sales-tax reduction into the elimination of tax in areas that would only help Quebec industry." In turn, federal officials "felt they had been suckered and betrayed...."[30] When the Mulroney government of the 1980s sought to reform the Manufacturers' Sales Tax and transform it into the GST, there were many expressions of provincial criticism. Furthermore, for a long time premiers stood far removed from federal proposals to blend or harmonize the GST with provincial sales taxes.

The division of powers and the differing financial resources available to the various governments (federal and provincial) make the process of governing complex and disaggregated. This reality may not always be peaceful, but Canada is a large and diverse country with underlying political and cultural tensions. Budgets at both levels of government help make the practice of federalism a reality oriented to Canadian circumstances, political culture, and intergovernmental relations. The use of budgetary instruments or remedies to facilitate a more smoothly working federation shows up in terms not only of transfers related to policy fields, but in other ways as well. Among the most prominent are the following. There are tax collection agreements whereby the federal government engages to collect taxes for interested provinces. Some provinces ultimately accepted sales tax harmonization. Quebec, New Brunswick, Nova Scotia, and Newfoundland all reached agreements with Ottawa. There is also the case of section 36 of the *Constitution Act, 1982,* which provides a commitment that Parliament and the provincial legislatures encourage comparable opportunities, economic development, and essential public services for all Canadians and that interprovincial equalization be supported. Equalization is now enshrined under section 36 (2). "Parliament and the government of Canada are committed to the principle of making equalization payments to ensure that provincial governments have sufficient revenues to provide reasonably comparable levels of public services at reasonably comparable levels of taxation." Equalization is a system of fiscal transfers paid out to the poorer provinces which is underwritten by the wealthier provinces (Ontario, British Columbia, and Alberta). There are also federal government payments for public services in the northern territories as well as for obligations to aboriginal peoples. In addition to all this it bears noting that provincial governments have responsibilities for local governments and in each province there is a network of transfer arrangements.

Both the federal and provincial governments are working to rein in budgetary deficits so as to turn attention to public services and debt repayment. Past years of deficit financing and debt payments have made interest payments a major budgetary expense. In 1998–99, 29.4 percent of federal expenditures are destined for interest payments.[31] Resulting federal restraint has forced provincial adaptation. Some have had to respond to this while also coping with the limits of being a have-not province. Among these, New Brunswick is an example of achievement. The provincial 1998–99 Budget (introduced in December of 1997), detailed the progress made in reaching annual surpluses and exhibiting financial discipline. Observers were reminded by provincial finance minister Edmond Blanchard that this had come despite cuts to federal transfers. He observed that "in 1986–1987, transfers from the federal government represented 40.1% of our total budgetary revenue. By 1998–1999, transfers are projected to decline to 36.2%."[32] Meanwhile for example, New Brunswick's eastern neighbour, Nova Scotia, is having a difficult time getting expenditures in order and there has been considerable budget unrest over the past decade.[33]

The ratio of federal transfers to provincial expenditures is an often used guide to estimating provincial dependence upon the federal treasury. As an indicator it is very helpful, but there are often political overtones accompanying its use. Declining numbers may, as in the New Brunswick example, be cited as restraint and blossoming provincial self-reliance. On other occasions such a trend may be cited as evidence of declining federal government interest in a province or region. There is now a growing trend for provincial governments, particularly in Quebec, to evaluate Canadian federalism in terms of the relative costs and benefits, that is to say the relationship between what the province contributes to the national government or economy compared to what the province receives from the federal government. Provincial grumbling over the costs of Confederation often runs into federal assertions of custodial responsibilities over the whole country which vary from year to year and region to region. Often dubbed the "battle of the balance sheets," such conflict continues without easy resolution. This is a complex area of calculation for a number of reasons such as—the difficulty of assigning a provincial value for benefits received from nationwide programs (national defence, the CBC), the arbitrary nature of the time period chosen for analysis (some years may feature major purchases such as ships or a large sum spent upon disaster relief), the difficulties posed by the mobility of taxpayers (How do we really assess how much a province contributed to the country?), and/or the problem of calculating the costs and benefits of governmental activity in areas which cross federal-provincial boundaries (the environment, tourism promotion, or immigration and resettlement), etc.

Such calculations would, of course, become critically important in the event of discussions over provincial separation from Canada. Matters such as distribution of responsibilities for debt, currency arrangements, cross-border trade, and national government assets within the discontented province would all need resolution. Robert Young has done the most sustained analysis of such thorny questions and he urges Canadians to remember the global pressures which will descend upon them as soon as separation seems imminent. Fluctuations in the value of Canadian currency, downgrades in the credit assessments for the two parts of the broken country, and the desire of investors to seek safe havens, will push events along faster than many may imagine. Canada is an open economy which is still coping with entrenched national and provincial government debt. Holders of this debt will demand proof of stability and repayment capacity. Interest rates may have to rise to keep investors interested in a divided Canada, thereby raising costs for domestic borrowers and homeowners. In the case of dealing with the national debt, for example, Young argues that "The domestic and international investment communities will require a quick resolution."[34]

Budgets and budgetary plans help shape Canadian federal arrangements. Steps taken at one level of government will reverberate across the constitutional divide, particularly in a country like Canada where the two levels are so intertwined. This would remain true even in the event of provincial separation. In fact, severe dislocations and adjustments would become the order of the day.

BUDGETARY DIRECTION AND MACROECONOMIC MANAGEMENT

Government actions have not only political and social, but also economic, consequences. The size of the public sector makes this virtually inevitable, but they also come about through the efforts of government to use budgetary direction to affect and shape the state of the national economy. This was seen most clearly in the post–World War II era through the application of Keynesian models which stressed that governments could play a role in guiding the overall economy. Since the latter 1970s this orientation has come under attack from those who question the ability of governments to respond to economic upsets in a timely or effective manner. In fact, there is the argument that the political context of government prevents the kind of fiscal responsibility which would allow solid economic management.

John Maynard Keynes was a brilliant British economist who directed his attention to the conundrum posed by the Great Depression of the 1930s. How could an economy which seemed so buoyant during the 1920s collapse and remain prone for such a long period of time? Earlier economists contended that the market functioned in a self-regulating fashion and that supply and demand would soon find a new equilibrium. Unfortunately the prolonged hardship and devastation of the Depression led many to question the ability of the economy to right itself. Keynes provided a new explanation as he "argued that equilibrium might in fact be reached at a point below full employment and that government could influence the level of economic activity through its spending and taxation policies."[35] Such a perspective offered governments an encouragement to monitor and fine-tune the economy. Fiscal policy, the use of government expenditure or taxation levels, became a primary federal government concern. Recession or depression could be countered through stimulus based on increased government spending and/or reductions in taxation. An overheated economy might be addressed through a reversal of these measures.

In the end few ever read the detailed analysis of Keynes, and the Depression was for many only brought to an end by World War II. Whatever the case, postwar governments imbibed the spirit of activism and intervened in the economy. Annual government budgets would come replete with references to overall economic conditions and the impact of the budget on the future of these conditions. There was a sustained postwar boom and the Keynesian-inspired orthodoxy became entrenched. However, by the mid to late 1970s unrest over stagflation (the combination of high rates of inflation coupled with high unemployment) and government debt levels began to surface.

Belief in the fine-tuning capacity of governments eroded in subsequent decades as a new, more right wing orthodoxy grew in strength. Politicians such as Margaret Thatcher of Great Britain and Ronald Reagan of the United States spoke out on the need for governments to cut back and unleash the marketplace. Governments were increasingly depicted as sluggish, captive to entrenched interests, and almost incapable of exercising restraint. This led to privatization of government functions, cuts to government spending, and a recasting of the role of government itself.

Governments and their budgets were now to set the scene for private-sector development. Formerly budget deficits and debts were understood as long-term investments in the country and were appropriate policy actions in times of recession. As the debt grew and governments seemed unable to restrain their growth, a change in outlook ensued. Debts were now characterized as drains on the national economy which forced up interest rates as governments struggled to borrow increasing amounts of money. As a result, they raised the cost of doing business as entrepreneurs had to compete with governments for capital and resources. Interventionist government was now portrayed as "big government," a force which stifled innovation and promoted psychological dependence upon the public sector. This revolution in intellectual and political orthodoxy had major repercussions upon governments all across Canada. As Peter Leslie asserts, "the primary fiscal goal is to balance the budget. The idea of using fiscal policy to achieve near-full employment without inflation ... has been all but abandoned...."[36] Compare this to the words of Paul Martin in his 1998 budget address to the House of Commons. "This budget will demonstrate that we have left the era of chronic deficits behind, that we are now on an irrevocable course to reduce the debt."[37]

The federal government has become absorbed in the task of reducing the size of government, promoting commercial development and job creation, and in being cautious about future spending commitments. Within this environment activist fiscal policy has passed from the scene. Government budgets still have importance for macroeconomic trends, but now the emphasis is upon creating the conditions for private sector growth.

BUDGETS AND DEFINING A POLICY AGENDA OR INITIATIVE

Budget speeches are closely monitored by domestic and international observers. Press coverage is extensive and the parliamentary calendar is designed to provide an extended debate upon the themes of the budget. These and other attributes make it a suitable venue for a government seeking to announce a major new program or policy direction. Budget addresses showcase finance ministers and prime ministers or premiers, thus facilitating their desires to get headlines and develop the "spins" on issues which they regard as politically desirable. Introduction within the budget permits easy reference to the associated resource needs and allows a government to show a skeptical opposition how the costs will be borne.

An example of a policy initiation twinned with a budget's introduction was the Trudeau government's National Energy Policy. The deputy minister (the senior bureaucrat advising the minister and directing the department's administration) of Finance, Ian Stewart, "saw that so many tax changes were being proposed, it made sense to merge the energy document with the Finance Department's annual budget."[38] More recently there is the case of the Millennium Scholarships and the 1998 Martin budget's references to educational development and student assistance.

While there are many good reasons to piggyback new policy or program announcements onto budget presentations, it remains true that introducing something at budget time is a high-stakes effort. Putting all your political eggs in the proverbial basket carries with it significant risks. An ill-considered proposal, a troublesome unfulfilled election promise, or angry interest group denunciation of budgetary proposals can all jeopardize credibility, a critically important political resource. Governments walk uneasily along the fine line between adherence to past promises and their understandings of new realities. Another risk for a government is loss of control over their preferred way of seeing issues and interpreting events.

Several readily available examples illustrate the problem of governments failing to navigate undamaged through the waters of public opinion at budget time. In their 1985 budget the Mulroney government called for partial deindexation of seniors' benefits. Coming after an 1984 election where the idea did not figure prominently and at a time when the debt did not yet rank highly with average Canadians as a priority, the Conservatives walked into a firestorm of protest. A retreat was effected, but control over the policy agenda was sacrificed and the effort to assert the importance of the debt issue was weakened. In the words of Edward Carmichael, it was one of a number of "costly dead-ends for a government groping for deficit-reducing strategies for which the electorate had little or no appetite."[39] The Liberal government elected in 1993 faced similar unrest as they failed to do away with the hated GST.

Perhaps the most damaged budget introduction of recent memory came in the Trudeau government's 1981 budget introduced by Finance Minister Allan J. MacEachen. Many of the budget's most novel features were overtaken by hostility from interest groups opposed to major changes. MacEachen and Stewart, his deputy, had developed innovations in regard to such issues as tax loopholes and business incentives, but they had not forged close associations with the business community. They were unable to mount an effective defence of their handiwork and the assault was on. "Day after day, newspaper headlines trumpeted the dissatisfactions of the business community. Night after night, on television news shows, representatives of interest groups, labour unions, and even charitable foundations could be heard lambasting the government ...."[40] Political retreat ensued and government credibility and agenda control were savaged.[41]

Because of the high stakes involved, modern governments approach budget preparations armed with surveys of public opinion, media strategies, and promotion efforts. In the case of the February 1998 federal budget, media preparations were detailed well in advance. Members of parliament had barely digested the budget's main themes when the public selling campaign commenced. Liberal MPs and cabinet ministers fled the Commons for a week to deliver the government's message. They were armed with a paid advertising campaign[42] and a common theme, promises of continued budget surpluses and selective government investments in human capital and education.

CONCLUSION

Budgets are about the finances of governments and the public sector, but they deserve to be read by an audience broader than simply accountants and economists. They have political implications and serve a variety of political functions. These functions touch upon most aspects of government. Examination of these functions and their implications will provide a richer understanding of budgetary politics and deepen the realization that government financial administration can never be seen as separate from political conflict and value choices.

The discussion found here should serve to prepare students for advanced debates about whether or not budgets and prevailing patterns of public sector resource allocation can be (or are) used to reinforce a particular social order and/or reflect ideological agendas. These debates arise in various ways but they share deep-seated concerns about social control, state-society relations, and the treatment by governments of groups within society. Two examples of this type of debate are briefly noted as a means of alerting readers to the existence and importance of such discussions. The first involves claims by feminist groups that their criticisms of the Mulroney government and its agenda produced budgetary cuts in funding for the political organization of women and for the programs they valued.[43] Evaluating such an assertion must involve reference to the trends in government expenditures as well as to the relations between the government in question and the proponents of a feminist agenda. Another example which can be cited arises from the literature that suggests that governments and their budgetary efforts are part of state structures which promote capitalist accumulation and maintain it through efforts at legitimation backed up by coercive capabilities. Leo Panitch, for example, has asserted that "one sees in terms of state functions that, from its very beginnings, the Canadian state has played a tremendously large role in fostering capital accumulation."[44] Evaluation of this and related themes touches upon many issues, one of which is the impact of government spending and taxation levels (budgetary variables) on capital accumulation and the distribution of societal wealth.

NOTES

1. Adam Smith, *The Wealth of Nations—Books I–III*, edited with an introduction by Andrew Skinner (Middlesex, England: Penguin Classics, 1977 reprint), 446.

2. John McMenemy, *The Language of Politics: A Guide to Important Terms and Concepts*, rev. ed. (Waterloo, Ontario: Wilfrid Laurier University Press, 1995), 15.

3. Andrew Heard, *Canadian Constitutional Conventions: The Marriage of Law and Politics* (Toronto: Oxford, 1991), 68.

4. C. E. S. Franks, *The Parliament of Canada* (Toronto: University of Toronto, 1987, reprinted 1989), 11.

5. John B. Stewart, *The Canadian House of Commons: Procedure and Reform* (Montreal: McGill-Queen's, 1977), 10.

6. J.M. Beck, *Pendulum of Power: Canada's Federal Elections* (Scarborough, Ontario: Prentice-Hall, 1968), 347.

7. See chapter 12 in Denis Smith's *Rogue Tory: The Life and Legend of John G. Diefenbaker* (Toronto: Macfarlane, Walter and Ross, 1995).

8. Ibid., 470.

9. Ibid., 480.

10. Ibid., 482.

11. Ibid., 485.

12. Bob Rae, *From Protest to Power: Personal Reflections on a Life in Politics* (Toronto: Viking, 1996), 70.

13. John Crosbie with Geoffrey Stevens, *No Holds Barred: My Life in Politics* (Toronto: McClelland and Stewart, 1997), 180. Crosbie also cites an article by an economic commentator which suggested that his budget was much more progressive than was commonly assumed in 1979.

14. Ibid., 180.

15. Jeffrey Simpson, *Discipline of Power: The Conservative Interlude and the Liberal Restoration* (Toronto: Personal Library, Publishers, 1980), 28–9.

16. Quoted in Simpson 36.

17. Heard, *Canadian Constitutional Conventions,* 71.

18. Aaron Wildavsky, *The New Politics of the Budgetary Process*, 2nd ed. (New York: Harper Collins, 1992), 2–3.

19. Craig McInnes, "Deficit Dashes NDP Pledge on B.C. Budget—Liberals Claim Government Hid Details in Bid to Win Recent Election Campaign," [Toronto] *Globe and Mail* 3 July 1996: A4.

20. Heather Scoffield, "Ottawa to Broaden Departure Tax," [Toronto] *Globe and Mail* 3 March 1998: B5.

21. Gene Swimmer, "An Introduction to Life Under the Knife," *How Ottawa Spends 1996–97: Life Under the Knife* (Ottawa: Carleton University Press, 1996), 15. The essays in this volume provide an excellent introduction into the program review exercise and the diverse experiences of various departments.

22. Herman Bakvis and David MacDonald, "The Canadian Cabinet: Organization, Decision-Rules, and Policy Impact," *Governing Canada: Institutions and Public Policy,* ed. Michael Atkinson (Toronto: Harcourt Brace, 1993), 68.

23. Hon. Paul Martin, "Budget Address to the House of Commons February 24, 1998," available through www.fin.gc.ca/budget98/speeche/speeche.txt: p. 7 of 21.

24. Edward Greenspon, "Millennium Scholarship Fund Details Scant," [Toronto] *Globe and Mail* 25 February 1998: A8.

25. Stephen Brooks, "Federal-Provincial Relations: The Decline of the New Centralism," *Canadian Public Policy: Globalization and Political Parties,* eds. Andrew F. Johnson and Andrew Stritch (Toronto: Copp Clark, 1997), 288.

26. Paul Barker, "Disentangling the Federation: Social Policy and Fiscal Federalism," *Challenges to Canadian Federalism,* eds. Martin Westmacott and Hugh Mellon (Scarborough: Prentice Hall Canada, 1998), 152.

27. "Budget Reaction," [Toronto] *Globe and Mail* 25 February 1998: A6.

28. "Budget Fact Sheet—Information: Canada Millennium Scholarships," available through www.fin.gc.ca/budget98/facte/millfte.html: p. 2 of 3.

29. Hugh Mellon, "The Complexity and Competitiveness of Fiscal Federalism: Blending the GST with Provincial Sales Taxes," *Challenges to Canadian Federalism*, eds. Martin Westmacott and Hugh Mellon (Scarborough: Prentice Hall, 1998), 159–60.

30. Graham Fraser, *PQ: René Lévesque and the Parti Québécois in Power* (Toronto: Macmillan, 1984), 165. Parizeau also sought for full compensation from the federal government for the tax cut.

31. Table titled "Where It's Spent," [Toronto] *Globe and Mail* 25 February 1998: A7.

32. *New Brunswick Annual Budget 1998–1999* (Fredericton: New Brunswick Dept. of Finance, 1997), 11.

33. For an interesting discussion of public finances in Nova Scotia see David M. Cameron, "Nova Scotia's Fiscal Challenge: Intergovernmental Relations and Structural Adjustment," in *Canada: The State of the Federation 1995,* eds. Douglas M. Brown and Jonathan W. Rose (Kingston: Institute of Intergovernmental Relations, 1995), 97–113.

34. Robert A. Young, *The Secession of Quebec and the Future of Canada* (Montreal: McGill-Queen's, 1995), 215.

35. Stephen Brooks and Andrew Stritch, *Business and Government in Canada* (Scarborough: Prentice-Hall, 1991), 46.

36. Peter Leslie, "The Economic Framework: Fiscal and Monetary Policy," *Canadian Public Policy: Globalization and Political Parties*, eds. Andrew F. Johnson and Andrew Stritch (Toronto: Copp Clark, 1997), 30.

37. Available from www.fin.gc.ca/budget98/speeche/speeche.txt: p. 1 of 21.

38. Christina McCall and Stephen Clarkson, *Trudeau and Our Times—Volume 2: The Heroic Delusion* (Toronto: McClelland and Stewart, 1994), 174.

39. Edward A. Carmichael, "The Mulroney Government and the Deficit," *Canada Under Mulroney: An End-of-Term Report* (Montreal: Véhicule Press, 1988), 229.

40. McCall and Clarkson, *Trudeau and Our Times,* 235.

41. See McCall and Newman, chapter 8, especially pp. 239-40.

42. William Walker, "Martin's Budget Sales Staff Hits the Road," [Toronto] *The Toronto Star* 26 February 1998: A6. For one of the few detailed studies of government advertising in Canada see Alasdair Roberts and Jonathan Rose, "Selling the Goods and Services Tax: Government Advertising and Public Discourse in Canada," *Canadian Journal of Political Science*, 28.2 (1995): 311-30.

43. See, for example, Sylvia Bashevkin, "Losing Common Ground: Feminists, Conservatives and Public Policy in Canada During the Mulroney Years," *Canadian Journal of Political Science*, 29.2 (June 1996): especially p. 236.

44. Leo Panitch, "The Role and Nature of the Canadian State," in *The Canadian State: Political Economy and Political Power*, ed. Leo Panitch (Toronto: University of Toronto, 1977), 9.

POLICY AND ADMINISTRATION— DEBATES IN EDUCATION: A Case Study

There have been many active controversies in recent years about matters of educational policy. Questions abound: What role should the state assume in the educational process? What should our educational goals be? Who should direct educational reforms? Is it time to consider how educational services are provided? The following group of readings offers food for reflection on these and other related issues.

Ronald Manzer explores the relationship between ideological outlooks and the role and place of education. The values and beliefs we bring to a discussion often lead us toward certain sets of assumptions. These assumptions then move us toward particular sets of policy recommendations. Manzer's commentary surveys how people working within different schools of thought see issues from varying perspectives. His insights should lead students to realize the significance of ideas and values, their connection to policy debates, and the linkage between ideological assumptions and the outlooks of people and groups on reform of policy and administration.

Peter Neary examines a particularly interesting instance of governmental intervention in the interest of making education available to deserving individuals. After World War II, intense efforts were made to affirm the contribution of members of the Canadian forces and to encourage their postwar opportunities. Actions were taken to improve educational accessibility and opportunity for this group of people who had given up much during the war. Neary's essay offers insights into an interesting case study and encourages continued inquiry into the historical record. This record contains much that merits ongoing consideration.

Paul Barker looks at the contemporary debate about the reform of educational services with particular reference to matters of administration and service delivery. These are issues of concern all over Canada and the United States. Across Canada provincial governments of diverse party affiliations have grappled with these challenges. How can educational programs best be organized amid shrinking budgets? Who should coordinate/direct the process? What can be learned from developments in other jurisdictions? Barker's essay offers useful background information on such topics and a framework for organizing ideas about administrative reform possibilities.

DISCUSSION QUESTIONS

1. Think back to your own high school education. What did you like best about your learning experiences? What complaints do you have? Why?

2. Should governments be involved in the provision of education? Why or why not?

3. Why do people with differing ideological outlooks see education issues from divergent perspectives? Why is this politically significant?

4. Which of the ideological outlooks surveyed by Manzer most appeals to you? Why?

5. Outline the measures taken by governments to make education more accessible to those involved with the war effort? Why were such affirmative steps taken?

6. Are there, or should there be, any parallels between the post–World War II experience and present day events? How accessible is education to contemporary students?

7. What are some of the alternatives to the way educational services are provided or administered? Do any particularly appeal to you? Why or why not?

8. What might or should guide decisions about the future of educational policy and administration? Why?

9. Why might debates about educational reform be affected by controversy over values or issues of political direction? How might these controversies be resolved?

POLITICAL IDEAS IN POLICY ANALYSIS: Educational Reform and Canadian Democracy in the 1990s

Ronald Manzer

In the 1990s, public education in Canada has been beset by political conflict and buffeted by policy change. School curricula have been attacked as grossly inadequate, both in the substance of what is taught and in the levels of attainment reached by the vast majority of young people in school. There are demands for high standards that focus on core academic subjects, formal assessments to measure educational results, and stricter accountability for educational results at every level of public education in classrooms, schools, and districts. At the same time there are harsh criticisms of the governance of public education, decrying the pathologies of educational bureaucracies and the selfishness of "special interests." Across the provinces, policies have been designed and implemented that purportedly will strengthen the teaching of core academic subjects, institute stricter procedures for evaluating outcomes, hold teachers and administrators more closely accountable for achieving predetermined results, enlarge school districts in order to cut costs and improve efficiency, strengthen local school councils in order to increase parental involvement, and create new partnerships between schools and their communities.

In the public debate about these policies the need to adapt public education to the imperatives of economic globalization and technological society has been largely taken for granted. Policy analysis has concentrated on redesigning curricula and restructuring governance in order to maximize individual and collective economic well-being. Less recognized, and hence less critically analyzed, are the changing assumptions about the aims and objectives of public education and the implications of changes in educational institutions and policies for the meaning and practice of Canadian democracy.

In order to raise questions about contemporary educational reform, not only as an instrument of economic progress, but also with respect to its expressive and constitutive meanings for Canadian democracy, I propose to examine, in turn, the importance of political ideas for understanding and evaluating public policies, the main competing ideological perspectives on the contemporary problem in the political economy of public education, and the transformation in terms of ideology and policy of provincial educational regimes from the 1960s to the 1990s. In my concluding section I shall raise questions about the potential significance of contemporary educational reform for our understanding and practice of liberal democratic politics.

POLICY ANALYSIS AND POLITICAL IDEAS

In defining policy analysis as "the disciplined application of intellect to public problems" Leslie A. Pal says, "The central distinction to keep in mind is between a style of policy analysis that is more explanatory and descriptive and a style that is more applied or prescriptive."[1] Each of these styles of policy analysis requires a distinctive approach to studying the connection between political ideas and public policies.

Policy analysis that aims to be descriptive and explanatory, now often designated by the term "policy studies," treats political ideas as causal determinants of public policies.[2] Public policies are assumed to result from a causal chain that involves not only the influence of ideas on the actions of policy makers, but also the networks formed by policy makers as they deal with each other in the policy process, the organization of political interests and consequent distribution of power resources, the arrangement of institutions that simultaneously enable and constrain policy action, and the contextual effects of the geographic, demographic, and socioeconomic environment.[3] In this approach to policy analysis, political ideas may involve modification of currently dominant ideas, displacement by rival ideas, or invention of new ideas, but the ideas are assumed already to exist. The problem of policy studies is describing and weighing the importance of ideas against process, institutions, interests, and environment as causal determinants of public policies.

Policy analysis that aims to be evaluative and prescriptive transforms the place of political ideas in policy arguments in three important ways. First, in this approach to policy analysis, ideas in the form of causal beliefs or theories are advanced, not as predictive or (more often) retrospective explanations of policy choices or outcomes, but as reasons—which also may be given either prospectively or retrospectively—for choosing particular courses of action on the grounds that they are feasible, effective, and efficient means to achieve given public purposes. Ideas advanced as instrumental reasons for policy action are open to rebuttal by challenges to their validity, relevance, or cogency. Second, ideas in the form of expressive signs or symbols that represent the fundamental principles, values, beliefs, or attitudes of a political community are advanced as reasons or justifications for the choice of policy goals, as well as to defend the means chosen to pursue those goals. Here the crucial tests of the rationality of public policies are basic political goods of legitimacy, justice, and democracy. Third, ideas in the form of constitutive meanings of public policy are disclosed or uncovered by translating the significance of policy actions, typically contained in the form of a complex narrative, into the terms of formal philosophical and theoretical language, thus revealing the changing discourse of democratic politics. Political ideas as constitutive meanings may be articulated by policy makers and analysts who are advocates for programs. Very often, however, they are advanced by political rivals and policy analysts who are their critics. Whether the result of advocacy or critique, as public institutions and policies are argued over time, interpretations are also advanced about consequent changes in the meanings of the political ideas, especially with respect to core concepts in the vocabulary of democratic politics, and judgments are made that condone or condemn the changing political morality or public philosophy.

POLITICAL ECONOMY AND EDUCATIONAL IDEOLOGY IN THE 1990S

This section originally appeared in "The Teachers vs. Bob Rae," The Literary Review of Canada *5, no. 8 (September 1996).*

In the late 20th century there has emerged a remarkably broad intellectual consensus that advanced industrial societies are undergoing a technological revolution comparable in its global impact and human implications to the "agricultural revolution" which began in the 17th century or the "industrial revolution" which dominated world economic development from the early 19th century past the middle of the 20th century.[4] Theorists differ in their overall characterizations of this "postindustrial" society. Those who focus on the revolutionary impact of computers and telecommunications refer to an emerging "knowledge" or "information" society. Neo-Marxists who are more concerned with the changing relations of production in technological society analyze the transition from "Fordism" to "post-Fordism." Theorists who give priority to the transformation of culture analyze the shift from "modernism" to "postmodernism." Nevertheless, a general consensus appears to exist regarding the basic features of this emerging technological society: the imperative of information technology, penetration of global markets, decentralization and deconcentration of bureaucratic organizations, erosion of state capacity, deconstruction of state legitimacy, and homogenization of popular culture.

Liberal, conservative, and socialist theorists largely agree on these basic features of postindustrial, post-Fordist, postmodern society. Liberals, conservatives, and socialists differ profoundly, however, in their assessments of the impact of technological society on human welfare, and in particular they disagree, both with each other and amongst themselves, on what should be the basic purposes of education, the proper role of the state, the structures of educational governance, the organization of schools, and the content of curricula.

Liberal theorists of technological society have an essentially optimistic view of the contemporary revolution in information technology and its consequences for human welfare. The revolution in information technology is simply the most recent and potentially most progressive achievement in the modern history of expanding scientific and technical mastery which has overcome natural scarcity, providing material abundance and leisure for both elites and masses. To reap the benefits of the new information technology, however, people must be prepared to reform their political, economic, and cultural institutions and practices, and on this liberal agenda educational reform is a high priority. Educational institutions and policies must be dedicated to achieving high levels of knowledge and skills in science, mathematics, and technological studies which form the technical foundation for lifelong learning in technological society, they must teach basic skills of effective communication, and they must instil the entrepreneurial spirit upon which individual and collective prosperity will in future depend.

Liberals broadly agree about the role of the state in creating the framework for education in technological society, but they have disagreements about structures of educational governance and provision. "Utilitarian" liberals favour a shift from state control to educational markets. State educational monopolies, which are bureaucratic, inflexible, and unaccountable, should be supplanted by private and/or public markets in which parents are enabled to choose educational programs for their children. "Ethical" liberals agree that existing state educational regimes are often bureaucratic, inflexible, and unaccountable, but they reject the utilitarian liberal conclusion that creating public or private markets for educational services would remedy these problems. Instead, they advocate the preservation of direct and equalized public provision for neighbourhood or community schools. A key feature of ethical liberal thinking is the establishment of school councils comprising representatives of teachers, parents, and (where appropriate) students as the basic unit of local educational governance. By strengthening the institutions of local democracy at the level of schools, as opposed to school boards, effective participation of parents (and students) in educational decision making can be combined with the professional competence of teachers. Thus a proper balance can be achieved between the private interests of families and the public interest of the liberal democratic state.

Socialists are much more pessimistic than are liberals about the impact of technological society on human welfare. The revolution in information technology does create highly skilled, highly paid jobs, but technological society is not characterized by a preponderance of such jobs. On the contrary, technological society is characterized by expansion of low-skilled, low-paid jobs and disappearance of low-skilled, high-paid jobs. The central problem of technological society is not achieving mass technical literacy and numeracy, as liberals contend, but creating a framework of political and economic institutions in which distributive justice is secured for people on both sides of the technological division of labour.

Since power relations favour technological elites, socialists focus on democratic politics as the way to protect workers and secure justice, but "social democrats" and "democratic socialists" pursue different political strategies. Social democrats focus on unemployment and underemployment as persistent, mass phenomena of technological society. The mix of strategies for overcoming the crisis of the labour market will depend on political relationships among state authorities, organized business, and trade unions. For democratic socialists the crisis of contemporary technological society is a crisis of democratic governance. In contrast with the tripartite corporatist partnerships envisaged by social democracy, democratic socialists see themselves confronted with a dual task: "to secure socialism against capitalist opposition and to do so in a way that will develop socialism's democratic potentials."[5] Full employment, humanly rewarding jobs, satisfaction of basic needs, and greater social equality are not thereby diminished as democratic socialist goals, but as public purposes they are subordinated "to support and enhance a sense of citizenship and common involvement in the doings of the society one inhabits."[6]

Conservatives recognize the potentially liberating effects of technological society in alleviating human "suffering from hunger, disease, overwork and conflict from scarcity," but they also fear "the threat to liberty and plurality posed by technique, the technical control of human nature, the danger of ecological or nuclear disaster, the decline of nurturing traditions, the banality of education, the deprivation of purpose and meaning to an increasing number of modern men and women."[7] Conservative educational ideology is generally agreed on the inevitability and desirability of educational hierarchy and academic elitism. The liberal project for public education in technological society is rejected because it is instrumental, not morally substantive. Nonetheless, there are important differences between "communitarian" and "liberal" conservatives in their priorities concerning basic education versus vocational training.

According to communitarian conservatives, there is an ancient tradition of "liberal education" that must be recovered as the foundation for educating young people in technological society. This tradition comprises not only the great texts of Western literature, philosophy, and science, but also the national heritage of language, literature, and history of the community in which students live. Liberal conservatives share the concern of communitarian conservatives for instructing young people in their Western and national heritage, but they give greater priority to the acquisition of vocational knowledge and skills relevant for work in technological society. Protecting the power and wealth of the state and its people in a global political economy depends on designing and implementing an educational regime that will successfully marry traditional and technological education. Hence, for liberal conservatives the separation of young people according to their potential talents for work in technological society must be an important part of the educational process. One approach to achieving such a separation involves adapting the communitarian conservative project of common education by streaming or tracking students based on their levels of achievement in the subjects of a common curriculum. An alternative approach to separating young people by their talents and prospects for work in technological society involves constructing class-structured programs that lead students to different occupational futures, starting in upper secondary school and extending into postsecondary academic, technical, and cooperative education.

IDEOLOGY AND POLICY: CANADIAN EDUCATIONAL REGIMES FROM THE 1960S TO THE 1990S

Tracing its origins in educational policy as far back as the 1930s, in the late 1960s and early 1970s a progressive ("ethical") liberal commitment to individual self-development as the primary purpose of public education became the core principle of provincial educational regimes.[8] Educational reforms based on ethical liberal educational ideology were never uncontested. Over the past decade, however, there has been a pronounced shift in the discourse of educational policy analysis and formulation that stems from the idea of technological change and economic globalization as the focal problem in the political economy of public education.[9]

Curriculum design in the ethical liberal educational regimes aimed to maximize the provision of learning experiences that would meet the self-developmental needs of each person in school. Among other policies, this meant breaking down the standard organization of schools by grades, emphasizing individual and small-group work involving teachers and students rather than whole-class instruction, and in high school ending the historical distinction between academic and vocational tracks in favour of credit systems with individual timetables and promotion by subject. Over the past decade, by contrast, policy analyses and curriculum reforms have assumed that the primary purpose of elementary and secondary education is acquisition of a common body of basic knowledge and skills. Official policy studies and curricular reforms have differed somewhat in their definitions of basic knowledge and skills, but they agree on the need for a common curriculum in primary and middle or junior high school and a core curriculum that emphasizes languages (English or French), mathematics, and sciences in senior high school. Ontario's Royal Commission on Learning, for example, neatly expressed the new ideal of curriculum design as a "curriculum for literacies," not only the basic literacies of reading, writing, and communicating, but also "advanced high-level literacies that enable people to continue to learn, not to be easily stuck when a new problem comes along."[10]

Ethical liberal educational regimes with their primary concern for individual self-development rejected the competition and ranking of students that was a standard feature of the traditional school's function of selection. As one indicator of this commitment, by the early 1970s all provinces except for Quebec and Newfoundland (historically, the two most conservative provincial educational regimes) had abolished provincial departmental examinations at the end of senior high school. Under the educational regimes of the 1990s, directly measuring and comparing the levels of knowledge and skills attained by young people during their schooling is the preferred way to evaluate how well they are being served by their education. Learning outcomes for basic stages of schooling—usually taken as the end of grades three, six, nine, and twelve—and standards of achievement have to be established by provincial ministries of education. Then appropriate methods of evaluating student progress, both individually and collectively by school and district, have to be implemented and must include external evaluation by provincial authorities. Provincially mandated testing at basic stages of schooling has been restored over the past decade, and national tests of achievement in mathematics, reading, writing, and science have been introduced for students aged 13 and 16.[11] The allegedly mediocre performance of Canadian students on international tests of mathematics and science also has been an important factor in stoking criticism and motivating reform of provincial curricula and testing.[12]

Ethical liberal educational regimes assumed that public education aiming at individual self-development should encompass the diverse cultural communities of a pluralistic society. Over the past three decades, progressive policies on religion and language have slowly institutionalized and legitimized provision for cultural pluralism in public education. Under the educational regimes of the 1990s the constitutional requirements and political realities of religion and language in Canadian education have not been disregarded, but there has been a visible shift toward a more conventional form of modern liberalism which emphasizes the political association of equal individuals rather than the collective protection of their cultural identities. The implementation of a substantially common curriculum, which is needed to make elementary and secondary education relevant for technological society and global economy, necessarily means putting limits on the accommodation of religious and ethnic differences. Constitutional amendments have transformed the historical foundations of public education in Newfoundland from a denominational to a nondenominational regime, and in Quebec the historical regime founded on the division of Roman Catholics from Protestants has been replaced by a regime based on linguistic dualism. Recent judicial decisions on religion in public education in Ontario have insisted on the secular standing of Ontario public schools, interpreting the constitutional provision for Roman Catholic separate schools as an historical anomaly rather than a legal precedent for expanding public provision for denominational schools.[13]

In ethical liberal educational regimes, the norm of provincial-local governmental relations was interdependent policy making. The dual aspiration of the 1960s for rational management and participatory democracy would be realized by reforming the historical domination of educational governance by provincial departments of education into an equal partnership between central and local educational authorities. Official policy analyses and reforms of educational governance in the 1990s have aimed to shift the balance of public authority in favour of ministries of education. Consistent with prevailing theories of the "new public management," the functions of policy and management are divided respectively between provincial and local educational authorities. The policy framework of public education involving decisions about overall resource allocation to public education, content of the common or core curriculum, provincial standards of educational achievement, and mechanisms of accountability is determined by provincial educational authorities. The function of management is devolved to school boards, school councils, and teaching staffs.

Under the ethical liberal educational regime, the norm for policy networks in provincial educational policy communities on such key issues as educational finance, collective bargaining, school organization, and curriculum design joined ministry officials and organized teachers and trustee associations together in a process of mutual consultation and bargaining. In practice, trilateralism varied among the provinces from quasi-corporatist partnerships in Ontario and Quebec, as well as Saskatchewan and Manitoba under NDP governments, to largely state-directed policy networks in New Brunswick, Prince Edward Island, and British Columbia. In the 1990s the rhetoric of educational policy reform paradoxically has emphasized the critical importance of committed teachers, while teachers' unions are widely portrayed as special interests threatening to block meaningful reform. At the same time, provincial trustees' associations have been weakened by the reorganization of school districts and the shift of policy-making authority from local to central authorities. Trilateral norms have been further undermined by the calculated expansion of "stakeholders" in educational policy making. In particular, institutionalized educational partnerships between government and business are now seen as essential to refit public education for the new era of global economic competition.

This consensus on the basic principles of educational reform in the 1990s has not been built on adherence to one hegemonic educational ideology. Rather there has been a revisionist merger of liberal conservative, utilitarian liberal, and ethical liberal ideas to construct what may be described as a "technological liberal" educational regime.[14] Widespread consensus on the principles of this technological liberal educational regime has effected a major shift in the discourse of educational policy analysis and the design of educational policies, but it has not thereby suppressed ideological conflict. Under the umbrella of technological liberalism, liberal conservatives continue to preach the need for inculcating moral virtues and rewarding academic merit; utilitarian conservatives advocate the efficiency of public markets and the liberty of parental choice; and ethical liberals urge the priority of cultural diversity and child welfare. Communitarian conservative and democratic socialist ideas have been generally excluded in the construction of the educational regimes of the 1990s. As a result, communitarian conservatives who attacked the "child-centred" education sponsored by ethical liberal educational regimes have continued to criticize emerging technological liberal educational regimes because they teach modern skills of communicating, analyzing, and problem solving without proper grounding in the liberal humanist tradition of Western civilization. Democratic socialists for their part reject contemporary educational reform as the work of "a neoconservative juggernaut" that exacerbates class divisions and destroys local democracy.[15] Finally, unreformed ethical liberals continue to defend the ideals of the 1960s. These diehard advocates of individual self-development and child-centred schools are found in some progressive parent associations but mainly in the teaching profession which, combined with the activism of social democrats and democratic socialists in organizing teachers' unions, makes it easy and inevitable that elite policy makers dismiss them as "special interests."

EDUCATIONAL REGIMES AND CANADIAN DEMOCRACY

Over the decade from the late 1980s to the late 1990s, public education in Canada has been reformed to meet the needs of young people who will be living and working in the 21st century. The effectiveness and efficiency of emerging technological liberal educational regimes have been argued from a liberal ideological analysis of the challenges and opportunities of contemporary technological change and economic globalization. The legitimacy of restoring hegemonic ministries of education has been defended by reference to the constitutional principle of public accountability through ministerial responsibility, the collapse of popular belief in school boards as legitimate representatives of public educational will, and the perverse power of teachers' unions to protect their selfish interests and block educational reform. The justice of imposing common and core curricula with high standards and rigorous testing rests on the argument that, not only has education become the main determinant of collective economic well-being, it also is a decisive influence on individual economic welfare.[16]

These claims for the justice, legitimacy, effectiveness, and efficiency of the new technological educational regimes are all contestable. In the technological educational regimes of the 1990s, "person-regarding equality" has been replaced by a concept of equality under which the educational lots of individual students would be essentially interchangeable.[17] Such an approach not only undermines care for individual differences in talents and interests, but also threatens recognition of communal identities as a central principle to ensure justice in our pluralist society. Restructuring school boards and reorganizing the teaching profession raise concerns about the propriety of centralizing educational decision making. School-business partnerships pose difficult issues about drawing the line between state and market, and between business as private enterprises and schools as public institutions. The place of parent councils raises the question of whether parents either want the type of participation being envisaged or, if they do, will be willing to settle for their projected role as school advisors or part of the local management of schools as opposed to being involved in substantive decision making about the education of their children. Can the commitments of volunteer parents on school councils compensate for the loss of the hours of educational policy development delivered by elected school trustees? Will a more centralized provincial educational regime really deliver public education more efficiently or effectively than the process of intergovernmental cooperation and conflict that characterized the ethical liberal educational regime?

The transformation of Canadian educational regimes in the 1990s also directly raises at least four issues about the meaning and practice of Canadian democracy at the turn of the century.

First, responding to the dynamic of technological change and economic globalization, contemporary educational regimes give priority to the economic role of individual learners as future producers rather than their political role as future citizens. In current policy analysis and political rhetoric, the traditional goal of public education for democratic citizenship is given formal consideration; in practice the education of democratic citizens has been subordinated to the demand for competitive workers.

Second, common and core curricula that are oriented to the imperatives of global capitalism threaten the inclusive recognition of communal identities that was central to the principles of the ethical liberal educational regimes and raise concerns, not only with regard to the capacity of contemporary educational regimes to respond to the countervailing pressures of localism in the era of the global economy, but also about representing and hence expressing the social diversity of a pluralist society in its public schools.

Third, restructuring of educational policy communities has weakened the participation of teachers' unions in policy making, forcing them back into a reduced role as policy advocates or even into outright political opposition, while strengthening the participation of organized business. This change in educational policy networks has broader implications for forging new relationships between state agencies and societal organizations in the political economy of technological society and global capitalism.

Fourth, restructuring school boards by amalgamating districts and centralizing policy, especially decisions about curriculum and finance, makes school boards into instruments of public management rather than agencies of communal self-government. Nor does the introduction of school councils repair the loss, in part because of their weakness as presently constituted, but also because the catchment areas of schools rarely coincide with the boundaries of local communities. Historically, in theory and practice, liberal democracy has been vitalized by local government. Hence, the evisceration of school boards under technological liberal educational regimes portends a major turning in Canadian democracy.

I offer no prescriptions, only questions. The history of Canadian educational regimes shows that old regimes can be broken and new ones constructed without efficiency, effectiveness, legitimacy, and justice—let alone democracy—being well served. For the basic principles of democratic educational regimes to be met, educational politics and policy making have to engage not only the instrumental economic benefits, but also the substantive political impacts of reforming public education. Only then can our reform of provincial educational regimes have the potential to contribute to the construction of an authentic Canadian democracy.

NOTES

1. Leslie A. Pal, *Beyond Policy Analysis: Public Issue Management in Turbulent Times* (Scarborough, Ontario: Nelson, 1997), 12–13.

2. For a discussion of the difference in approaches to studying political ideas and public policies between political ideas as causal determinants and political ideas as constitutive meanings of public policies, see Ronald Manzer, *Public Schools and Political Ideas: Canadian Educational Policy in Historical Perspective* (Toronto: University of Toronto Press, 1994), 4–7.

3. With the exception of "interests," these factors correspond to the five categories for explaining public policies—process, institutions, ideas, power, and environment—advanced by Richard Simeon in his classic article, "Studying Public Policy," *Canadian Journal of Political Science* 9 (December 1976): 385–92. Simeon's discussion of "power" does deal with pluralist, elitist, and class theories of interests and the distribution of power, and policy studies now commonly treat "organized interests" rather than "power" as the relevant factor for describing and explaining public policies.

4. The following paragraphs on contemporary political economy and educational ideologies are taken from my review article, "The Teachers vs. Bob Rae," *The Literary Review of Canada* 5 (September 1996): 24–25.

5. Frank Cunningham, *Democratic Theory and Socialism* (Cambridge: Cambridge University Press, 1987), 273.

6. Ronald Beiner, *What's the Matter with Liberalism?* (Berkeley: University of California Press, 1992), 167.

7. Edward Andrew, "George Grant on Technological Imperatives," *Democratic Theory and Technological Society*, eds. Richard B. Day, Ronald Beiner, and Joseph Masciulli (London: M.E. Sharpe, 1988), 301.

8. By "educational regime" I mean a stable ordering of political principles and public authority for the governance of education. An educational regime is constituted in the first place as a collective

response to a primary problem of political economy. By "political economy" I refer to understanding the relationships among state, market, and community (or voluntary sector) as basic modes of collective decision making. The generic problem of political economy is the proper relationship of state, market, and community, here with particular concern for the demand and supply of education. Second, its coherence and purpose depends on widespread acceptance of a core of political ideas that may derive from a dominant political ideology but more often will be created from conflict and compromise among the proponents of opposing doctrinal positions. Third, an educational regime implies a distinctive set of public policies covering both the governance and the provision of education. Hence, the concept of educational regime includes the established institutions and procedures for educational governance, allocation of public authority, and style of public decision making as well as the design and implementation of educational programs. For an overview of the ethical liberal regimes of the late 1960s and early 1970s see Manzer, Public Schools and Political Ideas, chapters 9–11.

9. My generalizations about official policy analyses that have contributed to educational reform in the 1990s are based primarily on George Radwanski, *Ontario Study of the Relevance of Education, and the Issue of Dropouts* (Toronto: Ontario Ministry of Education, 1987); British Columbia, Royal Commission on Education, *A Legacy for Learners: The Report of the Royal Commission on Education 1988* (Victoria: Queen's Printer for British Columbia, 1988); Ontario, Premier's Council, *People and Skills in the New Global Economy* (Toronto: Queen's Printer for Ontario, 1990); Canada, Economic Council of Canada, *A Lot to Learn: Education and Training in Canada* (Ottawa: Minister of Supply and Services Canada, 1992); Newfoundland and Labrador, Royal Commission of Inquiry into the Delivery of Programs and Services in Primary, Elementary, Secondary Education, *Our Children Our Future* (St. John's: Queen's Printer, 1992); New Brunswick, Commission on Excellence in Education, *Schools for a New Century* (Fredericton: Commission on Excellence in Education, 1992); and Ontario, Royal Commission on Learning, *For the Love of Learning: Report of the Royal Commission on Learning, 4 volumes* (Toronto: Queen's Printer for Ontario, 1994).

10. Ontario, Royal Commission on Learning, *For the Love of Learning, volume 2, Learning: Our Vision for Schools*, 8.

11. The School Achievement Indicators Project was approved by the Council of Ministers of Education, Canada in September 1989. A first round of national testing began in April 1993 with a test of mathematics achievement given to 47 000 students aged thirteen and sixteen and was completed by tests of reading and writing (1994) and science (1996). A second round of national testing in mathematics was held in April 1997 followed by reading and writing (1998) and science (1999).

12. The International Association for the Evaluation of Educational Achievement has conducted three mathematics and three science tests, and the International Assessment of Education Progress has run two studies of mathematics and science. Canada participated in the second and third IEA tests and in both of the IAEP studies. For an assessment of the Canadian results on these international tests see Philip Nagy, "International Comparisons of Student Achievement in Mathematics and Science: A Canadian Perspective," *Canadian Journal of Education* 21 (Fall 1996): 396–413.

13. Greg M. Dickinson and W. Rod Dolmage argue that recent cases in Ontario have major implications for other provinces. They conclude with respect to Ontario public schools, "Although it is permissible to teach about religion in public schools, it is not permissible to support or promote any particular religious view; to do so would inevitably violate the religious freedom of students who do not share the view being supported or promoted....Although such a position clearly does not support an assimilationist or indoctrinational approach to education (it supports educational programs that encourage students to learn and appreciate other cultures and cultural institutions), it has, to this point, fallen distinctly short of any active attempt to promote ethnic and cultural diversity.

It is probably also fair to conclude from these cases that the courts have supported an individual rights, as opposed to a group rights, approach to the resolution of these issues" (Greg M. Dickinson and W. Rod Dolmage, "Education, Religion, and the Courts in Ontario," *Canadian Journal of Education* 21 [Fall 1996]: 379).

14. For a discussion of the differences between "technological liberalism" and the educational ideologies of political, economic, and ethical liberalism, see Manzer, *Public Schools and Political Ideas*, 255–69.

15. See, for example, the critique of the educational reforms sponsored by the NDP government of Bob Rae in Ontario by George Martell, A New Education Politics: Bob Rae's Legacy and the Response of the Ontario Secondary School Teachers' Federation (Toronto: James Lorimer, 1995), and for a more general critique of contemporary educational reform from an essentially democratic socialist perspective, see Maude Barlow and Heather-jane Robertson, *Class Warfare: The Assault on Canada's Schools* (Toronto: Key Porter Books, 1994).

16. As George Radwanski put it, "In this new economic environment, our young people will not long feel fulfilled, nor will their self-esteem endure, if they find themselves unemployable or unqualified for other than the most menial, dead-end work because they lack the requisite knowledge or skills. And our collective sense of fulfillment and self-esteem as a society will scarcely be enhanced if our standard of living goes into steady decline because an under-educated population has made us uncompetitive in an increasingly rigorous global economy" (Radwanski, *Ontario Study of the Relevance of Education*, and the Issue of Dropouts, 3). © Queen's Printer for Ontario, 1987. Reproduced with permission.

17. By "person-regarding equality" in public education I refer to educational programs that have been designed to meet the individual needs of each person in school. Students are not given a uniform or identical education; they follow different educational programs, depending on their needs. Hence, the educational programs of individual students are not generally interchangeable, but all students get equal value from their different educational careers. By "lot-regarding equality" I refer to educational programs that are uniform or identical. Where all students follow essentially the same courses and program, no student would gain or lose value by exchanging his or her educational program for that of any other student. Hence, the educational lots of all students are equal. For analysis of person-regarding and lot-regarding equality in Canadian public education see Manzer, Public School and Political Ideas, 42–3, 97, 148, 161–63, 188–89, 265, 269–71. For a theoretical discussion of the concepts of lot-regarding and person-regarding equality see Douglas Rae with Douglas Yates, Jennifer Hochschild, Joseph Morone, and Carol Fessler, *Equalities* (Cambridge, Mass.: Harvard University Press, 1981), 85–101.

HOW THE VETERANS OF WORLD WAR II CHANGED CANADIAN UNIVERSITIES

Peter Neary

In the late 1940s Canadian universities were bursting at the seams with veterans of World War II. This influx was made possible by the *Veterans Rehabilitation Act* of 1945, one of the many pieces of creative legislation that constituted the Veterans Charter, Canada's comprehensive program of benefits for those who served in World War II. The contrast with the experience of university students today is striking.

The origins of the Veterans Charter can be traced to December 1939, when a cabinet committee was formed to study and make recommendations on future demobilization problems and issues. That Ottawa acted so promptly on this matter is attributable to the determination of Prime Minister Mackenzie King and his colleagues not to repeat mistakes made at the end of World War I, when demobilization had been a messy operation and veterans a sometimes menacing presence in a divided Canada.

On 1 October 1941 the Post-Discharge Re-establishment Order was issued. This promised all veterans of World War II rehabilitation assistance and specified that military service would constitute insurable employment under the *Unemployment Insurance Act* of June 1940. These provisions marked a big advance in veterans' benefits. In the case of the World War I generation, only disabled veterans had been eligible for comprehensive rehabilitation benefits. Now everyone who served would qualify.

Devising the program that would fulfil the promise of the Post-Discharge Re-establishment Order was the job of the Department of Pensions and National Health, principally of Walter S. Woods, a veteran of the Great War who became associate deputy minister in April 1941. Woods' philosophy of veterans' benefits derived from the "basic truth...that the great majority of veterans would rather work than receive relief in any form from the State."

Canada was obligated to provide long-term support for sick and disabled veterans, and for the dependants of those who had died in the service of their country. Able-bodied veterans, however, would need only short-term help to compensate for service rendered, opportunities lost, and interrupted life. Given the means to make a fresh start, they would soon be looking after themselves and their families, and building up the country they had so gallantly come forward to defend. In short, what the able-bodied veterans of World War II would need to re-establish themselves was "OPPORTUNITY WITH SECURITY." This meant—in the words of *Back to Civil Life*, the pamphlet that explained the completed benefit package to rank-and-file members of the armed forces—training that would position veterans "to earn a living."

It was this philosophy that inspired the *Veterans Rehabilitation Act,* which offered qualified veterans financial support to attend university or take vocational education. The Canadian educational benefits were discretionary and not (as in the United States under the *G.I. Bill of Rights)* entitlements. Under the American scheme, the colleges were the gatekeepers, whereas in Canada government officials decided who would go to university. This kept numbers down. Nonetheless, to 31 March 1951, of the more than a million Canadians who enlisted during World War II, 80 110 had been supported to receive vocational education and 53 788 to attend university. To 1954–55, spending in support of vocational and university education amounted to more than $194 million, an appropriation that helped fuel the robust postwar economy.

To prepare themselves for the rush of demobilization, the universities began planning in 1942 through the National Conference of Canadian Universities (NCCU). In 1944 the NCCU published the *Report of the National Conference of Canadian Universities on Post-War Problems.* This dealt with a range of issues but most importantly made the case for federal funding to the universities to accommodate the veterans. The argument was simple: though education was a provincial responsibility under Canada's federal constitution, the country had a national responsibility to the veterans which could only be met by national funding.

Ottawa agreed and eventually offered the universities a supplementary grant on behalf of each student veteran. Under the *Veterans Rehabilitation Act* the veterans were supported to attend university, and under the supplementary grant scheme the universities were given special funding to admit them. Each veteran had his or her fees paid and was given a living allowance, the amount of which varied according to marital circumstances and number of dependants. The amount of the supplementary grant paid on behalf of each student was initially set at $150, with a cap of $500 for fees and grant.

To get the supplementary grants, the universities had to agree to accommodate veterans by adjusting admission dates, arranging summer sessions, providing counselling and advisory services, avoiding excessively large classes, insuring adequate residence accommodation, engaging additional qualified instructors, establishing loan funds, adapting courses to the special needs of adults seeking to enter professions, and controlling incoming numbers of civilian students. The universities also agreed to work through an Advisory Committee on University Training for Veterans, appointed by Ottawa and chaired by Woods. This committee brought together key government officials and university presidents.

Not surprisingly, the effect of these changes was profound. Before VE-day (8 May 1945) about 250 000 individuals had been discharged from the armed forces. In the calendar years 1945 and 1946, total discharges were 395 013 and 381 031 respectively. These numbers created a huge demand for services for veterans, and university resources were soon stretched to the limit. Principal F. Cyril James of McGill, an economist, caught the flavour of the times when he wrote to an official in Ottawa on 12 October 1945: "My own class has grown from about 52 last year to 295 and will be over the 300 mark next week, which gives you an idea of what has happened at McGill."

By 15 February 1947, 40 143 veterans were being supported by the government of Canada to attend university or prepare themselves to do so. In Canada itself, 33 828 were registered in university, while 872 were registered in the United States and 218 in the United Kingdom and Europe. At the same time 5225 veterans were being supported to take pre-matriculation classes. By comparison, the entire full-time undergraduate enrolment in Canadian universities and colleges in 1939 had only been 35 164.

In November 1946 the seven universities in Canada most favoured by the veterans (75.5 percent of all such registrations) were, in order, the University of Toronto, McGill University, University of British Columbia, University of Saskatchewan, University of Alberta, University of Manitoba, and Queen's. In 1947–48 veterans accounted for 49 percent of the student body at the University of Toronto, and in 1948–49 they accounted for 42 percent. As late as 1949–50, veterans still accounted for 21 percent of all university students in Canada.

To 30 June 1950, the University of Toronto had received 23.3 percent of the supplementary grant payments made by Ottawa to all universities. The University of British Columbia stood second at 15.2 percent and McGill third at 11.6 percent. Significantly, francophone institutions fared very poorly indeed in the distribution of supplementary grants, despite the participation of prominent French-Canadian academic administrators in the work of the NCCU and the Advisory Committee. Laval University ranked 23rd in the list of universities receiving the grants and the University of Montreal 25th. The Maritime universities likewise lagged, though not as badly. Inevitably, this uneven distribution of benefits had lasting consequences, both political and educational.

To meet the new demand for their services, the universities improvised impressively. At the University of Toronto, first-year science and engineering students were taught in a surplus defence industry plant at Ajax, 25 miles from the city, where assembly lines were made into classrooms and laboratories. At the University of British Columbia, wartime huts were moved to the campus and a $5 million construction program started to provide a new physics building and new accommodation for pharmacy, home economics, and applied science, as well as a bigger library. At McGill, Sir William Dawson College was established in the former Royal Canadian Air Force No. 9 Observatory Training School. Like Canada itself in this period, universities had to adapt in myriad ways, and they not only coped but prospered. A big short-term demand allowed them to reinvent themselves and build for a brighter tomorrow. This was very much in keeping with the spirit of the times.

As a group, the veterans more than lived up to the academic expectations of the planners. Those who failed, however, lost government support. In 1946–47, 77 percent passed unconditionally, 10 percent were able to continue with one condition, and 13 percent failed to qualify for continued assistance. Anyone who failed was eligible for one reinstatement to benefits. To achieve this, an individual had to continue studying at his or her own expense for a year, meet all academic requirements, and be recommended for reinstatement by the university in question. Unusually, of 224 veterans registered in first-year law at Osgoode Hall, Toronto, in 1947–48 (50 of whom were university graduates), only 126 or 56.3 percent passed (the passing rate for non-veterans was 54 percent). Of the veterans who failed, moreover, 39 were repeating the year at their own expense. This was rough—but it was also out of character with the general performance of veterans.

Veterans who did well in their studies could have their benefits extended beyond their service entitlement. To qualify, the veteran had to complete at least one year of study, pass all subjects, either achieve second-class honours standing or be in the top 25 percent of his or her year, and be recommended for further support by the scholarship committee of the university attended.

The postwar boom also brought many more married students to Canadian campuses. An analysis of 9119 student veterans in receipt of allowances at 30 November 1945 showed that 2308 (25.3 percent) were married and 6811 (74.7 percent) were single. As time passed and the baby boom began, the percentages tipped dramatically in favour of the married category. By the fall of 1948, 50 percent of those being supported to attend university were married. In 1946–47, the average age of veterans attending the University of Saskatchewan was 25.4 years. Canadian universities were not only growing but were admitting students of very different outlooks and expectations.

Veterans ranged widely in their choice of subject but engineering and commerce were especially popular. Of the 33 828 being assisted to study in Canadian universities on 15 February 1947, fully 8093 (23.9 percent) were in engineering. Not all veterans, however, were able to study what they wanted. Admission to medical and dental faculties was especially difficult. Nevertheless, by November 1950, 1672 veterans had been admitted to first-year medicine; of these, 22 were being assisted to study in the United States and the United Kingdom. Some 759 veterans had likewise been admitted to dental faculties, of whom 44 were being assisted to study in the United States. These figures are indicative of the fact that a generation of Canadian professionals was quickly trained in the immediate postwar years.

The *Veterans Rehabilitation Act* not only enhanced the careers and lives of tens of thousands of individual Canadians but transformed the institutions through which its benefits were delivered. In the case of the universities, the Act stimulated action by the federal government to give the universities the means to acquire new faculty and provide urgently needed new facilities. These benefited post-secondary education in the country long after the great wave of veterans had been educated and re-established. A big short-term demand left behind it important long-term resources. Of necessity, the universities had to learn quickly after 1945 how to deliver new services in new ways to a larger and more diverse student body than ever before. In the public interest, they were able to work together through the NCCU and the government's Advisory Committee and this enabled them to innovate to an unprecedented extent. The legacy of the period was a university system that was more complex and capable than it had previously been.

The compact body of university leaders, all of them men, who responded to the needs of the times participated in stirring national events and acquired a distinctly pan-Canadian outlook. They had forcefully impressed on them the beneficent possibilities inherent in collective action organized by the federal state. This was something a later generation of Canadians, faced with mounting debt and influenced by anti-tax and anti-statist ideas, was inclined to forget. Far from subverting self-reliance, state intervention and subsidy of the sort provided for in the *Veterans Rehabilitation Act* was designed to have the exact opposite effect. In this case, government spending on individual Canadians fostered work, property holding, and traditional family life.

Today Canadian university students face restructuring of programs, ever higher fees, mounting debt, and the prospect of spending their early working years paying off income-contingent loans. The consequences of these developments for family formation and middle class life as it evolved in the affluent postwar decades will be profound.

Today's students can only dream of a time when the needs of the young were uppermost in the minds of policy makers and when a whole generation was launched on the high road of economic success through good planning and farsighted public investment. The very different educational experiences of the veteran generation and present-day undergraduates highlight just how much our prospects and priorities changed in the second half of the 20th century.

FURTHER READING

Morton, Desmond and Glenn Wright. *Winning the Second Battle: Canadian Veterans and the Return to Civilian Life, 1915–1930.* Toronto: University of Toronto Press, 1987.

Neary, Peter and J. L. Granatstein (eds.). *The Veterans Charter and Post–World War II Canada.* Montreal and Kingston: McGill-Queen's University Press, 1998.

EDUCATION IN CANADA:
Options for Change
Paul Barker

In Canada, responsibility for elementary schools and high schools rests with the provinces and territories. Accordingly, Canada has not one national education system but, in fact, a series of systems. However, in each of these systems, it is possible to find similarities. Typically, the provincial authority articulates the broad policies for education and supplies much of the necessary funding, and local school boards shape the policies to suit the needs of the area over which they have jurisdiction. Individual schools, of course, also play a role, which is to deliver the educational services to students. In the past decade, this set of arrangements has experienced a great deal of turmoil. Though schools have always been a focus of some attention, the intensity of interest in education in recent years has risen considerably. There is a fear among some that existing schooling arrangements fall well short of furnishing students with the skills necessary to compete successfully in the new global economy. Concern has also been expressed about the need to provide a greater role for parents and the community in the operation of schools, and many urge schools to do a better job of reflecting the increasing diversity of Canada. There also appears to be a preference for a greater range of choice of schools.

In response to these and other pressures, numerous reform proposals have been forwarded, some of which have already been implemented. In many provinces the movement has been towards giving provincial ministries of education greater authority, with the result that school boards have been relieved of some of their prime responsibilities. At the same time, territories and provinces have established structures which are intended to facilitate greater parental input into school decision making, a development which suggests that arrangements for education are being centralized *and* decentralized simultaneously. Also, the wish to expand the capacity of parents and guardians to choose where they shall send their children has been expressed in some locales. Traditionally, the child has been sent to the neighbourhood school, but this may now be too limiting. More generally, there has been a desire to think about how education might be provided or delivered in a way that diverges quite dramatically from the present situation.

Canada is not alone in the attention it is paying to its schools. In other English-speaking democracies, whose experience with schools is probably the most relevant for Canada, some important changes have taken place. In England, schools now compete for students; they no longer can assume that the children will enrol in the local school. The same has taken place in New Zealand. Schools in New Zealand are also required to enter into contractual agreements with national authorities for the purpose of ensuring that certain education goals will be met. In the United States there is a push for national education standards, and new decision-making bodies have emerged to provide for greater parental and community input into how schools are run. As well, parents, teachers, and other interested parties, working together, can now create their own schools which operate outside the established regulatory framework while still receiving public funding. For the most part, Canada lags behind these countries in its reform of schools, but much of the change taking place elsewhere is becoming evident in Canada.

The intent of this essay is to provide an overview of the changes now taking place in Canada's schools. To do this it is first necessary to understand the context for reform, and in so doing to appreciate what are the *problems* with the present arrangements for primary and secondary education in Canada. It would be helpful to report that a consensus exists on what ails Canada's education system, but such is not the case. Any would-be reformer of the Canadian education system has to understand that criticisms of the country's schools are multifaceted and are not always consistent with one another, and that some even deny the existence of any real difficulties with schools. The essay next examines some of the suggested *solutions* to the purported weaknesses in education. Here, too, agreement is missing, for there is no consensus on what should be done to make Canada's schools better. The best that can be done in a definitive sense is to survey and assess the most prominent options for change. However, the essay will suggest that the education system might benefit from giving officials at the school level more flexibility while at the same time offering parents greater choice in the selection of schools. This combination of reforms may act to enhance both the quality and fairness of education arrangements in Canada.

CONTEXT FOR CHANGE AND REFORM

In a recent review of education in Ontario, members of the province's Education Improvement Commission observe that "there is a large public appetite for change" in education.[1] Though meant only in relation to Ontario, the sentiment captures accurately the situation in all parts of the country. Such an appetite is whetted by many things, but arguably the most important is the concern over the quality of education in Canada's schools. It is believed that the education system is offering an inferior level of education compared to what it provided in earlier decades, and that the system in general is not performing very well. To support this claim, some point to the high dropout rates, the disappointing performance of Canadian students on national and international tests, and the low levels of literacy of recent graduates.[2] Over the past few years, this concern with quality has been expressed in one government report after another. A Newfoundland study notes that "there have been many indications that the education system in the Province is not performing as well as it should," and a discussion paper on schools in New Brunswick makes a similar point about schools in that province, saying that "there is a widespread view that our system is not performing any-where near its capability."[3] In Ontario a government report calls for "[f]undamental alter-ations" to the province's schools, and in Manitoba "new directions" in education are outlined by the governing authorities.[4] Concern over the quality of schooling is also reflected in the proliferation of parent groups and other organizations which demand excellence in schools. Parents in Action, the Quality Education Group, Albertans for Quality Education, and PAR-ENT are only a few of the groups which have arisen recently to influence policy on educa-tion. Polls, too, reveal an uneasiness about and a declining lack of confidence in the country's schools; and enrolments in private schools—schools which exist outside the fully financed public school system—have continued to increase in recent years.[5]

In some instances this apprehensiveness stems from a simple desire for the best possi-ble schooling. But more often it is a result of a belief that the schools are not preparing stu-dents for the new global economy. In the world of international trade and finance, in which Canada competes with all nations of the world, it is believed that the successful participant will be in possession of basic literacy and numeracy skills, be technologically proficient, and be able to adapt to a constantly changing economy. For too many Canadians the education system fails to meet these new international standards of education. If Canada as a whole is to prosper and if the children of today are to succeed in the world of tomorrow, then the schools will have to change. And in most minds the change must involve schools focusing on acquiring fundamental skills and knowledge, and spending less time on matters not cen-tral to preparing students for the challenge of globalism. As Manzer says in summarizing this type of thinking, "The only type of elementary and secondary education that is relevant in a technological society is a general, liberal education teaching basic knowledge and skills."[6]

Interestingly, some observers of education policy note that many criticisms of schools in Canada are unfounded, that there is a serious gap between perception and reality. An ex-amination of the relevant data does tend to show that on some indicators—dropout rates and literacy skills for example—the education system does fairly well, at least in compar-ison with the past.[7] As a result, the real problem may not be that schools are declining in qual-ity or performing poorly, but rather that they are not improving *fast enough* to salve the concerns of those who fear the competitiveness of the world economy.[8] Whatever the case may be, the fact remains that the appetite for reform revolves around concern—however defined—about the quality of schooling in Canada.

Another aspect of the context for education reform relates to the desire for a more open education decision process. Too often, it is argued, parents and other interested parties have little or no say in school policies and operations. In one respect this is a carryover from the concern about quality, especially among parents and business groups who feel that their input into the policy process might make for better schools. But there is another force operating here, one related to the rise of a well-educated generation, the baby boomers, who feel con-fident in commenting on education policy and who "shop for quality in education much as they shop for quality in other aspects of their lives."[9] This is a "postmaterialist" generation which rejects traditional authority patterns and feels less and less secure about the capaci-ties of established institutions.[10] It is also the first generation relieved of material concerns (hence the postmaterialist label) and with the opportunity and inclination to focus on mat-ters which go beyond meeting basic needs. From the perspective of this group, what is re-quired is an opening up of the education system, in terms of how decisions are made and what kind of choices are available for prudent consumers. The middle-class parents of today, says Lawton, are "not about to leave the education of their children in the hands of faceless bureaucrats who believe that the 'one best system' is suitable for all children."[11] The days of the accepting, deferential parent appear to be over.

The increasing diversity of the Canadian population is also a factor in education reform. New Canadians feel that the schools sometimes fail to reflect their beliefs and values. Similarly, certain marginalized groups—gays, Aboriginal people, blacks, women—complain about the offerings of the education system. And religious groups protest the increasing secularization of schools, and claim that the separate school systems, ones which give recognition to Protestant and Catholic faiths, discriminate against other religions.[12] As in the case of the baby boomer generation, this particular force works in a direction which endeavours to open up the education system further and offer a richer variety of schooling choices to parents. The diversification so evident in the larger Canadian society should, some claim, be reflected in the schools of Canada. Canada is "'the world's first international nation,'" so its schools should be similarly characterized and structured.[13]

The context of education change also encompasses dissatisfaction with the institutional structures of education. The education bureaucracies stand accused of insensitivity, inefficiency, and serving their own particular interests; they also represent a dollar cost which seems excessive in itself and certainly unwarranted in light of the educational returns. Receiving particular attention here are the school boards, which traditionally play an important role in the functioning of schools. Board trustees appear highly paid, yet are perceived as doing little beyond rubber-stamping the decisions of their administrative subordinates, and the latter seem intent on building up budgets and staff at no apparent gain to the paying public. Parents and communities once controlled the schools, but no longer; that job is now in the hands of monopolistic school boards who take little heed of their cost or their constituents.[14] More broadly, the education bureaucracies, which include not only school boards but also provincial ministries of education and teachers' unions, spend more than almost any other education system in the western world without apparently providing a discernably better product. This last point brings into play a related element in the context of education reform, and that has been, until recently, the deleterious fiscal situation of provincial governments. Faced with large budget deficits, governments have looked to the education sector for expenditure savings.

The preceding suggests a sympathetic context for education reform: the schools are indicted on grounds of poor quality, inflexibility, inefficiency, high cost, and a certain deafness to the demands of parents. Yet this impression is misleading, for there still exists a large reservoir of support for schools. Polls suggest that while respondents with school children are less than happy with the education system as a whole, they are satisfied with their own teachers and schools (which, in turn, suggests that the uneasiness with schools is unrelated to their actual performance).[15] Polling also indicates, in some provinces, support for *additional* spending on education.[16] Furthermore, even the harshest critics of Canada's schools concede that "education is held in moderately high regard."[17] What this all suggests is a complex context for educational reform, that schools suffer from various problems but at the same time they can still count on the support of parents and others in the electorate. If there is any doubt about this, then the 1997 teachers' strike in Ontario should be considered. Notwithstanding the illegal nature of the strike action and the government's constant reference during the strike to many of the highly publicized problems with education, the teachers seemed to win the battle of public opinion. By the end of the strike, the Ontario government was trying to substantiate its position, while the teachers returned to their classes with the support of the majority of the provincial population.[18] Any policy maker who thinks he or she can strip the education system of funds and introduce significant changes without extensive public consultation—a fair description of the policy of the Ontario government—misunderstands the context for education reform.

At the beginning of this section, it was noted that there was in Canada a large appetite for education reform. This appetite reveals a large number of concerns about Canada's schools. There are, in other words, some perceived problems with the education sector. However, these problems offer less than clear and consistent direction for governments. On the one hand, the context calls for a standardization of education, a type of education which equips young Canadians to do battle in the new global world; on the other hand, the context suggests a need for more choice and diversity in schools, and a system whose decision-making processes reach down into the individual schools. The context is also complicated by the fact that the perception of problems with schools is also accompanied by support for these same schools and a decided wariness about reform proposals. All in all, those who dare to tackle that area of public policy dealing with education, which this essay tries to do in the next section, must appreciate the full complexity of the issue.

POSSIBLE SOLUTIONS

When policy problems present themselves, governments and other interested parties sometimes react with reform proposals which represent only incremental change. The decision is to muddle through, to make marginal adjustments to existing policies and accompanying administrative arrangements. The response in Canada and elsewhere to perceived failings in public education, though, has been to reject incrementalism and to propose rather major reforms of the school system. In this section, three such reforms are considered: school councils and school-based management in the individual schools; parental choice, charter schools, and other initiatives which broaden the selection of schools; and standardized curricula and testing regimes set at the provincial level. As well, a fourth solution is examined, one which implores governments to resist the large adjustments inherent in the aforementioned options, and instead to focus more directly on continuing efforts to improve what takes place in the school classrooms. However, in a way this one, too, seeks major change, for it endeavours to accomplish the very difficult task of transforming the way teachers and others in the individual schools think about teaching and learning.

School-Based Management and School Councils

One possible response to the varied demands of the education sector is to effect a decentralization of authority down to the school level. If the education system suffers from a lack of choice and diversity, and if it appears ensnared in bureaucratic procedures and practices, then a possible solution is to give more influence to those at the local level. At a minimum, such a move would involve giving local school authorities and interests greater say over administrative matters or the means for accomplishing policy ends, and most likely would extend to include additional influence over education policies. It is also argued that the quality of education would improve because those closest to the students—and hence those best able to determine the needs of students—are given more authority and responsibility.

Though this particular option could entail many specific actions, there are two basic directions in which a decentralization of authority may and usually does take. One direction is related to an arrangement which is called school-based (or school-site) management. Under this particular arrangement, some authority over budgetary, personnel, curriculum, and operational matters is transferred from either the provincial ministry or (more usually) the local school board to the school level. Instead of school board trustees deciding how to spend certain monies or hire certain individuals, the principal and teachers at the individual schools are authorized to make these kinds of decisions. Typically, some type of formal decision-making body is set up in the school to exercise the newly acquired powers. In some cases, the principal assumes the lead, in others there is a more collegial decision-making process in which teachers take a full part. Up to this time, few Canadian provinces have embraced school-based management, but there have been some noteworthy exceptions. Since the late 1970s the public school board in Edmonton has operated along the principles of school-based management. In this district the province and board specify the broad purposes of education, and it is up to the schools to use the available financial and human resources in a manner that allows them to meet the goals of the provincial education system. For instance, each school is provided with a degree of discretion which allows them to specify the distribution of allotted revenues. Selected school districts in British Columbia have also introduced school-based management, and Alberta has recently announced the establishment of school-based management arrangements for the entire province.

The second direction involves the establishment of school or parent councils in the individual schools. With school-based management, there is a decentralization of authority *within* the organization, but with school councils the relevant authority is moved *out* of the school administrative apparatus and into the hands of parents and community members.[19] Usually, parents form the majority of school-council members, and their job is either to decide on matters relating to the core concerns of the school—budgets, curriculum, personnel— or to restrict themselves to advising the principal and the local school board on these concerns. In either guise, school councils are meant to go beyond traditional parent-teacher associations and the latter's focus on fund-raising and other non-academic matters. In the past few years, nearly all provinces and territories have established school councils. In most instances, parents do form the majority, and the responsibility of the councils is typically limited to an advisory role. However, the intent in some jurisdictions is for the councils eventually to assume a decision-making role, especially in light of the severe reduction in the number of school boards that has taken place in all provinces.

Expectations for both school-based management and school councils are quite high. In relation to the former, the belief is that "schools will become more effective only if teachers and principals gain a sense of personal responsibility for their students' performance."[20] In addition to improving the quality of education, school-based management is purportedly better situated to respond to the increasing diversity of Canada, and it reduces the role of the education bureaucracy in the daily operation of schools. As for school councils, they, too, are supposed to better the educational product. A Newfoundland report, echoing the views in other provinces, states that school councils are set up "for the purpose of enhancing the quality of school programs and improving the levels of student achievement in the school."[21] In theory, they also respond to parent demands for a greater voice in the operation of schools. The fact that school councils have sprouted in almost all provincial and territorial school systems suggests high hopes for this particular reform.

The question, though, is whether decentralization works in practice. With respect to school-based management, there are some encouraging signs. The relevant experience in Canada suggests that school-based management can result in greater diversity, enhanced flexibility, more teacher participation in decision making, and a "higher level of awareness of and concern for the school as a whole."[22] Some success has also been reported in other nations as well, and researchers have uncovered conditions which make for successful school-based management arrangements.[23] However, the brunt of the evidence suggests that school-based management *on its own* has only marginal utility. One of the problems relates to implementation: the degree of responsibility devolved to schools is often "remarkably limited." School-based management is expected to deal with curriculum, personnel, and other important matters, but usually it is limited to such "peripheral issues" as school climate, safety, campus beautification, and career education.[24] Perhaps more disconcerting, some studies show that even when properly implemented the benefits are few, that schools with and without school-based management differ very little on indicators relating to innovation and focus on academic matters.[25] On the overall effect of school-based management on student achievement, there is no clear indication of a positive relationship between the two.[26] Also, school-based management schemes may transform relations within the school in an undesirable manner, as principals become more managerial in their perspective and slight their role as partner with teachers in the education process.[27] All in all, school-based management struggles when introduced without any accompanying adjustments in the education process. However, as will be argued later, it may flourish if coupled with a policy—namely, parental choice—which provides an incentive for schools to become more diverse, flexible, and effective in their operations.

As for school councils, the preliminary indicators for Canada are disappointing. There seems to be some confusion about the exact purpose of the councils, and school officials appear resistant to the idea that parents and community members should have greater influence over the core operations of schools.[28] One examination of school councils in Alberta concludes that "none of the persons involved in the implementation of parental involvement was feeling successful: not parents, teachers, or administrators."[29] The experience with school councils in other countries suggests parents are rarely afforded a real say over matters relating to curriculum, personnel, and budgets.[30] There is as well some doubt that successfully implemented councils would have a positive effect on learning.[31] Moreover, studies indicate that parents have their greatest impact on student achievement when supporting the child in the home and helping teachers as classroom volunteers, and *not* when they become involved in school decision making.[32] It is also important to note that some parents themselves are not eager to assume a governing role, partly because of the time-consuming nature of this role and partly because they feel more comfortable leaving governance matters up to local school officials.[33]

Parental Choice

A second option for addressing the concerns with schools is parental or school choice. Like the first option, this one can come in different shapes and forms. It may involve only minor adjustments to the education process. For example, parents and guardians may be afforded an opportunity to send their children to a school other than the one located in the local neighbourhood. It may also involve facilitating the establishment of schools which recognize the demands of certain groups or religious interests. The separate or Catholic school system in some of the provinces is an example of this kind of parental choice. In its most extreme form, parental choice entails providing parents with a voucher—a cash coupon—which they can use to purchase a spot in any school within the school system. Though these manifestations of parental choice are different in some important respects, they are the same in the sense that they all give parents and guardians some degree of choice in the selection of schools for their children.

Parental choice is an option because it is felt to be a very effective policy. Indeed, some consider parental choice a "panacea," something which will cure the major problems which face public education systems around the world.[34] This confidence flows in part from the belief that choice deals a mortal blow to the major problem with the school system, which is its monopolistic character. Less effusive supporters recognize that nonschool factors, such as family background, must always be taken into consideration when discussing the effectiveness of any school reform, but they nevertheless argue that parental choice can have a positive effect on academic achievement and can lead to an education system which better responds to increasing diversity in the population. At a minimum, a policy of school choice responds to the desire of the postmaterialists for more say in education and, unlike school councils, it does so in a way that is not time-consuming. If parents are unhappy with a school, there is no need under a policy of school choice to haggle over the perceived problems at school council meetings, a not insignificant consideration for busy people. Instead, parents take their children out of the school and look for a better one.

In the present school system in Canada there is already an element of parental choice. Prospective users of schools can choose between English and French language schools, denominational schools, French Immersion programs, bilingual schools, Aboriginal schools, and private schools. Moreover, many school boards allow parents to select public schools outside the designated attendance area, and some boards enter into agreements with one another to facilitate choice among schools in different school districts. Notwithstanding this, the Canadian school system still appears to fall short of offering an acceptable degree of choice. Religious groups claim that government support of schools is limited to only a few belief systems, and public financing of private schools is limited. Also, boards which allow either intradistrict or interdistrict choice place restrictions on this type of choice (for example, no transportation is available or there is a lack of space in the school of choice). More generally, parental choice in Canada tends to be associated with a response to *group* rights (religion and language), with less attention being paid to *individual* rights—those of families, parents, and guardians.[35] A policy of parental choice in Canada would thus involve giving greater support to individual families in their choice of schools, which might mean providing transportation to the choice of school or simply making parents more aware of choice options. It might also mean giving parents (acting with teachers and others) the opportunity and the financial support to set up their own schools and to operate them with only minimal government regulation. These are called "charter schools," and the province of Alberta already has passed legislation authorizing such schools.[36] A policy of parental choice which responds to *both* individual and group rights would be the institution of a voucher system, in which parents apply government funding to any type of schooling.

As with decentralization, there is conflicting evidence on the usefulness of parental choice. In England a fairly expansive system of parental choice has been introduced, and the results so far are unsettling. It appears that the policy is leading to an increased segregation of schools by aptitude and social class, and the expectant diversity of schooling under parental choice has not emerged.[37] In general, what is happening is that well-off families are better able to take advantage of parental choice than their less well-off counterparts. In the United States, choice policies also bring up concerns of equity, for they "tend markedly to differentiate choosers from nonchoosers in ways that increase the social stratification of schools rather than reducing inequality."[38] Equally damning, there is little indication that enrolment in choice-based schools in the United States leads to a significant enhancement of academic performance.[39] There is also a concern that choice policies will result in curricula that forsake courses of study which are considered socially beneficial but of only direct limited value in the job market. Inherent in education is a tension between "enhancing individual well-being and ensuring an educated citizenry essential in a democracy," and the fear is that with school choice this tension may be resolved in a manner that greatly favours the private over the public interest.[40]

Despite these troubling results, there are some benefits associated with parental choice. For one, choice is popular with parents; thus this particular option appears to respond to at least one of the present problems with the education system, namely, its insensitivity to the wishes of parents. For instance, a policy of intradistrict choice in the Edmonton public school system had led to "far fewer parental complaints about schools," and the approach is popular in the United States.[41] Also, some challenge the contention that choice has no real effect on academic achievement, and provide some evidence in support of their claims.[42] As for complaints about the lack of diversity, this may reflect the fact that many parents *want* the same kind of education—one which focuses on the development of basic skills—and that parental choice allows parents to escape school boards determined to provide a different kind of education. Finally, with respect to the problem of equity, some studies show that disadvantaged families are aggressive users of policies of parental choice.[43] In a way, this is to be expected, for well-off families already are able to choose schools through residential location. What parental choice does is to extend this ability to select schools to those unable to pick and choose where they wish to reside.

Parental choice is a controversial policy option. In some eyes, parental choice threatens to produce a segregated school system which offers no real academic benefits to any child. The whole notion of a public school system, with its offering of a rich range of courses to all children, appears under attack. But choice also seems to speak to parents' need to have some input into school selection, and the very notion of opening up the school system to allow for more choice is on its own quite attractive. As well, it may make school-based management arrangements more effective, for now schools would have a greater incentive to pay more attention to their offerings in light of the existence of choice-conscious parents. Indeed, the two might naturally go hand-in-hand. Parental choice would only work well if schools were able to respond to the wishes of parents, and school-based management would rely on the demands of parents to prod it into serious consideration of curriculum and general overall orientation of the school. What the pairing of the two reforms does is create *within the public sector* more competitive or market-like conditions under which the forces of supply and demand—the schools and the parents respectively—are given more latitude in order to produce an education system which satisfies the wishes of all concerned parties.

Standardization and Centralization

Arguably the most important force driving education reform is the belief that students must become better fitted to compete in the new global economy. To meet this goal, it is commonly believed that the purpose of education should be the "acquisition of basic knowledge and skills," and that this can be achieved through the establishment of a common curriculum and an associated set of standards.[44] Moreover, to ensure that the basic skills are being learned, an extensive regime of testing ought to be established. Finally, given that these changes apply to all students, provincial ministries must assume a greater role in education policy making. What needs to happen is that much of the responsibility now lying with school boards must be transferred to provincial decision makers. A standardization of the education system implies a centralization of authority.

Accordingly, a third option is one which goes in a direction which is the opposite of that taken by the options considered so far. School-based management, school councils, and parental choice all assume a *decentralization* of authority is essential to solving any problems facing the education system. But the option under consideration here contends that a *centralization* of authority should take place. Interestingly, many provincial authorities support this latter contention, for nearly all provinces have begun to implement reforms which include common curricula, province-wide testing, standardized report cards, and enhanced teacher training. These same provinces have also drastically reduced the number of school boards, and in New Brunswick the boards have been eliminated altogether. In making these changes, provinces have objected to the claim that these changes amount to a centralization of power. What has happened, they say, is that the duties of provincial and local authorities has just been clarified, with the former setting the goals of education and the latter devising the most appropriate means for meeting the goals. But a close look reveals a centralization of power in the hands of provincial authorities and the consequent transformation of school boards into administrative agents of provincial departments of education.

Perhaps the province that best exemplifies movement in this direction is Ontario. In the past few years Ontario has effected a province-wide curriculum at the elementary-school level. The province's government says this new course of study "provides a solid foundation in the basics" and "sets out clear, challenging and consistent standards for what students should learn year-by-year."[45] Also, there will be regular testing on a province-wide basis, and standardized report cards "will give parents clear and concise information about their children's progress."[46] Moreover, a regulatory body has been set whose purpose is to ensure that teaching is of high quality. The province also enacted legislation which cut the number of school boards in half and placed limits on the number of board trustees and their remuneration. Most recently, it passed the *Education Quality Improvement Act*, which gives the province greater authority to regulate matters relating to class size, length of school year, and the amount of time teachers spend teaching on a daily basis. (It was this act which precipitated the Ontario teachers' strike.) The government has also reduced spending on education and taken away the power of school boards to levy education property taxes. All this has been done, says the government, to "provide our students with a strong grasp of the skills they'll need to have successful careers in today's competitive economy."[47] Critics claim, though, that the changes represent an unprecedented centralization of authority in the hands of the provincial department of education. If so, then nearly all provinces have experienced unique developments in education, for all have either already gone down the path that Ontario is taking or are in the process of doing so.

This widespread support for the standardization of education and an emphasis on the basics certainly implies that such action will address the problems facing education. In fact, there are indications that this might be the most desirable option for the education system.

Administrative and other nonclassroom costs at the school board level have increased quite significantly, so a reduction in the role of school boards might be in order. One Ontario report claims that for every dollar spent in the classroom by school boards, more than 80 cents is spent outside the classroom, which if true seems far too much.[48] Also, this course of action responds to the demands of those parents who believe that schools have strayed too far from the "three Rs" of education. Last, and perhaps most important, the establishment of academically focused, common curricula may enhance learning and achievement. In both international and national tests, Alberta scores the highest among the provinces. In attempting to explain this result, an education researcher observes that "Alberta has had, for a number of years, a very clearly set out curriculum and expectations for what students should be learning at every level from Grade 1 up," while an Alberta education official notes the importance of "a well-defined curriculum and a provincial testing program that gives feedback to classroom teachers."[49] Alberta is successful because it has been one of the first provinces to endorse a public education system with a common curriculum which concentrates on the basics and whose students are regularly assessed.

As with any purported policy solution, this one, though, is not without some possible pitfalls. The focus on basics may lead to a kind of education which prepares students for a career but teaches them little about democracy, morality and the society in which they live. Education is not just about the private interests of parents and students, but also strives to offer an educational experience which serves the public interest; as with a policy of parental choice, centralization increases the chances of taking the "public" out of the public school system. In addition, some parents may in fact want one common school with a focus on the fundamentals, but it seems highly unlikely that this will satisfy all families in a country which is becoming more and more diverse. Furthermore, the emphasis on testing might lead to a host of problems: teaching to the test, a devaluation of subjects which are difficult to test (such as music or art), and high costs associated with both the actual testing and the use of test results.[50] As well, analyses of international tests reveal that countries that do well "are not particularly focused on more assessment and have in fact given professional educators more autonomy in teaching and assessment than is the case in the English-speaking countries."[51] Most interestingly, this option assumes an economy which requires an educated labour force with a firm grasp of basic skills and knowledge. But some projections suggest that many jobs in the future will demand little education.[52] The rush on the part of provincial governments to produce students with fundamental skills may only lead to overeducated individuals mired in low-skill, low-pay jobs. This, of course, may be the fate of all the options considered so far, given that each values high-quality education. But this outcome seems particularly relevant to the standardization and centralization approach because of the emphasis of the latter on linking education and requirements of the economy.

Teaching and Learning

A fourth and final option to consider focuses on dealing with what transpires in individual classrooms. The key to a better education system, from this viewpoint, is to help teachers teach and students to learn. The other three options, of course, also focus on this, but only indirectly through structural changes which are eventually expected to have an impact on the classroom. But the emphasis here is to address the classroom *directly*, which means providing more support for teachers, enriching the training of teachers, developing more effective methods of pedagogy, and recognizing that students have diverse needs that have to be met in creative and innovative ways. More broadly, it also means changing the way all those participating in the classroom—teachers, students, parents—*think* about teaching and learning and about how classroom activities should be conducted. In other words, the culture of education must change, for a plan of structural change will meet with little success without a shift in how individual schools conceptualize their purpose and responsibilities.[53]

In some respects, this purported solution is less change-oriented than the others. It leaves existing institutional arrangements largely intact; it also builds upon existing practices— what takes place in the classroom—rather than supplanting them. School-based management, parental choice, and centralization of responsibilities are almost revolutionary in their implications, whereas the focus on teaching and learning is more in the incremental reform mode. This perception, which has some validity, stems from the belief that the problems facing the education system are not as great as some suppose. It also arises from the belief that school-based management, parental choice, and the like are equivalent to quick fixes that are doomed to fail, and that the only way to approach education is to understand that any successful change will involve a long and arduous process. In other respects, though, this option is just as revolutionary as the others. It seeks to make major changes in the classroom, such as encouraging more collaborative work, facilitating independent learning exercises, and exploiting the resources of the surrounding community in the class.[54] It also tries to place teachers in the class who "combine deep knowledge of subject matter and a wide repertoire of teaching strategies with intimate knowledge of students' growth, experience and development."[55] One would be hard-pressed to identify this with incremental change.

The focus on teaching and learning appears reasonable. Ultimately, the key to education lies in the classroom, so it seems sensible to start with those who are to be found in the classroom. One should refrain from imposing a solution on teachers and their classes, and instead work with teachers and turn them into agents of change. This approach maintains that reform is an inside-out process, whereby the transformation in education begins in the individual classroom and gravitates outwards to the larger education structures. The implicit rejection in this approach to large-scale structural adjustments is also attractive, for these structural changes do at times appear to be quick fixes. Most recognize that turning the education system into something better will not happen overnight, and the emphasis on teaching and learning accepts that change will in fact be long and arduous. Nevertheless, this approach is not without its own possible problems. For many, the emphasis on teaching, learning, and meeting the individual requirements of students has been the approach of the past, and it has clearly failed. The watered-down curricula, the absence of testing, and the lack of perceivable standards are all a result of too great a focus on the learning needs of students. Also, the option at times demands almost superhuman teachers; according to one proponent of this approach, teachers must "tak[e] into account the real knowledge and experiences of learners, including their cultures, their communities, and the conditions in which they live."[56] Finally, the option may be too optimistic in believing that change can take place in the class without making concomitant adjustments in the larger education structures. What the likes of parental choice, school councils, and common curricula do is to place pressure on the individual classroom to change. Supporters of the teaching and learning option are critical of the larger structural approaches because the latter fail to tell policy makers *how* the system should be changed, but at least these approaches provide a stimulus for change. It is not always clear where the stimulus for change resides in this last option.

CONCLUSION

Canada's education system is under pressure to reform itself. The way education services are delivered must undergo some kind of change. But the kind of change that needs to take place is not clear, partly because there is some difficulty in determining the problems with existing arrangements and partly because there is some uncertainty about the impact of the available alternatives. Provincial governments think they know what has to be done. They have acted in an almost concert-like fashion to produce a more standardized and centralized education system. But supporting evidence for such action is inconclusive, and there are some new problems that might emerge with this approach. This essay has suggested that a combination of school-based management and parental choice might be considered. Essentially, this recommendation relies on increased flexibility and competitiveness for effecting positive changes in the education system. With this option, those who are closest to the students—the schools— are better positioned to respond to the needs of students, and the policy of parental choice offers more say to parents and provides an incentive for schools to exercise the flexibility garnered through school-based management. But this could lead to what many most fear: namely, a school system divided into the academically able and the less academically able. The tentativeness with which this approach is offered may be well-advised.

This suggested combination of two approaches leads to a further proposal, which is that elements of all options be put into place. In a sense, this is what is happening in Canada now. Governments have centralized responsibility for the setting of curricula and tests, established school councils for the purpose of helping in the fine-tuning of centrally established policies, enlarged the range of choice available to parents and other users of schools, and continued efforts to make changes to classroom procedures. However, this bringing together of the various options has some built-in contradictions. Centralizing governments will be reluctant to share authority with parent-dominated school councils, and the diversity inherent in some versions of parental choice may conflict with the intention to provide for common curricula and schools. Moreover, a focus on teaching and learning exists uneasily with strategies which seek to make major changes to the basic structures of education. For one thing, the latter distracts reformers from dealing with the challenges associated with teaching and learning.

The appetite for change in education in Canada has indeed been whetted. But that is all that can be said with any degree of certainty. For the prudent observer of education policy, the problems which face education and the proposed solutions need to be examined and debated in more detail, and experimentation with some of the proposed changes seems sensible. Then the education system will be prepared to move forward with confidence.

NOTES

1. Education Improvement Commission, *The Road Ahead: A Report on Learning Time, Class Size and Staffing,* August 1997, 2.

2. Stephen B. Lawton et al., *Busting Bureaucracy to Reclaim Our Schools* (Montreal: IRPP, 1995), 26–27.

3. Government of Newfoundland and Labrador, *Adjusting the Course: Restructuring the School System for Educational Excellence* (25 November 1993): 2; New Brunswick Department of Education, *Towards a Quality Education Agenda As Part of a Renewed Education System for New Brunswick* (1996): 1.

4. Ontario Ministry of Education and Training, *New Foundations for Ontario Education: A Summary* (1995):3; and Manitoba Education and Training, *Renewing Education: New Directions, A Blueprint for Action* (July 1994).

5. Allan Gregg and Michael Posner, *The Big Picture: What Canadians Think About Almost Everything* (Toronto: MacFarlane, Walter and Ross, 1990), 64; Victor Dwyer, "Are We Cheating Our Kids?," *Maclean's* 14 March 1994: 47; and Statistics Canada, *Enrolment in Elementary and Secondary Schools and Schools for the Blind and the Deaf,* http://www.statcan.ca/english/Pgdb/People/education/educ01.htm.

6. Ronald Manzer, *Public Schools and Political Ideas: Canadian Educational Policy in Historical Perspective* (Toronto: University of Toronto Press, 1994), 213.

7. Philip Nagy, "Accountability in a Broader Context," *Canadian Journal of Education* 20:1 (Winter 1995): 93; and Francois Gendron, "Funding Public School Systems: A 25-Year Review," *Education Quarterly Review* 4:2 (1997): 29.

8. Murnane and Levy make this point in relation to U.S. schools. See Richard J. Murnane and Frank Levy, "What General Motors Can Teach U.S. Schools About the Proper Role of Markets in Education Reform: *Phi Delta Kappan* 78:2 (1996): 110.

9. Stephen B. Lawton, "Why Restructure? An International Survey of the Roots of Reform," *Journal of Education Policy* 7:2 (1992): 147.

10. See Neil Nevitte, *The Decline of Deference: Canadian Value Change in Cross- National Perspective* (Peterborough: Broadview Press, 1996).

11. Lawton, "Why Restructure?," 147 (reference in sentence omitted).

12. On these matters, see J. Anthony Riffel, Benjamin Levin and Jonathan Young, "Diversity in Canadian Education," *Journal of Education Policy* 11:1 (1996); Kari Dehli, "Travelling Tales: Education Reform and Parental 'Choice' in Postmodern Times," *Journal of Education* Policy 11:1 (1996); Bruce Wilkinson, *Educational Choice: Necessary But Not Sufficient* (Montreal: IRPP 1994), 24–25.

13. Barbara Ward quoted in Jerry Paquette, "Universal Education: Meanings, Challenges, and Options into the Third Millennium," *Curriculum Inquiry* 25:1 (1995): 27.

14. Lawton et al., *Busting Bureaucracy to Reclaim Our Schools* 40; and Lawton, "Why Restructure?," 149–50.

15. Virginia Galt et al., "Power Struggle Rocks Canada's Schools," [Toronto] *Globe and Mail,* 11 October 1997: A10. Polling in the United States also reveals that parents tend to be supportive of their own schools while being critical of the education system. See Tom Loveless, "The Structure of Public Confidence in Education," *American Journal of Education* 105:2 (1997): 140–42.

16. Virginia Galt et al., "Power Struggle Rocks Canada's Schools," A10; and D. W. Livingstone, D. Hart, and L. E. Davie, *Public Attitudes Towards Education in Ontario 1994* (Toronto: Ontario Institute for Studies in Education, 1995), 9–11.

17. Lawton et al., *Busting Bureaucracy to Reclaim Our Schools,* 25.

18. D'Arcy Jenish, "The Battle for Ontario's Schools," *Maclean's,* 17 November 1997: 23.

19. Bruce Bimber, *School Decentralization: Lessons from the Study of Bureaucracy* (Santa Monica: RAND, 1993), 8.

20. Paul T. Hill and Josephine Bonan, *Decentralization and Accountability in Public Education* (Santa Monica: RAND, 1991), 9.

21. Government of Newfoundland and Labrador, Department of Education, *Working Together for Educational Excellence: School Council Handbook* (Fall 1995, Revised June 1996): 1.

22. Peter Coleman, "Implementing School Based Decision Making," *The Canadian Administrator* 26:7 (1987): 9.

23. Priscilla Wohlstetter, "Getting School-Based Management Right: What Works and What Doesn't," *Phi Delta Kappan* 77:1 (1995): 23–25.

24. Priscilla Wohlstetter and Allen Odden, "Rethinking School-Based Management Policy and Research," *Educational Administration Quarterly* 28:4 (1992): 532–33.

25. Carol H. Weiss, "Shared Decision Making About What? A Comparison of Schools With and Without Teacher Participation," *Teachers College Record* 95:1 (1993).

26. Larry E. Sackney and Dennis J. Dibski, "School-Based Management: A Critical Perspective, " *Educational Management and Administration* 22:2 (1994): 107–8.

27. Geoff Whitty, "Creating Quasi-Markets in Education: A Review of Recent Research on Parental Choice and School Autonomy in Three Countries, " *Review of Research in Education,* 22, ed. Michael W. Apple (Washington, DC: American Educational Research Association, 1997), 26.

28. See Alice Collins, "School Councils: A Pilot Study," *Morning Watch* 23:3-4 (1996); Kathryn G. Skau, "Parental Involvement: Issues and Concerns," *The Alberta Journal of Educational Research* XLII:1 (1996).

29. Skau, 47.

30. See, for example, Viviane M. J. Robinson et al., "The Community-School Partnership in the Management of New Zealand Schools," *Journal of Educational Administration* 32:3 (1994); Viviane M. J. Robinson and Helen Timperley, "Learning to Be Responsive: The Impact of School Choice and Decentralization," *Educational Management and Administration* 24:1 (1996); Janet L. David, "School-Based Decision-Making: Kentucky's Test of Decentralization," *Phi Delta Kappan* 75:9 (1994); Betty Malen and Rodney T. Ogawa, "Professional-Patron Influence on Site-Based Governance Councils: A Confounding Case Study," *Educational Evaluation and Policy Analysis* 10:4 (1988); Kevin J. Brehony and Rosemary Deem, "School Governing Bodies: Reshaping Education in Their Own Image?" *The Sociological Review,* 43:1 (1995); and C.D. Rabb et al., "Devolving the Management of Schools in Britain, " *Educational Administration Quarterly* 33:2 (1997).

31. Michael G. Fullan with Suzanne Stiegelbauer, *The New Meaning of Educational Change,* 2nd ed. (New York: Teachers College Press, 1991), 237.

32. Ontario, Royal Commission on Learning, *For the Love of Learning, Vol. 4* (Toronto: Printer for Ontario, 1994), 107; Chandra Muller, "Parent Involvement and Academic Achievement: An Analysis of Family Resources Available to the Child," *Parents, Their Children, and Schools,* eds. Barbara Schneider and James S. Coleman (Boulder: Westview Press, 1993), 87; and Fullan, *The New Meaning of Educational Change,* 229–37.

33. See, for example, Raab et al., "Devolving the Management of Schools in Britain," 154-55; and Ontario Parent Council, *Report on the Establishment of School Parent Councils in Ontario* (15 July 1994): 63–64.

34. John E. Chubb and Terry M. Moe, *Politics, Markets and America's Schools* (Washington, DC: The Brookings Institution, 1990), 217.

35. Stephen B. Lawton, "Issues of Choice: Canadian and American Perspectives," *The Choice Controversy,* ed. Peter W. Cookson (Newbury: Corwin Press, 1992), 191–92.

36. Alberta Education, *Charter School Handbook* (Edmonton: Alberta Education, April 1995).

37. See Geoff Whitty and Sally Power, "Quasi-Markets and Curriculum Control: Making Sense of Recent Education Reform in England and Wales," *Educational Administration Quarterly* 33:2

(1997); and Anne West, Hazel Pennell, and Ann Edge, "Exploring the Impact of Reform on School-Enrollment Policies in England," *Educational Administration Quarterly* 33:2 (1997).

38. Richard F. Elmore and Bruce Fuller, "Empirical Research on Educational Choice: What Are the Implications for Policy-Makers?," *Who Chooses? Who Loses?: Culture, Institutions, and the Unequal Effects of School Choice,* eds. Bruce Fuller and Richard Elmore, with Gary Orfield (New York: Teachers College, Press, 1996), 190.

39. Bruce Fuller, "Is School Choice Working?" *Educational Leadership* 54:2 (1996): 38.

40. Martha McCarthy, "School Privatization: Friendly or Hostile Takeover?" *Journal of Education Policy* 12:1–2 (1997): 61.

41. Wilkinson, *Educational Choice,* 59; and Fuller, "Is School Choice Working?," 38.

42. Paul E. Peterson, "A Report Card on School Choice," *Commentary* 104:4 (1997): 31; Paul E. Peterson and Chad Noyes, "School Choice in Milwaukee," *New Schools for a New Century,* eds. Diane Ravitch and Joseph P. Viteritti (New Haven: Yale University Press, 1997), 144–46; and Joe Nathan, *Charter Schools: Creating Hope and Opportunity for American Education* (San Francisco: Jossey-Bass Publishers, 1996), 168–71.

43. Barbara Schneider, Kathryn S. Schiller and James S. Coleman, "Public School Choice: Some Evidence from the National Education Longitudinal Study of 1988," *Educational Evaluation and Policy Analysis* 18:1 (1996): 26–27.

44. Manzer, 236.

45. Ontario Ministry of Education and Training, *Excellence in Education: Ontario's Plan for Reform* (Toronto: Queen's Printer for Ontario, 1997), 1; and Ontario Ministry of Education and Training, *Putting Students First: Ontario's Plan for Education Reform* (Toronto: Queen's Printer for Ontario, 1997), 1.

46. Ontario Ministry of Education and Training, *Putting Students First,* 2.

47. Statement to the Legislature by John Snobelen, Minister of Education and Training on the *Education Quality Improvement Act, 1997* (September 22, 1997, http://www.edu.gov.ca/eng/document/statemen/sept22.html): 1.

48. James Rusk, "Paper Sets Stage for Shakeup of Ontario School System," [Toronto] *Globe and Mail,* 11 January 1997: A11.

49. Virginia Galt, "Alberta Students Rank High in Science, Math," [Toronto] *Globe and Mail,* 12 June 1997: A10; and Jennifer Lewington, "Young Canadians Lack Elite Skills, Science Test Finds," [Toronto] *Globe and Mail,* 30 January 1997: A6.

50. Nagy, 95, 98.

51. Benjamin Levin, "The Lessons of International Education Reform," *Journal of Education Policy* 12:4 (1997): 263.

52. Paquette, 35.

53. Michael Fullan, *Change Forces: Probing the Depths of Educational Reform* (New York: Falmer Press, 1993), 49–51.

54. Benjamin Levin, "Changing Basic Delivery Systems," *Advances in Educational Productivity: Organizational Influences on Educational Productivity,* eds. Benjamin Levin et al. (Greenwich: JAI Press Inc., 1995), 200–3.

55. Linda Darling-Hammond, "Reframing the School Reform Agenda," *Phi Delta Kappan* 74:10 (1993): 754.

56. Darling-Hammond, 758.

INFORMATION, TECHNOLOGY, AND GOVERNMENT ADMINISTRATION

Information management and technology may sound like relatively straightforward issues for government. It might be assumed that governments are routinely in favour of making information available and promoting technological development. While superficially appealing, such bland assumptions overlook much that is important. Further investigation and reflection are imperative.

There are a multitude of complex issues lurking beneath the general heading of "information management" issues. Governments and public sector agencies are, at one and the same time, collectors of voluminous mountains of information (vital statistics, criminal and health records, economic performance indicators, etc.), agents of information transmission (through educational enlightenment, provision of information on disease or lifestyle trends, publishers of statistical compendiums, etc.), protectors of private information (personal information gathered through health care or criminal law settings, personal income information gathered through tax collection, etc.), protectors of, or censors of, information on behalf of the general public (enforcers of laws about official secrets, enforcers of prohibitions against pornography, etc.) and the authors of legal regulatory arrangements governing accessibility to information in nongovernmental arenas (what information has to be made available for business incorporation, how often lobbyists have to report upon their efforts, definition of what constitutes truth in advertising, etc.). Each and every one of these roles poses responsibilities for public sector agencies. At issue in the essay by Colin Bennett and Robin Bayley are the questions of openness (access to information provisions) and privacy (protection of personal information and highly sensitive material). These are particularly important topics as they relate to fundamental questions about how societies determine what information should be publicly available and what should be restricted. Discussion of these issues can serve as a springboard to the larger agenda of information management concerns.

Technological advances also pose diverse complications for governments. Computers and newly emerging technologies provide promises of greater access to information and communication across vast geographic distances. Meanwhile, these same advances pose problems of confidentiality (protection of personal information), of costly technology upgrades, and of discernable gulfs between those in society who understand and can afford the technology and those who cannot. Jocelyne Bourgon offers an overview of the effects of new technologies and computerization on modern governance. Her insights can serve as a springboard for further study and reflection.

DISCUSSION QUESTIONS

1. What kinds of information have you provided to government agencies at different stages in your life? Have you ever tried to examine the files government agencies may possess about you? Why or why not?

2. What kinds of information should public officials have access to, for example: customs officials at national borders? tax collection officials? military leaders? university administrators? gatherers of statistical information for development of national economic indicators? Why?

3. Are there any suitable grounds for governments keeping certain kinds of documents or information confidential? Why or why not?

4. Should there be any exclusions when people attempt to access government records or files? If so, what sort? Who should oversee access deliberations?

5. What groups or types of people do you think would be most concerned by issues of access to government information? Why?

6. What sorts of challenges are raised for governments by advances in computerization and technology? How important are they?

7. Do you sense that governments will be able to respond to the challenges posed by emerging technologies and computerization? Why or why not?

8. Why do you think some people are worried about protecting privacy in the years ahead? Do you share their concerns? Why or why not?

THE NEW PUBLIC ADMINISTRATION OF INFORMATION: Canadian Approaches to Access and Privacy

Colin J. Bennett and Robin Bayley

Whilst preparing this chapter, a number of issues relating to access to information and protection of privacy have appeared in the media. In British Columbia, a special legislative committee is reviewing the operation of British Columbia's *Freedom of Information and Protection of Privacy* legislation, as is mandated in this 1992 statute. In Quebec, the Commission d'Accès à l'Information (the body established under the 1982 access and privacy protection legislation) is investigating the improper release of personal tax information from the Bouchard government. In Ontario, Metro Toronto is considering a new form of biometric identification system for welfare recipients. In Ottawa, the federal Privacy Commissioner has criticized the matching of immigration records with unemployment records. And his counterpart, the Information Commissioner, has issued his last annual report criticizing the culture of secrecy that is still pervasive in Ottawa government departments.[1]

Information policy issues rarely capture the attention of politicians and hardly ever influence the outcome of elections. Nevertheless, they are constantly beneath the surface of our most significant political challenges and conflicts, inspiring the passions of outside advocates and the constant attention of the media. Conversely, the implementation of information policies can frustrate politicians and officials, increasingly pressed to achieve existing policy goals with fewer public resources. Access to information and privacy protection are now constant features of the Canadian administrative landscape.

Yet 20 years ago, no freedom of information or privacy legislation existed in Canada. Only very recently have Canadian legislatures seen fit to establish statutory frameworks for the collection, retention, use, and disclosure of information. Access to information and privacy protection are very new policy areas—even though the underlying values and principles have always posed difficult dilemmas for democratic governments. How and why, then, in under 20 years, has this group of policies emerged? How do access and privacy laws attempt to regulate the use of information by public agencies? And what effects have they had on the day-to-day work of government employees? This essay attempts to address these questions.

THE INTERNATIONAL SPREAD OF FREEDOM OF INFORMATION AND PROTECTION OF PRIVACY LEGISLATION

Although freedom of information (FOI) and protection of privacy are treated in Canada within the same statutes, the two policy areas do have somewhat different origins. There are, therefore, some countries still that have one without the other.

Let us deal first with FOI. These laws were initially inspired by a perception of an uncontrolled growth in the size, power, and complexity of the modern state; by a "credibility gap" fuelled by incidents of secrecy and deception; and by a declining sense of trust in government. Demands for greater access to government information are consistent with what Guy Peters has called a "new individualism" in public administration, apparent in many advanced industrial states.[2]

There are now approximately a dozen liberal democratic states that have enacted laws to allow public access to government-held information (see Table 1). Apart from Sweden, whose *Freedom of the Press Act* dates from 1766, the first in modern times was the United States *Freedom of Information Act* of 1967. As all others have tended to follow this American example, there is a significant degree of cross-national similarity between FOI laws. Table 1 does not indicate that several other countries, including the United Kingdom, are seriously debating the introduction of such legislation.[3] Nor does it indicate those jurisdictions that allow access to narrowly specified types of information.

The central purpose of FOI is to provide a legal right for any person to inspect the records of public agencies. Any person who seeks an official record does not have to establish any right to seek access, or state the reasons why he/she may want that information. Typically, the information has to be reasonably described, and agencies may normally charge a modest fee for their time and effort. This "public's right to know" is qualified by specific and limited exemptions, the most important of which tend to relate to national security, commercial, law enforcement, and third-party personal information. The burden is placed squarely upon the agency to justify the withholding of that information.

The cross-national differences centre on the time limits within which an agency must respond, the permissible fees an agency may charge for providing the information, and the breadth of the exemptions. The legislation also differs with regard to the operation of the instruments of oversight and redress.[4] Most countries, including Canada, have established specialized review mechanisms in the form of access to information commissioners, whose decisions are normally subject to judicial review. The exception is the United States, where appeals are handled solely within the federal court system.

Turning now to privacy protection, we immediately confront a greater conceptual diversity, as there are a number of issues embraced by this ambiguous and controversial term. The concept of privacy can serve to justify a right to make private decisions about intimate sexual and familial matters (such as contraception or abortion); it can be invoked to limit surveillance by law enforcement agencies; it has a spatial dimension, referring to the claim for an exclusive physical space around individuals; and it can refer to the right to control the circulation of personal information. It is important, therefore, to specify clearly that this article is concerned with this last interpretation—"information privacy" (or "data protection," to use the European nomenclature).

The problems associated with the increased capability of organizations to collect, store, manipulate, and disseminate vast quantities of personal data using the latest technologies have been recognized since the 1960s. The principal policy response has been to enact "privacy" or "data protection" laws. These include the American *Privacy Act* of 1974, the Canadian *Privacy Act* of 1982, the British *Data Protection Act* of 1984, and the German *Data Protection Act* of 1978, among others. Table 1 also indicates that (by December 1997) some 24 Organization for Economic Cooperation and Development (OECD) states have passed some version of data protection law to regulate the personal data held in public and, in many cases, private organizations.[5]

All such laws are founded upon a common set of "fair information principles" for the treatment of personal information. These entail the following: that the existence of record-keeping systems for personal information should be publicly known; that individuals should have rights of access and correction to their own information; that personal information should only be collected for legitimate and openly stated purposes; that personal data should only be used (internally) in ways that are consistent with those purposes; that personal data should only be disclosed to other organizations in ways that are consistent with those purposes—unless the individual consents; and that there should be adequate and appropriate se-

TABLE 1	The Status of Freedom of Information (FOI) and Data Protection Legislation in OECD States (December 1997)	
	FOI	**Data Protection**
Sweden	1766 (1)*	1973 (1)*
Finland	1951 (2)	1987 (13)
Denmark	1970 (4)	1978 (5)
Norway	1970 (4)	1978 (5)
New Zealand	1970 (10)	1982 (11)
U.K.		1984 (12)
France	1978 (7)	1978 (5)
Portugal		1991 (18)
Australia	1982 (10)	1988 (14) [public sector]
Austria	1974 (6)	1978 (5)
Ireland		1988 (14)
Netherlands	1978 (7)	1988 (14)
Spain		1992 (19)
U.S.A.	1967 (3)	1975 (2) [public sector]
Canada	1982 (10)	1977 (3) [public sector]
Luxembourg	1979 (9)	1979 (9)
Germany		1977 (3)
Iceland		1981 (10)
Japan		1988 (14)
Belgium		1992 (19)
Switzerland		1992 (19)
Greece		1997 (23)
Italy		1996 (22)
Turkey		

*(The rank order for each state on each innovation is placed in parentheses after the year of adoption.)

curity safeguards to prevent unauthorized access or disclosure. At the level of the basic statutory principles, data protection policies have converged.[6]

The laws differ with regard to the extent of organizational coverage—those in North America mainly regulate the public sector, whereas those elsewhere (especially in Europe) encompass all organizations. They vary in the extent to which they regulate non-computerized files (i.e., the manila folder in the filing cabinet). Most notably, they differ with regard to the policy instruments established for regulation and oversight. Many countries (again with the notable exception of the United States) have set up small privacy or data protection agencies with varying oversight, advisory or regulatory powers.[7] Various international instruments, from the OECD,[8] the Council of Europe[9] and, most recently, the European Union[10] have motivated and will continue to motivate a further harmonization of the content and implementation of privacy protection policies.

THE DEVELOPMENT OF FREEDOM OF INFORMATION AND PROTECTION OF PRIVACY POLICY IN CANADA

Freedom of Information is not an issue that is generally characterized by partisan differences. Politicians of various political affiliations have actively supported reforms in this area. As in the United States, real impetus for change came from the legislature rather than from external pressure. Gerald Baldwin MP is normally given most of the credit for pushing the issue during the early 1970s. In 1974, his private member's bill (C-225) was given a second reading, and referred to the Standing Joint Committee on Regulations and Other Statutory Instruments. In February 1976, the Committee produced a report approving in principle the enactment of FOI legislation in Canada. This report was unanimously adopted by the House of Commons, leading to a Government response in the form of a Throne Speech pledge "to improve public access to government information," and a Green Paper which was very skeptical about diminishing ministerial discretion over the provision of information or giving more power to the courts.[11] These arguments were refuted in a report prepared for the Canadian Bar Association[12] and by the Standing Joint Committee which recommended expansive FOI legislation with a two-tier review process: at the first stage, an information commissioner would review complaints; at the second, the matter could be referred to the federal court system.

After much debate in the late 1970s, these proposals finally found their way into a bill introduced in 1979 by the short-lived Conservative government of Joe Clark (C-15) and, in a similar measure, introduced by a re-elected Trudeau Liberal government in July 1980 (C-43). Bill C-43 was granted a second reading in January 1981 and was referred to the Standing Committee on Justice and Legal Affairs, which finally reported the bill in June 1982; the committee's work had been suspended for seven months, due in large part to provincial objections regarding the perceived inadequacy of the exemption for information about federal/provincial relations. The bill was finally sent to third reading in the House on 28 June 1982 and passed by a vote of 193–21. It passed the Senate on 7 July, received Royal Assent the same day and came into effect in July 1983.

Privacy issues also tend to be nonpartisan. The forces that brought this issue to the agenda in Canada in the 1960s and 1970s were generally the same as those in other countries. The computerization of personal information systems, especially in the public sector, together with the development and expansive use of a universal identifier (the Social

Insurance Number) raised general fears about the state's increased capacity for surveillance and the concomitant erosion of personal privacy.[13] There followed a quiet and wide-ranging debate about privacy and computers over the next decade, focusing in part on the recommendations of a task force report from the Department of Justice.[14]

The first privacy legislation at the federal level was contained in Part IV of the 1977 *Canadian Human Rights Act*, which established the office of the Privacy Commissioner—a member of the Canadian Human Rights Commission—whose main responsibilities were to receive complaints from the general public, conduct investigations, and make recommendations to Parliament. While Part IV succeeded in codifying fair information principles in legislation for the first time, privacy arguably sat uneasily within a statute devoted to the question of discrimination, a related but obviously more controversial issue that tended to overshadow the importance of privacy protection.[15]

Parallel debates over a federal access to information statute in the early 1980s raised immediate questions about the compatibility between such legislation and the privacy standards within Part IV of the *Human Rights Act*. The current 1982 *Privacy Act*, therefore, flows from a belief that the protection of personal information should be a corollary to free-

TABLE 2	The Status of Canadian Information and Privacy Law	
Provinces	**Name of Act/Oversight Agency**	**Date Adopted**
Alberta	*Freedom of Information and Protection of Privacy Act* Office of the Information and Privacy Commissioner	1994
British Columbia	*Freedom of Information and Protection of Privacy Act* Office of the Information and Privacy Commissioner	1992
Manitoba	*Freedom of Information and Protection of Privacy Act* Office of the Manitoba Ombudsman	1997
New Brunswick	*Right to Information Act* *Protection of Personal Information Act* Office of the Ombudsman	1978 1998
Newfoundland	*Freedom of Information Act* Civil Law Division, Department of Justice	1981
Nova Scotia	*Freedom of Information and Protection of Privacy Act* FOI and Protection of Privacy Review Officer	1993
Ontario	*Freedom of Information and Protection of Privacy Act* Information and Privacy Commissioner/Ontario	1987
Quebec—public sector	*An act respecting access to documents held by public bodies and the protection of personal information* Commission d'Accès à l'Information du Québec	1982
Quebec—private sector	*An act respecting the protection of personal information in the private sector* Commission d'Accès à l'Information du Québec	1993
Saskatchewan	*Freedom of Information and Protection of Privacy Act* Information and Privacy Commissioner/Saskatchewan	1991
Northwest Territories	*Access to Information and Protection of Privacy Act* Information and Privacy Commissioner	1994
Yukon Territory	*Access to Information and Protection of Privacy Act* Office of the Ombudsman	1996

dom of information and that the various exemptions in both pieces of legislation should be consistent. Bill C-43, incorporating a new *Access to Information Act* and a *Privacy Act*, thus institutionalized the Canadian innovation of legislating access to information and privacy protection within the same statutory framework.[16]

The practice of legislating both policy areas within one statute was later copied by some of the provinces: by Quebec in 1982, by Ontario in 1988, by British Columbia in 1993, by Alberta in 1995 and by Manitoba in 1997. As of the end of 1997, only Prince Edward Island and New Brunswick lacked a legislated privacy protection policy for the personal information held by public agencies. Table 2 presents the current status of access to information and protection of privacy legislation in Canada.

All of this legislation applies only to federal and provincial *public* agencies. The passage in 1993 of Quebec's *Act respecting the protection of personal information in the private sector* (Bill 68) marked a departure from previous regulation limited to the public sector. This gave effect to the information privacy rights incorporated in the new Civil Code and made Quebec the first jurisdiction in North America to produce comprehensive data protection rules for the *private* sector. Bill 68 applies the fair information principles to all pieces of personal information collected, held, used or distributed by enterprises engaged in an "organized economic activity." The Commission d'Accès à l'Information du Québec, the body established under the 1982 public sector access and privacy law, oversees implementation of Bill 68, hears complaints and renders binding decisions.

After Quebec's action, Canada became the only country in which the scope of privacy protection in one of its member jurisdictions exceeds that of the central government. In the rest of the country, we find only a few isolated statutes relating to specific sectors, such as the consumer credit industry.[17] There are also limited common law remedies and constitutional provisions of potential relevance.[18] Canadian privacy protection policy has been described by the federal Privacy Commissioner as a "patchwork."[19] With the exception of Quebec, privacy protection in the private sector is largely dependent on the implementation of a set of voluntary and sectoral codes of practice developed according to the framework of the 1981 *OECD Guidelines* or the 1996 *Model Code for the Protection of Personal Information* from the Canadian Standards Association.[20] A number of political, international, technological, and legislative developments have now convinced federal policy makers that this incoherent policy cannot be allowed to continue.

First, the recently passed *Data Protection Directive* from the European Union[21] establishes minimum legal standards for the processing of personal data within Europe but also has extraterritorial consequences in that no personal information may be transmitted outside the European Union to jurisdictions that cannot demonstrate an "adequate level of protection." No jurisdiction in Canada (except Quebec) can plausibly make that claim; privacy protection therefore has some significant trade implications. Second, the passage of the Quebec legislation has created an "unlevel playing field" within the Canadian federation, creating uncertainties and transaction costs for businesses that operate in different provinces.[22] Third, the publication of a series of public opinion surveys has demonstrated that the general public regards privacy protection as a matter of major concern.[23] Fourth, the contracting-out or privatization of some governmental functions has undermined the implementation of public sector data protection law and the ability of Canada's privacy commissioners to ensure the protection of personal data when it leaves government.[24] Finally, the debates over the development and character of the Canadian "information highway" have exposed the need for a common set of "rules of the road" for the networked and distributed computing and communications environment of the 21st century.[25]

These forces have created an expectation that the patchwork of laws and codes will be replaced by a more coherent regulatory system for privacy protection, probably based upon the recently negotiated Canadian Standards Association's *Model Code for the Protection of Personal Information*.[26] In September 1995 the federal Advisory Council for the Information Highway (IHAC), operating under the auspices of Industry Canada, called on the federal government to:

> create a level playing field for the protection of personal information on the Information Highway by developing and implementing a flexible legislative framework for both public and private sectors. Legislation would require sectors or organizations to meet the standard of the *CSA Model Code*, while allowing the flexibility to determine how they will refine their own codes.[27]

On 23 May 1996 federal industry minister John Manley released the government's response to the IHAC report in which it was concluded that "the right to privacy must be recognized in law, especially in an electronic world of private databases where it is all too easy to collect and exploit information about individual citizens."[28] In September 1996, Justice Minister Allan Rock addressed the Annual Conference of the International Privacy and Data Protection Commissioners in Ottawa and clarified this commitment: "By the year 2000, we aim to have federal legislation on the books that will provide effective, enforceable protection of privacy rights in the private sector." The Government of Canada has thus reconsidered its two-tiered approach of legislation for the public sector and voluntary self-regulation for the private: "The protection of personal information can no longer depend on whether the data is held by a public or a private institution."[29] In an era of deregulation, privacy protection stands out as one of the few areas of public policy in which an extension of the scope of regulation is being seriously contemplated, even though there is likely to be much opposition to further bureaucratic "red tape." A federal discussion paper, released in January 1998, outlines the options for policy reform.[30]

THE ACTORS AND THEIR ROLES

The implementation of FOI and protection of privacy legislation in Canada can be understood by examining the roles, relationships, and responsibilities of four sets of actors: public bodies, coordinating agencies, information and privacy commissioners, and the general public and their representatives. With few exceptions, these generalizations apply to both federal and provincial levels of government.

The Obligations of Public Bodies

There are a number of obligations for public sector agencies under the typical FOI statute. All FOI laws make it clear that the primary responsibility for implementation rests with the "designated minister" or "head" of the agency in question. Each agency is also supposed to appoint an official responsible for the initial receipt of requests and wider tasks of information management. The law then embodies a significant degree of decentralized administration. Agencies must assist the applicant in defining what he or she requires, make a reasonable effort to search for requested records and respond to requests within the specified time-frame. There are also systemic implications for records management. The time limits for responding to FOI requests mean that it is essential for an agency to understand the nature and location of its record holdings.

Privacy protection policy requires more systemic and proactive implementation. Agencies need to ensure that no personal information is collected unless it relates directly to a program or activity. They need to ensure that, wherever possible, personal information shall be collected directly from the individual to whom it relates, and that the individual shall be informed of the purpose for which the information is being collected. Personal information shall be retained and disposed of according to the jurisdiction's regulatory regime, and shall be as accurate, up-to-date, and complete as possible. And government agencies can only use personal information for purposes to which the individual has consented and for other limited uses specified in legislation. Most laws, however, contain a rather vague exemption that allows for disclosure for "consistent uses." Most also express a principle of transparency by requiring the proper indexing and publication of "personal information banks."

Significant pressures for the more efficient management of resources, and new technologies, have brought a range of fresh challenges to the protection of personal privacy. Computer matching, for example, involves the comparison of different databases to identify those individuals who improperly appear in both (for instance social assistance recipients who may be "double-dipping") and has significant privacy implications. Some Canadian jurisdictions have contemplated the introduction of "smart" identification cards to assist in the delivery of social services and health care. A few municipalities are examining the potential benefits of video-surveillance cameras in public places. Agencies are required, before introducing any system that would require the collection of personal information (including visual images), to consider the privacy implications and preferably to consult with the central agency or the privacy commissioner.

The Role of Central Coordinating Agencies

Every jurisdiction requires the coordination of these various activities. Two types of agencies play crucial roles. The first is the central agency that provides advice, guidance, and coordination on the implementation of the legislation. At the federal level, this role is played by Treasury Board staff. In British Columbia it is played by the staff of the Information Science and Technology Agency and in Ontario by that of the Management Board. Typically these agencies perform a variety of functions crucial for the effective implementation of privacy and FOI. They will issue corporate policies and occasional interpretive bulletins, for example when a new technology, such as electronic mail, emerges. They will respond to questions about the interpretation of legislation and policy. They will maintain and update the legislation through periodic amendments to the statute, the schedules and regulations. They will conduct periodic evaluations of the legislation. They will try to identify and address inconsistent application of the statutes and policies and therefore play a vital role in cross-agency coordination. When new legislation, programs or information systems are being contemplated, they will try to ensure that FOI and privacy values are incorporated.

The second set of agencies provide legal guidance and counsel. The Ministry of Justice in Ottawa and ministries of the Attorney General in some provinces play a crucial role in providing legal services to agency officials on access and privacy matters. Legal opinions will often be sought on the meaning of particular provisions. They also help the public bodies prepare their cases when an applicant has asked the commissioner to review an agency decision or when a case is under judicial review.

Offices of the Information and Privacy Commissioner

At the federal level, there is both an Information Commissioner and a Privacy Commissioner, each with its own separate staff but sharing common management support. In Ontario, British Columbia, and Alberta, one commissioner "wears both hats" and has to balance the sometimes competing interests in his or her own mind. In the other provinces, review responsibility is granted to some other oversight agency, such as the Ombudsman (in Manitoba) or to single review officers (such as in Nova Scotia and Saskatchewan).

Responsibilities, on the FOI side, are mainly concerned with the review of decisions made by government agencies. In British Columbia, Ontario, and Alberta, the commissioner is granted order-making power and can therefore determine whether a record should be released or not, either in its entirety or in "severed" form. Out of these cases, a jurisprudence has developed (especially in British Columbia, Ontario, and Quebec) which assists in the interpretation of the principles and wording in the statutes. These orders may then be reviewed by the courts on limited grounds. The federal Information Commissioner, on the other hand, has only advisory and reporting powers, although he does have the option of appealing the decision of a ministry to the federal courts. While the recommendations of the federal Information Commissioner are not binding, they can exert a considerable force. Few matters over the years have therefore needed referral to the judicial level of review.

The privacy work is on the whole more advisory. All privacy commissioners are primarily "Ombudsmen" whose principal duty is to receive and investigate complaints. The federal *Privacy Act*, for example, specifies in considerable detail the procedures and powers for receiving, investigating, and reporting the results of complaints. Much of the work, then, is reactive and commands a significant amount of the often limited personnel and resources.

Privacy commissioners also conduct investigations and audits of government departments. These may be part of a formal audit program (as in Ottawa), or more ad hoc "site visits" to public bodies (as in British Columbia). In this role, commissioners and their staffs are often more "consultants" than "investigators." These activities can often lead to special reports on practices and technologies which have privacy implications. Reports on AIDS,[31] drug-testing[32] and genetic testing[33] have been the most prominent at the federal level. Other shorter factsheets are also released from time to time, to provide guidance to agencies about their responsibilities and education to the general public about their rights.[34] All commissioners are also obliged to file an annual report on their activities.

Commissioners are also authorized to comment on the privacy implications of pending legislation and other initiatives. The privacy commissioners constantly try to inject a privacy perspective at the earliest stages of the legislative process, technology development or service delivery. High-profile legislative changes that involve radical implications for the processing of personal information are often the circumstances under which consultation is the most serious; examples would be the proposal for a DNA data bank[35] or the new permanent voters' register.[36] Such developments are normally attended by significant media interest. On other occasions, however, privacy commissioners complain that privacy protection is a last minute "add-on" and that their staff are not consulted early enough in the policy development process. Agencies have a wide latitude to treat the issue in a perfunctory manner.

The Public and Public Interest Groups

The other actors within the community of regulators are, of course, individual citizens and their representatives. The importance of these laws would be undermined if citizens did not register complaints about the collection, storage, and dissemination of personal information. The operation of the entire regime also relies to some extent on individuals exercising their rights to access and correct personal information. Most jurisdictions report a consistent, if not increasing, exercise of access and privacy rights.

To a significant extent, the response of the general public to privacy issues allows the other actors in the process to determine the appropriate balance between privacy and competing interests. This balance will vary over time and jurisdiction. Acceptable intrusions in one context can spark civil protests and extensive media criticism in others. There has been recent publicity in British Columbia about the distribution of a letter to 75 000 recipients of social assistance benefits requesting their "consent" for verification of eligibility by matching individual records with a large and varied range of public and private data banks. Vociferous protests from antipoverty groups and others will influence the particular balance struck between surveillance and privacy in this particular case and ultimately the administration of the B.C. *Freedom of Information and Protection of Privacy Act.*

CONCLUSION: THE IMPLICATIONS FOR CANADIAN PUBLIC ADMINISTRATION

The implications of FOI and protection of privacy legislation in Canada for the conduct of public administration are still somewhat difficult to establish, even after 20 years' experience in some jurisdictions. We must also be cautious about over-generalization since federal and provincial bureaucracies operate within different political cultures. In some jurisdictions, citizens might be more ready to exercise their information rights than in others.

The implementation of FOI and privacy protection policy involves a considerable degree of mutual adjustment and readjustment to outside influences.[37] It is not characterized by a top-down process of command, control, and sanction. These laws should not be seen as a system producing outputs and outcomes, but as a process that involves organizational change and learning and that involves a large implementation network of persons and organizations besides the central actors in government.

Nevertheless, FOI and privacy protection policies attempt to provide a clear set of rules that reduce the discretion of agency officials. These rules enjoin openness in some circumstances and confidentiality in others and are designed to be perfectly flexible and adaptable to all possible situations and neutral and impartial in their effect. FOI and privacy statutes try to approximate what Deborah Stone calls the "rationality model" of rule-making.[38]

FOI policy embodies a tension between this rational pursuit and application of clear legal standards and opposing political pressures. Administering access and privacy protection is always difficult in a political context where information is the key to the exercise of power. For example, tensions will often mount when access requests under FOI begin to focus on an emerging scandal. The role of the public servant, as providing unquestioned loyalty to his or her minister, may sometimes be placed in considerable jeopardy by the "rational" administration of the FOI statute. FOI still sits uneasily within a constitutional system based on the principle (perhaps fiction) that the minister should be responsible to the legislature for the release of all official information.

One perennial criticism of access to information legislation is that its consequence is the opposite of that intended, in that it reduces the amount of information recorded. Access rights may only be exercised when a record exists. To circumvent the legislation, it would seem a natural tactic to record less information. On the other hand, the complexities of modern government organization demand extensive records. Evidence that FOI, far from rationalizing information management, reduces the amount of government records, tends to rely on anecdote. We know of no reliable empirical study that has effectively tested this interesting hypothesis.

On the privacy side of the legislation, political pressures stem from the pressing desire to use new technologies to enhance the effectiveness of programs. The federal Privacy Commissioner and his or her colleagues must now attempt to comprehend the implications of a staggering range of new surveillance tools and practices. These include computer matching and profiling, smart identification cards, genetic data banks, cellular telephones, call management services, video-surveillance, health information networks and, of course, the privacy-intrusive capabilities of the Internet.

The range of privacy issues has been extended beyond those contemplated when many of these laws were passed. The early FOI and Privacy Acts were generally written to respond to the problems inherent in a relatively manageable number of discrete "data banks" or "personal information systems," each maintained for precisely defined purposes. In the 1990s, the technological environment has become more distributed, networked, dynamic, and complicated. Information is not processed in distinct stages (collection, storage, disclosure, etc.) and it knows fewer organizational attachments. Responsibility for those data is now far more difficult to locate. The pervasive and adaptable application of these new technologies will make it increasingly difficult to determine which organizations in which location "hold" data and, therefore, which rules (if any) apply.

Many technology practices may also involve a variety of public and private organizations over which the federal and provincial commissioners may not have jurisdiction. The distinction between the public and the private is eroded whenever "private" organizations perform traditional "public" functions and require the use of "public" data to fulfil those obligations; for example, when smart cards and ATM machines are used for the dispensing of government benefits or when credit reports are used for security checks. Where the "public" sector ends and the "private" sector begins is increasingly difficult to determine. Questions raised about the application and meaning of the privacy provisions in all jurisdictions will have an evolving impact on Canadian business.

In summary, while it would be desirable to evaluate the impact of these laws in an objective way, such an evaluation would be misleading. The resource that FOI and privacy statutes seek to regulate (information) is an elusive and dynamic one.[39] We can probably conclude that "more" information has entered the public domain as a result of successful applications under FOI. But more in comparison with what? We can also probably conclude that privacy interests are more seriously considered in government when new systems are being planned. But as a result of statute, or as a result of a heightened sensitivity within the political culture to excessive secrecy and surveillance?

The values inherent in freedom of information law are multiple and inherently subjective. These laws are not designed to be evaluated with clear "outcome" measures of a substantive nature in mind. They establish procedures for the exercise of information rights if individuals wish to exercise those rights. In this respect, the continued complexity and dynamism of Canadian government will ensure that, with or without clear evaluation, FOI and privacy laws will continue to be an important feature of Canadian public administration.

NOTES

1. Information Commissioner of Canada, *Annual Report 1996–97* (Ottawa: Minister of Public Works and Government Services, 1997).

2. B. Guy Peters, *The Politics of Bureaucracy* (New York: Longman, 1978), 33–35.

3. U.K., Chancellor of the Duchy of Lancaster, *Your Right to Know: The Government's Proposals for a Freedom of Information Act* (London: HMSO, 1997).

4. *Public Access to Government-Held Information*, ed. Norman Marsh (London: Stevens, 1987).

5. Colin J. Bennett, "Understanding Ripple Effects: The Cross-National Adoption of Policy Instruments for Bureaucratic Accountability," *Governance* 10 (1997): 213–34.

6. Colin J. Bennett, *Regulating Privacy: Data Protection and Public Policy in Europe and the United States* (Ithaca, NY: Cornell University Press, 1992), 95–115.

7. David H. Flaherty, *Protecting Privacy in Surveillance Societies* (Chapel Hill: University of North Carolina Press, 1989).

8. Organization for Economic Cooperation and Development (OECD), *Guidelines on the Protection of Privacy and Transborder Data Flows of Personal Data* (Paris: OECD, 1981).

9. Council of Europe, *Convention for the Protection of Individuals with Regard to Automatic Processing of Personal Data* (Strasbourg: Council of Europe, 1981).

10. European Union, *Directive 95/46/EC of the European Parliament and of the Council on the Protection of Individuals with regard to the Processing of Personal Data and on the Free Movement of Such Data* (Brussels: OJ No. L281, 24 October 1995).

11. Canada, Department of the Secretary of State, *Legislation on Public Access to Government Documents* (Green Paper)(Ottawa: Minister of Supply and Services, 1977).

12. Murray Rankin, *Freedom of Information in Canada: Will the Doors Stay Shut?* (Ottawa: Canadian Bar Association, 1977).

13. Colin J. Bennett, "The Formation of a Canadian Privacy Policy: The Art and Craft of Lesson-Drawing," *Canadian Public Administration* 33 (1990): 551–70.

14. Justice Canada, *Privacy and Computers* (Ottawa: Information Canada, 1972).

15. Bennett, "The Formation of a Canadian Private Policy," 559.

16. *An Act to enact the Access to Information Act and the Privacy Act*, SC 1980–81–82–83, C. 111.1.

17. Colin J. Bennett, *Implementing Privacy Codes of Practice: A Report to the Canadian Standards Association* (Rexdale: CSA, PLUS 8830, 1995).

18. Ian Lawson, *Privacy and Free Enterprise: The Legal Protection of Personal Information in the Private Sector* (Ottawa: Public Interest Advocacy Centre, 1992).

19. Privacy Commissioner of Canada (OPC), *Annual Report 1993–94* (Ottawa: Canada Communications Group, 1994).

20. This agreement was negotiated between 1992 and 1995 between industrial, consumer and government representatives: Canadian Standards Association (CSA), *Model Code for the Protection of Personal Information* (CAN/CSA-Q830-96) (Rexdale: CSA, 1996). The CSA Model Code is at www.csa.ca. See also, Bennett, *Implementing Privacy Codes of Practice: A Report to the Canadian Standards Association.*

21. European Union, *Directive 95/46/EC.*

22. Colin J. Bennett, "Rules of the Road and Level Playing Fields: The Politics of Data Protection in Canada's Private Sector," *International Review of Administrative Sciences* 62 (1996): 479–91.

23. Ekos Research Associates, *Privacy Revealed: The Canadian Privacy Survey* (Ottawa: Ekos, 1993); Louis Harris and Alan F. Westin, *The Equifax Canada Report on Consumers and Privacy in the Information Age* (Ville d'Anjou: Equifax Canada, 1995); Public Interest Advocacy Centre (PIAC), *Surveying Boundaries: Canadians and their Personal Information* (Ottawa: PIAC, 1995).

24. Privacy Commissioner of Canada (OPC), *Annual Report 1995–96* (Ottawa: Canada Communications Group, 1996).

25. Information Highway Advisory Council (IHAC), *Communication, Community, Content: The Challenge of the Information Highway* (Ottawa: Minister of Supply and Services Canada, 1995); Ann Cavoukian and Don Tapscott, *Who Knows: Safeguarding your Privacy in a Networked World* (Toronto: Random House Canada, 1995).

26. Canadian Standards Association (CSA), *Model Code for the Protection of Personal Information.*

27. Information Highway Advisory Council, 141.

28. Industry Canada, *Building the Information Society: Moving Canada into the 21st Century* (Ottawa: Industry Canada, 1996): 25. [http://info.ic.gc.ca/info-highway/ih.html].

29. Allan Rock, *Address to the 18th International Conference on Privacy and Data Protection* (Ottawa: September 18, 1996).

30. Industry Canada and Justice Canada, Task Force on Electronic Commerce, *Building Canada's Information Economy and Society: The Protection of Personal Information* (Ottawa: Industry Canada, 1998) at: http://strategis.ic.gc.ca/privacy.

31. Privacy Commissioner of Canada, *AIDS and the Privacy Act* (Ottawa: Minister of Supply and Services, 1989).

32. Privacy Commissioner of Canada, *Drug-Testing and Privacy* (Ottawa: Minister of Supply and Services, 1990).

33. Privacy Commissioner of Canada, *Genetic Testing and Privacy* (Ottawa: Minister of Supply and Services, 1992).

34. For example, Ontario Information and Privacy Commissioner, *Privacy Protection Principles for Electronic Mail Systems* (Toronto: OIPC, February 1994); *Privacy Alert: A Consumer's Guide to Privacy in the Marketplace* (Toronto: OIPC, May 1994).

35. Privacy Commissioner of Canada, *Annual Report 1994–95* (Ottawa: Canada Communications Group, 1995): 19.

36. Privacy Commissioner of Canada, *Annual Report 1995–96*: 47.

37. Charles D. Raab, "Data Protection in Britain: Governance and Learning," *Governance* 6 (1993): 43–66.

38. Deborah Stone, *Policy Paradox: The Art of Political Decision-Making* (New York: Norton, 1997), 300.

39. Charles D. Raab and Colin J. Bennett, "Taking the Measure of Privacy: Can Data Protection Be Evaluated?" *International Review of Administrative Sciences* 62 (1996): 535–56.

ADDRESS ON CONNECTING CANADIANS: Public Service in the Information Age

Jocelyne Bourgon
Clerk of the Privy Council and
Secretary to the Cabinet

An address given in Ottawa, Ontario, on 20 October 1997 for Technology in Government Week.

INTRODUCTION

Thank you for the invitation to be with you today.

This annual conference is always an important event because it brings together professionals of information technology and information management from all levels of government, the private sector, and from many countries around the world. It brings together experts and users equally committed to the use of information technology for improving services to the public.

We all want to make the most of this unique opportunity. We want to learn, to exchange, and to challenge each other to set ambitious goals for ourselves.

The theme of this year's conference is *Serving Canadians Better: Building for the 21ˢᵗ Century*. This theme could not be more timely. It is at the heart of the role of all governments on the eve of the millennium. It was the central focus of the Speech from the Throne presented by the Government of Canada on 23 September 1997.

In the hope of making a useful contribution to your discussions and deliberations, I would like to:

(1) sketch some of the *challenges* ahead of us;

(2) draw some *implications* for the role of Government in the future; and finally,

(3) make some personal observations about a *career* in information technology and information management in the public service.

PART I: PREPARING FOR THE 21ST CENTURY—THE CHALLENGE

In less than 3 years—802 days from now—Canadians will be celebrating the beginning of the year 2000. The Speech from the Throne has set the course and the priorities that the Government of Canada will be pursuing *to prepare Canada and Canadians for the 21ˢᵗ Century:*

- It will invest in *education, knowledge,* and *innovation*;
- It will invest in good *health and quality care;*
- It will expand opportunities for *young Canadians;* and
- It will help prepare *children* to learn and succeed in a modern and complex society.

What is the common link between these priorities? They are strategic investments *in people.* Taken together they provide the essential elements to prepare Canada and Canadians for a knowledge-based society.

The challenge ahead of us is well described in the Speech from the Throne. Allow me to quote from it:

> Canada is well-positioned to be a world leader in the global knowledge-based economy of the 21ˢᵗ century. We have the talent, we have the resources, we have the technology and we have the institutions.
>
> We will make the information and knowledge infrastructure accessible to all Canadians by the year 2000, thereby making Canada the most connected nation in the world.
>
> A connected nation is more than wires, cables, and computers. It is a nation in which citizens have access to the skills and knowledge they need. It is…a nation whose people are connected to each other.

This is the challenge for all of us in this room. Success will require a truly pan-Canadian effort; it will require everyone's contribution. The question before us is how can we best make a contribution toward this goal— whether we are from the private sector, the public sector, or governments? How can we best work together?

To develop a concerted plan of action, we need to ask what does it mean "to become the most connected nation in the world"? What is the meaning of connectedness?

1. Connecting Citizens

Hundreds of years ago, connecting citizens meant coming together in the village square to exchange information, to debate, and to make decisions of collective interest. That's how democracy was born.

As society became more complex and because of the limitations imposed by distance, representative democracy emerged as the most viable model to ensure a permanent link and a proper oversight by citizens over political institutions.

On the verge of the 21ˢᵗ century, technology is allowing us to imagine new ways of connecting citizens, of eliminating the disadvantage of physical distance—and of giving a fuller, richer meaning to democracy and citizenship. We can foresee:

- people sharing a community of interest, coming together to pursue common goals;

- linguistic minorities overcoming physical isolation and building stronger alliances to protect and promote their culture;

- Aboriginal nations reaching native people on reserves or in urban centres; and

- citizens across Canada and abroad sharing the treasures of the National Gallery or the Museum of Civilization located in Ottawa.

The basic infrastructures needed to connect Canadian citizens are already in place. The challenge will be to provide universal access and equal opportunities of access for all Canadians.

2. Connecting Communities

Information technology can help us ensure that all the institutional knowledge in the hands of the three levels of government is put to the service of our communities. Canadians have already paid for this information; it is rightfully theirs.

To achieve this goal we will need to address the legitimate concerns of Canadians about privacy, to provide adequate protection for commercial information, and to address security issues. I do not underestimate the difficulties, but it is possible to properly balance the need for openness and access with the need for confidentiality and protection.

The potential benefits are worth the efforts. Information technology could break down the barriers imposed by distance, change the relationship between rural and urban areas of Canada, and allow community groups to take charge of their own development. For instance:

- Connecting all schools, and every library and learning institution would help make lifelong learning a reality in Canada. This is an essential element for a well performing knowledge-based society;

- Students wherever they live could conduct research in libraries all over the world and participate in schools and universities far from home, thus bringing to all what used to be the purview of a few;

- Patients in towns and villages could receive medical attention once available only in metropolitan centres; and

- Voluntary sector organizations could find new willing hands and strengthen our community capacity for self-help and mutual help.

We are making connectedness happen in Canada—Schoolnet and the Community Access Program are two prominent examples. The governments of Canada and Prince Edward Island have entered into a Knowledge Economy Partnership. The governments of Canada and New Brunswick have signed a memorandum of understanding to make information from both governments available at more than 200 access points in the province. The challenge will be to develop a concerted approach among all governments—federal, provincial, and municipal—to do likewise across the country.

3. Connecting Businesses

Information technology has created many new opportunities for businesses. It holds special promise for small- and medium-sized businesses. For the first time, local businesses are freed from the limitations of place and the exclusionary economics of global marketing. A lot could be said about the potential of IT for businesses; I will limit my comments to *electronic commerce*.

To reap the benefits of a knowledge-based economy, it is important to eliminate the barriers to commerce on the information highway. This is especially important in the case of small businesses which often face significant challenges in adapting to information technology.

The challenge will be to provide some measure of certainty in the marketplace by ensuring that the legal, policy, and regulatory framework for electronic commerce is in place.

By creating the best environment for electronic commerce, Canada will have a considerable competitive advantage in the global competition for talents and investments.

It will require a concerted effort by the departments of Justice, Industry, Revenue, and Heritage, and the Treasury Board.

Let me summarize the first part of my remarks:

The challenge is to make Canada "the most connected nation in the world." It is a very exciting challenge; one that holds many promises for the future.

To be successful will require a truly pan-Canadian effort and everyone's contribution. If we rise to the challenge, our work:

- will help prepare Canada for the future;

- will empower citizens;

- will create opportunities for businesses; and

- will provide Canada with new comparative advantage among nations.

PART II: WHAT DOES IT MEAN FOR GOVERNMENTS?

Governments have long understood, though sometimes imperfectly, the importance of information technology to build a strong knowledge-based society.

At first, governments used information technologies to improve *productivity* and *efficiency* (tax processing, payroll, and accounting systems).

Then, IT became an essential tool in our quest to *improve services to Canadians*. The role of governments is not limited to bricks and mortar or to issuing cheques. It is increasingly to provide information—useful and timely information provided in a user-friendly way.

We are now entering a new phase where technology will increasingly be used by governments to support the *acquisition of knowledge* and the process of innovation. This is of a different order of complexity altogether. It will require a profound change of culture in governments. It will also change the relationship between governments and citizens.

Before focusing on the changes to come, let's acknowledge the progress to date, since it provides the foundation from which we will build as we enter the new phase.

1. Governments have created networks allowing them to be present, relevant and adapted to local needs.

For instance, Human Resources Development Canada delivers services electronically at about 5000 kiosks. Their network alone is comparable to that of Canada's largest financial institution.

"Ropin' the Web," Alberta Agriculture, Food and Rural Development's website, provides high quality agricultural information and direct communication with departmental specialists.

2. Citizens and businesses can transact electronically with governments.

One hundred million payments are made electronically every year, representing half the payments made by the Receiver General.

There are eight million electronic clearances of customs annually.

3. Governments have become more accessible.

There are on average 2.5 million hits per month on the Canada site on the Internet—21 million hits since the beginning of 1997.

There are 200 000 hits per day on Strategis which contains 20 000 electronic documents relevant to businesses.

4. Government departments and public servants are better coordinated.

PWGSC has created a government-wide e-mail infrastructure allowing 160 000 public servants nationwide to exchange information electronically.

The Regional Municipality of Peel has implemented a secure high-speed network to support social services, public safety, and recreational interests in the region.

There is no denying it. We have come a long way and a lot has been accomplished over the last ten years. But looking ahead, what we can accomplish over the next five years is even more impressive.

First, government departments and agencies should move from being independent providers of service toward an integrated approach to service delivery. We still have a lot of progress to make for the Government of Canada to project a common image—for departments to share and operate from common infrastructures—for the Government of Canada to provide single windows centred around citizens and citizen needs. This is an essential step for governments to move from the role of provider of information to the more complex role of contributing to the acquisition of knowledge. In many ways, provincial governments are further ahead; we could all learn from their experience:

- The Government of Manitoba has established "Service First" and "Better Systems." The goal of Better Systems is to create a single window to government.

- The Government of Saskatchewan is in the process of developing a Health Information Network that will see all health services contact points in the province connected.

- The Government of New Brunswick is implementing a high speed network connecting all government offices across the province.

- The Government of British Columbia has used the B.C. Electronic Highway Accord to rethink the way in which it will deliver services to British Columbia.

- The Government of the Northwest Territories is leading the way in system sharing by working with the Government of Alberta in the development of a revised version of the Alberta Child Welfare Information System.

Second, during the coming years we will be called upon to redefine the relationship between governments and citizens. The most important breakthrough would be the coming together of municipal, territorial, provincial, and federal governments— respectful of their individual responsibilities but united in their effort to serve Canadians.

Last year, I issued a challenge at the close of the Gala Dinner; the challenge was that at this year's conference all levels of governments be properly represented. This year, eight sessions are specifically targeting the issues of partnership and interdependence. There are 166 provincial and territorial delegates registered; there are 17 delegates from municipalities. There are over a dozen nominations for innovation awards from the provinces, territories, and municipalities.

Municipal governments are the closest to the daily preoccupation of citizens and therefore their participation would be the key to the success of this effort

We are making progress. There is so much we could do together. A *single window for all government services can be a reality in Canada—that is the challenge.*

Third, governments should show *leadership* to ease the transition toward a knowledge-based society. This is the role that the Information Highway Advisory Council (IHAC) has described as "*Government as a Model User.*" Governments are the owners and the operators of many information systems. They are the users of many more. Government can also play a *leadership* role that could help accelerate the transformation of the Canadian society, set an example, and help Canadians to adjust to the use of information technology.

It is not easy to be a leader; it requires that governments continuously adjust their role to focus on the areas of highest need. Let me explain. For the public interest to be well served, governments do not need to do it all. As the Canadian society becomes more mature, others are able and willing to take on more responsibilities. There must be an orderly process of transfer of responsibilities from the public sector to the private sector, so that at all times governments focus their scarce resources and the energy of their employees in those functions that can only, or can best, be provided by the public sector. For instance, today the private sector is providing us with the basic IT infrastructure across the country—maybe not in every community, but the capacity is there. *We must build on it.* Similarly, the private sector is providing us with many off-the-shelf software and commercial systems relevant to government needs. We *should exploit this potential.* No one has the time nor the resources to reinvent the wheel.

For Canada to become the most connected nation in the world by the year 2000, and to become a strong knowledge-based society, *we need a strong private-public partnership.* As the private sector takes on more responsibilities, we in government must refocus our work on higher areas of need, in areas of greater complexity, or of higher value added.

Which leads me to my last topic. Is there a future for IM/IT in the government or should the field be abandoned to the private sector? Will it be possible to pursue a rich and rewarding career in this field in the public sector? Will it be possible to attract, but even more importantly, to retain young bright professionals?

In today's world the IM/IT functions are not severable from others. In government, it is part of the development process; the design of policy and programs; the delivery of service.

The IM/IT function cannot be privatized. The issue is what is the best way to *share* responsibility between the public and the private sectors. Let me venture a personal opinion. An IM career in the public sector should be *different* from one in the private sector. If it was the same, I would worry about the future because the public sector is unlikely to match

the salary conditions available in the private sector. I believe that an IM career in the public sector is different and will be increasingly different in the coming years. IM professionals in government:

* must understand the public sector and public sector values;

* must know how to get things done in government;

* must know about our many legal requirements—from laws of specific applications like the *Income Tax Act* to laws of general application like the *Privacy Act*
  or the *Official Languages Act;*

* must be versed in their specialty in order *to broker* the best of the private sector to
  meet public sector needs. They must build partnerships and strategic alliances.

This kind of knowledge can only be acquired through experience. It must be grown. It
cannot be bought at market price.

The attractiveness of an IM career in government must be built around:

* the diversity of experience the breadth of the challenge;

* the potential to make a difference in the life of Canadians;

* the excitement of contributing to making Canada a better place.

I worry about the number of experienced professionals we are losing each year. If the reforms needed to modernize the public service, and in particular the IM functions, are not introduced in a timely way, we should all worry about the consequences.

We have many reasons to remain optimistic. One of them is the person who will follow
shortly on this podium. The Chief Information Officer has made the renewal of the information
community in government his top priority. He has been working in collaboration with the
Treasury Board and every department at developing a plan of action ranging from recruitment, training, outsourcing, and the year 2000 computer problem. We will hear from him
shortly. He will need, and can be assured of, our full support.

CONCLUSION

Tonight at the Awards Dinner, as we honour the winners, let their work inspire us to greater
heights.

We are only at the beginning of creating a truly connected country. The complexity of
our task is sometimes overwhelming. But we have the commitment, the skills, and the ingenuity to make it happen. It holds great promise for the future, including the promise of a
challenging and rewarding career for those who serve in the public sector.

This conference couldn't come at a better time. Each year this intensive IT environment brings together a critical mass of technologies, people, and ideas. And each year a
tremendous energy flows out as we come back to the task refreshed, reenergized, and eager
to push ahead.

I look forward to our discussions, our exchanges, and our celebrations tonight. I also
look forward to our meeting next year to celebrate our achievement toward making Canada
the most connected nation in the world.

SENIOR PRACTITIONERS' INSIGHTS

Experience is often said to be a tremendous teacher. Those who have hands-on experience enjoy a degree of knowledge and insight which few possess. Their achievements serve as the basis for study and guidance to students. In an effort to provide commentary marked by the insights born of experience, the following essays are offered. They reflect the views of two prominent public servants whose work has shaped the evolution of public service in Canada. Their essays offer encouragement for the next generation of public administration students, as well as for those who aspire to political or bureaucratic leadership. Gordon Osbaldeston had a long and celebrated career culminating in receipt of the Order of Canada. Jocelyne Bourgon currently holds the position of Clerk of the Privy Council, one of the most (if not **the** most) important positions in the Canadian bureaucracy. She, too, has had an impressive career and has earned professional recognition.

Gordon Osbaldeston offers advice to governments on the importance of the structure of the cabinet. When first ministers design their cabinets, they are presented with a myriad of opportunities, challenges, and competing interests. Osbaldeston urges them not to lose sight of the fact that the structure of the cabinet will have a major impact on the quality of their government's decision making. He makes useful suggestions as to how they can enhance the cabinet's effectiveness while accommodating the various interest groups clamouring for attention.

Jocelyne Bourgon discusses the work of the public service and the challenges of administrative leadership. These remarks are drawn from a speech specially tailored to a student audience. Note how the work of the Clerk of the Privy Council is described. This post is at the apex of the Canadian bureaucracy and its impact extends throughout the political system.

DISCUSSION QUESTIONS

1. What is the role of a cabinet minister? a cabinet? How many cabinet ministers can you name?

2. Why might a new cabinet minister be interested in the observations offered by Osbaldeston? What kinds of challenges await a new minister?

3. Explain Osbaldeston's key pieces of advice. Why are they important?

4. Would you like to be a cabinet minister? a prime minister? Why or why not?

5. What is the role of the Clerk of the Privy Council? Why is this position considered to be so important?

6. What are the key points of Bourgon's message? Why are they significant?

7. Would you be interested in a public service position? in a leadership role such as the Clerk of the Privy Council? Why or why not?

ORGANIZING TO GOVERN: Getting the Basics Right

Gordon Osbaldeston

> We have too many departments of government, and as a corollary, have split natural decision centres. For example, by creating the Department of Communications we denied the Department of Regional Development and Industrial Expansion a high technology role and it has become a "smokestack" department.
>
> —G. F. Osbaldeston, Personal Diary, 20 July 1984

> I am convinced that the government is too large, too complicated and that decision points have been fractured.

> We need a Glassco Commission 1984.
>
> —G. F. Osbaldeston, Personal Diary, 3 August 1984

By fracturing key decision points, often in well-intentioned attempts to demonstrate political responsiveness, governments in Canada have hampered their own ability to deliver what the electorate wants—comprehensive, coherent and timely policies on issues that matter to them. This is one of the central conclusions I reached during my 32 years in the federal public service and, in 1992, documented in a study of how governments have organized to govern.

During the past decade, the structure of the federal government has been the object of more public attention, analysis and debate than it has for the past 50 years. I am pleased to see this public debate on the structure of government. As the excerpts from my personal diary illustrate, the size and complexity of the government have been of concern to me for many years. But the structural debate, like its subject, is complex, its angles and arguments profuse. For example, consider that the term "structure" as applied to government can refer to the number of ministers in the ministry, the number and mandates of cabinet committees, the number and mandates of departments and agencies, and the distribution of public servants and authority across Canada and throughout the world. The permutations and combinations of

211

these (particularly when complicated by personalities, partisan agendas, cost effectiveness and so on) present a daunting array of possible futures.

So, where does one start?

I suggest that there is one fundamental objective: to build a structure that can carry out the primary role of government—the allocation of scarce resources among unlimited needs and desires in a comprehensive, coherent and timely manner. The achievement of that objective requires the establishment and maintenance of key decision points.

In the past, the key decision points were fractured by the organizational practices of federal governments. The task of Prime Minister Chrétien's government is to restore policy coherence by reestablishing a strong-decision making structure. It made a good beginning and then faltered.

HOW DECISION POINTS ARE FRACTURED

The allocative role of government is fundamental:

> All societies, however primitive, possess some form of government. It is logical, therefore, to assume that there must be some common underlying function (or set of functions) which is performed by such institutions. There are two simple reasons for the existence and nature of the governmental or political function: human beings have a multitude of basic needs and wants which must be satisfied if the species is to survive and if individuals are to attain happiness; second, the resources necessary for the satisfaction of these needs and wants must be extracted from an environment that is limited. The combination of virtually unlimited wants and limited resources produces a situation where an individual must compete with others to maximize personal satisfaction. The function of government is to resolve the conflict which arises over who gets what resources in a given society.[1]

The output of this allocative process is policy. "In other words a policy is the intention to produce a certain allocative output, and the process of policy making involves deciding what that output should be."[2]

Policy makers need information to make policy (allocative) decisions. Therefore, they must arrange for information to flow into the political system and for policy outputs to be delivered to the electorate. The structure of government consists, first, of arrangements for channelling information to policy makers and having it arrive in a usable form and, second, of arrangements for delivering the outputs to the population. Given the vast amount of information that enters the policy making system, a process of sorting, reducing and ordering the endless flow of information must be in place if a government is to avoid information gridlock. Critical decisions must be made about the nature of the problem that could be cured by government action and the policy decision that will effect the cure. It is these decisions that determine the coherence, comprehensiveness and timeliness of government policy.

The fracturing of key decision points—chiefly through the addition of ministerial portfolios—has brought a complexity to government that makes this task increasingly difficult to perform in a manner acceptable to the electorate.

HISTORY OF GROWTH—1940 TO 1992

The federal government has proved particularly adept at creating organizations. Since Confederation, Canadian governments have established more than 700 of them. Some of those organizations have now been wound down, others have changed their goals and their names, and still others have gone through a series of structural evolutions. As of 1992, over 300 organizations existed in the federal public sector. In the past few years, new organizations concerned with constitutional affairs, forestry, multiculturalism, children, taxes, international competitiveness and several other policy areas have been announced. And in the face of increasing demands for imaginative political responses to the problems facing the country, it is inevitable that more new organizations will emerge.

During my time in the public service, I observed, criticized, and ultimately participated in the process of changing, fracturing and rearranging the structures of government. The result of all this activity has been hard to assess, in part because until 1992 there had not been a comprehensive compendium of these organizational changes. In the absence of a well-documented history of organizational change, and the reasons for it, it was very difficult to arrive at an informed view about the merits or otherwise of the existing structure. It was for that reason that I undertook, with a small team, a two-year study of organizational change in the federal government during the period 1940 to 1992. In 1992, the results of that study were published by the National Centre for Management Research and Development and McGraw-Hill-Ryerson under the title *Organizing to Govern*.

ORGANIZING TO GOVERN

The research for the book pursued four major questions:

(1) How have governments organized to govern over the last 50 years?

(2) Why did governments organize the way they did?

(3) What were the political and administrative outcomes of organizing decisions?

(4) What lessons can future decision makers learn from 50 years of organizing to govern?

In support of these questions our research goals were, first, to document the evolution of government organization in the postwar period and, second, to increase understanding of the goals, forces and processes at play in the organizing environment of the federal government. In essence we wanted to gather together what is known about organizing to govern. We pursued these goals through document research and interviews with nearly one hundred political and public service decision makers active in the period under study.

In the interviews, we explored two major areas: the factors and forces that motivated governments to take specific organizational decisions, and the political and administrative outcome of those decisions. To cover these areas, our interviews drew from the following groups:

Operators: Ministers and deputy ministers of new or reorganized departments and agencies.

Planners: Former cabinet secretaries, machinery of government officials and political advisers who counselled prime ministers on organizational issues.

Administrators: Line managers in regions and departmental headquarters, personnel and finance officers and task force leaders—those who dealt with the implementation of change.

Observers: Politicians and public servants who, throughout their careers, maintained an analytical outlook on the environment in which they worked.

Focus Groups: As the study progressed, we tested our research approach, findings and recommendations with groups of senior officials who had extensive experience with organizing in government.

ORGANIZING IN THE GOVERNMENT ENVIRONMENT

Broadly speaking, work is organized in the public sector much as it is in the private sector—objectives are set, staff are hired, offices are leased or built and so on. However, several factors make government a unique and difficult environment in which to organize.

Organizing to Govern is an attempt to capture the history of organizing in the federal government over a 50-year span and, thereby, identify the forces at play when the task is carried out. It was not meant to be a prescriptive document. Rather, I wanted it to be a reference work for all who engage in the task of organizing governments. It was my intention to convey my own prescription on how to organize in a separate article.

The key findings of the *Organizing to Govern* study were:

(1) First and foremost, governments are political instruments. A decision to establish or restructure an organization is subject to the same range of considerations as any other government decision—public policy considerations, such as the capacity of the organization to contribute to regional development (by locating the organization's offices in an area of high unemployment), and partisan considerations, such as giving a job in the organization to someone loyal to the party. As shown, all these considerations are added to the body of work originally proposed for an organization, whether it be a department of communications, a transportation safety board or a space agency. The organization that ultimately emerges is encumbered not only with the objectives associated with the original body of work, but also with objectives added through the political decision making process.

(2) The organizing of government is not driven solely by the logic of efficiency but rather by a wide variety of forces related to policy, partisan politics and personalities.

(3) Organizations tend to accumulate, because for every organization created there is a constituency dedicated to its survival. As a result, it is impossible to explain or justify a government structure on the grounds of the pursuit of its primary allocative role, let alone on the basis of administrative efficiency.

(4) Governments tend to launch organizations prematurely. Usually, organizations in government come into being because of some real or perceived political need. There is enormous pressure on the organizers to get the particular organization up and running. This leads to less than optimal results.

(5) Implementation planning is often impeded by secrecy. Frequently, the government does not want its own ministers to know about a pending organizational change since the power of some will be diminished even as that of others will be increased. Also, the government likes to surprise the opposition parties. If the opposition parties learn too early of the intent of the government, they will begin to attack (that is a key function of the opposition). It is difficult to carry out the task of organizing when you can consult very few people.

(6) The legislative process to effect organizational change is antiquated. Most organizing is completed months before Parliament is asked to authorize it.

(7) During the process of organizational change, the work of organizing frequently replaces the work of government.

IMPACT OF INCREASING SIZE AND COMPLEXITY

Examining what has occurred in the field of industrial development policy, the study revealed the important impact of this unique organizational process on the structure of government.

From 1892 to about 1960, responsibility for industrial development rested almost exclusively with the Minister of Trade and Commerce. In 1960, the process of fracturing that decision point began with the hiving off of the Economic and Technical Assistance Office to the External Aid Office. Then, in rapid succession, the Industry Branch went to the newly formed Department of Industry, the Energy Branch to Mines and Technical Surveys, and the Standards Branch to Consumer and Corporate Affairs. At about the same time, the National Productivity Council (which later became the Economic Council of Canada) and the Science Council of Canada were formed, as well the Anti-Dumping Tribunal and the Textile and Clothing Board. In the 1970s, the Ministry of State for Science and Technology and the Foreign Investment Review Agency were brought into being. The pace at which the responsibilities of the old Department of Trade and Commerce were being scattered across the government speeded up toward the end of the 1970s with the creation of the Ministry of State for Economic Development followed closely by the transfer of responsibility for International Trade to the Department of External Affairs.

During much of this period, the responsibility for regional economic development rested outside the department responsible for industrial development policy. So, as we entered the 1990s, policy and program responsibility for industrial development, which previously had rested almost exclusively with one minister, now rested with:

- the Minister of State for Science and Technology;
- the Minister of Energy, Mines and Resources;
- the Secretary of State for External Affairs;
- the Minister of Forestry;
- the Minister of Fisheries and Oceans;
- the Minister responsible for the Western Diversification Office;
- the Minister responsible for Atlantic Canada Opportunities Agency; and
- the Minister for International Trade.

This listing does not include the Ministers of State to Assist, such as:

- the Minister of State (Small Business and Tourism); and
- the Minister for External Relations.

One former minister, upon assuming office and looking at the evolution of this policy stream, commented, "Now I understand why the government has never been able to produce a coordinated economic development strategy."

ATTEMPT TO REGAIN POLICY COHERENCE

Two major organizational moves attempted to address the need to bring coherence back to industrial development (as well as other policy fields that had been fractured). The first was to create an inner cabinet (later named the Cabinet Committee on Priorities and Planning), thereby reducing the number of ministers involved in the key decision making process. This committee was at the apex of what eventually became a rather forbidding array of cabinet committees (approximately twelve), including a committee on economic development policy. This unwieldy structure (which was eventually bypassed almost totally with the creation by Prime Minister Mulroney's government of the Operations Committee) was mirrored by a set of deputy ministerial committees. Extensive interdepartmental negotiation became a fact of everyday life, since the authority required to act decisively on industrial development issues was now spread among numerous departments. This fracturing of the core decision point also occurred in other fields such as social affairs.

Given the obvious problems caused by fracturing core decision points, what were the offsetting benefits expected from this proliferation of departments and agencies and the creation of ministerial portfolios?

THE CAUSES OF GROWTH

Our study indicated that the government of the day anticipated several benefits, such as:

- being seen to be responsive to changing conditions, values and societal needs;

- demonstrating government priorities;

- providing a political response to interest groups;

- implementing the personal vision of a politician or a bureaucrat; and

- providing a ministerial portfolio to a member of the government caucus.

One of the most common reasons given in defence of the large size of the ministry—the need to provide adequate representation to Canadians in all regions of the country—was not cited by those we interviewed as a significant source of the increase in the number of ministers. It appears to be an argument advanced after the fact to explain the size of the Canadian cabinet. Given the size and diversity of Canada, there is a certain validity to the argument. But for most of our history (until the 1960s), the need to provide adequate representation for all Canadians has been met by having a cabinet consisting of fewer than 25 ministers.

The second most common reason advanced in defence of a large ministry is that it provides a higher level of representation to particular groups such as seniors (Minister of State [Seniors]), youth (Minister of State [Youth]), or the Atlantic region (Minister for ACOA). This acknowledgment of a particular group is usually coupled with the expectation on the part of the group that the assignment of a minister to look after their needs will advance the interests of that group. It has been my experience, however, that this is often not the case. Frequently, the resources (power and authority) transferred from a core department to create the new entity are not sufficient to alter the balance of power in the ministry. The most important impact is to reduce the authority and power of the core minister from whom the resources were taken. If sufficient power is taken away from core ministers, the capacity of the government to govern is seriously impaired.

TOO MANY COOKS

In the period under study, the chief lesson to be taken from the structural adventures in the industrial policy field—at least with respect to the decision making capacity of the federal government—is that when authority and power are concentrated in a single department of government it is far easier to discharge the government's allocative responsibility in a coherent, comprehensive and timely fashion than it is if responsibility is dispersed across many departments. This lesson was repeated in the other policy fields studied.

In the absence of such a centre or decision point, governments are in constant search of a substitute, giving rise to the creation of powerful central agencies (e.g., Privy Council Office, Department of Finance and the Treasury Board). They are charged with instilling coherence in the divergent plans of departments and using the fiscal weapon to enforce their views. Powerless coordinating agencies (superministries, horizontal coordinating departments, etc., etc.) all have failed or fallen dramatically short of their announced objectives because they lack the means to enforce their views.

Experience tells us that the greater the number of people involved in a decision, the more likely it is to give rise to a suboptimal solution as a result of the compromises needed to gain group support. The decision will also be less timely because of the negotiations involved. The drawbacks of decision making in large groups make it essential to create (under whatever name) an inner cabinet. In a sense, you undo that which you have done by reestablishing the power and the authority of core ministers. It is a long and cumbersome way to arrive back at your starting point!

THE ROAD TO REFORM

While conducting the study, we were constantly asking ourselves, "If one were to start with a clean slate, what would the key decision points be? How many ministers does the federal government require?" As a starting point, consider what other governments have done. In 1992, the results were surprisingly consistent.

	Number of Cabinet Ministers	**Number of Departments**
United Kingdom	25	25
France	21	21
Germany	22	22
Israel	20	20
Sweden	21	21
Japan	21	21
United States	20	20
Australia	17	17
Spain	18	18
Italy	21	21
Switzerland	7	7
CANADA	**35**	**32**

Despite differences in geographical size and population, there were remarkable similarities in numbers of cabinet ministers and departments. Canada was the exception. It is true that some of these countries (notably the United Kingdom) have junior ministers who assist the core cabinet ministers. But these ministers are not cabinet ministers and do not participate as a matter of right in the key decision making process of cabinet. They do not have power independent of the core minister to whom they report.

FUNCTIONS OF GOVERNMENT

On further reflection, these similarities are not as surprising as they first appear. The fact is that the number of functions a government (any government) must perform is limited. An examination of the departments (a proxy for the functions of government) established in other countries reveals that the following are considered core functions.

Finance/Treasury	Culture
Justice	Defence
Agriculture/Food	External Affairs
Environment	Industry/Resources
Transport	Human Resources
Aboriginal People	House Leader
Prime Minister	Government Services

This list gives rise to the oft-repeated view that the Canadian government could be reduced to as few as a dozen ministers. In my view, that number is unrealistic. For example, to suggest that the present Department of Fisheries can be wrapped into a newly created Department of Food, given the *present* turmoil in the fishery industry, is unrealistic, not because it doesn't make sense in policy terms, but because it would be political suicide. I expect politicians to be courageous, but not suicidal. It would appear, from the experience of these governments, that between 20 and 25 ministers are required to meet the management needs of government and to satisfy the various special interest groups that exert pressure on all governments. As we have seen, however, the demands of special interests can soon get out of hand.

MANAGING SPECIAL INTEREST DEMANDS

How can a government demonstrate its concern for a particular issue, and devote resources to its resolution, short of establishing a new department or agency? Once again, it is instructive to see how other governments deal with this problem.

When the Government of the United Kingdom faced the need to address the issues of energy, international trade, industrial policy, corporate affairs, science and technology, and small business, it did not follow the Canadian example of appointing a new cabinet minister and/or creating a new department or agency of government to handle each task. Instead, it created a number of junior ministers with responsibility for these various matters within the Department of Trade and Industry portfolio.

This difference in approach gives rise to two major differences. First, the junior minister is not a cabinet minister and therefore does not usually participate in cabinet meetings. The cabinet of the United Kingdom is still small enough to act as a decision making body, unlike the Canadian cabinet which had become so unwieldy that it had been displaced by an inner cabinet (the Priorities and Planning Committee) that acted as the real decision making body. In the United Kingdom the government can dispense with the plethora of cabinet committees that served to give all Canadian cabinet ministers a sense of participating in cabinet deliberations by reviewing the regular business of the government before it went to the Committee on Priorities and Planning. Needless to say, this layering of committees (Cabinet, Priorities and Planning, and the functional committees) imposed on ministers a demanding work load simply to process the material. The most common complaint of ministers was the amount of time spent in committees. Their United Kingdom colleagues were more fortunate in that regard.

The second difference arises from the fact that, in the United Kingdom, the decision point associated with economic development remains whole—under the guidance of a single senior minister. He or she has responsibility for those matters critical to a given area of concern to a far greater degree than Canadian ministers do.

Operationally this means that senior ministers undertake the essential task of making the tradeoffs between competing interests as presented by their junior associates. Unlike the Canadian system, which diffused legal responsibility for a single policy field among many ministers, the U.K. Minister of Trade and Industry remained concerned with and responsible for the overall coherence of the government's economic development policy. The relative ease of achieving agreement in an intradepartmental forum is much to be prized. It reduces the amount of log rolling and the time required to reach a decision.

HISTORY OF GROWTH—1993 TO 1997

In 1992, we published our report on *Organizing to Govern*. In that year, a series of events occurred that reversed the Canadian history of cabinets getting larger and larger with every passing decade:

- The Mulroney government announced in the February 1992 budget that several organizations would be dissolved, including the Economic Council of Canada, the Law Reform Commission, and the Science Council of Canada. In total, 46 separate organizations were wound up, privatized, or consolidated with other organizations; 13 Ministerial Advisory Councils were brought to an end; and three new agencies were put on hold.

- Later in 1992, at the request of Prime Minister Mulroney, the Honourable Robert de Cotret formed a team (in which I participated) to assist him in examining options for restructuring the government.

- In late December, Prime Minister Mulroney shuffled his cabinet. Among other moves, the portfolios of National Defence and Veterans Affairs were combined under one minister, as were the portfolios of the Minister of State (Small Business and Tourism) and Science and Technology, as well as the Minister of State (Indian Affairs and Northern Development) and Consumer and Corporate Affairs. In total, the number of cabinet ministers was reduced from 39 to 35. In New Year's interviews, the Prime Minister suggested that more structural changes were on the way.

- In the election of 1993, structural change was incorporated into the electoral platforms of all national parties.

In 1993, Prime Minister Kim Campbell announced the largest downsizing in the history of the Canadian government. She reduced the number of cabinet ministers to 25. The number of cabinet committees were reduced from 11 to six. Final decision making was returned to the full cabinet with the elimination of the Cabinet Committee on Priorities and Planning. Overall, 15 departments of government were either wound up or consolidated into other organizations.

After the 1993 election, Prime Minister Jean Chrétien announced that "for the first time a clear distinction will be drawn between Ministers who are members of Cabinet and 'Secretaries of State' who are not members of Cabinet." He appointed a cabinet of 23 ministers and he appointed eight Secretaries of State. He reduced the number of cabinet committees from six to four. Once again, there was no Priorities and Planning Committee. This was one of the smallest cabinets in modern times.

In January 1996, his cabinet increased to 24 ministers and there were nine Secretaries of State. In October 1996, the number of ministers increased to 25, and in June 1997, the number of cabinet ministers increased to 28.

It is instructive to review what has happened in the other jurisdictions since we did our study in 1992.

Country	Number of Ministers:	1992	1997
United Kingdom		25	22
France		21	17
Germany		22	17
Israel		20	18
Sweden		21	22
Japan		21	21
United States		20	15
Australia		17	15
Spain		18	16
Italy		21	20
Switzerland		7	7
CANADA		**35**	**28**

It is striking that, with few exceptions, the trend has been to reduce the size of cabinets. However, in 1993, Prime Minister Chrétien's first cabinet had only 23 ministers, while it now has 28.

It is instructive to note the functions given prominence since 1993 by the appointment of five new ministers. The ministerial portfolios added are:

- Solicitor General of Canada (previously the responsibility of the Leader in the House of Commons);

- Minister for International Cooperation and Minister Responsible for Francophonie;

- Minister of Labour (previously the responsibility of the Minister of Human Resource Development);

- Minister of the Environment (previously the responsibility of the Deputy Prime Minister);

- Minister of Veterans Affairs (previously the responsibility of the Minister of National Defence).

One can only speculate as to the combination of need, personalities and politics that gave rise to these changes.

OBSTACLES TO REFORM

In my judgment, over the past 60 years the most serious impediment to restricting the size of Canadian cabinets has been the relatively modest importance attached to good governance—making allocative decisions in a comprehensive, coherent and timely fashion—as opposed to good politics.

As with most institutions, the federal government is hierarchical in its decision making and structure. At the highest level (prime minister and cabinet), allocative decisions must be made between the private and public sector. Within the public sector, allocative decisions concerning rights (legislation) and resources (money and people) must be made between the various interests that make up society (policy fields). Finally, allocative decisions must be made between competing needs and desires within the policy field. If the policy field has been fractured by the creation of multiple departments, then many departments are competing for the available resources. This means that below the level of cabinet there is no one responsible for the overall coherence of the allocative process in a given policy field. This allocative free-for-all within a given policy field gives rise to delay and confusion.

The lowest level of decision making, the departmental level, is highly visible to the public. The department and its minister, are seen by the public as the critical decision making authority. Groups with their "own" department and minister believe that they are in a preferred position. As we have seen, this may or may not be the case, but in politics perception is reality. Therefore, at the level of special interest politics, there is political mileage to be gained by creating new departments and appointing more ministers.

Unfortunately, this puts the government's capacity to govern coherently and competently at the mercy of a sequence of organizational decisions that does not have good governance as its primary focus. As previously noted, governments have tried to regain the necessary coherence by establishing coordinating committees at the ministerial and officials level.

Even if a government is committed to establishing an effective organization, it will encounter resistance. Reorganizing government is not a task for the faint of heart! There will be gains and losses among stakeholders, including the clients of the department, the officials in the affected departments and the ministers involved. The present distribution of power (rights and resources) will be disturbed—to the perceived benefit of some and detriment of others.

The difficult position of the reformer was understood by Machiavelli, who said:

> It must be considered that there is nothing more difficult to carry out, nor more doubtful of success, nor more dangerous to handle, than to initiate a new order of things. For the reformer has enemies in all those who profit by the old order, and only lukewarm defenders in all those who would profit by the new order, this lukewarmness arising partly from fear of their adversaries, who have the laws in their favour; and partly from the incredulity of mankind, who do not truly believe in anything new until they have had actual experience of it. Thus it arises that on every opportunity for attacking the reformer, his opponents do so with the zeal of partisans, the others only defend him half-heartedly, so that between them he runs great danger.[3]

Change is usually seen, by those affected, as a criticism of their past performance rather than an evolutionary process fuelled by experience. Those involved have a heavy psychological investment in the status quo, not the least of which may be a sincere belief in the efficacy of the existing structure.

Finally, the easiest part of reorganizing a government is deciding what should happen. The most difficult part is making it happen. Too many reformers believe their task is accomplished when the announcement is made. In fact, it has only begun!

The announcement must be accompanied by a considerable investment of political will, for reasons stated so eloquently by Machiavelli. Second, the announcement must carry with it a commitment of adequate resources to see the process through to a successful conclusion. Third, there must be some form of continuing institutional support (involving politicians and officials), that is, an implementation team or task force whose purpose is to oversee execution of the plan that has sufficient "clout" to get the job done. Fourth, sufficient time must be allotted to accomplishing the task, including a recognition that major reforms must usually proceed in stages and that time must be available for meaningful involvement of all stakeholders, if reform is to succeed.

There are formidable barriers in the way of administrative reform. It should be undertaken only if there is a powerful belief in the benefits of a leaner, more coherent and agile government. Otherwise, the reformers' determination to reestablish the key decision centres will falter as their resolve fades in the face of opposition, or with the passage of time.

NOTES

1. R. J. Van Loon and M.S. Whittington, *The Canadian Political System* (Toronto: McGraw-Hill Ryerson, 1981), 3.

2. Ibid., 16.

3. Niccolo Machiavelli, "The Prince" in Niccolo Machiavelli, *The Prince and the Discourses* (New York: The Modern Library, Random House, Inc., 1950), 21—22.

ADDRESS ON CANADIAN STUDENT LEADERSHIP

Jocelyne Bourgon
Clerk of the Privy Council and
Secretary to the Cabinet

An address given in Ottawa, Ontario, on 24 January 1997 for the Canadian Student Leadership Conference.

I. INTRODUCTION

I would like to thank Sally Campbell, your conference organizer, for inviting me to speak today. This is a rare opportunity to address students in leadership and some of the nation's future leaders.

I was asked:

- to tell you what it means to be the Clerk of the Privy Council, the Secretary to the Cabinet and the Head of the Public Service;

- to talk briefly about the qualities I think are needed to be a leader and, in particular, a public sector leader;

- to turn to the future of the public service and the role you might play in it as tomorrow's leaders.

As I thought you might be especially interested in the latter, I have saved it for last.

II. A DAY IN THE LIFE OF THE CLERK OF THE PRIVY COUNCIL

Let me start with a few words about my job. The Public Service of Canada serves Canadians and their elected representatives. The Clerk has broad responsibility for the two primary roles of the Public Service: policy development and service to Canada. I therefore have an overall responsibility:

- to ensure that the Prime Minister and his Cabinet receive sound and thoughtful policy advice upon which to base their decisions;

- as a result of those decisions, to ensure that public servants provide citizens with high-quality programs and services.

As Head of the Public Service, I must ensure that the Public Service constantly adapts to respond to the needs of the Government of Canada and of Canadians. I must help ensure that the Public Service of Canada will remain a modern, vibrant, national institution, staffed with highly competent and committed professionals ready and able to face the challenges of their time.

So what does this mean on a practical, day-to-day basis?

As Clerk, I work every day with the Prime Minister, ministers, deputy ministers, interest groups, and the citizens of Canada. I am an appointed official, not an elected one. Therefore, my function is very much different from that of a minister. My role is to "prepare the foundation" for the work of the Prime Minister and ministers. This means ensuring that the Public Service comes up with the best research, the best analysis, and the most thoughtful options possible—so that the Prime Minister and ministers have the tools they need to make the decisions which set the course for Canada. Their job is to lead the evolution of the country; mine is to lead the Public Service of Canada. In my role, one is in a good position to learn about Canada and to marvel at the commitment of ministers and the dedication of public servants.

Every week, the Privy Council Office is expected to provide advice covering the entire spectrum of policy questions and operational issues facing the Government.

Officials bear great responsibility. Public servants are responsible for the quality of their advice and for their professional work. And the quality of their work determines how well ministers will be able to fulfil their role, how many reforms they will have the time to introduce, and how efficiently the reforms will be implemented. To fulfil this advisory role requires:

- strength and competence in every department and agency;

- a team of highly competent staff in the Privy Council Office to respond to needs and to ensure the whole operation runs smoothly.

In my job, one learns quickly about the importance of relying on the strength of others and of removing the obstacles that prevent ministers and officials from contributing to the fullest.

The Prime Minister and his cabinet have the ultimate responsibility for making the final decisions. The cabinet system, as you know, is where the elected officials who collectively run our country make the decisions that will ultimately affect the life of every Canadian. Through that system, ministers are collectively responsible for government decisions.

Once decisions are made, I must work with my colleagues in the various departments and agencies of government to ensure that the decisions are implemented in a way that best meets the needs of Canadians. As you know, implementation is never easy. In fact, implementation often reveals the real quality of a proposed reform.

Implementation is achieved through a network of 24 departments; 37 crown corporations; 26 tribunals and quasi-judicial bodies; and at least 48 service agencies of different types. Each organization has its own purpose, role, culture, and management style.

III. WHAT ABOUT LEADERSHIP?

Although I have briefly described my role, I have yet to say something about leadership. In a nutshell:

- All people in public office exercise power, but all are not necessarily leaders.

- All people in charge of organizations practise management, but that does not automatically make them leaders.

In other words, some people in authority, some managers, go beyond the routine of setting priorities, organizing the work, achieving results, appointing and firing, making decisions, and issuing orders. Some create among the people around them a desire to follow, to be part of it, to join in, to make a contribution. Creating this desire is one of the signs of leadership.

There are many who know how to exercise power and authority, and who do it well. But only a few practise the art of leadership.

For the evidence of outstanding leadership, look for the followers. Without them, there are no leaders.

At the risk of boring you, since you are all students of the art of leadership, a word on my personal observations about leadership. Over the last 20 years, I have been fortunate to observe leaders in action—in politics, in government, in the private sector, in the not-for-profit sector and in private life. Leaders have a number of characteristics in common:

- They think clearly.

- They can articulate their beliefs and values.

- They have established their own assumptions about human nature—because leadership is about people.

- They understand the role of their organization.

Managers who practise the art of leadership share a concept about people. It begins with an understanding of individual gifts, talents, and skills. It recognizes that the organization's needs are best met when each and every one in the organization is allowed to make his or her special gift a part of the corporate effort.

Each of us, no matter what our rank in the hierarchy, wants similar things. We want:

- to be needed and to apply our talents towards making a contribution;

- to be involved in the collective effort;

- to understand corporate needs;

- to be accountable for our contribution to the group;

- to make a difference and be proud of the results achieved.

Managers who are also leaders are those who help create an environment that satisfies these needs. But let's be modest. Any manager knows there are days when we succeed, or play a leadership role, and there are days when we are simply good managers. On the latter days, we rely on the strength of others and follow their lead.

Leaders in the public service need all these qualities and a bit more.

Leaders in the public service need a sense of country. They must be loyal and committed to the public interest as represented and interpreted by the duly elected government of the land. They must be strong believers in the importance of democracy and of the rule of law in meeting the needs and protecting the rights of citizens.

Public servants hold a public trust. At all times, they must put the common good ahead of any private or individual interest. Public servants serve citizens, not customers. Citizens are equal bearers of rights as members of a community where competing interests must constantly be balanced.

Finally, public servants must be able to serve in a neutral and nonpartisan manner.

IV. A CAREER IN THE PUBLIC SERVICE OF THE FUTURE

As Head of the Public Service, I have a responsibility to ensure that we have the people we will need to meet the challenges of our time—today and in the future.

Let me close, then, by addressing my next few remarks to those of you in this room who are contemplating a career in the Public Service or, perhaps what is even more important, to those of you who have not thought about the Public Service as a possible career choice but who might be persuaded to do so.

The public sector makes a significant difference to the performance of nations. The public sector contributes to competitiveness, provides countries with a comparative advantage in their competition for trade and investment, and contributes to citizens' quality of life and standard of living.

Any country would be handicapped if it could not rely on a strong, competent, and professional public service. Any government would be handicapped if it did not have a high-calibre public service to carry out its policies and programs.

Canadians and their elected representatives have always been able to rely on a public service that is one of the best in the world. People in public life and in the Public Service are committed to taking the necessary steps to ensure that Canadians will continue to live in a country that is considered among the best in the world. This will mean that:

- Canada must continue to regain its fiscal sovereignty;

- Canada must give itself competitive advantages to succeed in the community of nations (e.g., education, learning, information technology);

- Canadians must modernize the social union of Canada, the sharing community;

- the Public Service must rethink its ways of serving (e.g., new technology, partnerships, service delivery);

- we must renew the ranks of the Public Service.

To meet these challenges, the Public Service must be able to attract highly skilled, talented, and motivated people to lead us into the future.

A career in the public sector is exciting. No other career offers the same diversity, breadth of experience, or complexity—and all within the same organization. And there has never been a more interesting time to work for the Public Service. This is our opportunity to ensure that Canada will enter the next millennium as a united country and as one of the best countries of the world.

So why might you want to join the Public Service of the future? I will mention a few reasons:

- First, to serve. The role is to serve the Government and the citizens of this country—to contribute to the public good and to make a difference.

- Second, to work with those who are reinventing the role of government—to integrate the global scene, national policies, and citizens' needs.

- Third, to learn and be challenged. No other organization in this country can give you the diversity that exists within the Public Service of Canada, or the breadth of experience.

- Fourth, to join an exceptional team. To work with colleagues from across the country, who are equally talented and committed.

- Fifth, to discover the richness of this country and its people. Very few employers in Canada can offer you that.

- A sixth reason, and I will stop there, is the opportunity to be involved in major issues. When you sit down tonight and watch the news, or tomorrow when you read the newspaper, remember that someone in the Public Service of Canada has been working on many of the issues that you are reading about or seeing on *The National* or on *CBC News World*. The issues could be national unity, job creation, or the health care system. And you could be a part of the team that works on these critical issues.

Now this career is not for just anybody. The people we need:

- are not looking to get rich, though you should be able to expect fair compensation;

- are not looking for fame or for prestige (you would work behind the scenes);

- are not looking to have an easy, carefree job.

But if you are looking for a sense of giving to your country in a unique way and an exhilarating sense of contributing to the future, then consider the Public Service of Canada.

In the end, one of the best reasons to consider a career in the Public Service is that the leadership qualities I described are exactly what the Public Service will need. If you have these qualities, we need you to help us carry the country into the future.

Thank you.

LIST OF CONTRIBUTORS

Donald E. Abelson is an Associate Professor in the Department of Political Science at the University of Western Ontario where he teaches courses on American domestic and foreign policy. He is the author of *American Think Tanks and their Role in U.S. Foreign Policy* (Macmillan and St. Martin's Press, 1996) as well as several articles and book chapters on the domestic sources of American foreign policy.

Paul Barker is Associate Professor of Political Science at Brescia College, The University of Western Ontario. He has written on health policy, cabinet decision making, and Canadian federalism. His current interests include education policy in Ontario and Canada.

Robin Bayley obtained from the University of Victoria a Bachelor of Arts in Political Science in 1986 and a Master of Public Administration in 1989. Since 1989 she has worked in policy and legislation in central agencies in the British Columbia government. Most recently, Ms. Bayley acted as Project Manager for a government-wide review of the *Freedom of Information* and *Protection of Privacy Act* which produced the government's submission to the Special Committee of the Legislative Assembly reviewing the Act.

Colin J. Bennett received his PhD in Political Science from the University of Illinois in 1986. He is now Associate Professor of Political Science at the University of Victoria. He has researched information policy issues for approximately fifteen years and is the author of *Regulating Privacy: Data Protection and Public Policy in Europe and the United States* (Cornell University Press, 1992) and the co-editor of *Visions of Privacy: Policy Choices for the Digital Age* (University of Toronto Press, 1998, forthcoming). He has also published numerous articles on privacy and the protection of personal information, as well as policy reports on these issues for the Canadian Standards Association and Industry Canada.

Jocelyne Bourgon is the first woman to be appointed to the position of Clerk of the Privy Council and Secretary to the Cabinet. She fulfils three main functions in that position: Clerk of the Privy Council, Secretary to the Cabinet, and head of the Public Service of Canada. Ms. Bourgon holds the most important position in the Canadian Public Service. Born in Papineauville, Quebec, she studied at the Université de Montréal and the University of Ottawa. From 1975 to 1989 Ms. Bourgon held various positions of increasing importance at the Department of Fisheries and Oceans, the Department of Regional Industrial Expansion, the Federal-Provincial Relations Office, and the Department of Energy, Mines and Resources. From 1989 to 1994 she was, in turn, Deputy Minister of Consumer and Corporate Affairs, Associate Secretary and Secretary to the Cabinet for Federal-Provincial Relations, President of the Canadian International Development Agency, and Deputy Minister of Transport. In February 1994 Ms. Bourgon was appointed to her present position of Clerk of the Privy Council and Secretary to the Cabinet.

Keith Brownsey teaches Political Science at Mount Royal College in Calgary. He is the co-editor of *The Provincial State* and has published a number of articles on provincial politics in Canada.

Peter Clancy is a member of the Political Science Department at St. Francis Xavier University. His research interests include politics in the Canadian North, business-government relations in Canada, and the political economy of forestry.

Peter Desbarats, writer, broadcaster, journalist and educator, was Dean of the Graduate School of Journalism at The University of Western Ontario when he was appointed in 1995 to be one of three Commissioners of the Commission of Inquiry into the Deployment of Canadian Forces to Somalia. The Commission reported in July 1997, and Professor Desbarats took early retirement from the University at that time. Before his academic appointment in 1981 he had spent three decades as a journalist in Montreal, London (U.K.), Winnipeg and the Ottawa Press Gallery, working for such media concerns as the *Montreal Gazette*, Reuters, the *Winnipeg Tribune,* the *Montreal Star,* the CBC, the *Toronto Star,* and Global Television. In 1980–81 he was senior consultant and associate research director for the Royal Commission on Newspapers and has provided commissioned research for a number of federal inquiries since then. A frequently quoted expert on media, he has written extensively on this topic and lectured in Canada, the United States and overseas. His eleven books include a best-selling biography of René Lévesque, the authoritative *Guide to Canadian News Media,* as well as several volumes of stories and verses for children. His book *Somalia Cover-Up: A Commissioner's Journal* was published by McClelland & Stewart in October 1997.

David C. Docherty is Assistant Professor of Political Science at Wilfrid Laurier University in Waterloo, Ontario. His main areas of research interest are the Canadian Parliament, comparative legislative studies, and political careers in Canada, the United States and Great Britain. He is the author of *Mr. Smith Goes to Ottawa: Life in the House of Commons* (UBC Press, 1997), a comparison of party discipline and representational styles of members of the 34th and 35th Parliaments of Canada. He has also published in the *Canadian Journal of Political Science* and *Canadian Parliamentary Review.*

Katherine A. Graham is Associate Dean of the Faculty of Public Affairs and Management at Carleton University. She is the co-author of the book *Urban Governance in Canada: Representation, Resources and Restructuring.*

Ronald Manzer is Professor of Political Science in the Division of Social Sciences and the Department of Political Science at the University of Toronto. He is author of *Teachers and Politics* (1970), *Canada: A Socio-Political Report* (1974), *Public Policies and Political Development in Canada* (1985), and *Public Schools and Political Ideas: Canadian Educational Policy in Historical Perspective* (1994).

Hugh Mellon is Associate Professor in the Department of Political Science at King's College, The University of Western Ontario. His teaching interests include Canadian government and public policy. His work has been published in *Canadian Public Administration* and the *Journal of Canadian Studies*. He recently co-edited (with Martin Westmacott) *Challenges to Canadian Federalism* (Prentice Hall, 1998).

James R. Mitchell is a founding partner of Sussex Circle, Inc., an Ottawa consulting firm which provides advice on policy, strategy and government organization. He began his government career in 1978 in the Department of External Affairs and later served in the Privy Council Office and the Treasury Board Secretariat. As Assistant Secretary to the Cabinet (Machinery of Government), Mr. Mitchell was a principal advisor on the 1993 reorganization of the federal government. Mr. Mitchell holds a BA (Hons.) from the University of British Columbia and a PhD in Philosophy from the University of Colorado. Before joining government, he held positions as Visiting Professor of Philosophy at universities in Canada and the United States. He has written and lectured on a wide range of public policy and public administration issues.

Peter Neary is Dean of the Faculty of Social Science and Professor of History at The University of Western Ontario. He was born at Bell Island, Newfoundland, in 1938 and is a graduate of the Memorial University of Newfoundland and the London School of Economics and Political Science, University of London. His publications include *Newfoundland in the North Atlantic World, 1929–1949* (Kingston and Montreal, 1988) and *White Tie and Decorations: Sir John and Lady Hope Simpson in Newfoundland, 1934–1936* (Toronto, 1996). He has co-edited (with J. L. Granatstein) *The Good Fight: Canadians and World War II* (Toronto, 1995) and *The Veterans Charter and Post–World War II Canada* (Montreal and Kingston, 1998).

Michael Nolan teaches Journalism at The University of Western Ontario and Political Science at King's College, a Western affiliate. A former CTV network news commentator, he has written three books including *Alan Plaunt and the Early Days of CBC Radio* (CBC Enterprises, Toronto, 1986) and *Walter J. Blackburn: A Man for All Media* (Macmillan of Canada, Toronto, 1989).

Gordon Osbaldeston joined the Public Service of Canada in 1953 and has occupied many influential positions including Secretary of the Treasury Board (1973), Secretary to the Minister of State for Economic Development (1978), Under Secretary of State for External Affairs (1982), and Clerk of the Privy Council (1982–85). He resigned from the Public Service of Canada in 1985 and was appointed Senior Fellow of the Richard Ivey School of Business, The University of Western Ontario, in 1986. In 1995 he was appointed Professor Emeritus of the Ivey Business School and he currently serves on the board of directors of several corporations.

Susan D. Phillips is Associate Professor in the School of Public Administration, Faculty of Public Affairs and Management, Carleton University. She is co-author of the book *Urban Governance in Canada: Representation, Resources and Restructuring*.

Sharon L. Sutherland is Professor of Political Science at Carleton University. She received her BA and Master's degrees from the University of Alberta and her PhD from the University of Essex. Professor Sutherland was a member of the faculty at Dalhousie University, at the Schools of Public Administration at both Dalhousie and Carleton, and at the University of Essex. She has also worked in a number of federal government departments. She has published widely in the areas of political psychology and Canadian government, and particularly on issues related to bureaucracy and ministerial responsibility in Westminster systems. Professor Sutherland was elected a Fellow of the Royal Society of Canada in 1995. In 1988 she received an Ontario Confederation of University Faculty Associations award for excellence in university teaching. James Mitchell and Sharon Sutherland are co-authors of "Relations between Politicians and Public Servants," in M. Charih and A. Daniels (eds.) *New Public Management and Public Administration in Canada* (IPAC, 1997) and "Parliament and Administration," in J. Bourgault, M. Demers, C. Williams (eds.) *Public Administration and Public Management: Experiences in Canada* (Publications du Québec, 1997).

Martin Westmacott is Associate Professor of Political Science, Department of Political Science, at The University of Western Ontario. His teaching interests include the introductory course in Political Science, Canadian politics, and constitutional reform. He has co-edited two books of readings on Canadian federalism and recently co-edited (with Hugh Mellon) *Challenges to Canadian Federalism* (Prentice Hall, 1998).